*The Palgrave Gothic Series*

Series Editor: **Clive Bloom**
Editorial Advisory Board: **Dr Ian Conrich**, University of South Australia, **Barry Forshaw**, author/journalist, UK, **Professor Gregg Kucich**, University of Notre Dame, USA, **Professor Gina Wisker**, University of Brighton, UK, **Dr Catherine Wynne**, University of Hull, UK, **Dr Alison Peirse**, University of York, UK

This series of gothic books is the first to treat the genre in its many inter-related, global and 'extended' cultural aspects to show how the taste for the medieval and the sublime gave rise to a perverse taste for terror and horror and how that taste became not only international (with a huge fan base in places such as South Korea and Japan) but also the sensibility of the modern age, changing our attitudes to such diverse areas as the nature of the artist, the meaning of drug abuse and the concept of the self. The series is accessible but scholarly, with referencing kept to a minimum and theory contextualised where possible. All the books are readable by an intelligent student or a knowledgeable general reader interested in the subject.

Timothy C. Baker
CONTEMPORARY SCOTTISH GOTHIC
Mourning, Authenticity, and Tradition

Dara Downey
AMERICAN WOMEN'S GHOST STORIES IN THE GILDED AGE

Barry Forshaw
BRITISH GOTHIC CINEMA

Margarita Georgieva
THE GOTHIC CHILD

Derek Johnston
HAUNTED SEASONS
Television Ghost Stories for Christmas and Horror for Halloween

David J. Jones
SEXUALITY AND THE GOTHIC MAGIC LANTERN
Desire, Eroticism and Literary Visibilities from Byron to Bram Stoker

Sian MacArthur
GOTHIC SCIENCE FICTION
1818 to the Present

Emma McEvoy
GOTHIC TOURISM

Lorna Piatti-Farnell and Maria Beville (*editors*)
THE GOTHIC AND THE EVERYDAY
Living Gothic

Aspasia Stephanou
READING VAMPIRE GOTHIC THROUGH BLOOD
Bloodlines

Catherine Wynne (*editor*)
BRAM STOKER AND THE GOTHIC
Formations to Transformations

Catherine Wynne
BRAM STOKER, DRACULA AND THE VICTORIAN GOTHIC STAGE

---

**The Palgrave Gothic Series**
**Series Standing Order ISBN 978–1–137–27637–7   (hardback)**
(*outside North America only*)

You can receive future titles in this series as they are published by placing a standing order. Please contact your bookseller or, in case of difficulty, write to us at the address below with your name and address, the title of the series and the ISBN quoted above.

Customer Services Department, Macmillan Distribution Ltd, Houndmills, Basingstoke, Hampshire RG21 6XS, England

# Bram Stoker and the Gothic

Formations to Transformations

Edited by

Catherine Wynne
*University of Hull, UK*

Selection, introduction and editorial matter © Catherine Wynne 2016
Remaining chapters © Individual authors 2016
Softcover reprint of the hardcover 1st edition 2016 978-1-137-46503-0

All rights reserved. No reproduction, copy or transmission of this publication may be made without written permission.

No portion of this publication may be reproduced, copied or transmitted save with written permission or in accordance with the provisions of the Copyright, Designs and Patents Act 1988, or under the terms of any licence permitting limited copying issued by the Copyright Licensing Agency, Saffron House, 6–10 Kirby Street, London EC1N 8TS.

Any person who does any unauthorized act in relation to this publication may be liable to criminal prosecution and civil claims for damages.

The authors have asserted their rights to be identified as the authors of this work in accordance with the Copyright, Designs and Patents Act 1988.

First published 2016 by
PALGRAVE MACMILLAN

Palgrave Macmillan in the UK is an imprint of Macmillan Publishers Limited, registered in England, company number 785998, of Houndmills, Basingstoke, Hampshire RG21 6XS.

Palgrave Macmillan in the US is a division of St Martin's Press LLC,
175 Fifth Avenue, New York, NY 10010.

Palgrave Macmillan is the global academic imprint of the above companies and has companies and representatives throughout the world.

Palgrave® and Macmillan® are registered trademarks in the United States, the United Kingdom, Europe and other countries.

ISBN 978-1-349-55468-3      ISBN 978-1-137-46504-7 (eBook)
DOI 10.1057/9781137465047

This book is printed on paper suitable for recycling and made from fully managed and sustained forest sources. Logging, pulping and manufacturing processes are expected to conform to the environmental regulations of the country of origin.

A catalogue record for this book is available from the British Library.

Library of Congress Cataloging-in-Publication Data
Bram Stoker and the Gothic: formations to transformations / Catherine Wynne, University of Hull, UK [editor].
  pages cm
 1. Stoker, Bram, 1847–1912—Criticism and interpretation.  2. Gothic fiction (Literary genre), English—History and criticism.  3. English literature—19th century—History and criticism.  4. Horror tales, English—History and criticism.  I. Wynne, Catherine, 1971– editor.
 PR6037.T617Z575  2016
 823'.8—dc23                                                                        2015025943

Typeset by MPS Limited, Chennai, India.

*This book is dedicated to my mother,
Rose Wynne*

# Contents

*List of Figures* ix

*Acknowledgements* x

*Notes on Contributors* xi

Introduction 1
Catherine Wynne

1 On the Origins of the Gothic Novel: From Old Norse to Otranto 14
  Martin Arnold

2 Wollstonecraft's *Wrongs of Woman* to Stoker's *Dracula*: You've Come a Long Way Baby, or Have You? 30
  Bettina Tate Pedersen

3 Stoker, Poe, and American Gothic in 'The Squaw' 48
  Kevin Corstorphine

4 Bram Stoker and Gothic Transylvania 63
  Marius-Mircea Crişan

5 'Labours of Their Own': Property, Blood, and the Szgany in *Dracula* 78
  Abby Bardi

6 Invasions Real and Imagined: Stoker's Gothic Narratives 92
  Carol A. Senf

7 'Gay Motes that People the Sunbeams': Dust, Death and Degeneration in *Dracula* 105
  Victoria Samantha Dawson

8 The Imprint of the Mother: Bram Stoker's 'The Squaw' and *The Jewel of Seven Stars* 118
  Sara Williams

9 'Empire of the Air': Ireland, Aerial Warfare and Futurist Gothic 138
  Luke Gibbons

10 Bram Stoker, Ellen Terry, Pamela Colman Smith and the Art of Devilry 159
   Katharine Cockin

| 11 | Beyond 'Hommy-Beg': Hall Caine's Place in *Dracula*<br>*Richard Storer* | 172 |
|---|---|---|
| 12 | The Du Mauriers and Stoker: Gothic Transformations of Whitby and Cornwall<br>*Catherine Wynne* | 185 |
| 13 | The Un-Death of the Author: The Fictional Afterlife of Bram Stoker<br>*William Hughes* | 207 |
| 14 | Gallants, Ghosts, and Gargoyles: Illustrating the Gothic Tale<br>*Jef Murray* | 222 |

| *Works Cited* | 253 |
|---|---|
| *Index* | 270 |

# List of Figures

| | | |
|---|---|---|
| 12.1 | George du Maurier, 'A Powerful Quartet', *Punch*, 24 September 1881 | 194 |
| 12.2 | George du Maurier, 'A Little "New Woman"', *Punch*, 1 September 1894 | 200 |
| 14.1 | Bram Stoker Conference Image | 224 |
| 14.2 | The Human Figure | 225 |
| 14.3 | The Magic Ring – Sir Otto | 227 |
| 14.4 | The Magic Ring – Bertha and the Mirror | 228 |
| 14.5 | Romance | 230 |
| 14.6 | The Heroine | 231 |
| 14.7 | The Byronic Figure | 232 |
| 14.8 | The Gothic Setting | 234 |
| 14.9 | The Coffin | 235 |
| 14.10 | The Supernatural | 236 |
| 14.11 | The Grotesque | 238 |
| 14.12 | The Religious Element | 239 |
| 14.13 | Medieval Trappings | 240 |
| 14.14 | Clerics and Conjurors | 242 |
| 14.15 | The Magic Ring | 243 |
| 14.16 | Zelotes and Sir Hugh | 245 |
| 14.17 | The Crowning of Bertha | 246 |
| 14.18 | The Demon of Brockenheim | 247 |
| 14.19 | Seer: A Wizard's Journal | 249 |
| 14.20 | The Lady of the Shroud | 250 |

# Acknowledgements

With warmest thanks to the British Academy for supporting the Bram Stoker Centenary Conference in 2012 in Hull and Whitby. The essays in this collection have emerged from the conference and Stoker Birthday symposia.

# Notes on Contributors

**Martin Arnold** is Reader in Old Northern Studies at the University of Hull specialising in early Germanic languages, literature and beliefs. He has authored books and articles on Icelandic sagas, Viking Age history and Old Norse mythology. His study of the reception history of the Norse god Thor – *Thor: Myth to Marvel* – was listed in *The Times Literary Supplement* as one of the 2011 Books of the Year.

**Abby Bardi** is Professor of English at Prince George's Community College in Largo, Maryland, USA. Her work on the Gypsy trope in British fiction has been published in *Critical Survey*, *Romani Studies* and the anthology *Gypsies in European Literature and Culture* edited by Valentina Glajar and Domnica Radulescu. She is also the author of the novel *The Book of Fred*.

**Katharine Cockin**, University of Hull, England, is Professor of English and Principal Investigator and editor of the British Academy-funded project, The Collected Letters of Ellen Terry (8 vols, 2010–17). Her publications include *Ellen Terry, Lives of the Shakespearian Actors* (2012), *Ellen Terry, Spheres of Influence* (2012) *Women and Theatre in the Age of Suffrage: the Pioneer Players 1911–25* (2001) and *Edith Craig* (1998). She is the Principal Investigator of the AHRC Ellen Terry and Edith Craig Database (2006–08), online catalogue of the National Trust's archive at Smallhythe Place, one of the most significant theatre archives in Britain. She is working on Edith Craig and the Theatres of Art.

**Kevin Corstorphine** is Lecturer in English at the University of Hull. His research interests are in the Gothic, the reception of science in literature, American Literature, ecology, and theories of spatiality. He has published chapters and articles on Ambrose Bierce, H. P. Lovecraft, Robert Bloch and Stephen King. He is working on the spaces and places of Gothic fiction and the popular imagination, and is writing a book on Haunted Houses in fiction and culture.

**Marius-Mircea Crişan** is a senior lecturer at the West University of Timişoara, Romania. He holds a PhD from the University of Turin, Italy. He is the author of *The Birth of the Dracula Myth: Bram Stoker's*

*Transylvania* and *Impactul unui mit: Dracula și reprezentarea ficțională a spațiului românesc* [*The Impact of a Myth: Dracula and the Fictional Representation of the Romanian Space*] (2013) – nominated for the Debut Prize of the Union of the Romanian Writers – Timișoara Branch, as well as of *Sinteze de didactica limbii și literaturii române: Coordonate introductive și perspective de cercetare* [*Syntheses of Didactics of Romanian Language and Literature: Introductory Coordinates and Research Perspectives*] (2014). He has written several articles on the Dracula myth, imagology, reception theories and didactics, and is co-author of *An Imagological Dictionary of the Cities in Romania Represented in British Travel Literature* (coordinators Carmen Andraș and Cornel Sigmirean Mentor, 2012) and *Dicționarului Scriitorilor din Banat* [*Dictionary of the Writers of the Banat*] (2005, general coordination: Alexandru Ruja).

**Victoria Samantha Dawson** is an AHRC Collaborative Doctoral Award holder pursuing her PhD in social and cultural history at De Montfort University. A scholar of literature and history, she previously studied for an MA in English Literary Studies at the University of York. Her research interests are primarily literary and historical, especially issues of class, gender, science, and social and cultural identity.

**Luke Gibbons** is Professor of Irish Literary and Cultural Studies at the School of English, Drama and Media Studies, National University of Ireland, Maynooth, and formerly taught at the University of Notre Dame, USA, and Dublin City University. He has published widely on Irish culture, film, literature, and the visual arts, as well as on aesthetics and politics. Publications include *Limits of the Visible: Representing the Great Hunger* (2015), *Gaelic Gothic: Race, Colonialism and Irish Culture* (2004), *Edmund Burke and Ireland: Aesthetics, Politics and the Colonial Sublime* (2003), *The Quiet Man* (2002), *Transformations in Irish Culture* (1996), and co-wrote (with Kevin Rockett and John Hill) *Cinema and Ireland* (1988), the pioneering study of Irish cinema. He was a contributing editor to Seamus Deane, ed., *The Field Day Anthology of Irish Writing* (1991).

**William Hughes** is Professor of Gothic Studies at Bath Spa University. He is the author, editor or co-editor of 17 books, almost all of which concern the Gothic. These include the monographs *Beyond Dracula: Bram Stoker's Fiction and Its Cultural Context* (2000) and *That Devil's Trick: Hypnotism and the Victorian Popular Imagination* (2015), as well as two student guides to *Dracula* (both 2009) and *The Historical Dictionary of Gothic Fiction* (2013). With Andrew Smith, he has edited a number of ground-breaking essay collections including *Empire and* the Gothic (2003), *Queering the Gothic* (2009), *Ecogothic* (2013), and *The Encyclopedia of the Gothic* (2013, with Andrew Smith and David Punter). He is the editor of *Gothic Studies* and Past-President of the International Gothic Association.

**Jef Murray** is an artist, author and illustrator. In terms of his Gothic work he has produced book jackets and illustrations for Bram Stoker's *The Lady of the Shroud* (2012), *The Demon of Brockenheim* (2012) and *The Magic Ring* (2009).

**Bettina Tate Pedersen** is Professor of Literature at Point Loma Nazarene University in San Diego, California. Her research interests are women writers, British literature, feminist theory, and the relation of feminism and Christianity. She has published essays on British and Canadian women writers, feminism, and teaching. She is co-author and editor, with Allyson Jule, of *Being Feminist, Being Christian* (2006) and *Facing Challenges: Feminism in Christian Higher Education and Other Places* (2015).

**Carol A. Senf** is a professor and Associate Chair of the School of the Literature, Media, and Communication at the Georgia Institute of Technology (Atlanta, GA). She has been exploring Bram Stoker's works for over 40 years and has written two critical studies of Stoker and one critical study of *Dracula*. She has also edited a volume of essays on Stoker's work and annotated two of Stoker's novels: *The Mystery of the Sea* and *Lady Athyne*. She has also written a number of essays on Stoker's novels and their film adaptions as well as essays on Charles Dickens, George Eliot, the Brontës, and Stephen King.

**Richard Storer** is Senior Lecturer in English at Leeds Trinity University. He has published several essays on the popular Victorian 'Manx' authors Hall Caine and T. E. Brown. He is also the author of the volume *F. R. Leavis* (2009).

**Sara Williams** is an honorary research associate at the University of Hull. She completed her doctorate on the 'The Maternal Gaze in the Gothic' in 2012. She has published a scholarly edition of Georgiana Houghton's *Evenings at Home in the Spiritual Séance* (2013), an essay on H. P. Lovecraft in *New Critical Essays* (2013) and an article on *The Exorcist* in *Lit: Literature, Interpretation, Theory* (2011) which was republished in *The Evil Child in Literature, Film and Popular Culture* (2013).

**Catherine Wynne** is Senior Lecturer in English at the University of Hull. She is author of *Bram Stoker, Dracula and the Victorian Gothic Stage*

(2013) and editor of two volumes of Stoker's theatrical reviews and theatrical writings, *Bram Stoker and the Stage: Reviews, Reminiscences, Essays and Fiction* (2012). In 2012 she organized the Bram Stoker Centenary Conference at the University of Hull and in Whitby. This conference was supported by a grant from the British Academy.

# Introduction

*Catherine Wynne*

## I

**Gothic heritage and disease narratives**

In August 1665 in the village of Eyam in England's Peak District, a tailor bought a bale of cloth from London to make clothes. What resulted was an unleashing of the bubonic plague in this small community. The disease allegedly killed 260 of Eyam's residents before it abated over a year later. Although having little knowledge of the spread of infection, the villagers sealed off their community and this self-imposed quarantine prevented the disease from spreading into the surrounding district (www.eyammuseum.org.uk). Eyam is, Patrick Wallis argues, 'the epicentre of Europe's plague heritage' (2005: 2). Almost forgotten in subsequent centuries, it was not until the late 18th century that the plague story of Eyam was recreated and largely reimagined through folklore and literature finding its 'fullest expression' in literature produced in the mid-19th century (Wallis, 2005: 2). By the time of its bicentenary in 1866, the Eyam plague was firmly embedded in cultural heritage and Eyam itself became, and remains to this day, a sombre tourist site.

In Charles Dickens's *All the Year Round*, for instance, an 1869 article entitled 'The Plague at Eyam' describes how the 'journeyman of the tailor ... opened the box ... and at once observed a peculiar smell; for exclaiming "How very damp they are!" he hung [the cloth] before the fire to dry. Even while attending to them a violent sickness seized him' and he died after a '[l]arge swelling rose on his neck and groin' and the 'fatal plague spot appeared on his breast' (17 July, 1869: 161). By June the following year, the article continues, the local vicar, William Mompesson, urged the locals not to depart the village, 'warn[ing] them against the guilt of carrying the plague far and wide' (162). By August 1866 Mompesson lost his wife to the disease. The vicar, according to this account, had by that summer instituted a plan with the Duke of Devonshire at Chatworth (five miles from the village) to organize supplies to be sent to Eyam and points near to the village where such goods could be left were arranged near rivulets and here money left by the villagers could be cleansed by running water or by vinegar: 'Here, very early in the morning, supplies were left .... And here would be left the record of deaths, with other information for the world outside Eyam' (162). Through this narrative of heroic self-sacrifice Eyam provided a 'framework around which ... a fragment of the past could be woven: a tamed catastrophe that, like medieval or modern wars, became a tableau for unproblematic heroism' (Wallis, 2005: 13). Wallis cautions, however, that the Eyam plague was not a 'romantic interlude' but an event whose 'bloody weight' is testified by the parish registers of the death toll (Wallis, 2005: 36). Whether Mompesson and his acquaintances saved the extended area from infection through quarantining remains unresolved but the event serves to aid an interpretation of how 'heroic or romantic narratives continue to permeate accounts of epidemics' (Wallis, 2005: 37).

These points have a contemporary relevance to the Ebola outbreak (a viral disease which spreads through contact with bodily fluids and blood of infected individuals) which has devastated West Africa since 2014. Here isolation measures are in place and foreign aid workers, who have contracted disease, are airlifted home to special units and achieve heroic status. Literature is often used to attempt to reach an understanding of such catastrophes and with rapidly spreading infectious disease Gothic provides a rich source of speculation, if not, explanation. A medical article relating to pre-2014 outbreaks of the Ebola epidemic, for example, draws on Edgar Allan Poe's 'The Masque of the Red Death' (1842) – a Gothic tale of an infectious disease spreading through a walled abbey where the ruling Prince and his nobles have secluded themselves to avoid this unidentified disease called the red death (Vora and Ramanan, 2002). Equally, contemporary Gothic narratives are fuelled by the fear of the spread of infection as they transform real fears into Gothic nightmares.

In 'The Plague at Eyam' from *All the Year Round*, the event, in line with a 19th-century interpretation of infectious disease, is also gothicized. The article describes how a

> line was drawn around the village, marked by well-known stones and fences; and it was agreed upon by all within it that the boundary

should not be overstepped. No need to caution those beyond it! The fear of entering Eyam was general, and its inhabitants were left to meet their enemy alone. (162)

The article continues in this Gothic register. As the death toll mounts over the course of the summer, 'Coffins and shrouds were no longer provided. An old door or chair would serve as a bier .... Day saw dead bodies hurried along the village; night heard the frequent footsteps of those who bore them out' (162). The nineteenth century was a period characterized by what Faye Getz describes as a 'Gothic epidemiology' (1991: 279) emerging from Justin Hecker's *History of the Black Death* (1832) where the

> miasma of plague ... rolled like a fog out of the mysterious East; a crawling miasma exhaled by earthquakes and volcanoes, by the rotting dead in graveyards ... by decaying matter in marshes and swamps. Plague leveled all those who stood before it and spared no person. It seeped into churches, castles and cottages. (1991: 276–77)

Even a genre like travel writing could be 'infected' by the Gothic in its description of the spread of disease. Gertrude Bell's *Persian Pictures* (1894) – a text contemporaneous with *Dracula* – describes a cholera outbreak in Tehran: 'The cloud of dust that hung forever over the desert and the city assumed a more baleful aspect; it hung now like an omen of the deeper cloud which was settling down upon Tehran' (2005: 32). Fleeing into the desert and into the mountains, the 'fugitives' could not escape and [w]herever they went they bore the plague in the midst of them; they dropped dead by the roadside' (33). Disease takes on a racist tone – while the inhabitants succumb to 'Oriental fatalism' (33) and fail to impose systems of quarantine, Europeans and American missionaries work to halt the spread of infection 'in a land where Ignorance is forever preparing a smooth highway for the feet of death' (37). Disease is drawn into the prevailing late 19th-century discourse of progress. Dracula, too, is both a throwback and a contaminator from the East.

As Martin Willis notes, competing theories on the spread of infection filled the medical discourse of the 19th century: contagionism (the spread of disease through human contact – the treatment of which resulted in quarantining and one which was instituted in Eyam centuries earlier) competed with miasmatic theory which postulated that poisonous vapours in the air caused infection and could be treated by sanitary improvements until the more modern understanding of disease, germ theory, took root in the later 19th century. Stoker's use, as

Willis argues, of the miasmatic theory of disease is evident in *Dracula* (1897) and in his earlier short story, 'The Invisible Giant' (1882). In 'The Invisible Giant', an imaginary land is infected by disease in the form of a 'montrous gothic figure' (2007: 303) or miasma but the dereliction of the duties of the angels on the portal to the land allows the disease to enter so the principles of contagionism (quarantine) have been relaxed with serious consequences (2007: 309). In *Dracula*, Willis argues, Stoker presents all three theories of disease. Vampires appear from clouds of dust which 'draws considerably on miasmatic conceptions of infection' (2007: 311). In Whitby Lucy becomes exposed to the disease by her 'unforeseen expedition to the place of infection' (315) but it is her mother who inadvertently brings about her death by 'privile[ing] her knowledge of sanitary science over Van Helsing's more sophisticated understanding of germ theory' (315). Mrs Westenra opens the window of Lucy's bedroom and removes the garlic and when Dracula bursts in through the window her final act before her sudden death by heart attack is to clutch at the garlic around her daughter's neck and tear it away. Lucy or Lucy's body is, of course, the site of the novel's focus on various types of dis-ease (infection, cultural anxiety about the sexualized 'New Woman,' and fear of empire). However, Harker is, as Willis argues, responsible for enabling the transmission of infection 'suggest[ing] the necessity for greater medical and governmental control of foreign trade through the restrictive practices of disease control recommended by the contagionists' (321).

The first biography of Stoker, Harry Ludlam's 1966, *A Biography of Dracula: The Life Story of Bram Stoker*, reads gothicized disease narratives as 'infecting' Stoker's childhood. Furthermore the young Bram Stoker was, until he reached the age of seven, bed-ridden. In *Personal Reminiscences of Henry Irving* (1906) Stoker notes this fact:

> In my babyhood, I used, I understand, to be often at the point of death. Certainly until I was about seven years old I never knew what it was to stand upright. I was naturally thoughtful and the leisure of long illness gave opportunity for many thoughts which were fruitful according to their kind in later years.
>
> This early weakness, however, passed away in time and I grew into a strong boy and in time enlarged to the biggest member of my family. (vol. 1: 31–2)

In the opening paragraph of the first chapter of his biography which Ludlam entitles, 'The Boy Who Refused To Die', the biographer presents

Stoker as a 'sick and feeble child' who 'was expected to die' (1966: 11). However,

> Bram Stoker did not die. For months he hovered on the brink of death, and as the months stretched into long years he maintained a patient, painful struggle to keep himself alive; a struggle that brought eventual triumph only in his eighth year, when for the first time he was able to leave his bed and experience the precarious thrill of standing upright on his own two legs. (1966: 11)

Stoker's own comment in *Personal Reminiscences* that his illness 'gave opportunity for many thoughts which were fruitful according to their kind in later years' (1906, vol. 1: 31) is both suggestive and suitably ambiguous. Ludlam locates the development of Stoker's gothic imagination in the stories that his mother told to him of the cholera outbreak that she had witnessed in County Sligo, Ireland, in 1832. The material, collated in a letter in 1875, and first published in Ludlam's biography, recounts the outbreak as a Gothic nightmare, reminiscent of Bell's later account of the spread of infection in Tehran: 'Rumours of the great plague broke upon us from time to time, as men talk of far-off things which can never come near themselves, but gradually the terror grew on us as we heard it coming nearer and nearer' (1966: 26). One 'poor traveller was taken ill on the roadside some miles from the town' and the locals 'dug a pit and with long poles pushed him living into it, and covered him up quick, alive' (26). Then in a 'very few days the town became a place of the dead. No vehicles moved except the cholera carts or doctors' carriages (26). The local infirmary turned into a cholera hospital and a Catholic priest was 'obliged to sit day after day, and night after night, on top of the [hospital's] great stone stairs with a horse whip, to prevent' the 'wretches' of women who had replaced the dead nurses from 'dragging the patients down the stairs by the legs with their heads dashing on the stone steps, before they were dead' (1966: 27). One man brought his wife to the hospital and by evening he was told she was dead but when he went to recover her corpse he found her under several bodies still alive and brought her home where she recovered (27). One former soldier, Sergeant Callan, was too big for his coffin, so a hammer was used to break his legs, the blow from which 'roused the sergeant from his stupor, and he started up and recovered' with Charlotte confirming that she 'often saw the man after' (27). The townspeople deployed 'constant fumigation' and 'plates of salt on which vitriolic acid was poured' were placed outside windows and doors (28).

The coffin-maker used to knock on doors to see if his services were required and Charlotte threatened him with a jug of water if he refused to desist. When he came again she fulfilled her promise. Charlotte's account, though similar in its gothic tone to the 'The Plague at Eyam' in *All the Year Round*, bears no resemblance to the heroic self-sacrifice of the accounts of the earlier plague.

Charlotte's testimony suffuses Stoker's early short stories in his collection *Under the Sunset* (1882), which includes 'The Invisible Giant'. These were published as children's stories and dedicated to his son Noel. Stoker, influenced by his mother's cholera stories during his early childhood illness, perpetuated this tradition for his own child. Indeed, the *Academy's* review of *Under the Sunset* recoiled from the graphic description of disease advising 'judicious' mothers to 'omit' some of the text's 'dismal doings which might banish sleep from the children's pillows' (10 December 1881: 431). The reviewer warns against a 'terribly grim picture' of the coming of the plague in 'The Invisible Giant' and wishes that these 'lurid passages had been expunged' (432). Stoker's interest in the disease narrative culminates in *Dracula*, a text which has, of course, been transformed in the 20th century and beyond.

The most significant of these transformations from the perspective of disease is Richard Matheson's 1954 vampire novel *I am Legend*. Here Robert Neville is the last human survivor after dust storms from obscure bombings have unleashed what looks like a vampire pandemic amongst Neville's family, neighbours, his city and, by implication, the rest of the planet. In Neville's world, there are two types of vampires: the living and the dead. Rooted in fears of Soviet Russia in Cold War America, Matheson's text is set 20 years in the future. His vampires are not supernatural but rather products of some type of vague chemical warfare. While others succumb to the disease Neville attributes his immunity to a bat bite that he received when he was a soldier in Panama. In *I am Legend* Neville's ordinary suburban home, fortified against the vampires who come out only at night, is the last bastion of survival. As the victims behave like vampires, Neville reads *Dracula* in order to understand them and they conform to the some of the stereotypes of vampire behaviour in *Dracula*, but not to others:

> They were strange, the facts about them: their staying inside by day, their avoidance of garlic, their death by stake, their reputed fear of crosses, their supposed dread of mirrors.
>
> Take that last, now. According to the legend, they were invisible in mirrors, but he knew that was untrue. As untrue as the belief that

they transformed themselves into bats. That was a superstition that logic plus observation had easily disposed of. (1999: 21–2)

Neville becomes a self-trained scientist, a type of Van Helsing figure, locating the cause of the pandemic in a germ. Under a microscope 'there, fluttering delicately on the slide, was a germ. I dub thee *vampiris*' (1999: 79). Like the vampire hunters in *Dracula* Neville initially deploys the stake in order to dispose of the vampires resting by day. While it works, his discovery of the germ brings the realisation that the stake is effective in that it lets air into the body. 'The bacillus', as he explains to Ruth, an alleged survivor of the pandemic,

'is a facultative saprophyte. It lives with or without oxygen; but with a difference. Inside the system, it is anaerobic and sets up a fresh symbiosis with the system. The vampire feeds it fresh blood, the bacteria provides the energy so the vampire can get more fresh blood'. (135)

However, when air enters, Neville explains, '"the situation changes instantaneously. The germ becomes aerobic and, instead of symbiotic, it becomes virulently parasitic ... and eats its host"' (135). Cutting the wrists of vampires is just as effective to eliminate them as staking them through the heart. Although he identifies the germ as the cause of the pandemic, Neville only realises too late that '[B]acteria can mutate' (147) and that Ruth is a living vampire, who with others, has learned to adapt with the aid of a pill, 'a combination of defebrinated blood and a drug .... The blood feeds the germs, and the drug prevents its multiplication. (145). She explains that it was the discovery of this pill that saved us from dying, that is helping to set up society again slowly' (145). Incarcerated in his suburban castle, the living vampires come for Neville at night. As readers we identify with Neville as the last man on earth – we understand his hunting of vampires, his desire for self-preservation. But what shocks us is that Neville is not the norm; he is Other. As the 'last of the old race' he must be destroyed because he is both different and antithetical to the new regime (160). For them, Neville becomes 'a new terror, a new superstition entering the unassailable fortress of forever' – in other words, a new Dracula (160). Like the Count trapped in his castle, Neville's attempt to forge a future is in vain. Like Dracula, who tries to understand and adapt to the modern world, Neville discovers that the modern world of medical development has outpaced him.

That disease continues to be a potent force in gothic narratives is evident in Danny Boyle's *28 Days Later* (2002) which, with its desolate and pandemic-ravaged urban and suburban landscapes, draws its impetus from *I am Legend*. In Boyle's film, disease is no longer just a threat but has consumed. Produced in the context of the 'foot and mouth' epidemic which ravaged British livestock in 2001, the film's opening scenes focus on animals in a laboratory. Animal rights activists storm a Cambridge laboratory (Cambridge Primate Research laboratory) dedicated to animal testing where a chimpanzee is attached to electrodes and strapped to a table. Injected, as we later discover, with the 'Rage' virus the chimpanzee is surrounded by TV monitors projecting violent riots within a global context. Conforming to traditional Gothic ambiguities about scientific experimentations, the scientist explains in a *Jekyll and Hyde* manner that, 'In order to cure you must first understand', before succumbing to the infected apes, released from their cages.

The film shifts its focus to a hospital bed as a young man, Jim, awakens from a coma to discover that he is the sole inhabitant of an empty hospital with residue of hospital equipment indicating that the hospital has been abandoned in panic. Like its early Gothic predecessors, the film interrogates state institutions – the laboratory (a place of danger since *Frankenstein*, 1818) and the hospital (its counterpart in *Dracula* is the asylum which operates as a place of dubious experimentation by its resident psychiatrist, Dr Seward, and where vampire disease can be spread through the patient Renfield). Outside the hospital Jim discovers that while the architecture of a post-apocalyptic London remains intact, people have retreated from this urban space. Seeking answers in a Catholic church, Jim finds dead bodies heaped in the pews (a deliberate reference to the Rwandan genocide of 1994) and encounters his first 'resurrected', a priest. Similarly, in *The Castle of Otranto* (1764) the church is perceived as a place of sanctuary. However, surrounded by the symbols of the resurrection (the ordering principle of Christianity) in an ornate window and cross, Jim finds the newly 'resurrected' zombies who emerge from the heaps of bodies as threatening his very survival. Church is not a place of salvation but one of threat. When he is rescued by survivors, Selena and Mark (who is later infected and killed) Jim still believes in state institutions: 'there's always a government'. The family, the focus of early Gothic, also functions as a place of danger. Frank and his daughter Hannah lead Selena and Jim to what they believe is the security of an army outpost near Manchester after Frank picks up a radio message which promises that 'the answer to infection is here'. The last word in the broadcast is 'salvation' – a word which unites all the state and societal apparatuses – laboratory, hospital, church and army.

The journey to the army outpost invokes Emily's journey to captivity in *The Mysteries of Udolpho* (1790) and the survivors (Jim, Selena and Hannah) discover in the outpost, a country mansion, a despotic patriarchy presided over by a commanding officer Major Henry West. West seeks to create what Jordan S. Carroll describes as a 'regulated space of unquestioned, sovereign patriarchy' (2012: 53). Here he conducts crude experimentation on one of his infected soldiers. In this Gothic mansion, the formerly capable Selena loses her 'non-gendered survivalist persona' (Williams, 2007: 33). This is a place of potential violation, a trap for women and a place of madness. Here the teenage Hannah, drugged into a zombie-like state by Selena (a chemist) in order to protect her psychologically from the soldiers' planned assaults wanders through the mansion's labyrinthine corridors like the threatened heroine, Isabella, in *Otranto*. Jim, forced outside the perimeter walls of this new regime, has to adapt. He becomes zombie-like and unleashes an army of zombies into the grounds of the mansion in order to save his companions. Like *I am Legend*, the notion of the norm becomes reversed. The Other – the army gone mad – is within.

The closing scene sees the survivors in a country cottage as Jim awakens in a metal bed which recalls the hospital bed of the film's opening and the next frame sees Selena sewing. Wearing knitted cardigans the two females project a stereotype of pastoral femininity. Selena has been sewing a giant sheet with the word 'Hello', the first words Jim utters in the film, and which, rather ironically, first alerted the zombies to his presence. When they hear a military plane, Selena, Jim and Hannah spread the 'Hello' onto the field outside the house. Despite its hopeful ending Jordan suggests that there is an implicit fear that 'the second time the characters call upon military saviors will be like the first' (2012: 55).

The film's bucolic ending and much of its narrative conforms to a conservative Gothic. In this regard, it is similar to *Dracula* where capable women (Mina and Selena) retreat to domesticity and less capable men (Jonathan and Jim) become heroes. In the film's alternative ending, Jim dies in a deserted hospital as Selena desperately pumps drugs into him in an attempt to save him. The final scene shows Selena and Hannah leave the hospital with Hannah picking up Jim's gun. The fully armed women, still clothed in red dresses which the soldiers forced them to wear, walk down the corridor 'fully bent on their survival as individuals' (Williams, 2007: 34). But Boyle noted that rather than seeing this as a moment of female empowerment, audiences perceived the women as heading 'towards their own doom' (34). What this suggests is that the conservative gender politics of the Gothic merely reflects that of contemporary society.

Both *28 Days Later* and *I am Legend* articulate the fear of pandemic. *28 Days Later* draws both on the menstrual cycle and infection through blood. Dracula's desire to walk through a mighty London is associated with devastating consequences, but his attacks in Britain result in the contamination of only two individuals: Lucy succumbs to the vampire disease, while Mina survives. The vampire threat does not materialize in a pandemic as the children Lucy attacks on Hampstead Heath seem to survive the encounter, and their residual memory of the infection is positive as the children describe how they were playing with the '"bloofer [beautiful] lady"' (1997: 160). However, the vampire's attack on Lucy Westenra is symbolic of an attack on the west, just as Henry's West's name in *28 Days Later* signifies that degeneracy is already within. All three texts explore disease as a materialization of fear in the culture.

Apart from its resonances and transformations across Gothic productions, Dracula, has left his deathly imprint on Whitby. The plague village of Eyam commemorates an actual plague after all, if indeed, the history of its events have largely become an invented tradition. The tablets outside the village houses in Eyam, recording like tombstones the victims who resided within, service this grim heritage. In Whitby, the actual tombstones of St Mary's Churchyard which, with the exception of the suicide's grave where Dracula rests on landing in the town, are, as old Mr Swales explains, largely empty tombs for the bodies lost at sea, rather than those lost through disease. From the suicide's grave, Dracula is resurrected to transform the town into a place of Gothic heritage.

## II

### 'My revenge is just begun'

'My revenge is just begun! I spread it over centuries, and time is on my side' (1997: 267), warns Dracula to the group of vampire hunters. In many ways this statement is descriptive of the genre. Like the Count, the Gothic encompasses and has manifested itself in many forms since *The Castle of Otranto*. Its revenge has just begun. It has spread over centuries and time is on its side. Early Gothic, much like its 21st century transformation in *28 Days Later*, reveals the corruption that lies behind authority and questions the dominant cultural values of its age, even as it reconstitutes them. As Clive Bloom argues, the genre is 'at once escapist and conformist' and 'speaks to the dark side of domestic fiction: erotic, violent, perverse, bizarre and obsessively connected with contemporary fears' (2007: 2). He continues: 'It could hardly be otherwise and the debate over gothic's power to be subversive or conservative by turns is testimony to its immediacy as well as to its archaic (or 'eternal') elements' (2). Between *Otranto* and *28 Days Later* lies *Dracula*. Stoker's novel, as this collection of essays testifies, marks a key moment in the transformation of the Gothic. *Dracula* harks back to early Gothic's preoccupation with the supernatural, decayed aristocracy and incarceration in gloomy castles in foreign locales as well as a 19th-century Gothic preoccupation, as we have seen above, with science and disease. The novel speaks to its own time but also transforms the genre, a revitalization that continues to sustain the Gothic today.

*Bram Stoker and the Gothic: Formations to Transformations* explores the formations of the Gothic, the relationship between Stoker's work and some of his Gothic predecessors and presents new readings of Stoker's fiction. The collection concludes by focusing on aspects of transformation. Martin Arnold opens by tracing a European Gothic literary heritage before *Otranto*. The European Romantic Revival, Arnold argues, demonstrated an enthusiasm for the myths of medieval Scandinavia which have underpinned the Gothic novel as it emerged in the late 18th century. Walpole, influenced by his friend the poet Thomas Gray, was known to have studied Old Norse myths just before he started writing *Otranto* and Stoker, born in Clontarf, Dublin (the site of a famous battle between the Irish and the Vikings) also romanticized the figure of the Viking in his fiction. Bettina Pedersen's essay draws Mary Wollstonecraft's *The Wrongs of Woman; or Maria* (1796) into dialogue with *Dracula*. Although published a century apart, Pedersen argues that while Wollstonecraft makes an 'unapologetic and progressive critique of the wrongs of woman', Stoker, although 'seemingly positive' about the rise of the New Woman, in fact re-inscribes a 'paternalistic essentialism.' Kevin Corstorphine concludes the section on Gothic formations by examining the influence of Edgar Allan Poe on Stoker's fiction. Focussing on Stoker's little-known story, 'The Squaw', Corstorphine examines the influence of America in Stoker's fiction and reveals rich transatlantic cultural exchanges.

The next essays in the collection shift the terrain to aspects of Transylvania. As Stijn Reijinders argues, Transylvania has 'become synonymous with Dracula Country: a land of howling wolves, vampires, bats and gloomy castles' creating a Transylvania in the popular imagination that is on the 'mental periphery of Europe – a kingdom where superstitions and ancient rituals are still widespread' (2010: 231). Marius-Mircea Crişan's essay examines Stoker's reading on Transylvania and the representation of Transylvania in nineteenth-century travelogues. Stoker,

Crişan argues, creates a mythic Transylvania that is both superstitious and outside of time. Abby Bardi focuses on the Szgany in *Dracula* in relation to the Count's accumulation of property in Britain. As 'facilitators of the Count's project' the Szgany, perceived as wandering and outsider figures, aid the count in his assault on English identity.

Carol A. Senf moves the discussion into new approaches to Stoker's work. Senf argues that while Stoker has been perceived as producer of Gothic fiction, his broader oeuvre undermines this simple designation. Stoker's fictions, including his non-Gothic, Senf argues, can be read as 'invasion narratives' which articulate contemporary fears of invasion or 'reverse colonization' in a period when 'England was intent on preserving her colonial holdings.' Victoria Samantha Dawson offers a scientific reading of dust in *Dracula*. While on one level the undead Count's transformation into dust raises anxieties about 'human stability', on a Christian level this may also allow for his reintegration into the 'taxonomic order of matter'. Sara Williams examines the 'devouring mother' in Stoker's *The Jewel of Seven Stars* and 'The Squaw.' Read in the context of gynaecological beliefs of the *fin-de-siècle* Williams explores how the mother in these fictions leaves its mark or imprint on the foetus as an act of appropriation that has psychic and colonial ramifications. Luke Gibbons' essay examines an aerial Gothic, a host of aerial fictions produced in the early twentieth century, including Stoker's *The Lady of the Shroud*, which engaged in war and colonization. Gibbons draws Stoker and the focus of his essay into an Irish and European context.

The next two essays in the collection focus on the cultural influences on Stoker's fiction. Certainly the 'climate of supernatural plays and melodramas' (Wynne, 2013: 9; 41–77) produced by Henry Irving and Ellen Terry at the Lyceum Theatre where Stoker worked as business manager cultivated Stoker's Gothic imagination. Katharine Cockin's essay engages in this broader climate looking at the occultist predilections of the period and Stoker's association with the illustrator, Pamela Colman Smith, who designed tarot cards and provided the lurid illustrations for Stoker's final novel, *The Lair of the White Worm*. Richard Storer draws on archival materials to examine the relationship between Stoker and the best-selling novelist Hall Caine, the dedicatee of *Dracula*. Storer explores Caine's 'liminal presence' in *Dracula* and further examines the characters in Caine's fiction who 'can be identified as transformed portraits of Bram Stoker'.

The final set of chapters in the collection engage with transformations. My essay examines the du Maurier family's relationship with Whitby as well as Stoker's. George du Maurier holidayed in Whitby in the 1880s and 1890s and produced numerous illustrations of the town. The essay uncovers new connections between Stoker and George and focuses on how Daphne du Maurier and Stoker transform Whitby into a Gothic place in their writings. It concludes with an examination Daphne's Gothic Cornwall and briefly addresses Stoker's fictions set in that county. William Hughes examines the 'fictionalisation' of Stoker arguing how the 'apparently uncomplicated masculine heartiness of the author's Victorian and Edwardian image' is transformed by critics and biographers into a 'façade' hiding 'alleged personal and sexual traumas'. Hughes further examines a number of contemporary novels which feature and transform Stoker for a 20th- and 21st-century audience. The final essay in the collection is a reflective piece by a working artist whose inspiration is derived from a Gothic literary heritage. Jef Murray's illustrated essay concludes with a reflection on the book jacket image of Stoker's Lady of the Shroud. *Bram Stoker and the Gothic: Formations to Transformations* testifies to Stoker's centrality to the Gothic genre. Like Dracula, Stoker's 'revenge' shows no sign of abating.

# 1
# On the Origins of the Gothic Novel: From Old Norse to Otranto

*Martin Arnold*

> A primary vehicle for the literary Gothic in the late eighteenth to early nineteenth centuries was past superstition. The extent to which Old Norse tradition provided the basis for a subspecies of literary horror has been passed over in an expanding critical literature which has not otherwise missed out on cosmopolitan perspectives.

This observation by Robert W. Rix (2011: 1) accurately assesses what may be considered a significant oversight in studies of the Gothic novel. Whilst it is well known that the ethnic meaning of 'Gothic' originally referred to invasive, eastern Germanic, pagan tribes of the third to the sixth centuries AD (Sowerby, 2000: 15–26), there remains a disconnect between Gothicism as the legacy of Old Norse literature and the use of the term 'Gothic' to mean a category of fantastical literature. This essay, then, seeks to complement Rix's study by, in certain areas, adding more detail about the gradual emergence of Old Norse literature as a significant presence on the European literary scene. The initial focus will be on those formations (often malformations) and interpretations of Old Norse literature as it came gradually to light from the sixteenth century onwards, and how the Nordic Revival impacted on what is widely considered to be the first Gothic novel, *The Castle of Otranto* (1764) by Horace Walpole (1717–97). As will be argued, although Walpole was ambivalent in his opinions on the growing influence of Nordic antiquity in the latter half of the eighteenth century, it is quite clear that it played an important role in stimulating his 'Gothicised' imagination, not least due to his close association with the poet Thomas Gray (1716–71), an unabashed enthusiast for the Old North. The essay will conclude with an examination of how, over a hundred years later, this material and all things Viking, along with the attendant glamorisations, had become an accepted and uncontroversial cultural reference point in the novels of Bram Stoker (1847–1912).

## The Scandinavian recovery period from the sixteenth to the early eighteenth century

The manuscripts containing myths and legends concerning pagan Scandinavia fall broadly into three areas. The first and most mythologically informative area includes *The Poetic Edda*, an anonymous collection of over thirty poems, many of which were preserved from oral tradition, and *The Prose Edda*, a systematised account of Old Norse mythology set down in the early thirteenth century by the Icelander Snorri Sturluson (1178/9–1241). As Iceland had converted to Christianity over two hundred years earlier, Snorri's *edda* takes particular care not to offend biblical orthodoxy, so providing a euhemerised introduction which explains the error of Norse paganism in terms of naïve Scandinavians mistaking northward migrating descendants of heroes of the Trojan wars for gods. The second area includes medieval histories, such as Adam of Bremen's late eleventh-century *Gesta Hammaburgensis Ecclesiae Pontificum* (Deeds of the Bishops of the Hamburg Church), Saxo Grammaticus's late twelfth-/early thirteenth-century *Gesta Danorum* (The History of the Danes) and Snorri Sturluson's *Heimskringla*, an early thirteenth-century history of the kings of Norway. Explicit disapprobation of pre-Christian practices is most apparent in the histories by Adam and Saxo. The third and by far the largest area is the Icelandic sagas, which range from the seemingly historical to the wildly imaginative. The sagas also preserved the majority of skaldic poetry, an occasional verse-form using a highly complex metre. Whilst Old Norse manuscripts continued to come to light from the Renaissance onwards, it was the interpretations placed on them and the various medieval histories by patriotic Scandinavian scholars that characterised their early reception history.

Initially, there were three main problems for the Scandinavians in their efforts to reclaim their respective country's pre-Christian history. Firstly, there was the widespread perception elsewhere in Europe that Scandinavia was a cultural backwater, one where Christianity was late in arriving and where Greco-Roman Classicism had had little impact and, so, had left the European north culturally impoverished. Endorsing this view was Giorgio Vasari (1511–74), whose influential *Lives of the Artists* (1524) included a 'philippic against the Gothic style' which denounced north European medieval architecture as barbaric compared to the Classical Revival of his own time (Pearsall, 2001: 2). Secondly, as was the case with Snorri Sturluson's *edda*, any attempt to recover the pagan past needed to be reconciled with biblical history, hence the continued need for euhemerisation. Thirdly, political relations between the Dano-Norwegian coalition, which included Iceland as a Danish colony, and Sweden were very strained. The, perhaps inevitable, consequence of these problems was that interpretations placed upon the Scandinavian past were invariably convoluted and typically determined to belittle their political opponents. Ethnographic insults and counter-insults were aimed across the Baltic inlets throughout the early recovery period.

In sixteenth-century Denmark, two printed editions of Saxo's *Gesta Danorum*, one in the original Latin and one in Danish translation, formed the basis of Danish insights into their early ancestors but, for further insight, the Danes needed to look to Iceland and its vast store of medieval manuscripts. The most influential Icelander on future Danish and Icelandic scholars was Arngrímur Jónsson (1568–1648), who referred to Old Norse as 'Old Gothic'. Arngrímur used Icelandic saga sources to write a now lost history of the Danish kings, and perturbed by the poor reports Iceland had received from visitors, wrote the chauvinistic *Brevis commentarius de Islandia* (Defence of Iceland) and *Crymogæa* (On Iceland). Given such efforts by learned Icelanders, the Danes would always be better informed than the Swedes and, as a result, somewhat more sober in the significances they attached to manuscript evidence. Lacking such resources, the Swedes were largely dependent on Adam of Bremen's unflattering history of their pagan past, which they combined with early Roman histories, notably Tacitus's first-century, often approving, history of the Germanic tribes, *Germania*, and Jordanes's sixth-century history of the Gothic tribes, *Getica*, which they construed as meaning exclusively Swedish tribes. The main significance of Swedish interpretations of their past lies in the impact they had on Danish scholars, whose responses were typically belligerent and not a little hyperbolised.

Setting the tone for future rivalries with the Danes were the Swedish brothers Johannes Magnus (1488–1544), the last Catholic Archbishop of Uppsala, and Olaus Magnus (1490–1557), who as a consequence of the Lutheran Reformation, inherited his brother's title in name only. According to Johannes's posthumously published *Historia de omnibus Gothorum Sveonumque regibus* (A History of All the Kings of the Goths and the Swedes) of 1554, the Swedish Goths were originally led by the biblical Magog, Noah's grandson. Fortunately, Magog had taken his tribe to Sweden before the destruction of the Tower of Babel, the upshot being that the Goths spoke the language of God and had therefore succeeded in spreading civilised values across Ancient Greece on through to the birth of Christ. It was these divinely ordained virtues that had enabled the Goths to triumph over the Roman legions, as recounted in Jordanes's *Getica*. Moreover, claimed Johannes, the surviving evidence of the *ur*-language of the Goths is Gothic script, otherwise known as runes, which, on the one hand, he wrongly asserted to be uniquely Swedish, and on the other, implied them to be a common form of manuscript writing. This extraordinary theory was one that Olaus Magnus not only fully endorsed but also used to remind enemies of the Swedes, i.e. the Danes, how unwise it would be 'to join battle with the elements themselves' (Johannesson, 1991: 189).

Pursuing a similar, if less excessive, line of what had become known as Gothicism was the Dane Ole Worm (1588–1654). Here again, doubtless in response to Swedish assertions, runes were the issue. For Worm, runes provided not only an insight into Danish origins, character and vocation but also into the origins of language, for, he argued, Danish runes, that is to say all runes, are derived from Hebraic script. With the help of the Icelanders, most notably Magnús Ólafsson (1574–1636), Worm's *RUNIR seu Danica literatura antiquissima ... eller literatura runica* (Runes or the Most Ancient Danish Literature) of 1636 drew particular attention to 'Krákumál', a heroic poem rendered by Worm in both runic script and Latin that became widely translated in Britain in the seventeenth and eighteenth centuries as 'The Death-Song of Ragnar Lodbrok'. In this, the hero, Ragnar, has been cast defenceless into a Northumbrian snake-pit, where he proudly reflects on his many triumphs as a Viking warrior. 'Laughing shall I die', concludes Ragnar, for he is sure of his glorious transportation to Valhalla by Odin's Valkyries, where, according to Worm's text, he will drink ale from the skulls of his fallen enemies. However, while the arresting idea of a human skull-cup is one that would become widely quoted by future enthusiasts for 'runic poetry', the text provided for Worm by Magnús Ólafsson had misinterpreted the Old Norse phrase *or bjúgviðum hausa* as signifying a human skull, whereas it actually means 'from the curved branches of skulls', a poetic locution for 'drinking-horns' (Gordon, 1981: lxix–lxx).

Such solecisms apart, the latter half of the seventeenth century presented even greater opportunities for the Danes to advertise the literary genius and indomitable spirit of their ancestors. The discovery of the manuscripts of *The Poetic Edda* in Iceland in 1634 and the presentation of them to King Frederick III of Denmark in 1662, led the Danish scholar

Bishop Peder Resen (1625–88) to include Danish and Latin translations of the eddic poems 'Völuspá' (The Seeress's Prophecy), a Creation to Ragnarök augury, and 'Hávamál' (The Sayings of the High One), an extensive articulation of Odin's wisdom, alongside Resen's landmark translation of the whole of *The Prose Edda* (Faulkes, ed., vol. 2: 1977–79). For Resen, Norse mythology contained 'certain higher spiritual truths, to be apprehended intuitively', which recent scholars have perceived as a shift from the 'pragmatic' to the 'metaphysical' (Malm, 1996; Clunies Ross and Lönnroth, 1999: 7). From here on, reconciling Norse paganism with the bible could be done on a philosophical basis rather than in terms of tortuous arguments concerning the divinely blessed origins of the Goths, not that this stopped such desperate efforts entirely.

The final decades of the seventeenth century marked the high point in antipathies between Danish and Swedish scholars. Setting aside, for now, the highly influential 1672 translation of the Icelandic *Hervarar saga ok Heiðreks* (The Saga of Hervar and Heidrik) by the Swedish scholar Olaus Verelius (1618–82), which included the much vaunted heroic poem that became known in English circles as 'The Waking of Angantýr', it was both national politics and the often deeply personal rivalry between the Dane Thomas Bartholin the Younger (1659–90) and the Swede Olof Rudbeck (1630–1702) that coloured scholarly judgements.

Olof Rudbeck's four-volume, three-thousand page treatise *Atlantica* (Swedish: *Atland eller Manheim*), which he began in 1679 and continued to work on until his death in 1702, was clearly inspired by the theories of Johannes and Olaus Magnus, and, indeed, Ole Worm. Rudbeck argued that Sweden was the cradle of civilisation named by Plato as 'Atlantis' and that the Swedish language was inherited from Adam and was, therefore, the forerunner of Hebrew. The logic of this, insisted Rudbeck, is that Greek and Roman mythology had originated in Atlantian Sweden. The proof for Rudbeck is to be found in the *edda*s, which, in painstaking detail, he interpreted as an allegorical code, one that Plato had cleverly remodeled. So it is, for example, that when Plato refers to elephants, what is actually being signified are Swedish wolves (Malm, 1994: 12).

Thomas Bartholin's response to Rudbeck was to ignore any distinction between the Swedish and the Danish past and refer to all Scandinavians as Danes. As for Rudbeck's *Atlantica*, Bartholin was an unsparing critic, accusing him of 'having no more purpose in all the heap of his work than to attack the history of the Danes' and adding, 'Oh, wretched condition of the History of the Northern Lands, if, indeed, upon the testimony of the Greek poets it shall stand or fall', which conveniently ignored Bartholin's own tendency to do likewise when it suited his argument (Bartholin, 1689: 324–6: author's own translations). Nonetheless, here again, while the Swedes were obliged to resort to extravagant theorising in order to assert their ancestral superiority over their Scandinavian neighbours, the Danes had the benefit of far greater manuscript resources.

As had been the case with Ole Worm, Bartholin was highly dependent on the Icelanders in order to substantiate his views. In Bartholin's case, it was his highly industrious assistant Árni Magnússon (1633–1730), who collected together and translated thousands of pages of Icelandic manuscripts. Notably, Árni also acquired the entire manuscript collection of his deceased countryman Þormóður Torfason (1636–1719), whose Latin translations of Icelandic sagas concerning Viking settlements across the North Atlantic, including the eastern seaboard of North America, had a major impact on many Catholic-averse North Americans during the nineteenth century (Barnes, 2001). Bartholin's use of this material was to focus was on Viking machismo and derring-do. His *Antiquitatum danicarum de causis contemptae a Danis adhuc gentilibus mortis* (Danish Antiquities Concerning the Reasons for the Danes Disdain for Death) of 1689, adduces as much evidence as was then available to highlight the nobility of Danish mentality, which, Bartholin suggests, was directly inherited from the Vikings and their devotions to the Norse gods.

Inevitably, as the title of Bartholin's study indicates, it was the death-defying Ragnar Lodbrok who epitomised Bartholin's lionisation of the Danish past. In effect, what Bartholin was ultimately set on validating was the manly virtue of that individual who, through no fault of his own, had not benefited from the revealed faith of Christianity but who nonetheless lived according to the principles of a blame-free precursor to Christian conversion. This rehabilitation of the Scandinavian pagan, mooted in the works of Worm and his Icelandic informants, marked another significant step toward Romanticist interpretations of Norse myth and legend that would come to dominate enthusiasm for the Old North.

Despite the tendency toward patriotically overwrought 'medievalisms' from both the Swedes and the Danes, the wealth of manuscript information they collectively gathered together and translated, both into Latin and their native tongues, gave many scholars and literary artists throughout Europe access to the Old Norse legacy. During the early eighteenth century, with theories of a Rudbeckian nature now largely dismissed, less nationalist and better informed studies emerged in both Denmark and Sweden, although euhemerisation continued to be regarded as essential when it came to any discussion of the origins of Norse paganism.

## Old Norse reception in England in the seventeenth and early eighteenth centuries

For a number of English scholars during the seventeenth century, knowledge about the pre-Christian Germanic practices, which became available through the publications of Worm and Bartholin particularly, stimulated several studies aiming to shed further light on the Anglo-Saxon past. Even before the Scandinavian material impacted on English antiquarians, William Camden (1561–1623) had perceived the ethnic and religious similarities between Bede's eighth-century description of pre-conversion Anglo-Saxons and Adam of Bremen's description of Scandinavian pagans (Quinn and Clunies Ross, 1994: 189–90). Adding to this, in 1605, was Richard Verstegen (c. 1550–1640), an English-born Dutch national whose *A Restitution of decayed Intelligence in Antiquities, concerning the most Noble and Renowned English Nation* had somewhat censoriously offered as detailed a study as was then possible of ancient Saxon beliefs.

Once vastly more documentary evidence came to light, the term 'rune' came under particular scrutiny by Sir Henry Spelman (c.1562–1641), who having corresponded at length with Ole Worm and been sent a copy of his *RUNIR*, deduced that in Old English the significance of 'rune' (*rún*) was 'a secret' or 'a mystery', a point that Worm noted in his future studies. Expanding on this was Robert Sheringham (1602–78), who, having read Resen's translations of the *eddas*, particularly 'Hávamál', commented insightfully on Odin's mastery of runes and also cited two verses from Worm's 'Death-Song of Ragnar Lodbrok' in Latin, including, of course, the mistranslation made by Magnús Ólafsson. Clearly influenced by Sheringham, Aylett Sammes (c. 1636–c. 1679) in his compendious account of Anglo-Saxon and Old Norse beliefs, the first to be published in English translation, also cites the egregious 'Death-Song' verse, the key lines of which he renders, perhaps with deliberate drollery, as, 'There we shall Tope our bellies full / Of Nappy-Ale in full-brim'd Skull' (Sammes, 1676: 436; Fell, 1993: 88–9; also Fell, 1996: 29–35). Adding further insight into the ideological significance of Old Norse poetry were the essays 'Of Heroick Virtue' and 'Of Poetry' published in 1690 by the British diplomat Sir William Temple (1628–99) (Omberg, 1976: 18–20).

While none of the scholars noted above could read Old Norse and were therefore reliant on Latin translations, a basis had been formed for a more rigorous and philologically accomplished approach. This was delivered by George Hickes (1642–1715), whose *Linguarum vett. septentrionalium thesaurus grammatico-criticus et archæologicus* (Treasury of the Old Northern Language, 1703–05) included the first English translations made directly from Norse poetry. Although making good use of Bartholin's work, it was Hickes's translation of 'The Waking of Angantýr', which he took from Olaus Verelius's edition of 1672, that would come to rank alongside Ragnar's 'Death-Song' in the fascination it held for scholars, poets and novelists of the latter half of the eighteenth century and beyond. This poem tells of the shield-maiden Hervor visiting the haunted grave of her 'berserker' father, Angantýr, in order to retrieve his magical but cursed sword, Tyrfing. Despite Angantýr's warning that the sword would bring Hervor nothing but misfortune, he reluctantly gives it to her. Ghosts, magic swords and supernatural curses were the very ingredients to excite the Romantic imagination.

The relatively marginal influence of Norse aficionados on mainstream English culture of the time was in many ways reflected in the generally poor reception that all things Gothic were given by English literary artists of the Enlightenment establishment. Andrew Marvell (1621–78) in his poem 'A Letter to Doctor Ingelo' (1653), ostensibly a tribute to Queen Christina of Sweden, nevertheless notes the 'sins the Goth ... committed against the liberal arts' (Donno, ed., 1983: 123, l. 71). Similarly, John Dryden (1631–1700) in his 'To the Earl of Roscommon' (1684) suggests that Gothic travesties 'Debas'd the majesty of Verse to Rhymes' (Hammond, ed., 1995, vol. II: 219, l. 12), and in his 'To Sir Godfrey Kneller' (1694) that 'Goths and Vandals, a rude Northern race, / Did all the matchless Monuments deface' (cited in Omberg, 1976: 86). However, judging from his 'Epistle to Dr Charleton' (1663), Dryden had not always been so critical of Germanic antiquity, for when it came to celebrating King Charles II allegedly taking refuge at Stonehenge in 1651, he evidently subscribes to Ole Worm's view, via Charleton (see Charleton, 1663), that Stonehenge was built by the Danes, a people, says Dryden, of 'mighty visions' (Hammond, ed., 1995, vol. I: 74, l. 56). Far less equivocal about the Gothic past and, in this case specifically, the scholarship of Ole Worm was Alexander Pope (1688–1744), who, in 1742, published the third of four versions of 'The Dunciad'.[1] The following deliberately archaised lines from it reveal exactly what Pope thought about such matters:

> But who is he, in closet close y-pent,
> Of sober face, with learned dust besprent?

Right well mine eyes arede the myster wight,
On parchment scraps y-fed, and Wormius [Ole Worm] hight.
To future ages may thy dulness last,
As thou preserv'st the dulness of the past!
(Rumbold, ed., 1999, Bk 3: 243–44, ll. 185–90)

If nothing else, Pope's ridicule does, at the very least, suggest that Worm's work was of sufficiently high profile to be worth an eminent English satirist's attention. Yet, while the impact of Scandinavian efforts to rehabilitate their past remained merely latent in England, matters were about to change and when they did so, the outcome was nothing short of dramatic.

## Mallet's Histoire de Dannemarc and Macpherson's Ossianic poetry

Underlying the Romantic Revival were three interrelated oppositions: northern or, more precisely, Germanic Europe versus Latinate southern Europe; Protestantism versus Catholicism; and the medieval versus the Classical. At the heart of these matters were issues concerning ethnic, religious and national identity, which, for Protestant countries, entailed establishing a cultural lineage to rival that of Greco-Romanism. While tensions between Denmark and Sweden had subsided by the mid eighteenth century, Scandinavians continued to resent anti-Gothic sentiments that still prevailed elsewhere in Europe. Determined to correct this was King Frederick V of Denmark (r. 1746–66), who commissioned the Swiss pedagogue and historian Paul Henri Mallet (1730–1807) to produce a new history of Denmark, one, as it turned out, that would also offer an aesthetic perspective.

Written in French and therefore much more accessible to Europe's bourgeoisie, Mallet published the initial fruits of his research in 1755 as *Introduction à l'Histoire de Dannemarc, où l'on traite de la Religion, des Loix, des Moeurs et des Usages des Anciens Danois*. In 1756 he published an expanded edition as *Monumens de la Mythologie et de la Poésie des Celtes, et particulièrement des anciens Scandinave, pour server de supplement et de preuves à L'Introduction à l'Histoire de Dannemarc'*, and in 1763 he published his comprehensive *Histoire de Dannemarc* in six volumes, this last having considerable impact in Britain. Mallet draws on all previous research in Denmark and Iceland but disdains unsubstantiated theorising, referring to Swedish scholars of the sixteenth and seventeenth centuries as 'pretended guides' (Percy, trans, 1809, vol. 1: 39). Sections are devoted to the legal, military, and religious beliefs and practices in the Old North, and, in this last respect, include his French rendition of Peder Resen's Latin translation of Snorri Sturluson's 'Gylfaginning', an interrogation of Odin's wisdom by a certain King Gylfi, as contained in *The Prose Edda*.

Mallet, however, did not entirely abandon earlier religious cautions, for despite finding Snorri's euhemerised introduction to his *edda* to be absurd, he nonetheless gives his own tendentious explanation for the origins of an Odinnic cult. This, he argues, had its beginning in the first century BC, when King Odin of Scythia – a territory which lay between the Black Sea and the Caspian – had fled north in the face of advancing Roman legions. Moreover, one obvious shortcoming of Mallet's research was his inability to distinguish between the Celtic and Nordic peoples, a confusion that would not be put right until Bishop Thomas Percy (1729–1811) published his *Northern Antiquities* in 1770, an English translation of *Histoire de Dannemarc*. Nonetheless, Mallet's *Histoire* chimed well with the dawning spirit of Romanticism and did more to bring respectability to early Scandinavian history than anything previously written. Informing and giving credibility to Mallet's later editions of his *Histoire* were Jean-Jacques Rousseau's notion of the 'noble savage' (1754), an idea that Bartholin had hinted at almost a hundred years previously, and Edmund Burke's notion of the 'northern sublime' (1756), a boreal challenge to a perceived Greco-Roman monopoly when it came to describing nature's wonders (Clunies Ross and Lönnroth, 1999: 15). It is, then, not a little ironic that a good deal of the interest that Mallet's work stimulated in the Germanic past arose from what might rightly be called one of the greatest literary frauds ever perpetrated.

In 1760, the patriotic Scot, James Macpherson (1736–96), published his *Fragments of Ancient Poetry, Collected in the Highlands of Scotland, and Translated from the Gaelic or Erse Language*. Two years later came the sequel *Fingal* and, in 1763, the concluding volume *Temora*. These allegedly authentic verse epics concerned the lives, beliefs and tribulations of the Highland tribes as told by the blind bard Ossian, a Caledonian Homer. Set, wholly improbably, in the third century AD, Ossianic poetry tells of the wars between the Celts and the barbarous sea-borne Scandinavians, who were worshippers of the brutal god Loda, a deity that Macpherson equated to Odin. What is more, said Macpherson, he had the manuscripts to prove it, although despite repeated requests, he never produced them, the simple reason being that they did not exist.

Delivered in a form to suit eighteenth-century tastes, Ossianic poetry was the first literary creation in the English language to pay any significant attention to the ancient Scandinavians, albeit that Macpherson's grasp of Old Norse mythology was at best superficial. Although Macpherson claims familiarity with Mallet's work, citing it on several occasions, it is most likely that he was getting his Scandinavian material second-hand from Hugh Blair (1718–1800), Professor of Rhetoric and *Belles Lettres* at the University of Edinburgh. It was Blair who wrote the preface for *Fragments* and published his *Critical Dissertation on the Poems of Ossian* in 1763, which Macpherson read in 1762, thus prior to publishing *Temora*. In whatever case, Macpherson both misrepresents and misreports Mallet's studies. It is also apparent that 'The Death-Song of Ragnar Lodbrok' played an increasingly large role in Macpherson's descriptions of the Scandinavians and this he most certainly sourced from Hugh Blair's translation of Worm's text. Blair, however, was no great fan of Old Norse poetry, which when compared to Ossianic poetry, he thought to be 'like passing from a savage desart [sic] into a fertile and cultivated country' (Omberg, 1976: 31–2; Hall, 2007: 14, *fn.* 50).

The impact of Macpherson's fraud cannot be underestimated, for despite it being identified as such by a number of eminent critics, including Dr Samuel Johnson (1709–84), it became a literary sensation across Europe, for example, in Germany, serving as an inspiration for the *volkspoesie* enthusiasms of Johann Gottfried von Herder (1744–1803) and Johann Wolfgang von Goethe (1749–1832) (see Gaskill, 2003: 95–116). Set together, Mallet's *Histoire de Dannemarc* and Macpherson's Ossianic poetry established much of the literary basis and inspiration for the Romantic Revival and, as will now be examined, for the Gothic novel.

## Gothicism and Horace Walpole

The 'frenzied enthusiasm for "antique poetry"' (Wawn, 2005: 326) that began in England in the early 1760s included two major figures, both spurred on by Ossian and Mallet: the celebrated poet Thomas Gray and the industrious antiquarian Thomas Percy, noted above for his translation of Mallet's *Histoire* in 1770.

In 1761, having absorbed himself in not only Mallet's early studies of Old Norse literature but also the studies of Bartholin and, via Bartholin, the Latin translations of Þormóður Torfason, Gray wrote embellishments of two 'odes' derived from *eddic* poetry, with plans, later abandoned, to write more from these sources. The first was 'The Fatal Sisters', which had been included in the medieval Icelandic *Njáls saga* as *Darraðarljóð* (The Lay of Dörruð [or Battle]). The setting is the Battle of Clontarf in Ireland in 1014, where, as the Vikings enter combat, a group of supernatural females, who Gray identifies as Valkyries, are depicted seated and chanting, while weaving the guts of the slain on a loom laden with severed heads. The second was 'The Descent of Odin' which was based on the poem known both as *Baldrs draumar* (Baldr's Dreams) and *Vegtamskviða* (Vegtam's, i.e. Odin's, Lay). This tells of Odin's journey into the realm of the dead to question a certain prophetess (*völva*) about the future of his knowingly ill-fated son, Baldr (Lonsdale, ed., 1969: 210–28; see also Finlay, 2007: 1–20).

While Gray was toying with further sorties into the realms of Old Norse poetry, Thomas Percy was preparing his own Mallet-inspired Nordic miscellany, *Five Pieces of Runic Poetry*, which he, too, put together in 1761 but delayed publication until 1763. This included two poems that had already found favour with English scholars: firstly, 'The Incantation of Hervor', for which he credits both Hickes's 'The Waking of Angantýr' and Hickes's own source, Olaus Verelius; secondly, 'The Dying Ode of Regner Lodbrok', for which he credits Worm and, as a consequence, replicates Magnús Ólafsson's error regarding drinking vessels in Valhalla.[2]

The question, then, is this: how much of the increasing fashion for Old Norse literature impressed itself on Horace Walpole, as between June and September 1764, prompted by a nightmare, he wrote *The Castle of Otranto*? Firstly, it is worth noting that Walpole clearly did not share Giorgio Vasari's contempt for Gothic architecture, having spent several decades and a small fortune painstakingly restoring Strawberry Hill, his country seat, in flamboyant Gothic style (see Miles, 2007: 11). Significantly, Walpole regarded Strawberry Hill as a place where he was 'always impatient to be back with my own Woden and Thor, my own Gothic Lares' (Vol. 21: 433. To Horace Mann, 28 August 1760).[3] Secondly, as Gray's close friend, often acting as his amanuensis, there was no possibility of Walpole being ignorant of Gray's fascination with the literary products of Germanic antiquity. Yet Walpole does not appear to be appreciative of Gray's efforts, for in a letter to George Montagu in 1761, he writes, 'Gray has translated two noble incantations from the Lord knows who, a Danish Gray, who lived the Lord knows when' (Vol. 9: 364. 5 May 1761). Moreover, in another letter to Montagu in 1768, the same year that Walpole's Strawberry Hill printing press published Gray's odes, he declares that, although they are 'grand and picturesque', unlike his other poetry, they are 'not interesting' and 'do not touch any passion'. He concludes, 'Who can care through what horrors a Runic savage arrived at all the joys and glories they could conceive, the supreme felicity of boozing ale out of the skull of an enemy in Odin's Hall?' (Vol. 10: 255. 12 March 1768).

Yet, in later years, Walpole was not consistent in these views, perhaps either because he no longer prized a literary flourish and wit over critical objectivity or because the untimely death of Gray now obliged greater respect. Whatever the reason may have been for Walpole's apparent *volte-face*, in 1776 he wrote to William Mason, who, apparently, had delivered him a drawing of 'The Fatal Sisters', saying, 'I hope you will draw *The Descent of Odin*, too, which I love as much as any of Gray's works' (Vol. 28: 271. 20 May 1776). Similarly, in another letter to Mason in 1784, wherein Walpole expresses broad approval of a recent collection 'on the doctrines of the Scandinavian bards', he nonetheless adds that the author 'seems to have kept *The Descent of Odin* in his eye, though he had not the art of conjuring up the most forceful feelings as Gray has done in a subject in which there is so much of the terrible' (Vol. 29: 331. 2 February 1784).[4]

As for whether Walpole read Percy's *Runic Poetry*, the quote noted above regarding 'boozing ale out of the skull of an enemy' is likely to have been prompted by Percy's translation of Ragnar's 'Death-Song'. Indeed, Walpole was much enamoured of Percy's folkish antiquarianism, as seemingly was Percy of Walpole's interest. Accordingly, on the publication of Percy's *Reliques of Ancient English Poetry* in 1765, Percy instructed his publisher, James Dodsley (1724–97), to send Walpole a copy, on receipt of which Walpole wrote to Percy thanking him and expressing his pleasure in reading the contents (Vol. 40: 372. 5 February 1765). However, it is also quite possible that Walpole derived his knowledge of Ragnar's 'Death-Song' from reading extracts of early editions of Mallet's *Histoire*, which, as already noted, Gray had studied and would, therefore, almost certainly be known to Walpole (Omberg, 1976: 36–47). Nevertheless, when Walpole read the 1763 edition of Mallet's *Histoire*, which he did in 1765, he found it something of a chore:

> I have been ... buried in Runic poetry and Danish wars ... written by one Mallet, a Frenchman, a sensible man, but I cannot say he has the art of making a tiresome subject agreeable. There are six volumes, and I am stuck fast in the fourth.
> (Vol. 10: 148. To George Montagu, 19 February 1765)

While Walpole may have been equivocal about 'Runic poetry' in the early 1760s, his influence on the emerging Gothic scene in England was not only manifest in terms of his architectural enthusiasms but also in terms of the effect that his creative imagination had on Gothic-inspired visual arts. 1763, a year in which many of the elements of Gothicism came together in England, is also marked by the arrival in London of the young Henri Fuseli (1741–1825), a painter who would go on to become the most celebrated, indeed, controversial artist of Gothic 'otherness' in the latter eighteenth and early nineteenth centuries. According to one anecdote, Fuseli declared that Walpole was 'the first patron I ever had', the commission in question being a scene from Boccaccio's Theodore and Honorio (Spooner, 1853, vol. 2: 72), and in 1797, along with William Blake (1757–1827), he was commissioned to illustrate a new edition of Gray's poetry, including his Gothic odes (O'Donoghue, 2007, 120–1). It is, then, curious that Walpole considered certain of Fuseli's paintings to be disturbingly excessive. One instance of this is apparent from Walpole's scribbled note in the margins of his 1785 exhibition catalogue that judged Fuseli's exhibit 'The Mandrake: A Charm' to be 'shockingly mad, madder than ever: quite mad'. This verdict, as one recent critic has pointed out, 'Coming from the author of ... a phantasmagorian Gothic novel inspired by a bad dream ... was a classic case of the pot calling the kettle black' (Blanning, 2010: 68–9). Indeed, it seems very likely that Walpole's *The Castle of Otranto* was, either directly or indirectly, an inspiration for many of Fuseli's wilder imaginings, most notably his vision of sexual terror 'The Nightmare' (1781).

There can, however, be no doubt that both Gray and Walpole were utterly enthralled by Ossianic poetry and, at least in the first place, convinced of its authenticity, as the following letters from 1760–61 indicate: Walpole corresponds with the Scottish historian Sir David Dalrymple (1726–92) on behalf of Gray, asking him to supply more information about Macpherson's 'Erse' poems and quoting Gray as saying, 'Is there any more to be had of equal beauty, or at all approaching it?' (Vol. 14: 106. *c.* April, 1760); Gray asserting elsewhere, 'I am gone mad about them ... I am resolved to believe them genuine, spite of the Devil and the Kirk' (To Thomas Wharton, July, 1760, in Mitford, ed., 1835: 249); and Walpole's report to Dalrymple that, for clarity's sake, he has advised Macpherson to 'have the names prefixed to the [poem's] speeches' and adding, 'My doubts of the genuineness are all vanished' (Vol. 15: 71–72. 14 April 1761). In this respect, and despite their later circumspection about Macpherson's sincerity, Walpole and Gray were very much of their time.

In conclusion, the significant extent to which matters runic and Ossianic were on Walpole's literary horizons when he wrote *The Castle of Otranto* seems undeniable. With this in mind, a plot involving a descent into secret chambers, the hostile presence of ghosts and giants, and the indefatigable, noble and manly hero seeking justice amid moribund Gothic 'gloomth', as Walpole was wont to call it, might well have been taken from the Icelandic *eddas*. Moreover, as Rix convincingly points out, that oversized sword that exhausted so many at Otranto was most likely to have been inspired by the sword Tyrfing in 'The Waking of Angantýr' (2011: 7). As Rix also demonstrates, beyond *The Castle of Otranto* English literary culture became fully aware of Old Norse literature as a resource for plot-lines and atmospherics, consciously and conspicuously so by the last decade of the eighteenth century, as is apparent in Matthew Lewis's *The Monk* (1796) (Rix, 2011: 13–15).

So deeply embedded and fashionable did the Old Northern worldview become that, by the end of the nineteenth century, Stoker presents the Viking biological heritage as a worrying trait in respect of his most famous Gothic villain but as an admirable one in respect of his stalwart heroes. So it is that Dracula boasts of his descent from Icelandic 'Berserkers' (Auerbach and Skal, eds, 1997: 34), in other words, those like Angantýr, while Quincey Morris is praised as 'a moral Viking' (Auerbach and Skal, eds, 1997: 156), a gentlemanly Ragnar Lodbrok, maybe. Stoker's view that the Vikings had endowed their descendants with formidable doughtiness is again apparent in his *The Gates of Life* (1908).[5] In this, the tellingly named young Harold An Wolf is lectured at length by his parson father, a man proud of his 'Gothic through the Dutch' ancestry (32) and a keen student of Icelandic sagas:

> There never was, my boy, such philosophy making for victory as that held by our Vikings. It taught that whoever was never wounded was never happy. It was not enough to be victorious. The fighter should contend against such odds that complete immunity was impossible ... Why, their strength, and endurance, and resolution, perfected by their life of constant hardihood and stress, became so ingrained in their race, that to this day, a thousand years after they themselves have passed away, their descendants have some of their fine qualities. (33)

As Stoker was born and raised in Clontarf, which, as previously noted, was the early eleventh-century scene of what, in effect, was the last gasp of Viking belligerence on Irish soil and the setting for the widely anthologised 'The Fatal Sisters', for example, Volume 2 of Matthew Lewis's *The Tales of Wonder* of 1801,[6] it likely that Viking fervour was instilled in him from an early age. Nonetheless, Stoker was far from unique among his contemporaries in this respect and few of his readers would have failed to appreciate what was being signified by his references to Viking machismo. In certain respects, the Nordic past and Gothic fantasies had become tantamount to synonymous.

While Rix's study makes useful progress in reconnecting Gothicism with the Gothic novel, it is hoped that this survey of the emergence of Gothicism as a key presence in English literature helps by providing even more context. It nevertheless remains the case that opportunities for further research into the Gothicism of the Gothic are worthy of investigation.

## Notes

1. The previous two versions of the 'The Dunciad' were published in 1728 and 1729, and the final version in 1743. In the two earliest versions, the same lines were targeted at the English antiquarian Thomas Hearne (1678–1735).
2. The three other poems Percy included in his *Five Pieces* are 'The Ransome of Egill the Scald', 'The Funeral Song of Hacon' and 'The Complaint of Harold'.
3. All correspondence to and from Walpole has been accessed via *Horace Walpole's Correspondence*, The Lewis Walpole Library, Yale University Library, online site http://images.library.yale.edu/hwcorrespondence/
4. The work referred to by Walpole is Edward Jerningham, *The Rise and Progress of Scandinavian Poetry: A Poem in Two Parts* (1784). The poem is dedicated to Walpole.
5. *The Gates of Life* is the US title of Stoker's *The Man*, which was initially published in the UK 1905. The full text of *The Gates of Life* can be found at https://archive.org/stream/gateslife00stokgoog#page/n42/mode/2up/search/Northern Accessed 25th November, 2014.
6. For Lewis's *The Tales of Wonder*, see https://archive.org/details/taleswonder02scotgoog: 'The Fatal Sisters': 347–51. 'The Descent of Odin' is also anthologised in this volume: 352–57. Accessed 29th November, 2014.

# 2
# Wollstonecraft's *Wrongs of Woman* to Stoker's *Dracula*: You've Come a Long Way Baby, or Have You?

Bettina Tate Pedersen

Two gothic novels written a century apart, Mary Wollstonecraft's *The Wrongs of Woman; or Maria* (1796) and Bram Stoker's *Dracula* (1897), grapple with powerful issues in the lives of their characters and their fictional worlds. Both appear as *fin de siècle* novels, and their anxieties deal with the stability of society and its institutions. In *Wrongs* these anxieties centre on women's autonomy, the nature of marriage, and patriarchy's power. In *Dracula* they focus on the need to restore Christian belief and establish the institution of marriage as the ultimate reward. In setting these two gothic novels side by side, we see that Wollstonecraft's 18th-century gothic vision is meant to critique traditional views of women and the patriarchy that supports them; whereas Stoker's later 19th-century tale looks to re-establish the familiar patterns and institutions of a declining religious and gender status quo.

Wollstonecraft's unfinished novel arises in the context of the emerging gothic novel and in the company of Ann Radcliffe, who was key in developing and popularizing the form. Typical gothic novels were filled with seductions, threatening sexual relations, predatory lovers, sensational entrapments, forced marriages, monstrous husbands, and compelled or coerced insanity. Their settings included remote castles, insane asylums, and family estates with their secret rooms and passages. Indeed most of these characteristics appear in *Wrongs*, but Wollstonecraft's novel also bears the marks of realism and of the aesthetic debate about the nature of the novel and its relation to the woman reader and the woman writer. Wollstonecraft's contemporaries, Anna Barbauld and Clara Reeve, both attempted to articulate a theory of the nature of the novel and its influence, in contrast to the more unrealistic romance genre that had predated it. They were particularly interested in defining the novel in contrast to the romance for the sake of their young female readers and the rising influence novels had on a growing reading public. Reeve's *Progress of Romance, through Times, Countries, and Manners, with Remarks on the Good and Bad Effects of It, on Them Respectively, in a Course of Evening Conversations* (1785) constructs a dialogue to lay out, through the voice of Euphrasia, one of the women speakers, the distinction between the novel and the romance:

> The Romance is an heroic fable, which treats of fabulous persons and things. –The Novel is a picture of real life and manners, and of the time in which it is written. The Romance in lofty and elevated language, describes what never happened nor is likely to happen. – The Novel gives a familiar relation of such things, as pass every day before our eyes, such as may happen to our friend, or to ourselves; and the perfection of it, is to represent every scene, in so easy and natural a manner, and to make them appear so probable, as to deceive us into a persuasion (at least while we are reading) that all is real, until we are affected by the joys or distresses, of the persons in the story, as if they were our own. (1996: 154)

Whether she read Reeve's statement or not, its logic is present in Wollstonecraft's picture of women's real lives under the legal and customary systems of her day. Wollstonecraft's vision harmonizes with the distinction Reeve draws between the romance and the novel. Barbauld, too, values realism as the defining characteristic of the novel. In 'On the Origins and Progress of Novel-Writing' (1810) she argues that '[a] good novel is an epic in prose, with more of character and less (indeed in modern novels nothing) of the supernatural machinery' (1996: 172).

Reeve and Barbauld also elevate the didactic import of novels as a genre, a key element in considering the influence of novels on young female readers. Barbauld, however, seems conflicted over whether or not novels should be written solely for entertainment (1996: 176) with little restraint laid upon their characters or plots (177), and with the potential negative effects on the morals of readers if they are:

> it must be desirable that the first impressions of fraud, selfishness, profligacy and perfidy should be connected, as in good novels they always will be, with infamy and ruin. At any rate, it is safer to meet with a bad character in the pages of a fictitious story, than in the polluted walks of life; but an author solicitous for the morals of his readers will be sparing in the introduction of such characters. (1996: 177–8)

Barbauld seems to acknowledge the need to tell the truth about nefarious individuals who appear in fiction, despite the possible tantalizing appeal, but still prefers that such characters not appear in novels at all. Without doubt, Barbauld recognizes the careful balance that must be struck between realism, which would expose young women readers to untoward content and characters, and entertainment, which would capture the minds and interest of a purchasing public. While novelists over the course of the 19th century became more committed to using their fiction as a means of advancing social change, in 1796 Wollstonecraft clearly shares this commitment in *Wrongs*. Her novel falls between Reeve's and Barbauld's criticism, but is more in line with Barbauld's acknowledgement of the novel's power to outstrip other vehicles of social activism – 'Let me make the novels of a country, and let who will make the systems?' (2004: 180) – than with a primary goal of entertaining readers.

Wollstonecraft's project was not to write a cautionary tale about bad women to encourage chastity in young women, but rather to critique the evils of a society and its institutions that drove women to transgressive behaviours as their only recourse in the first place. Though there are characters who appear in *Wrongs* who would have been censured as bad women when measured against 18th- and 19th-century social mores: prostitutes, unchaste women, thieves and violated servants. Wollstonecraft saw their plights, however, as entirely predicated on the horrors of societal constraints that made women's lives a veritable prison with no possibility of honourable living. These horrors she saw as virtually the same as those of gothic fiction.

*Wrongs* possesses some obvious tropes of the gothic genre as it existed in the late 18th century. In Anne Mellor's view,

> Wollstonecraft explicitly invokes the genre of the Gothic romance, the horror story of pure imagination, in which ghosts and apparitions haunt ruined castles. But she immediately rejects the romance ... in order to write a "true story," the plausible or realistic representation of the sufferings of women in eighteenth-century England. (1996: 418–9)

Cynthia Richards remarks on the way in which *Wrongs'* content and tone bears striking resemblance to Wollstonecraft's polemical prose in *A Vindication of the Rights of Woman* and *Letters on the Management of Infants*. (2004: 1, 5, 6). Diane Hoeveler observes that while Wollstonecraft 'exposed and at the same time reified the tyranny of sentimental literary formulae for women, Wollstonecraft also revealed that for women of all classes, life really was the way it was depicted in sentimental fiction – a series of insults, humiliations, deprivations, beatings, and fatal or near-fatal disasters' (1999: 387). Indeed these critics call attention to the connection Wollstonecraft herself avowed in her preface to *Wrongs* between gothic fiction and the realism of contemporary women's lives: 'In many instances I could have made the incidents more dramatic, would I have sacrificed my main object, the desire of exhibiting the misery and oppression, peculiar to women, that arise out of the partial laws and customs of society' (2004: 39). Despite her avowed realist aim, her use of gothic tropes is unquestioned.

The novel's setting opens in true gothic fashion with its female heroine, Maria, imprisoned in an insane asylum. From behind the 'small grated window of her chamber' (2004: 45) she looks out over a 'desolate garden and ... a huge pile of buildings, that, after having been suffered, for half a century, to fall to decay, had undergone some clumsy repair, merely to render [the place] habitable' (2004: 45). Indeed, Wollstonecraft emphasizes the enclosure and threat of the gothic from the novel's opening words by situating Maria within '[a]bodes of horror [that] have frequently been described, and castles, filled with specters and chimeras, conjured up by the magic spell of genius to harrow the soul, and absorb the wondering mind' (2004: 41).

Maria's entrapment is rearticulated and so re-emphasized 100 pages later in pages of her own memoir, which functions as an embedded story – also a characteristic feature of gothic novels. Here, Maria herself describes the confines and spectres of her gothic prison in the account she is writing to her infant daughter, whom she imagines reading it at some point in the future:

> The gates opened heavily, and the sullen sound of many locks and bolts drawn back, grated on my very soul, before I was appalled by the creeking of the dismal hinges, as they closed after me. The gloomy pile was before me, half in ruins; some of the aged trees of the avenue were cut down, and left to rot where they fell; and as we approached some mouldering steps, a monstrous dog darted forwards to the length of his chain, and barked and growled infernally. (2004: 177)

Maria's descriptions are much the same as the narrator's earlier ones, but Maria describes her gothic setting with more emotionally intense images.

Maria's account not only functions as an embedded narrative, itself encased in the asylum prison with Maria, but it also operates as didactic literature addressed to a young woman. With the purpose of instructing her daughter to different conduct from Maria's own, Wollstonecraft emphasizes the need to expose the repressed experiences, personal risks, and physical entrapments that characterizes her protagonist's life and, by extension, the lives of 18th-century women. S. Leigh Matthews associates these aspects of the novel with 18th-century, non-fiction, conduct literature: 'The memoirs are an active appropriation by Wollstonecraft of the very popular conduct and advice books of the period, which were often written to orphaned girls and which, like Maria's narrative, were meant to constitute textual presences to replace the absent mother' (2001: 94). This conduct literature reveals the cultural anxiety over young women and the influences that should shape their lives. A mother's influence was revered as paramount, but if no live mother were to hand, conduct books were a practical way to secure and pass on the wisdom of mothers (and fathers) all the same. Wollstonecraft's weaving together of non-fiction prose, realist fiction, and gothic entrapment tale makes the connection between gothic horror and real-life horror in women's lives closer still.

As *Wrongs* unfolds, the reality of Maria's gothic incarceration is revealed as ubiquitous. Even were she to escape the confines of her asylum prison – which she does – she would still be imprisoned by the legal and social control her husband exerts over her in a patriarchal system. Thus, the mysterious tenor of the gothic novel, which is usually explained over the course of most gothic plots, is not so satisfyingly dispatched in *Wrongs*. Though Maria is locked up in an asylum, the mystery about who put her there or why, is revealed early on, and there is little relief or resolution in the discovery, nor does her escape offer readers any satisfying plot resolution. Thomas Ford notes that

> while the novel was incomplete at the time of Wollstonecraft's death in 1797, enough remains for us to find it probable that Maria's struggle was to end tragically. Four of the five fragments with which Wollstonecraft's manuscript end give progressively more complete variations of a story of renewed betrayal, failures, and decline. (2009: 192)

Wollstonecraft found it almost impossible to imagine a plot trajectory ending in a satisfying resolution of freedom and autonomy for her heroine (Mellor, 1996: 419).[1] Although William Godwin published *Wrongs* as the unfinished manuscript and partial notes that Wollstonecraft had left behind, her message about patriarchy and women's entrapment, inside or outside of marriage, is hardly incomplete.

Maria's eventual, though harrowing, escape from the insane asylum is more in keeping with the terror readers expect from gothic novels, but the closing courtroom scene in the novel and what Wollstonecraft intends for it to communicate is not. Wollstonecraft designs this scene to make two unapologetic demonstrations of female competence and autonomy; one of behaviour, the other of philosophy. First, Maria's behaviour in acting as legal advocate for her would-be rescuer, Darnford, materially embodies Wollstonecraft's vision that women were fully capable of operating in traditionally masculine arenas and roles. In this scene Maria performs the function of a barrister in the court of law in making the defence against the charges of adulterous intention and action against Darnford. Second, in the ideas that Maria sets forth in defending Darnford, she makes a powerful, three-point, philosophical statement about women's value and autonomy: (1) she redefines sensibility as woman's chief value as 'a false morality ... of chastity, submission, and the forgiveness of injuries' (2004: 190); (2) she argues that a woman's legal stature should be determined by her adult age (2004: 191) alone and not by the decrees of her male relatives; and (3) she declares that choosing divorce may be a woman's truest action of conscience (2004: 192) in the face of a corrupt marriage (even though divorce was viewed as an evil and was essentially impossible for women to obtain in the 18th century).[2] Nowhere in this scene does Maria communicate that defiant or unchaste women deserve whatever punishment they receive or that they should return to their families willing to be quietly submissive; rather, Wollstonecraft gives her female protagonist an unabashed voice that articulates a revolutionary vision for women of her time.

The unfavourable outcome of the court proceedings for Maria, however, pointedly illustrates the novel's failure to achieve its revolutionary aim, illustrating just how ineffectual a resource the legal system was for women and how unattainable was female autonomy:

> The judge, in summing up the evidence, alluded to 'the fallacy of letting women plead their feelings, as an excuse for the violation of the marriage-vow. For his part, he had always determined to oppose all innovation, and the new-fangled notions which incroached (sic.) on the good old rules of conduct ... if women were allowed to plead their feelings, as an excuse or palliation of infidelity, it was opening a flood-gate for immorality. What virtuous woman thought of her feelings? – It was her duty to love and obey the man chosen by her parents and relations, who were qualified by their experience to judge

better for her, than she could for herself .... Too many restrictions could not be thrown in the way of divorces, if we wished to maintain the sanctity of marriage' (2004: 193)

The closing statement of the judge – meant to be received by readers as crippling irony – reaffirms the inviolable power of patriarchal systems. Scholars of the novel have identified the disappointment of the final scene as evidence linking Wollstonecraft's gothic fiction to what she saw as the real conditions of women's lives. Edna Kenton interprets it as Wollstonecraft's revolutionary vision for women grounded on the:

> plane of self-ownership and personal responsibility [... as Maria] proclaim[s] proudly her voluntary participation in what the world called crime, she as proudly proclaims her refusal to participate, without desire, in what the world called duty. She does this in a period of society when all the laws were against women's self-expression, and when ways for their self-support were non-existent. (1914: para. 8)

Critical assessment across the 20th century has agreed about the frustrating closure of *Wrongs*. Hoeveler argues: 'In every possible ending, the heroine is never a self-contained individual acting in her own right, although she has spent the text demanding just such a birthright' (1999: 404). Perhaps our frustration is the best index of the entrapment Wollstonecraft wanted to convey.

With the failure of Maria's argument to secure its aims as well as her own full autonomy, Wollstonecraft reveals marriage to be no safe haven for women and a morally bankrupt institution. Escape from asylum or not, Maria is still imprisoned within a patriarchal fortress of marriage and a legal system which supports it as such. Godwin's comment, following the several sketched-out notes that Wollstonecraft had written as possible endings to the novel, confirms her didactic intent 'to make her story subordinate to a great moral purpose, that of exhibiting the misery and oppression, peculiar to women, that arise out of the partial laws and customs of society' (Wollstonecraft, 2004: 197). When Wollstonecraft invokes the fictional gothic genre in *Wrongs* in the milieu of rising 18th-century democratic ideas, she does so, not to tell a fantastical *fin de siècle* escapist narrative, but rather to depict the realistic horrors of women's 'gothic' lives, to proclaim her didactic and democratic censure of woman's oppression, and to awaken a vision for a new paradigm for woman.

A century later Stoker's gothic vision in *Dracula*, though it may be didactic on some level, appears quite different from that which characterized *Wrongs*. With the industrialized state virtually complete by the end of the 19th century, its increasingly prosperous middle class had first-hand experience with the intractable and complex problems that attended the rise of industrial England. They were also familiar with the outcry for greater democratic freedoms for the working class and for women. In this democratic spirit – the same as Wollstonecraft's 1790s arguments for women's autonomy – the period witnessed the appearance of the New Woman who continued to challenge patriarchy as Wollstonecraft's Maria had done in her courtroom diatribe against women's marital imprisonment.

The New Woman intensified anxieties over the continuing disappearance of traditional societal, religious, political, legal, domestic, and sexual values. The New Woman was an identifiable figure in her dress and mode of travel, and in her progressive views of women and women's roles. She was frequently caricatured in *Punch* cartoons of the 1890s as a 'cultural icon of the *fin de siècle*' and stereotypically depicted 'in the guise of a bicycling, cigarette-smoking Amazon' (Richardson and Willis, 2002: 13). She engendered strong and sometimes vicious debates between women and men writing in major Victorian periodicals: about the nature of womanhood; about her marriageable qualities or lack thereof; about her effect on homes, families, and children; about her challenge to societal and political roles and paradigms; and about her disrupting of distinctions between English women and those of other national identities. Perhaps even more disturbing, her existence gave rise to serious questions about masculinity. Most of the periodical writers who weighed in on the debate over the New Woman eventually addressed the question about what changes in masculinity would arise if new womanhood took hold in society.

Stoker does not begin his gothic novel by addressing the New Woman and masculinity directly; instead *Dracula* conveys them indirectly through an inversion of the standard gothic trope from a century earlier. The novel begins not with an incarcerated woman controlled by calculating and predatory men, but with an incarcerated man who becomes the prey of vampire women. Jonathan Harker is unwittingly on his way to entrapment in Count Dracula's Transylvanian home. Unlike Maria in *Wrongs*, Harker is not unjustly ensconced as a hysteric woman mental patient; rather, he is depicted as an autonomous and culturally naïve young businessman, who is frighteningly obtuse, even stupid, in his failure to interpret all the ominous signs and warnings punctuating his journey to Dracula's castle. Harker proceeds with complete faith in the nature of the businessman–client relationship and possessing little fear of anything atypical which might challenge the nature of that relationship. Harker seems to lack the business acumen a man needs to read this professional relationship accurately. Once Harker realizes that Dracula has deceived him, it is too late to escape. Entrapped in this 'dreadful place' (2000: 85), he grows increasingly mentally distraught, but, by meticulously observing and recording Dracula's habits as well as the rhythms of the castle, he comes to understand his environment and manoeuvres his escape. The threat of the vampire women who seek to devour him intensifies this need and forces him to acquire the shrewd and decisive resolve of a man executing business:

> I am alone in the castle with those awful women .... I shall not remain alone with them: I shall try to scale the castle wall farther than I have yet attempted. .... At least God's mercy is better than that of these monsters, and the precipice is steep and high. At its foot *a man may sleep – as a man.* (2000: 85, emphasis mine)

Harker's manly resourcefulness and independence are finally awakened by these threatening women which enables him to reclaim a sense of English manhood. Stoker's focus on these assertive characteristics as the means of escape for Harker highlights their importance in establishing Harker's masculine strength of character and in awakening a more astute assessment of the people around him.

In Stoker's treatment, Wollstonecraft's gothic trope of trapped woman and predatory man is completely reversed. Although Stoker's project in *Dracula* is communicated indirectly, it is nonetheless clear: to re-establish a more potent masculinity for Harker and to make him acutely aware of the threats to that masculinity in a prison circumscribed by vampire women. Harker is behaving too much like a chaste young woman, and the announcement of his need to act 'as a man' serves as a strong corrective to this nature and behaviour. The vampire women, though ultimately trapped as well, pose a more immediate threat to Harker than Dracula since Dracula wishes to protect Harker temporarily and use his naïveté to establish a residence in England.

Stoker's gothic vision is also antithetical to Wollstonecraft's in its horizon of escape and restoration. Even though Harker's imprisonment renders him – like Maria – mentally unstable, temporarily incapacitated, and needing recovery, these effects result exclusively from his incarceration. They are temporary. Harker's full escape from them is not only possible, it is accomplished by the end of the novel. None of these same effects, experienced by Maria in *Wrongs*, are permanently overcome. Indeed, escape in *Wrongs* proves to be futile because the entire world – not just her asylum cell – is a prison for women ruled by patriarchy. In terms of restoration, both incarcerated protagonists require the assistance of a woman to achieve it: Harker needs his fiancé Mina's care giving alongside that of the nuns at the Hospital of St Joseph and Ste Mary Buda-Pesth. Maria needs her asylum guard Jemima's street knowledge and skill in breaking away from entrapments. Both female aides are aligned with their respective protagonists in terms of a marital relationship. While Harker's female aide is a source of help and recovery, Maria's serves both as aide and as a constant reminder that one woman's freedom is usually acquired at the expense of another woman's entrapment. Stoker's bachelor/husband protagonist, who is nursed back to health by his fiancé/wife, is the direct inverse of Wollstonecraft's married protagonist who is at constant threat from her husband whether she is incarcerated by him or not and whose female aide must put her own self at risk to help Maria.

The contrast of the two female aides signifies the progressive/regressive difference in the way Wollstonecraft and Stoker address the formation of gender communities. Wollstonecraft focuses on a community of women through Jemima and Maria's relationship. Maria's separation from her infant daughter and subsequent incarceration provokes a hysteria which threatens to incapacitate her. Unlike Jonathan Harker, she cannot rely solely upon her own personal devices and independent actions to recover her senses and devise a means of escape. Her guard, Jemima, who has become an asylum guard to stave off her own destitution as an abused and discarded working-class woman, must help Maria. Jemima has been more thoroughly traumatized by the ideological and material strictures of patriarchy than Maria. She has been financially and physically abused, raped, and abandoned with no recourse to the law or to wealthy and sympathetic male relatives. She has had to rely solely on her own wit and courage to secure a series of situations preventing her from starvation and death. In several of these instances, she has secured her own protection at the expense of another woman losing hers. 'Betrayal of one woman by another', Diane Hoeveler points out, 'suggests the lateral violence that equally victimized females practice on one another when they are forced to compete for an increasingly smaller share of the goods and resources of a society that stigmatizes them' (1999: 400). The alignment between Maria and Jemima illustrates the fraught nature of women's communities under patriarchy.

These communities may form, nonetheless, but competing risks and claims often persist within them. In spite of the personal risk Jemima faces in losing her employment in the asylum if she helps Maria escape, she is willing to do so because of the sympathy she shares with Maria as a mother. Once Jemima learns that Maria's nursing infant 'only four months old, had been torn from her' (2004: 48) her alignment shifts: 'the woman awoke in a bosom long estranged from feminine emotions, and Jemima determined to alleviate all in her power, without hazarding the loss of her place, the sufferings of a wretched mother, apparently injured, and certainly unhappy' (2004: 48–9). Mary Nyquist observes this tension between the women's competing needs and their need to align:

> Though the two women do escape, *Wrongs of Woman* can hardly be accused of sentimentalizing female–female relations. Throughout, numerous women are portrayed as abusing their power over other women. By having Jemima liberate Maria from the madhouse, however, *Wrongs of Woman* strategically has her provide the protection Maria has been awaiting and that Darnford has gallantly promised. It is also Jemima who makes sure they both actually get through the garden gate, ghastly Gothic apparition notwithstanding. (1997: 85)

Women's communities, then, though far from ideal, appear to be one of the only means of resisting male threats.

Women's alliances with each other are portrayed as more trustworthy than male–female ones. Laura Mandell notes, 'Whether the male characters be the worst of men (Mr Venables and Mr S – in Wollstonecraft's *Wrongs of Woman*) or the best (Darnford in *Wrongs* …) it is only the women who can keep their word' (2008: 66). The community Maria and Jemima form is typical in its opposition to male adversaries but atypical in that it forms across class boundaries. Nyquist suggests that Wollstonecraft 'drives a cross-class nail in the coffin of the ideology of patriarchal protection' (1997: 85) in aligning Jemima and Maria not solely because they are women, but also across class lines. Here Wollstonecraft is clearly reiterating her view from her 1790s polemics on the rights of men and of women[3] that a truly egalitarian society will be a corrective not only to gender hierarchies but to class ones as well.

Stoker's construction of community in his gothic vision is for men, not women; where women's communities in *Wrongs of Woman* are always troubled by women's competing gains and losses, the male community in *Dracula* is strikingly untroubled by such tensions. Although there are significant women characters in *Dracula*, it is the community of male friends that triumph in the novel, and the early focus on Harker's individual feats gives way to a communal brotherhood that is unified and victorious. This male union coheres around the mutual adoration of a threatened, beautiful, young woman, Lucy Westenra. Lucy is desired by virtually all the men in the novel except Harker, who is already married to her best friend, Mina. Lucy is first pursued by three honourable men, Dr John Seward, Mr Quincey Morris, and Arthur Holmwood (soon to be Lord Goldalming), before she is trapped by the rapacious Count Dracula. All three mortal men propose marriage to Lucy on the same day. When Holmwood's suit is accepted over those of Seward and Morris, there is no rancour or resentment among these men regarding Lucy's preference. Both Seward and Morris immediately shift their personal romantic affections to a courtly adoration of and loyalty to their friend Holmwood's fiancée, and they are ready to do whatever is required to protect and defend her without receiving any romantic favours in return.

In the three-proposal scene, Stoker codifies a vision of honourable manhood. Lucy's comments to Mina elevates men above women: '"My dear Mina, why are men so noble when we women are so little worth of them?"' (2000: 91). Later, when Dr. Van Helsing arrives, he too offers his own courtly adoration for Lucy. All these men are willing to give Lucy repeated blood donations, to sacrifice sleep and stand guard through the night at her bedroom door, and to risk their own well-being to take up arms in pursuit of the creature who threatens her. Van Helsing articulates the devotion the men feel most clearly when he states that he wants '"to help [Lucy,] a sweet young lady, whom, too, I came to love"' (2000: 245). Van Helsing goes on to compare his personal sacrifice to that of her fiancé even though he was her doctor, not her husband-to-be: 'I gave what you gave: the blood of my veins; I gave it, I, who was not, like you, her lover, but only her physician and her friend' (2000: 245).

The loyal male community continues to cohere in admiration of Lucy even after she has been corrupted by Dracula's bite. The men's continued loyalty to each other in seeking to aid Lucy serves to confirm the superior male status Lucy had attributed to them. Once Lucy has been put to eternal rest by the brotherhood of Holmwood, Seward, Morris, and Van Helsing, the men shift their attention to Mina. Mina's purity and goodness outshine Lucy's, and all Harker's friends quickly and willingly make her the object of their unconsummated devotion. In both cases, Stoker depicts the female protagonists as virtuous and pure but at risk of losing their chaste status without male protection. These women in their otherworldly purity and goodness embody several female literary tropes: the elevated lady of the courtly tradition, the virginal gothic heroine, and the angel in the house idol of the Victorian separate spheres ideology. In each, the construction of womanhood rests on its need for male protection and adoration. The fact that the creature threatening these women is male is minimized by making him supernatural. Thus, Stoker maintains his depiction of the male brotherhood as a superior version of masculinity.

Lucy, awaiting marriage and being pursued by a predatory vampire, most fully embodies the virginal gothic stereotype. As a wife, Mina (somewhat less stereotypical a heroine) appears to retain her virginal quality even though she is a married woman and is technically not sexually innocent when Dracula pursues her. By rendering her status as a married woman bereft of sexual knowledge, Stoker maintains in both Lucy and Mina the conventional virginal quality of the gothic heroine.

In this virginal depiction of women, Stoker's gothic vision for his heroines contrasts sharply with Wollstonecraft's. Regardless of their marital status, Stoker's women are chaste; whereas, Wollstonecraft depicts all women – married or not – as sexually compromised. Mina, a model of exemplary womanhood, is the angel in the house. In these regards her sexuality is unquestionably valued and esteemed. Maria, Wollstonecraft's married heroine, is depicted as unvalued and held in low regard, a diametrical opposite to Mina. Indeed, Maria's sexual and moral purity is held as essentially worthless by her husband, Venable. She is first assaulted by his profligate behaviour and sexual demands, and later by his nonchalant attempt to prostitute her to his friend simply because a husband who may do with his wife what he pleases. Wollstonecraft's depiction of a husband and his male friends portrays a sexually abusive male community. Wollstonecraft also includes portrayals of other minor female characters, all of whom are victims of male disregard or out and out abuse. There are virtually no virtuous women in the eyes of the male characters in her novel.

In *Wrongs* men neither adore women's chastity nor labour to preserve it. Neither do they respect the fidelity of the marriage bond. Indeed, they appear to be far more like the predatory Dracula than like the noble men with whom Lucy and Mina fall in love. Maria does fall in love, but she is deceived in the character of the man she loves, and it becomes quickly apparent to her that he is not noble in character and he does not appreciate her virtue or fidelity. In fact Maria's one value to her husband is her money. If her money proves difficult to secure, her chastity becomes little more than a second rate sexual commodity that he can consume himself or disburse to his friends if he wishes. As Barbara Taylor notes, 'This sexual objectification of women was a target of all Wollstonecraft's writings' (1997: 26). In varying degrees, Wollstonecraft's heroine is attacked on all sides by the men in her world. The way in which the heroines are viewed as mothers in these two gothic novels is also diametrically different. *Wrongs* focuses on the mothering of children with the underlying view that the mother–child bond is tremendously important. When she depicts Maria's mothering being abruptly interrupted and terminated by her husband, Wollstonecraft means to horrify her readers with the disrespect men show to mothers: their care of children is viewed as dispensable, and their emotional and nurturing attachment to them unimportant. Women's maternal feelings and commitments are utterly disregarded, and children can apparently be farmed out to other women with no harm done. In short, Wollstonecraft dramatically depicts the negative way men view the qualities and merits of women's mothering. Stoker's depiction of mothering, though not focused on children, elevates the value it has for the nurturing of men. The male characters who receive such care are physically and emotionally restored by it. Mina is nurse wife to her husband and consoling mother to her adult male admirers. Her maternal affections are not spent on children but rather on distraught men. When attending to the grieving Arthur, Mina expresses the thoughts that undergird and motivate such mothering care:

> We women have something of the mother in us that makes us rise above smaller matters when the mother-spirit is invoked; I felt this big sorrowing man's head resting on me, as though it were that of the baby that some day may lie on my bosom, and I stroked his hair as though he were my own child. (2000: 268–9)

Thus, even in mothering Stoker places the focus on men and the benefit men, not children, derive from such female nurturing.

In the children born to the heroines of these two novels, we see Wollstonecraft's focus on women and Stoker's focus on men sustained. Maria gives birth to a daughter and immediately 'lamented [that] she was a daughter, and anticipated the aggravated ills of life that her sex rendered almost inevitable' (2004: 44). Mina is given consummate traditional praise when Stoker resolves her story in the birth of a son whose 'birthday is the same day as that on which Quincey Morris [the American fellow in the brotherhood] died,' who is called Quincey but has a 'bundle of names [that] links all our little band of men together,' and whom Mina believes carries 'some of [their] brave friend's spirit' (2000: 419) in his own boyish temperament. Any actual nursing or mothering of her son goes unmentioned, but the fact that she has a son instead of a daughter, serves again to illustrate the importance and value of men.

Stoker's depiction of Mina suggests his tentative fascination with a self-determining and professionally competent woman. While Lucy only possesses beauty and chastity, Mina is praised for her attributes of intelligence, efficiency, professional skills, decisiveness, analytical thinking, keen insight, sound judgment, and calm rational control – all traits more conventionally masculine than feminine. Indeed, all these characteristics accrue to the 1890s New Woman who was routinely reviled for manliness. Stephanie Demetrakopoulos interprets Stoker's portrayal of Lucy and Mina as 'two conflicting concepts of Victorian womanhood,' one in which he is 'nostalgic about the woman of the 1850s' and the other in which he 'admires and venerates Mina who represents the "New Woman" of the 1890s' (1977: 108–9).Van Helsing comments on the cross-gendered quality of Mina's intelligence: '"Ah, that wonderful Madam Mina! She has a *man's brain* – a brain that a man should have were he much gifted – and a woman's heart. The good God fashioned her for a purpose, believe me, when He made that so good combination"' (2000: 274, italics mine). Van Helsing acclaims Mina for her ability able to discern, master, and use crucial information and skills, without which it is doubtful her male protectors could have defeated Dracula. She learns and uses shorthand on her own; is an excellent typist; functions as amanuensis to Harker, Seward, and Van Helsing; transcribes multiple copies of journal accounts so that a backup copy is always to hand; identifies and memorizes complicated train schedules; observes and records the details of interactions and events; works with surprising efficiency and accuracy; and in turn, helps all the men sift through an enormous catalogue of detail to clarify what knowledge is crucial to defeating Dracula and which is not. Clearly, Stoker has combined some of the traditional womanly virtues he gave to Lucy with the more modern New Woman attributes that only Mina possesses.

Stoker's heroes clearly rely on Mina's 'man-brain' but as the plot progresses, the ambivalence in Stoker's treatment of this exceptional woman increases. Mina, who has been an equal participant in strategizing against Dracula for the majority of the novel, is later sequestered from such plans in an effort to protect her, in spite of the fact that Harker conveys the ambivalence of this move: 'It took all my courage to hold to the wise resolution of keeping her out of our grim task' (2000: 306).

Eventually, the men must reject this paternalistic sheltering of Mina since her isolation has exposed her to Dracula's attacks on her body and mind: the very first thing we decided was that Mina should be in full confidence; that nothing of any sort – no matter how painful – should be kept from her' (2000: 330).

In this re-involvement of Mina in the men's planning, her 'man brain' and determined will are her most highly valued attributes. Stoker's plot development has gone too far in creating Mina's New Woman character to abort it here. Indeed, he seems to admire, even elevate, the New Woman over the traditional woman in replacing Lucy with Mina. He sustains Mina's New Woman characterization until the very end of the novel suggesting that Mina and her modern womanhood has superseded Lucy and her conventional womanhood. Further, in these character and plot developments, Stoker seems to share Wollstonecraft's earlier revolutionary view for women, and is using the gothic genre to that same end. As a New Woman of sorts, Mina appears to embody the challenge to patriarchy that Maria did in Wollstonecraft's novel although Maria is a far more outspoken challenger than is Mina. Though evoking the New Woman, Stoker retreats into the Victorian angel in the house ideal, repositioning Mina as the object of male adoration and praise and removing her from active participation in men's endeavours. In the scene in which Mina rejoins the male brotherhood in her New Woman competence, Stoker leaves traces of his ambivalence with such modern womanhood. Mina and her 'eyes [that] shone with the devotion of a martyr' are manoeuvred into silence at the novel's close.

Finally, the conclusions of these two gothic novels give readers the clearest sense of the difference between Wollstonecraft's despairing and Stoker's reassuring vision for women's futures. If there is optimism to be found in the possible endings Wollstonecraft imagined for her novel, it lies not in traditional marriage but rather in the relationships between women. In the longest of Wollstonecraft's possible endings sketched out for *Wrongs*, Jemima is unconvinced that Maria's daughter is truly dead and leaves Maria to go in search of the child. Jemima finds the toddler and brings her back to Maria admonishing Maria that she has a hope and a future: '"I left you (at a fatal moment) to search for the child! – I snatched her from misery – and (now she is alive again) would you leave her alone in the world, to endure what I have endured?"' (2004: 196). Jemima's admonition and Maria's recovered daughter exclaiming '"Mamma!"' is exactly what gives Maria the motivation to assert, '"The conflict is over! – I will live for my child!"' (2004: 196). Wollstonecraft anticipates the aims of subsequent woman's fiction that depicts women forming female communities for the benefit of their daughters and eschewing marriage

For Stoker, Christianity and marriage are upheld as the institutions offering both the ultimate protection from harm or destruction and the greatest adulation for women. Stoker's gothic vision participates in both the violent destruction of demonic women and the paternalist protection and marriage of angelic ones. Not only is Dracula defeated and the accompanying ominous threat to a Christian world view demolished, but the women who participate in Dracula's vampiric power by attacking defenceless children are morally condemned and violently dispatched as well. At the novel's close all of the heroes are ensconced in happy marriages to silent wives, except for the bachelor Van Helsing, who readers understand to be monastically wedded to academic life. Mina's strong voice is replaced by Van Helsing's report of the praises others have for her:

> We want no proofs; we ask none to believe us! This boy will someday know what a brave and gallant woman his mother is. Already he knows her sweetness and loving care; later on he will understand how some men loved her, that they did dare much for her sake. (2000: 419)

Her bravery exists as a story; whereas her active role in her son's life becomes only 'sweetness and loving care' (419). As Nancy Armstrong argues, 'In order to become the traditional reproductive woman, she [Mina] ceases to manage information and leaves the work of cultural reproduction to men' (2005: 12). The gothic vision of *Dracula* elevates the sanctity, safety, and honour of heterosexual marriage, especially for women.

While Wollstonecraft portrays a world in which patriarchy's ubiquitous and deleterious power over women's lives is exposed and critiqued, Stoker creates a world where threats to Christian patriarchy are thwarted and traditional gender values reaffirmed. Maria desires and strives for autonomy over her mind and body, despite traditional Christian belief and marriage vows. Male protection is no protection at all since Maria may be incarcerated based solely on her husband's claim that she has succumbed to hysteria, and Darnford, her would-be rescuer, cannot, in fact, help her without impugned or actual adulterous motives. Ultimately, in *Wrongs* women simply cannot trust or rely upon men to do them good. Conversely, in *Dracula*, female autonomy puts women at tremendous risk and is eschewed in favour of a benevolent chivalric surveillance. Here men's protection of women is everything. Indeed, it is so virtuous and effectual that it can save Lucy's and Mina's imperilled souls. Without male defenders Lucy is sacrificed to Dracula's rapacious male appetite and her soul is damned. Only her mortal male protectors stand between heaven and hell and can set her soul free. Mina, too, can only be saved from Dracula by the men's valiant efforts. This juxtaposition of two roles – defenders of women and vanquishers of demons – conflates a set of traditional gender expectations with a priest-like role for these men and makes them not only heroes but also saviours. In *Dracula* women are most definitely in need of their saviours' beneficent rescuing. The opposite is true in *Wrongs*, where women are not rescued by men but pursued or imprisoned by them, and where a working-class, abused, and cast-off woman becomes the effectual saviour of the imperilled Maria. In this gothic vision, women are the protectors of other women. In addition Wollstonecraft works to depict women as both capable and requiring autonomy, even if that autonomy challenges both traditional gender roles and traditional Christian beliefs. Maria advocates for a new morality outside and superior to that prescribed by patriarchy and Christian marriage; and hope, however tentative, lies in women's communities and control over their own destinies. A century following Wollstonecraft's *Wrongs*, Stoker's *Dracula*, rather than extending her critique of patriarchy, re-inscribes, under cover of a fantastical gothic tale, a Christian world order and patriarchy's masculine dominance. While Wollstonecraft's gothic novel makes an unapologetic and progressive critique of the wrongs of women, Stoker's, though seemingly positive about the emerging New Woman, in the end re-inscribes an anti-progressive and paternalistic essentialism at the dawn of the 20th century.

## Notes

1. See also Brock, 2009: 20, 26; Hoeveler, 1999: 389, 391, 404; Johnson, 'Mary ... Novels,' 2002: 204.
2. The outcome of the court proceedings is also unsurprising given the fact that laws regarding married women's autonomy and divorce were not significantly examined or altered in England until mid- to late-19th century: 1857 Divorce and Matrimonial Causes Act, 1878 Matrimonial Causes Act, 1870 and 1882 Married Women's Property Acts, 1886 Maintenance of Wives (Desertion) Act, and 1895 Summary Jurisdiction (Married Women) Act of 1895. (See Lyndon Shanley's 'Divorce' (223-24) and 'Marriage Law' (477-78) in Mitchell's *Victorian Britain: An Encyclopedia*).
3. *A Vindication of the Rights of Man* in 1790 and in *The Vindication of the Rights of Woman* in 1792.

# 3
# Stoker, Poe, and American Gothic in 'The Squaw'

Kevin Corstorphine

Edgar Allan Poe claims in the preface to his 1840 collection *Tales of the Grotesque and Arabesque* that 'terror is not of Germany, but of the soul' (Poe, *GA*: xxiv). Bram Stoker's 1893 short story 'The Squaw' illustrates this point perfectly. Written by an Irishman living in England, it is set in Europe's Gothic heart of Germany and concerns a (presumably) English couple and their meeting with an American frontiersman, demonstrating the 'cross-cultural exchange' (Elbert and Marshall, 2013: 1) that critics have recently identified in Gothic fiction. Stoker had a special admiration for the United States, and, as aspects of the story would suggest, for Poe. This is an aspect of Stoker's fiction that has not been widely discussed, but provides a revealing lens through which to read his earlier fiction, which demonstrates this influence strongly.

Stoker toured the United States with Henry Irving in the autumn of 1883; the first of eight Lyceum tours of the country that he organised as business manager of the theatre. He was so inspired by his trips that after a five-month tour between November 1884 and April 1885 he delivered the lecture 'A Glimpse of America' at the London Institution in December 1885, and published it the following year. It is remarkably detailed for 'a glimpse', and even the great explorer of the African continent, Henry Morton Stanley, told Irving that the lecture, 'had more information about America than any other book that had ever been written' (Dalby, 2002: 1). In the lecture, Stoker enthuses about such topics as the fire brigades, the freedom of women, and how well-dressed the working classes are in comparison to Britain. He claims of America that, 'we are bound to each other by the instinct of a common race, which makes brotherhood and the law of brothers a natural law' (Dalby, 2002: 30). It is reasonable to assume, given his enthusiasm, that American themes and characters would work their way into his fiction, and they do, notably in the form of *Dracula*'s Quincey Morris, who achieves the honour of stabbing the Count in the heart at the conclusion of the novel, and in the figure of Grizzly Dick, the rough frontiersman and bear hunter of *The Shoulder of Shasta* (1895). The connections between Quincey Morris and the United States have been discussed by Louis S. Warren, who connects the origins of the character, and many of the ideas behind Dracula himself, to William F. 'Buffalo Bill' Cody, who had been brought to perform at the Lyceum by Irving and Stoker in 1887 (Warren, 2002: 1124). It is tempting to read Elias P. Hutcheson, the American of 'The Squaw', as a mere prototype for these later characters, but an analysis of this short story in the light of Stoker's development as a writer, particularly with regard to the influence of Poe, reveals a deep connection to the mood and themes of what we might now refer to as American Gothic, which Eric Savoy characterises as displaying the ways in which the American 'national "self" is undone by the return of its repressed Otherness' (Martin and Savoy, 1998: vii). Despite not being written by an American author, Stoker's story follows this template exactly, and explores the preoccupations of the American Gothic in fascinating ways.

As an enthusiastic reader of the weird and macabre, Stoker was drawn to Poe. The latter's reputation, however, had suffered in the decades following his death in 1849, beginning with a brutal assault on his character in the New York *Tribune* by Rufus W. Griswold (writing as 'Ludwig'). Perhaps this is one reason that Stoker abandoned an early plan to turn 'The Fall of the House of Usher' into a stage play. He had previously noted the story as a 'subject for drama' in his journal in 1872 (Miller and Stoker, 2012: 66). Interestingly, this was the same year he wrote a gushing letter of praise to Walt Whitman, but 'shrank from mailing it' and did not send it until four years later, having passionately defended the American poet's work in debates at Trinity College Dublin (Murray, 2004: 64). Stoker later referred to himself and his friends as 'Walt-Whitmanites' (Stoker, *Personal Reminiscences*, vol. 2: 95). With regards to his own relationship to Whitman, Stoker claims in the letter that 'I would be towards you as a brother and as a pupil to his master' (Murray, 2004: 64). Clearly this was a time when he was immersing himself in American writing. The same year 'he was pained when an attempt to recite "The Raven" by an ill-educated local man produced only laughter from the audience at a poetry reading in Greystones, a seaside village outside of Dublin' (Murray, 2004: 184). The man's clumsy reading was not the only indignity inflicted on Poe's name. Dudley R. Hutcherson gives an account of his reputation around this time with reference to Henry James:

> Henry James, in 1878, digressing briefly in his essay on Charles Baudelaire, offered perhaps the best-known comment on Poe made during these years, with his assertion that 'an enthusiasm for Poe is the mark of a decidedly primitive stage of reflection.' James also stated that 'it seems to us that to take him with more than a certain degree of seriousness is to lack seriousness one's self'. (Hutcherson, 1942: 219)

These are charges, perhaps, that a young man like Stoker could be sensitive to. His hesitation to post the letter to Whitman suggests a certain reticence in being perceived as overly naive. Nonetheless, Stoker could take heart in the fact that French critics, notably Baudelaire, also recognised Poe's unique imaginative power. A shared love of Poe, also, was one quality that enabled Stoker to bond with none other than Alfred, Lord Tennyson, then Poet Laureate, whom he visited in 1878, only a year after James's essay. Paul Murray explains that, 'they shared an interest in the macabre, with Stoker noting that Tennyson regarded Poe as, "the most original genius that America had produced"' (2004: 117). He was not alone in this opinion. In 1886 'Andrew Lang called Poe "the greatest poet, perhaps the greatest literary genius" of America' (Hutcherson, 1942: 223). Stoker's friend, Arthur Conan Doyle, in a 1908 essay declared Poe to be 'the supreme original short story writer of all time' (Conan Doyle, *Through the Magic Door*: 117). Whitman himself was the only poet, among several who were invited, to attend the public reburial of Poe's remains in 1875; an occasion also noteworthy for a public reading of a poem composed for the event by Tennyson.

This is not the last time the connection would be relevant, as an enthusiasm for Poe was also shared by a young politician and one-time fiction writer called Winston Churchill, interviewed by Stoker in 1908 for the *Daily Chronicle*. Stoker's own reputation was established, and the interview was 'mainly brought about by Churchill's great liking for, and admiration of, *Dracula*' (Dalby, 2002: 121). During the interview Stoker, like any keen reader, was quick to cast an eye over Churchill's bookshelf:

> Here, in addition to the heavier works of history, philosophy and those bearing on politics and public life, are fine editions handsomely bound of Edgar Allan Poe, Carlyle, Richardson, Jane Austen, Dean Milan, George Grote, the Brontes, &c. (Dalby, 2002: 123)

Stoker continually places emphasis on the physical. In his youthful letter to Whitman he describes his own appearance at length, including such self-effacing comments as 'I am ugly but strong and determined and have a large bump over my eyebrows' (Miller and Stoker, 2012: 125). Claiming to know something of Whitman's character from his photograph he says 'I am a believer of the science [physiognomy] myself and am in a humble way a practicer [sic] of it' (Miller and Stoker, 2012: 62). This belief has clearly not been lost in the intervening years, as he considers the following level of detail to be necessary in describing Churchill's person:

> The forehead is both broad and high, with a fairly deep vertical line above the nose; the chin strong and well formed. His hands are somewhat remarkable: a sort of index to his life as well as to his general character .... Broad in the palm, with that breadth which palmists take as showing honesty; fingers both long and fairly thick, but tapering; the thumb slightly bent backward at the top joint. The man with such a hand should go far. (Dalby, 2002: 125)

Stoker turns out to be right, of course, although we might be quicker today to credit a combination of Churchill's background, talent, and ambition for his successes. That Stoker was well-versed in the physiognomic theories of his day is evidenced not just in his letter to Whitman, but in his description of Count Dracula, on Jonathan Harker's first meeting with the vampire:

> His face was a strong, a very strong, aquiline, with high bridge of the thin nose and peculiarly arched nostrils, with lofty domed forehead, and hair growing scantily round the temples but profusely elsewhere .... The mouth, so far as I could see it under the heavy moustache, was fixed and rather cruel-looking, with peculiarly sharp white teeth. These protruded over the lips, whose remarkable ruddiness showed astonishing vitality in a man of his years. For the rest, his ears were pale, and at the tops extremely pointed. The chin was broad and strong, and the cheeks firm though thin. (Stoker, 1997: 23–24).

Dracula's hands, in contrast to Churchill's, are 'coarse, broad, with squat fingers', and the palms are hairy. This analysis is prefigured somewhat curiously in Poe's description of Roderick Usher:

> A cadaverousness of complexion; an eye large, liquid, and luminous beyond comparison; lips somewhat thin and very pallid, but of a

surpassingly beautiful curve; a nose of a delicate Hebrew model, but with a breadth of nostril unusual in similar formations; a finely moulded chin, speaking, in its want of prominence, of a want of moral energy; hair of a more than web-like softness and tenuity. (Poe, *Tales of Mystery and Imagination*, 2000: 151)

Usher, like the Count, has a hooked nose (commonplace anti-semitism rearing its head here) and his chin, unlike Churchill's, shows a lack of moral character. He also shows characteristics of the exotic Other, his face having an 'arabesque expression' which lacked 'any idea of simple humanity' (151). The East, as in *Dracula*, is associated with cruelty. Usher may be an aristocrat, but generations of inbreeding have enfeebled his family line. Here he departs from Dracula, in whose blood is mingled many different tribes and nations:

> We Szekelys have a right to be proud, for in our veins flows the blood of many brave races who fought as the lion fights, for lordship. Here, in the whirlpool of European races, the Ugric tribe bore down from Iceland the fighting spirit which Thor and Wodin gave them, which their Berserkers displayed to such fell intent on the seaboards of Europe, aye, and of Asia and Africa too, till the peoples thought that the werewolves themselves had come. (Stoker, 1997: 33–34)

Dracula gains strength from the comingling of the blood of different races in his veins. The picture is a Mendelian one; these characteristics are passed down through inheritance, and express themselves in the Count. This race-mixing is certainly a good thing, at least for Dracula, as it is the very source of his power.

Stoker's views on race were relatively progressive, albeit steeped in the essentialist thinking of his day, and this comes to the fore in his opinions of America. In his 1909 article, 'Americans as Actors', he lays out his views on the future of the nation, also a 'whirlpool' of immigrant peoples:

> The ultimate fusion of these many races must create what will be practically a new type. But such is as yet far off; so we need only glance at it as a possibility, and confine ourselves to things as they are. How each of the various races named will supplement each other is an ethnological problem. In race-fusion the lower as well as the higher races have benevolent part, adding physical strength, endurance, fecundity, though they may lack moral and intellectual strength. (Dalby, 2002: 86)

This coheres with Stoker's belief in America as a bright hope for the future, as well as his identification as 'a believer in' Home Rule (Stoker, *Personal Reminiscences*, vol. 1, 1906: 343), where Ireland would throw off the yoke of tyrannical landlords, but remain a vital (in the sense of life-giving) part of the British Empire. The spectre of decadent, or degenerate, culture (as envisioned by Max Nordau) lurks in the background. Stoker believed that America was in danger of becoming decadent, and would be revived by this healthy influx of race and culture from countries such as Ireland, whose passionate temperament was akin to Mediterranean cultures, as opposed to the phlegmatic Scots, English, and Germans. This is also aligned to the dangerous yet invigorating force of the frontier. Frederick Jackson Turner in his 1893 lecture, 'The Significance of the Frontier in American History', saw the frontier as 'the westward-moving source of America's democratic politics, open society, unfettered economy, and rugged individualism' (Tindall and Shi, 1997: 598). Yet his thesis was delivered with the premise that this period had already passed. A new vision was needed for the future of the United States.

If Stoker was forward looking in his politics, he retained a habit of looking to the past in literature. Poe lurks in the background as a major figure of the literary Gothic in Stoker's imagination, and perhaps a literary father figure from whose shadow he had not escaped before doing so spectacularly with his most famous novel, *Dracula*. His mother Charlotte, on its publication, praises him in a letter by claiming that, 'no book since Mrs Shelley's *Frankenstein* or indeed any other at all has come near yours in terms of originality, or terror [;] Poe is nowhere' (Murray, 2004: 204). We must, of course, admit the possibility of a certain bias here. There is a measure of anxiety in here too. Stoker may have changed the original ending of *Dracula*, where the castle was to be destroyed, due to it being too similar to 'The Fall of the House of Usher' (Miller and Stoker, 2012: 57). If Stoker's mother is to be believed in her assessment, then this is the moment when he breaks free of the chains of influence that hang over most authors, particularly authors who are also avid readers like Stoker. It might even be said that some of the most important events in his life, such as becoming business manager of Irving's Lyceum Theatre were founded on a profound admiration for others. Indeed Elizabeth Miller and Dacre Stoker point out the indebtedness of Stoker to Poe and Tennyson for the metre of his poetic efforts in the early 1870s (Miller and Stoker, 2012: 16). It is certainly with a debt to Poe that he produces his short story, 'The Squaw' in 1893.

'The Squaw', a tale of seemingly accidental cat murder and subsequent ironic revenge, bears startling resemblance to Poe's 'The Black Cat' (1843) This is not just shown in the incidents of plot, but in their shared concerns with perversity, guilt, and what Freud would later term displacement. 'The Squaw' reads very much like the American magazine short stories contemporary with Stoker, displaying the hallmarks of what we might term the American Gothic. Teresa Goddu has argued that this constitutes the hallmarks of a distinct tradition:

> The nation's narratives – its foundational fictions and self-mythologizations – are created through a process of displacement: their coherence depends on exclusion. By resurrecting what these narratives repress, the gothic disrupts the dream world of national myth with the nightmares of history. (Goddu, 1997: 10)

This, of course, can be seen in Poe's famous short story, where a drunkard tortures and eventually hangs his beloved cat, Pluto, through sheer perversity. Another cat appears which may or may not be a reincarnation of the first. It too, has only one eye, but also displays a tuft of hair in the shape of a gallows on its chest. The increasingly manic narrator attempts to slay this one with an axe, but when his wife intervenes he 'buried the axe in her brain' (*Mystery and Imagination*, 2000: 194) and walls up the body in his basement in a kind of physical manifestation of repression. He is discovered when the police hear the howling of the cat, which has been accidently sealed up with the wife's corpse, and tear down the wall to reveal his crime.

Stoker's story features a young couple on honeymoon in Nuremburg, plus a 'cheery stranger' who joins them: the preposterously American Elias P. Hutcheson, 'hailing from Isthmian City, Bleeding Gulch, Maple Tree County, Neb' (*Dracula's Guest*, 2006: 37). Nebraska at this time was very much a frontier state, and its population had been increasing due to homestead acts granting land to migrants. Even today the state sells itself to tourists on the basis of being 'America's frontier' and offering 'the good life'. Hutcheson is brash and swaggering, not unlike *Dracula's* Quincey Morris, whom he clearly anticipates. Clive Leatherdale, among others, reads these characters as 'clones' of each other and remarks of the 'stereotypical' qualities (1993: 133). The young bridegroom even seems to realise this, telling us that they, 'much enjoyed the remarks of our transatlantic friend, who, from his quaint speech and his wonderful stock of adventures, might have stepped out of a novel' (*Dracula's Guest*, 2006: 37). The party are in Nuremberg to see the famous torture tower, which contains the Iron Virgin, now more commonly known as an Iron Maiden. This device itself has an interesting provenance: largely considered by historians to be a fake, the iron maiden fulfilled its purpose in drumming up tourism in Nuremburg among travellers keen to see the kind of Germanic excess they had read about in the Gothic novels of Walpole, Lewis, and Radcliffe. More recently, Poe had shown a fascination with the violent excesses of the past in his torture fantasy 'The Pit and the Pendulum' (1842). Notably, a copy of the Nuremberg Maiden was exhibited in America at the Chicago World's Fair in 1893, a few months before the publication of 'The Squaw', before being taken on a tour of the States. In late 1893 *The New York Times* reported ghoulishly (and inaccurately) that 'thousands of persons have gazed upon these terrible relics of a semi-barbarous age. All the instruments in the collection have been in actual use' (*New York Times*). The device, along with over a thousand others, had been purchased by the Earl of Shrewsbury in 1890 and exhibited in London. Stoker would have been familiar with the Virgin from these events, and also from Henry Irving's trip to Nuremberg itself in 1895, to conduct research for his production of *Faust*. Murray claims it unlikely that Stoker went on this trip but 'probably used his ability to describe places he had never actually visited, so ably demonstrated in *Dracula*, to paint a convincing picture of the medieval German city' (2004: 153). He was clearly fascinated, as in *Dracula* Mina compares the red rooftops of Whitby (a place he had visited in 1890) to Nuremberg (1997: 63). In 'The Squaw,' Stoker takes the opportunity to promote Irving's legendary status by claiming that the events in the story take place when the city was not well known, as Irving had yet to perform there.

The young couple of 'The Squaw', now accompanied by their American friend, encounter a cat playing with her kitten at the bottom of a large wall: an idyllic scene which is shattered when Hutcheson decides it will be amusing to playfully drop a stone at them, misjudging his aim:

> The stone fell with a sickening thud that came up to us through the hot air, right on the kitten's head, and shattered out its little brains then and there. The black cat cast a swift upward glance, and we saw her eyes like green fire fixed an instant on Elias P. Hutcheson; and then her attention was given to the kitten, which lay still with just a quiver of her tiny limbs, whilst a thin red stream trickled from a gaping wound. With a muffled cry, such as a human being might give, she bent over the kitten licking its wounds and moaning. Suddenly she seemed to realise that it was dead, and again threw her

eyes up at us. I shall never forget the sight, for she looked the perfect incarnation of hate. Her green eyes blazed with lurid fire, and the white, sharp teeth seemed to almost shine through the blood which dabbled her mouth and whiskers. (Stoker, *Dracula's Guest*, 2006: 39)

The scene would be disturbing for the kitten-crushing alone, but Stoker's description seems to transcend the level of horror we are supposed to feel at the death of an animal. Hutcheson, a rugged frontiersman, shrugs off the incident, worried only that he has upset the young bride. Any potential fears of feline revenge are put to rest by the pistol that he carries in his pocket. This is against German law but he ignores it due to what he sees as his rights as an American citizen: a wry piece of satire on Stoker's part. There is an uncanny anthropomorphism here, with the cat clearly demonstrating the human emotion of hatred (the description of the cat's eyes and teeth, too, show another prototype for Stoker's emerging vampire Count). This has an interesting post-Darwinian aspect, what Kate Hebblethwaite refers to as, 'the deep unease expressed in much later nineteenth-century popular literature about the need for the reassessment of the boundaries that separate human and animal.' (Stoker, *Dracula's Guest*, 2006: xix) This had already featured in Poe's fiction. In 'Murders in the Rue Morgue' (1841), published 18 years before Darwin's *On the Origin of Species* (1859), a similar motif is at work. An orang-utan steals its master's razor and attempts to shave a woman in imitation, accidently killing her, then throttles her daughter and stuffs the body up a chimney in an attempt to hide its murderous deeds. The guilt felt by the creature is unbefitting of a non-human animal, but compelling and powerfully uncanny.

Hutcheson, in response to the cat's fury, relates a frontier tale that is somewhat darker than the ones that have amused the young couple so far. This concerns a 'half-breed' called Splinters who was tortured to death by an Apache squaw. From a postcolonial perspective it is relevant that Stoker chooses to give this character a hybrid identity. Although according to Hutcheson Splinters 'should have been a white man, for he looked like one' (*Dracula's Guest*, 2006: 40), the savage part of his nature comes through. Stoker's voice, however, should not be confused with Hutcheson's, as the story complicates the issue of where savagery truly lies. The Iron Virgin, the ultimate 'instance of the horrors of cruelty of which man is capable' (38), is European, and supposedly centuries old. Splinters's mother, however has suffered from New World horrors, and was 'given the fire-torture' by Apache Indians. Contemporary literature often relished in a lurid Gothic mode of storytelling regarding alleged

Indian practices, as with this politically driven narrative about the Apache written by the Governor of Arizona in 1871:

> He is inventive in his means of torture. Women are often made captives, and subjected to a life worse than death. Children are placed on spears and roasted over a slow fire, and writhe in misery until life is extinct. Men are hanged by the feet and a slow fire kindled at the head, and gashed with knives and pierced with arrows until death gives relief. Reader, these are stubborn facts. Do you wonder the people clamor for protection, and feel deeply wronged when their brethren, far removed from these horrid scenes, denounce them as barbarous because they want peace and these Indians subdued? (Safford, 1871: 23)

In revenge for his mother's treatment, Splinters is said to have 'fixed up' a squaw's baby, presumably impaling it somehow (this is how he has gained his nickname). The squaw, Hutcheson says, tracked Splinters for years before having him taken captive and torturing him slowly until he was glad of death. The look of implacable hatred on her face, Hutcheson says, was like that of the mother cat. This is disturbing not only for the horrors related, but the breezy manner in which Hutcheson relates his own part in proceedings: 'the only time I saw her smile was when I wiped her out' (40). Immediately following the tale, the narrator claims that, 'Hutcheson was a kind-hearted man – my wife and I had both noticed little acts of kindness to animals as well as to persons – and he seemed concerned at the state of fury to which the cat had wrought herself' (40). This shows the double-thinking inherent in the denial of full human subjecthood to the colonised, that the narrator can recoil at the horror of the story, but still see Hutcheson as 'kind-hearted'. The notion of the merciful killing is quite a common trope in Indian warfare narratives, and occasionally extends to genocide. L. Frank Baum, later famous for his *Oz* series, wrote two now-infamous editorials for the *Saturday Pioneer* relating to the death of Sitting Bull at Wounded Knee. In the 1890 piece he praises the great Chief's spirit, and in contrast notes that his white enemies 'were marked in their dealings with his people by selfishness, falsehood and treachery' (Baum, 1890). It is no wonder, he suggests, 'that a fiery rage still burned within his breast and that he should seek every opportunity of obtaining vengeance upon his natural enemies' (Baum, 1890). He then goes on, however, to advocate 'the total annihilation of the few remaining Indians' (Baum, 1890) in order to preserve their dignity in the historical record. His reasons are made even clearer in the 1891 piece, where he offers his final solution to the problem:

> The Pioneer has before declared that our only safety depends upon the total extirmination [sic] of the Indians. Having wronged them for centuries we had better, in order to protect our civilization, follow it up by one more wrong and wipe these untamed and untamable creatures from the face of the earth. (Baum, 1891)

Baum's views are steeped in the racial pseudo-science of his day, and echoes almost exactly Alfred Russel Wallace's claim in *Natural Selection: A Series of Essays* (1870) that there occurs 'an inevitable extinction of all those low and mentally undeveloped populations with which Europeans come in contact' (2006: 222). It is testament to the normalisation of such beliefs that they are to be taken for granted in Stoker's narrative. 'The Squaw', however, allows for no such sentimental fading away of the native, instead offering a grisly reversal of fortunes.

Hutcheson, on finally seeing the Iron Virgin, has an urge to climb inside, bribing the attendant to tie him up and slowly allow the door to close, so that he can experience the feeling of a victim's last moments. This is immediately evocative of Poe's description of perversity, as laid out in 'The Imp of the Perverse' (1845). Here, the narrator imagines the condition of a person staring into an abyss. He claims that what we fear most is not accidentally falling, but that we have a secret urge to jump:

> It is merely the idea of what would be our sensations during the sweeping precipitancy of a fall from such a height. And this fall – this rushing annihilation – for the very reason that it involves that one most ghastly and loathsome of all the most ghastly and loathsome images of death and suffering which have ever presented themselves to our imagination –for this very cause do we now the most vividly desire it. (Poe, Complete Tales, 1982: 282)

It is this very feeling that Hutcheson craves, although he stops short (at least consciously) of the desire of actual death. He says that he wants 'to feel the same pleasure as the other jays had when those spikes began to move toward their eyes' (47). The ironic use of the word 'pleasure' is perhaps revealing of his underlying desire for what he calls 'the experience I've been pinin' and pantin' fur' (47). As with *Dracula*, Stoker shows his tendency to introduce strange sexual undercurrents to the horrific. This is all part of the imaginative appeal of the Iron Virgin in the first place: it enables a kind of perverse return to the womb followed, of course, by penetration of the victim. This thematic conflation of sexuality, death, and motherhood suffuses the story and lends it a particularly uneasy atmosphere. There is a dramatic irony in that everything that happens, despite the protestations of the characters, is inevitable from the reader's perspective.

Stoker was writing around the same time as Freud was developing his theories of the unconscious mind, and psychoanalytic readings would no doubt point out that the frontiersman's unconscious desire for punishment stems from the guilt that he has repressed under his cheerful manner. He claims to be 'as tender as a Maine cherry-tree' when discussing his plans to drop the stone, and somewhat disturbingly (given that he does hurt the kitten greatly), that 'I wouldn't hurt the poor pooty little critter more'n I'd scalp a baby' (39). Accident it may have been, but failure to predict the bloody outcome is an exceptionally poor error of judgment on Hutcheson's part. It is far more likely that it is Hutcheson's consistent disregard for the value of life, born of the harsh frontier, that leads to his actions. In contrast to the sensitive young bride, he appears to find the cat's mournful anguish amusing. When he sees its face spattered with the blood of its own offspring 'his eyes positively sparkled with fun' and he declares 'darned if the squaw hain't got on all her war paint!' (48). The contrast between his declarations of tenderness and his evident love of bloodshed is reminiscent of the narrator of 'The Black Cat' who claims that 'from my infancy I was noted for the docility and humanity of my disposition. My tenderness of heart was even so conspicuous as to make me the jest of my companions' (189). He claims to have been 'especially fond of animals' (189), and yet goes on to neglect and torture his large menagerie of animals, killing, of course, his most beloved cat. This stems from alcoholism, he claims, although this too could easily fall under the banner of the self-destructive urge of the perverse.

These ideas clearly affected Stoker. A strikingly similar motif occurs in 'The Secret of the Growing Gold' (1892). Here, the protagonist kills his wife and buries her under a hearthstone, which cracks open as her hair grows through it and proceeds to kill him and his new lover. He is driven mad with visions of the hair, and it appears for a while, as seems to be the case with the beating heart in Poe's 'The Tell-Tale Heart' (1843), that the visions are hallucinations brought on by guilt. Stoker takes this further than Poe into the realm of the supernatural, however, by revealing in the end that the killer hair is real. Stoker's stories also reveal an interesting return to the idea of women turning the tables on men. Geoffrey Brent, the murderer of this story, has like Dracula and Usher a lustful and cruel appearance, although 'certainly handsome, with that dark, aquiline commanding beauty which women so generally recognise as dominant' (Stoker, *Dracula's Guest*, 2006: 51). It is Mina's psychic connection that enables the destruction of the Count, and Usher is destroyed by his revenant sister. So too is Brent punished by a symbolic femininity in the form of the vengeful hair. The narrator of 'The Squaw' articulates his admiration for Hutcheson when the mother cat is briefly calm:

> 'See!' said I, 'the effect of a really strong man. Even that animal in the midst of her fury recognises the voice of a master, and bows to him!'
> 'Like a squaw!' was the only comment of Elias P. Hutcheson. (41)

The word 'squaw' is an Algonquian term used crudely in English to mean any Indian woman. Its use by Hutcheson, in keeping with contemporary norms, signifies submissiveness and inferiority. Given that the squaw of his own frontier narrative was far from pliant in the face of male power, the dismissive comment is given an irony that foreshadows the climax of the story.

The cat in 'The Squaw', then, becomes likewise an agent of female revenge. Having stalked Hutcheson down in the manner of the squaw's pursuit of Splinters, it appears in the torture chamber and launches an attack. This is directed not at Hutcheson as might be expected, but more cunningly at the attendant, scratching at his eyes until he drops the rope, which then slams the door of the Virgin shut. Hutcheson's skull is pierced so deeply that when the narrator opens the door his body swings out with it before crashing to the floor. What he sees confirms the intentionality of the deed: 'sitting on the head of the poor American was the cat, purring loudly as she licked the blood which trickled through the gashed socket of his eyes' (49). The narrator then seizes an executioner's sword and cleaves the cat in two, claiming that, 'no one will call me cruel' (49). This evokes the rather dubious claim of the narrator in 'The Black Cat' that he is not mad. Both reveal an underlying self-doubt and anxiety. The narrator's pseudo-merciful killing of the cat shadows the memory of Hutcheson's killing of the squaw. The squaw has returned, like Poe's Pluto, perhaps literally possessing the cat. The native rises up to take revenge for past wrongs, and the cycle of violence continues, repeated again and again. Joan Dayan has made this reading of Poe's 'The Black Cat', claiming that the symbolism of blackness produces a subtext relating to slavery in the American South: 'a black pet loved and owned by an increasingly cruel master, effects a damning conversion: the once benevolent owner utterly bestialized, reduced by the very thing he brutalized' (Dayan, 1999: 412) The cat performs as a signifier, here for the immanent presence of past guilt, re-emerging in the present. Likewise, the cat in 'The Squaw' becomes a vessel for past trauma to make its presence felt. Poe's cat returns with the imprint of a gallows on its chest, and when the young bride in Stoker's tale becomes a mother, the child is imprinted with a birthmark in the shape of the Iron Virgin. As Hebblethwaite points out, 'Stoker was much taken with the notion that birthmarks were either a direct result of "maternal impression" (the representation of an event experienced by a mother during pregnancy) or a physical manifestation of a past-life memory' (Stoker, *Dracula's Guest*, 2006: 385). This is the negative side of *Dracula's* positive ending, where Mina and Jonathan name their son Quincey. Jonathan notes that 'his mother holds, I know, the secret belief that some of our brave friend's spirit has passed into him' (1997: 326). This is despite (we assume) a genetic link. With Stoker, as with Poe, it is not just Mendelian inheritance at work, but the collision of contemporary ideas of race, culture, and the complex ways in which we are bound by blood.

This, after all, is the heart of the American Gothic, that the nation of hope, equality, and freedom is founded upon mass murder of natives, the brutalities of slavery and the bloody crucible of war. The idea that the past will catch up the present is a spectre that haunts American fiction. In his influential critique, Leslie Fiedler poses the question:

> How could one tell where the American dream ended and the Faustian nightmare began; they held in common the hope of breaking through all limits and restraints, of reaching a place of total freedom where one could with impunity deny the Fall, live as if innocence rather than guilt were the birthright of all men. (1960: 143)

The Faust legend itself, Fiedler asserts, was seized on immediately as far back as the 1680s, when the English translation of the German 'Faust Book' sold record numbers of copies (143), a full two centuries before Irving performed his version on stage. The play, Stoker notes, was wildly popular in the cities of Boston, Philadelphia, and New York. He attributes this to them all having been founded by devout Christians. In Chicago, however, 'which as a city neither fears the devil nor troubles its head about him or all his works, the receipts were not much more than half the other places' (Stoker, *Personal Reminiscences*, vol. 1, 1906: 184). Stoker clearly identifies this tension in the American literature and culture he devoured so avidly. In 'The Squaw', Elias P. Hutcheson plays the part of the Faustian over-reacher. Like Poe's protagonists, however, he puts himself willingly into restraints. He even goes so far as to compare this to a 'necktie party', in other words a lynching (*Dracula's Guest*, 2006: 46). This hints at the dark events of his era and country, but also a perversity born of guilt that appears to lie behind his affable manner. Stoker is brutal in his portrayal. It is not just the kitten's skull that is shattered, but the pre-Lapsarian naivety of the young honeymooners. Stoker's message is clear: that the stain of guilt lies heavily on nations as well as individuals, even should they, as with the United States, imagine themselves young.

# 4
# Bram Stoker and Gothic Transylvania

Marius-Mircea Crișan

Analysing the influence of Bram Stoker's readings about Transylvania on the representation of this region in *Dracula* can shed a new light on the construction of this famous fictional place (Leatherdale, 1987: 97–9, 108–110; Frayling, 1991: 317–20, 331; Goldsworthy, 1998: 77–82; Miller, 2006: 122–7; Crișan, 2013: 214–26). As Stoker never visited Transylvania, his representation of this space is partially inspired by the sources he consulted on the region: five books – William Wilkinson, *An Account of the Principalities of Wallachia and Moldavia* (1820), Charles Boner, *Transylvania: Its Products and Its People* (1865), Andrew F. Crosse, *Round About the Carpathians* (1878), A Fellow of the Carpathian Society [Nina Elizabeth Mazuchelli], *'Magyarland': Being the Narrative of Our Travels Through the Highlands and Lowlands of Hungary* (1881), Major E.C. Johnson, *On the Track of the Crescent: Erratic Notes from the Piraeus to Pesth* (1885) – and an article, 'Transylvanian Superstitions' by Emily Gerard, published in *The Nineteenth Century* (1885) and included in the volume *The Land Beyond the Forest* (1888). However, there is no doubt that it is Stoker's originality which created the successful image of the fictional Transylvania.

As Carol Senf points out, Transylvania is 'a mysterious region – an embodiment of the past, more mythic than real' and *Dracula* is 'far more about religion' than politics (2000: 52). The novel has been subject to several religious readings (Starrs, 2008; Rarignac, 2012), and Clive Leatherdale's interpretation marks one of the main tendencies in this direction:

> It might seem superfluous to claim that *Dracula* is a Christian parody. Everything that Christ is meant to be Dracula either inverts or perverts. Christ is Good: Dracula is Evil – an agent of the devil. Christ

was a humble carpenter: Dracula a vainglorious aristocrat. Christ offers light and hope, and was resurrected at dawn: Dracula rises at sunset and thrives in darkness .... Christ offered his own life so that others might live: Dracula takes the lives of many so that he might live .... The link between Christ and Dracula is made explicit through the Count's recoiling from crucifixes, holy water, and other symbols of Christianity. (2001: 193)

Besides a religious reading, the essence of the novel lies in its ambiguous symbolism. The fact that it begins in Transylvania in the spring and ends (in the same setting) in late fall symbolizes, according to Thomas Walsh, 'a reversal of the traditional seasonal death and rebirth cycle of the pastoral structure' (1979: 230). As Leatherdale notes, 'Stoker's Transylvania ... is not only a land beyond the forest; it is also a land beyond scientific understanding' (2001: 112). The rich symbolism in the construction of this fictional space opens the story to countless interpretations. This chapter, then, analyses some features which move the Transylvanian world from its referential status, and transform this geographical space into a gothic construction. I focus on the mythical dimension of time and space, and refer to the use of motifs (which are, according to David Punter (2014), essential for the gothic) such as the supernatural, the sublime, transgression, imprisonment, terror and the spectacular.

In *Dracula*, entering Transylvania marks the experience of a different world, and both time and space are endowed with supernatural features. From the beginning the reader can observe Jonathan Harker's obsession with time. The word *time* is frequently mentioned in the opening paragraphs. The English young lawyer wants repeatedly to check the 'the correct time' and is satisfied to note that the train left Budapest 'in pretty good time' (1994: 9). However, as Harker advances on his way to Castle Dracula, he departs gradually from the historical dimension of time and approaches the mythical one. From Munich to Bistritz – *Bistrița* in Romanian – (via Vienna, Budapest and Cluj) the trains are later and later: 'It seems to me that the further east you go the more unpunctual are the trains' (1994: 11). Travelling on the Transylvanian railway, Harker's impression is that he dawdles all day long. The same concern for punctuality is expressed in the dialogue with the landlady in Bistrița, when the Englishman stresses the fact that he 'must must go at once', as he is 'engaged on important business' (1994: 13). Deficiencies in time management in Transylvania were also noticed in Stoker's sources on the region. In '*Magyarland*', for instance, Elizabeth Mazuchelli describes the city of Oradea: 'almost every church steeple possesses four dials; but none of them agree as to the time, all maintaining a particular time of their own, and none of them being right' (1881: 75). Stoker, however, transforms this motif into a door to the world of the gothic fantastic.

Harker's impression that he experiences a different dimension of time increases after his encounter with Count Dracula. During the night coach ride to Dracula's castle, Jonathan worries again that he cannot know how time is passing, and strikes a match in order to look at his watch. Losing the control of time symbolizes the loss of self control: this is why he is so concerned about temporal details, and during his stay in the vampire castle he constantly winds the watch before going to bed. The encounter with the three vampire women can be interpreted as both an episode of seduction and an instance of losing control of time: when Harker wakes up in his room, after this tumultuous night, he notices that his watch is still unwound.

In the beginning of his diary, Harker has an obvious fascination with the past. He is delighted to be accommodated in an old fashioned hotel and seems extremely interested in the history of Transylvania. The references to Bistriţa's history (stormy existence, great fires, long sieges, thousands of victims, famine and disease) are significant in this regard. The working notes for *Dracula* demonstrate that the historical details about Bistriţa are borrowed from Charles Boner's *Transylvania: Its Products and Its People*. Although Stoker paraphrases Boner, the intentions of the two authors are different: while the latter tries to offer a precise historical background, Stoker is more allusive. Bistriţa is described in *Dracula* as a symbol of the past, though Boner noted in his volume that 'it has nothing of that medieval look which distinguishes Hermannstadt or Schassburg; the streets are straight and broad, and nearly every building is of modern date' (1865: 377).

The people of Stoker's Transylvania are detached from daily problems, and their only concern seems to be deterring evil spirits. The portraits of the owners of the inn are depicted in a mythological manner, and their clothes are coloured in black and white (unlike the colourful costumes of the region). The tone of the landlady, who desperately tries to prevent Harker from going to the Castle Dracula, and the landlord's fear of the mysterious count, also suggest a mythical perspective. Transylvanian time seems to be measured rather in holidays with spiritual significance: the Englishman should postpone his departure, because it is the eve of St. George's Day, and 'when the clock strikes midnight, all the evil things in the world will have full sway' (1994: 13). The only moment when the Transylvanian travellers feel the pressure of time is the drive to Borgo Pass, when the coachman hopes to avoid the meeting between

Harker and Count Dracula. The speed suggests the tension of Harker's dramatic situation.

The time of Dracula is also mythical. During his stay in the castle, Jonathan observes the opulence which reminds him of the medieval epoch: the table service is of gold, the curtains and upholstery of the sofas made of wonderful fabrics 'are centuries old' (1994: 30). Although similar furniture at Hampton Court is moth-eaten, the pieces possessed by the vampire count have not been affected by the passing of time. When Harker first enters the room of the vampire women, he imagines it as a place where medieval ladies waited for their lords to return from war: 'I determined not to return tonight to the gloom-haunted rooms, but to sleep here, where, of old, ladies had sat and sung and lived sweet lives whilst their gentle breasts were sad for their menfolk away in the midst of remorseless wars' (1994: 50).

Stoker's strategy to remove the historical dimension of time is more obvious in the invention of Dracula's history. As Elizabeth Miller (2006: 92-3) observes, although the Western characters refer to the vampire king with his aristocratic title, Dracula does not usually call himself a count. The creation of the character Dracula is a work which mixes Stoker's readings and his imagination. To understand his choice better, one needs to find clear answers to the questions: why Transylvania and why Dracula?

The working notes for the novel show that the novelist initially intended to place the action of the vampire story in Styria (Miller, 2006: 124; Eighteen-Bisang and Miller, 2008: 28-9). The vampire had already been a character of the English theatre for about a century. John Polidori's 'The Vampire' (1819) was adapted for the stage in 1820 by J. R. Planché. *The Vampire, or the Bride of the Isles* was, however, set in Scotland. A Styrian bloodsucking female was the main character of Sheridan Le Fanu's *Carmilla* (1872) so Stoker was well aware of the vampire's rich symbolism. Le Fanu's story certainly inspired Stoker. But the novelist clearly wanted to learn more about the belief in vampires, and, armed with encyclopaedic appetite, he consulted several works about the folklore of different people.

Of all sources on vampires, none was more fruitfully used by Stoker than Emily Gerard's article 'Transylvanian Superstitions.' In an interview with Jane Stoddard, Stoker declared: 'No one book that I know of will give you all the facts. I learned a good deal from E. Gerard's "Essays on Roumanian Superstitions," [sic] which first appeared in *The Nineteenth Century*, and were afterwards published in a couple of volumes' (Miller, 2009: 276). Not a proper anthropologist, the author of

'Transylvanian Superstitions' was the Scottish wife of a Polish officer in the Austro-Hungarian Army, who was employed at Sibiu for a few years. Gerard wrote a book of memories about her stay in this region, *The Land Beyond the Forest*, which was published in two volumes. While Stoker refers to this book in the interview his working notes do not prove that he consulted it. Gerard travelled in the rural areas of Transylvania and took notes about local beliefs (Crişan, *The Birth of the Dracula Myth*: 171–173). In spite of her critical attitude towards *superstitions*, she often expressed her admiration for the creativity of Romanian peasants, for the 'rich vein of their own folk-lore' (1888: 173). Gerard considers that Romanian legends, rooted in the Latin origin of the people, could be a useful source of inspiration for literature:

> the old stones around them will begin to speak, and the old gods will let themselves be lured from out their hiding-places. Then will it be seen that Apollo's lyre has not ceased to vibrate, and the lays of ancient Rome will arise and develop to new life. (1888: 173)

Stoker took several notes from Gerard's 'Transylvanian Superstitions,', and there is no doubt that the references to the vampire interested him most:

> More decidedly evil, however, is the vampire, or *nosferatu*, in whom every Roumenian peasant believes as firmly as he does in heaven or hell. There are two sorts of vampires – living and dead. The living vampire is in general the illegitimate offspring of two illegitimate persons, but even a flawless pedigree will not ensure anyone against the intrusion of a vampire into his family vault, since every person killed by a *nosferatu* becomes likewise a vampire after death, and will continue to suck the blood of other innocent people till the spirit has been exorcised, either by opening the grave of the person suspected and driving a stake through the corpse, or firing a pistol shot into the coffin. In very obstinate cases it is further recommended to cut off the head and replace it in the coffin with the mouth filled with garlic, or to extract the heart and burn it, strewing the ashes over the grave. (1885: 142)

The word *nosferatu* was used in *Dracula* as referring to the vampire. However, no such word exists in Romanian. Gerard's lack of precision is revealed by such instances. She may have heard the word *necuratu'* / *năcuratu* (the unclean one), which is used in Transylvania, for the Devil, or nefărtatu' / nefârtatu' – a symbol of evil in Romanian mythology. Other details are also used by Stoker in his vampiric novel: each person bitten by a vampire becomes a vampire, and the vampires are exorcised by driving a stake through the heart and cutting off the head.

However, the term *vampir* ('vampire') is rather a neologism in Romanian, and it is impossible to have been known by peasants in the nineteenth century. In Gerard's accounts, the belief in *strigoi* is *translated* as belief in vampires. A *strigoi* is a ghost who haunts the places where he lived. While the vampire is defined by the act of sucking blood, the *strigoi* is not explicitly described as an aggressive entity: he may have marks of blood on his mouth, but the bite is never described. Its presence is a question of mystery (Hedeşan in Crişan, *Impactul unui mit*, 2013: 8, 26). The motif of the vampire in Romanian folklore is rather a problematic issue (Crişan, *Impactul unui mit* ...: 21–25), and many folklorists state that there are more differences than similarities between the ghost of the Romanian folklore and the vampire: 'Romanians do not recognize Dracula as their hero, nor do they identify themselves with his basic life concepts .... It is significant and obvious that Romanian tradition forbids to "eat up" the raw essence of life, the blood, as a token of absolute respect for everything alive' (Ispas, 2010: 428).

Stoker's notes prove that the name Dracula is borrowed from William Wilkinson's book *An Account of the Principalities of Wallachia and Moldavia*, but they do not show if the novelist found the reports on the Transylvanians' belief on vampires (in Gerard's article) first, or the word Dracula. It is likely that he found Gerard's article first, and, as he saw essential information on vampires here, he did further investigation on this region. Therefore, during his holiday at Whitby, he found Wilkinson's book about the two provinces which neighbour Transylvania (Wallachia and Moldavia). An item of information found here made Stoker change the name of the vampire count from *Count Wampyr* to *Count Dracula*. The novelist was particularly attracted by a footnote, which explained that in Romanian 'Dracula means the Devil' (Wilkinson, 1820: 19). He underlined this item of information: in his source only D is capitalised, in the working notes for the book, the whole name is written in capital letters: DRACULA (Miller, 2006: 156; Eighteen-Bisang and Miller, 2008: 244–5). Stoker had the intention to write a novel about the eternal fight between good and evil, and the name Dracula shows that he chose it in order to create a character that symbolises the Devil. He jotted down a few notes about Voivode Dracula, but this information holds little relevance for the complex character of Dracula.

Voiovode Dracula is known in Romanian history as Vlad Ţepeş (Vlad the Impaler). In spite of endless pages of speculation and suppositions, there is no proof that Stoker knew about Voivode Dracula's nickname. As Elizabeth Miller (2006: 150–57) claims, all the information the novelist had in this regard is limited to the knowledge he found in Wilkinson. The Wallachian voivode was nicknamed 'the Impaler' because he used to impale his enemies, a practice borrowed from the Germans of Transylvania (Rezachevici, 2006). In his fights against the Germans or the Turks, he used this practice frequently. Impalement was also used as a means of establishing honesty in Wallachia, against thieves or beggars. His political enemies, the Germans, took a long lasting revenge on the voivode, by demonising his figure in several pamphlets which had great success in the German world of the fifteenth and sixteenth centuries. Although this form of medieval literature presented him as a cruel tyrant, since the nineteenth century, several historical studies depict Voivode Dracula as a hero of the Anti-Ottoman fight, a defender of Christendom (Andreescu, 1998: 9, 99–100; Treptow, 2000: 166, 178; Cazacu, 2008: 187–210). However, such details were probably unknown to Stoker, as there is no proof that he had any other source on Voivode Dracula than William Wilkinson.

Instead of basing his story on Romanian history, Stoker keeps the Gothic tradition in having an aristocrat as the evil character. Although the Wallachian voivode was born in Transylvania (at Sighişoara), he ruled (as his forerunners and inheritors did) over Wallachia. There are no counts in the history of Wallachia, and the aristocrats are called *boyars*. The Irish novelist 'moves' Voivode Dracula from Wallachia into Transylvania and transforms him into a Szekler count. The English travellers who inspired Stoker were fascinated with the Szekler community of Transylvania: they stressed their warlike qualities and rich history, adhering to the theory of the Szeklers' descent from Huns (Boner, 624; Mazuchelli, 1881: 140; Johnson, 1885: 205). This detail is speculated on by Stoker as Dracula tells Harker:

> We Szekelys have a right to be proud, for in our veins flows the blood of many brave races who fought as the lion fights, for lordship. Here, in the whirlpool of European races, the Ugric tribe bore down from Iceland the fighting spirit which Thor and Wodin gave them, which their Berserkers displayed to such fell intent on the seaboards of Europe, aye, and of Asia and Africa too, till the peoples thought that the werewolves themselves had come. Here, too, when they came, they found the Huns, whose warlike fury had swept the earth like a living flame, till the dying peoples held that in their veins ran the blood of those old witches, who, expelled from Scythia had mated

with the devils in the desert. Fools, fools! What devil or what witch was ever so great as Attila, whose blood is in these veins? (1994: 41)

As he talks to Dracula, Jonathan realises that the count comes from a different period: he speaks about medieval battles as if he had participated in them, and the story of his pedigree seems to be his own story. The past of Dracula is moved down in history to the beginnings of the world. Historical detail is overwhelmed by mythical elements: the comparison with devils and witches as well as the intercontinental dimension of the account suggest primordial roots.

The slip into myth suggests that Dracula is a correspondent of the fallen angel. Literary criticism has argued that one of Stoker's models for Dracula was Goethe's demonic character Mefistofel, in *Faust* (Milburn, 1998: 43–4; Murray, 2004: 181–3). Van Helsing explains that Dracula is a symbol of the Devil:

> he is devil in callous, and the heart of him is not, he can, within his range, direct the elements, the storm, the fog, the thunder, he can command all the meaner things, the rat, and the owl, and the bat, the moth, and the fox, and the wolf, he can grow and become small, and he can at times vanish and come unknown. (1994: 283)

At the close of the novel, the fallen angel returns to God. Mina describes the end of Dracula as 'a miracle', because, as the whole body 'crumbles into dust', his soul finds the eternal peace: 'I shall be glad as long as I live that even in that moment of final dissolution, there was in the face a look of peace, such as I never could have imagined might have rested there' (1994: 447).

Stoker's Transylvania is not, then, subject to historical time, but to *eternal time*, which has two dimensions in *Dracula*: *the serene course*, suggested by the slowness of trains, the slowness of the Transylvanian peasants, their detachment from the outer world and *the apocalyptic awareness*. The apocalyptic dimension of time implies a dramatic growing speed. The speed of the Transylvanian carriage towards Borgo Pass is followed by Harker's fight against time in Castle Dracula, which culminates with his last days there, when he understands that he has to escape from that place urgently before he is transformed into a vampire.

The existence of the vampire is described as fake eternal life, carried under the power of evil, whereas the real eternal life is the everlasting existence in God. Death is preferred to becoming un-dead: Harker thinks that for the unhappy mother whose child was kidnapped by

Dracula it is better to die torn by wolves, than become a vampire. When Van Helsing leaves Mina alone near Castle Dracula, he has a similar reasoning while hearing her shouts: 'the maw of the wolf were better to rest in than the grave of the Vampire!' (1994: 439).

Harker's attitude towards time changes during the novel. Although his scepticism is obvious in the beginning, he also feels a strong attraction towards the past, and is happy to be accommodated in one of the old buildings of Bistrița, 'Golden Krone Hotel, which I found, to my great delight, to be thoroughly old-fashioned' (1994: 12). He gradually perceives the dimension of the apocalyptical time. During the imprisonment in Castle Dracula, he starts to think in a symbolical way, similar to the landlady in Bistrița and to the Transylvanians who accompanied him to Borgo Pass. His transformation is obvious when he is ready to accept the supreme sacrifice, choosing death rather than remaining with the vampire women in the castle: 'At least God's mercy is better than that of those monsters, and the precipice is steep and high. At its foot a man may sleep, as a man' (1994: 69). The belief in the life after death is subtly expressed in sentences such as: 'the the worst it can only be death, and a man's death is not a calf's' (1994: 61).

As narration advances, the Western characters gradually feel the pressure of time. The hunting of Dracula in the final chapters of the novel is a fight against time: they have to get to the castle before the count arrives there, and to kill him before the sun sets. If these conditions are not fulfilled, the battle is lost forever. This apocalyptic perception of time is obviously expressed in Van Helsing's memorandum:

> It is now not far off sunset time, and over the snow the light of the sun flow in big yellow flood, so that we throw great long shadow on where the mountain rise so steep. For we are going up, and up, and all is oh, so wild and rocky, *as though it were the end of the world*. (1994: 432, my italics)

Stoker's Transylvanian world is devoid of human justice, as neither Dracula's nor the westerners' crimes are evaluated by any judge. Exorcising Dracula has an apocalyptic dimension, because justice is done by God.

Another gothic transformation is that the perception of time is influenced by the evolution of Harker's feelings from fear to terror. The English young man experiences fear after he hears rumours about Dracula's evil force. It increases during the night drive to Castle Dracula, while hearing the wolves: 'The baying of the wolves sounded nearer and nearer, as though they were closing round on us from every side. I grew dreadfully afraid, and the horses shared my fear. The driver, however, was not in the least disturbed' (1994: 22) Entering the realm of Dracula marks the experience of terror, and the view of the wolves increases the fear considerably:

> But just then the moon, sailing through the black clouds, appeared behind the jagged crest of a beetling, pine-clad rock, and by its light I saw around us a ring of wolves, with white teeth and lolling red tongues, with long, sinewy limbs and shaggy hair. They were a hundred times more terrible in the grim silence which held them than even when they howled. For myself, I felt a sort of paralysis of fear. It is only when a man feels himself face to face with such horrors that he can understand their true import. (1994: 23)

The gothic horror is increased by the motif of continuous tests of the senses: before entering Dracula's castle, Harker rubs his eyes and pinches himself to see if he is not in the middle of a horrible nightmare. As he discovers the identity of the vampire, his fear overwhelms him: 'This was all so strange and uncanny that a dreadful fear came upon me, and I was afraid to speak or move' (1994: 24). Harker's greatest fears are his own thoughts: 'imagination must not run riot with me. If it does I am lost' (1994: 37).

In Stoker's construction of Transylvania, space is also endowed with a mythical dimension. As Harker departs from the familiar world of Western Europe, the contrast between the West and the East reflects the relationship between *the known* and *the unknown*:

> the district he named is in the extreme east of the country, just on the borders of three states, Transylvania, Moldavia, and Bukovina, in the midst of the Carpathian mountains; one of the wildest and least known portions of Europe. I was not able to light on any map or work giving the exact locality of the Castle Dracula, as there are no maps of this country as yet to compare with our own Ordance Survey Maps. (1994: 9–10)

The novelist chooses a border place for the location of the vampiric castle, because the whole novel is constructed on the idea of border transgression, a theme (Punter 2014) typical of gothic literature. Besides geographical frontiers, transgressions occur between states such as dream–reality, self-control–lost control, human–animal, fear–courage, sex, cultures.

## Gothic Transylvania 73

In spite of a seeming tendency to imitate the geography of the real Transylvania, Stoker's concern for authenticity is rather simulated. The novelist was inspired by some accounts in his sources on the region and probably by a few drawings he found in those books. The description of the Transylvanian women was inspired by the cover image of Charles Boner's *Transylvania*, the description of the Castle Dracula by the drawing of Bran Castle (Terzburg at that time) in the same book, the representations of the Slovaks from a sketch in Major E. C. Johnson's travelogue. (Crișan, 2013: 74, 79, 109–110). Many details were borrowed from the travellers' journeys in the Banat: landscape descriptions, slivovitz, robber steak, the hay-ricks in the trees and the leitter-waggon.

However, the Transylvanian landscape in *Dracula* does not reflect a geographical reality but a mythical construction. The comparison of the Transylvanian castles and towns (noticed by Harker on his journey to Bistrița) to images in old missals is representative in this regard. At the first perception of the Transylvanian landscape, the foreign visitors are impressed with its beauty. Although Mina feels the terrible pressure of time when she enters this region, she cannot help admiring the scenery: 'The country is lovely, and most interesting. If only we were under different conditions, how delightful it would be to see it all.' (1994: 427). In Mina's diary, Transylvania is perceived as a realm of fairytales: 'It is a lovely country. Full of beauties of all imaginable kinds, and the people are brave, and strong, and simple, and seem full of nice qualities' (1884: 429). As Harker's diary shows, the beauty of the landscape is perceived even from the windows of Castle Dracula: 'The view was magnificent, and from where I stood there was every opportunity of seeing it' (1994: 38).

Stoker's Transylvania is an ambivalent mythical space based on the opposition between a paradisal realm – from Bistrița to Borgo Pass – and a hellish topos – Castle Dracula – (Crișan, 2013: 216–26, 246–54). On his way to Borgo Pass, Harker perceives the Transylvanian scenery as an earthly paradise:

> Before us lay a green sloping land full of forests and woods, with here and there steep hills, crowned with clumps of trees or with farmhouses, the blank gable end to the road. In and out amongst these green hills of what they call here the 'Mittel Land' ran the road, losing itself as it swept round the grassy curve, or was shut out by the straggling ends of pine woods, which here and there ran down the hillsides like tongues of flame. (1994: 15–16)

The landscape has a synthetic character, as it is composed of several forms of relief. In line with gothic tradition, the scenery is sublime, and nature is endowed with a metaphysical dimension. The hills are followed by the 'mighty slopes of forest' and 'the lofty steeps of the Carpathians', upon which the sun falls in 'glorious colours'; the traveller is impressed to notice 'the white gleam of falling water' through 'mighty rifts in the mountains' (1994: 16). The magnificence of nature is associated with the awe for God. In these surroundings, there is a 'lofty, snow-covered peak of a mountain', which is perceived by the Transylvanian peasants who accompany Harker to Borgo Pass as a sacred place: '"Look! Isten szek!" – "God's seat!" – and he crossed himself reverently' (1994: 16). In this spiritualised world, the peasants pray to God in the middle of nature: 'Here and there was a peasant man or woman kneeling before a shrine, who did not even turn round as we approached, but seemed in the self-surrender of devotion to have neither eyes nor ears for the outer world' (1994: 17).

While the scenery which precedes Borgo Pass mirrors heaven, Castle Dracula is a literary representation of the inferno. Dracula is depicted as a symbol of the Devil. When the count stops the three vampire women from sucking Harker's blood, the English man becomes aware of his satanic features:

> But the Count! Never did I imagine such wrath and fury, even to the demons of the pit. His eyes were positively blazing. The red light in them was lurid, as if the flames of hell fire blazed behind them. His face was deathly pale, and the lines of it were hard like drawn wires. (1994: 52)

The three vampire women's laughter is compared to 'the pleasure of fiends' (1994: 53), and the whole castle is described as hell: 'And then away for home! Away to the quickest and nearest train! Away from the cursed spot, from this cursed land, where the devil and his children still walk with earthly feet!' (1994: 69).

Castle Dracula is one of the typical castles of Gothic literature. Its exterior aspect (isolated position, inaccessibility, ruined aspect, heavy entrance door) is completed by its gothic interior. The building has several secret rooms, galleries, forbidden places, underground chambers, and it hides many terrible secrets. A motif typical for gothic literature is the interdiction: Harker is forbidden to enter the rooms which are locked. By breaking the interdiction, he can discover the secrets of the castles. A heavy door in Dracula's room leads through stone passages and dark circular stairways to the subterranean world of Dracula. The dark tunnel-like passage goes to a ruined chapel, the graveyard where the vampires lie during the day. Carfax, the ruined English estate bought by Dracula in England, is an extension of the Transylvanian castle. It is isolated from the outer world; its gloomy courtyard is surrounded by stone walls, and the large house has a mediaeval aspect, being made of thick stone and having only a few windows 'high up and heavily barred with iron' (1994: 35). The gothic scenery is completed by an old chapel nearby.

The motif of imprisonment is another gothic transformation. During his stay in Castle Dracula, Harker observes that he is surrounded by locked doors, and 'the castle is a veritable prison' (1994: 38). He realises that he also is a prisoner of his own fear:

> When I found that I was a prisoner a sort of wild feeling came over me. I rushed up and down the stairs, trying every door and peering out of every window I could find, but after a little the conviction of my helplessness overpowered all other feelings. When I look back after a few hours I think I must have been mad for the time, for I behaved much as a rat does in a trap. (1994: 39)

Only by changing his vision of life can Harker escape from his own terror and from Castle Dracula.

The connection of Stoker's Transylvania with the supernatural also conforms to gothic literature. Superstition is the first step towards the supernatural. This is why Transylvania is described in the beginning of the novel as 'the centre of some sort of imaginative whirlpool', a place where 'every known superstition in the world is gathered' (1994: 10). It becomes the place where Stoker synthesised world superstitions on vampires. The supernatural is anticipated by queer dreams (which Harker had at the hotel in Cluj) and by the rumours of the Transylvanian peasants. The strange behaviour of the frightened horses which signal the mysterious coming of Dracula's caléche suggests the approach of the supernatural. Magic is another element of the supernatural: during the night drive to Castle Dracula, the coachman manipulates the wolves in a magic way, by moving his arms. Besides animals, Dracula is also able to control meteorological phenomena in a magic way.

The vampire Dracula is one of the most famous supernatural characters of fantastic literature. With his multiple identities, the un-dead Dracula is a symbol of transgression. The physiognomy of Dracula marks the transgression between man and animal: he has strong face, aquiline thin nose, arched nostrils, massive eyebrows, 'lofty domed forehead', and the hair grows 'scantily round the temples but profusely elsewhere' (1994: 20). His mouth is 'cruel-looking', the sharp teeth 'as white as ivory' (1994: 20) protrude over the ruddy lips, his ears are pale, and 'extremely pointed' at the tops, his hands are 'coarse, broad, with squat fingers', there are hairs in the centre of the palm, the nails are 'cut to a sharp point', and his breath is rank (1994: 28). When he discovers Dracula's multiple identities, Harker's feelings change to repulsion and terror. The fury of the vampire when seeing the cut on Harker's face while shaving also suggests animal-like behaviour. In the description of the vampire women in the castle, the animal features and behaviour are also emphasized:

> The fair girl went on her knees, and bent over me, fairly gloating. There was a deliberate voluptuousness which was both thrilling and repulsive, and as she arched her neck she actually licked her lips like an animal, till I could see in the moonlight the moisture shining on the scarlet lips and on the red tongue as it lapped the white sharp teeth. (1994: 52)

An exchange of identity also occurs between Harker and Dracula: Dracula wears Harker's clothes and wants to learn from him how to behave like an Englishman. Harker sees only himself in the mirror when Dracula is behind, and he follows the vampire's behaviour by climbing the walls of the castle. This transfer of identity makes the unhappy woman whose child was kidnapped by Dracula to call Harker 'monster' (1994: 60). Carol Senf observes 'a marked similarity' between Harker and Dracula, and 'the most significant revelation' of the similarity between the two characters 'is that they share attitudes as well as clothing' (1998: 43).

This fictional Transylvania, the most famous space created by the theatre manager Stoker, is influenced by the world of the spectacle, and has a cathartic dimension. The Transylvanian peasants are perceived by Harker as actors on a stage; the Slovaks would play the role of brigands: 'on the stage they would be set down at once as some old Oriental band of brigands' (1994: 11), and the women costumes are compared to ballet dresses (1994: 11). When it is necessary, these imaginary peasants can also recite in German verses from Burger's *Lenore*. The scenery is composed as a background for a play, and after several descriptions of sublime landscapes, the conclusion is (as the truth teller Van Helsing writes) that 'nature seem to have held sometime her carnival' (1994: 433).

In *Dracula*, the time of the story is the eternal time of fiction, and the reader can constantly find references to the motif of the endless story, which is also suggested by some literary echoes. Being constantly aware of the literary character of his diary, Harker writes that it 'seems horribly like the beginning of the "Arabian Nights", for everything has to break off at cockcrow, or like the ghost of Hamlet's father' (1994: 42). The characters are frequently concerned with the aesthetic quality of their texts. When Mina and Van Helsing recognise the Transylvanian landscape from Harker's diary, they also evaluate its stylistic quality: 'By and by we find all the things which Jonathan have note in that wonderful diary of him' (1994: 432).

Besides the spectacle of the theatrical world, Stoker's Transylvania also implies the spectacle of reading. Books are essential in the creation of this gothic space, and the aesthetic dimension of reading is also emphasized in Dracula's discourse: '"These companions", and he laid his hand on some of the books, "have been good friends to me, and for some years past ... have given me many, many hours of pleasure"' (1994: 31). The spectacular dimension of Stoker's Transylvania contributed significantly to the success of the novel and to its countless sequels in different media. By transforming some referential representations of a geographical space into a gothic reality, Stoker opened one of the greatest doors to the continuous flourishing of gothic literature.

## Note

This work was supported by a grant of the Romanian National Authority for Scientific Research, CNCS – UEFISCDI, project number PN-II-RU-PD-2011-3-0194

# 5
# 'Labours of Their Own': Property, Blood, and the Szgany in *Dracula*

Abby Bardi

> In the morning come the Szgany, who have some labours of their own here. (Stoker, 2003: 57)

In *Dracula* (1897), as Jonathan Harker and Professor Van Helsing are discussing ways of gaining access to the London house of Count Dracula, the professor tells a strange and seemingly unimportant story:

> I have read of a gentleman who owned a so fine house in your London, and when he went for months of summer to Switzerland and lock up his house, some burglar came and broke window at back and got in. Then he went and made open the shutters in front and walk out and in through the door, before the very eyes of the police. Then he have an auction in that house, and advertise it, and put up big notice; and when the day come he sell off by a great auctioneer all the goods of that other man who own them. Then he go to a builder, and he sell him that house, making an agreement that he pull it down and take all away within a certain time. And your police and other authorities help him all they can. And when that owner come back from his holiday in Switzerland he find only an empty hole where his house had been. (Stoker, 2003: 313)

This anecdote, related as an aside, signals the central role anxiety about property plays in the narrative: it is not only through the occupation of its bodies that Count Dracula plans to invade and colonize England, but also through the occupation of its houses. The properties he purchases in the greater London area are intended as repositories of the fifty boxes he ships from Transylvania, just as the boxes are potential repositories for the vampire's body; houses, boxes, bodies, and soil are conflated in this transaction, all material manifestations of and vehicles for the Count's attempted invasion. In this project, Dracula is abetted by several key associates: his lawyers, including the unwitting Harker, and a group of Gypsies – 'Szgany' – who appear at the beginning and end of the novel to serve as accomplices.

Throughout the novel, the linchpin of Dracula's attack on Britain is its real estate: by conducting a variety of legal transactions with the help of solicitors, he plans to acquire properties and thus infect British national identity, creating hybridity like that of his native land. The houses he purchases are placed in strategic points around London that will enable him to colonize the entire city: the positioning of Dracula's real estate sets up a comprehensive framework whose geography mirrors the novel's preoccupation with the dichotomy between the 'civilized' west and the Orientalized east (Ridenhour, 2013: 69; Davies, 2014). At the same time Dracula intends to infect British blood with the contagion of vampirism, he also aims to infiltrate the British landscape with foreign soil. Like a cholera epidemic, such as the one Stoker's mother described to him in a letter (in Hindle, 2003: 412–18), the spread of vampirism is a terrifying prospect, not only because of its potential harm to individual bodies, but also because of its potential to infect and destroy an entire society.

Van Helsing's anecdote, related in a conspicuously 'foreign' syntax that calls attention to these threats to British homogeneity from without, is a parable about this powerful undercurrent in the text, the fear of disruption to property. His story in which a clever burglar is able to reduce a 'fine house' to an 'empty hole' with the aid of 'police and other authority' (Stoker, 2003: 313) suggests that the incursion of the burglar-like Count into England is an opening gambit in a vast project of 'reverse colonization' such as that adumbrated by Stephen Arata. For Arata the Count's assault on Britain expresses a dominant fear of the period, expressed by popular literature, of being 'colonized by "primitive" forces' that 'originate outside the civilized world' (1990: 623). He adds, 'In the marauding, invasive Other, British culture sees its own imperial practices mirrored back in monstrous forms' (1990: 623).

Along these lines, Dracula's monstrous, marauding invasion will foment the decline of the British Empire house by house, body by body, leaving only an 'empty hole' in its place (Stoker, 2003: 313). The gynophobic implications of the phrase 'empty hole' echo the novel's anxiety about women: apart from the Count himself, the novel's vampires are women who threaten the British body politic with contagion of the blood. In this fascination with blood, whose odor, noted by Harker

(Stoker, 2003: 45), has struck some readers as vaguely menstrual (Shuttle and Redgrove, 1990: 295), *Dracula* consistently conflates revulsion, terror, and erotic desire in which women are the primary agents. The houses of London parallel these female bodies: they stand empty, ready to be invaded by foreign matter, mimicking sexual reproduction by spreading vampirism and thus literally altering the blood of British subjects, and ultimately, their ethnicity; the 'empty holes' of London function as empty signifiers that may soon be occupied by the 'whirlpool' (Stoker, 2003: 36) of races that constitute Transylvanian national identity.

While *Dracula* is clearly a novel about the mechanics of vampirism, it is also about the mechanics of the transfer of property: British houses may legally be purchased by foreigners (Dracula has an ample supply of gold) so they may be used as a means of infiltration or 'reverse colonization.' Indeed, it is a real estate transaction that causes Jonathan Harker to journey to Transylvania to meet with the Count: according to his journal, Harker has been 'sent out to explain the purchase of a London estate to a foreigner' (Stoker, 2003: 22). The elaborate legal process of the Count's various transactions is demonstrated in the variety of documents of which the novel is composed, including papers referencing the purchase of houses and the shipping of boxes. There are also letters, as well as an invoice, between Dracula's Whitby solicitor and the firm receiving the London delivery of the boxes and routing them to Dracula's estate in Purfleet; a letter to Arthur Holmwood from Dracula's London estate agent; two telegrams to Arthur regarding the process of Dracula's getaway ship, the *Czarina Catherine*, from a representative of Lloyd's of London; and virtually incessant discussion of real estate, importation, and other business matters, including a meeting with Dracula's representative, a Mr. Hildesheim whose own threat to British ethnic homogeneity is suggested by a rather frankly anti-Semitic description of him as 'a Hebrew of rather the Adelphi Theatre type, with a nose like a sheep, and a fez' (Stoker, 2003: 371). Hildensheim relates his transactions with Dracula, or rather, 'Mr de Ville of London,' regarding the last of the fifty boxes, one in which the Count ultimately flees London, suggesting that perhaps Jews, like the other diasporic foreigners of the novel, such as the Szgany, have been accessories to the international conspiracy to pollute British blood with that of distastefully foreign others: and at the novel's end, while Dracula may have fled, the fez-wearing and thus Orientalized Hildensheim remains in Britain.

But it is not just 'foreign' Others who abet the Count's project: when Dracula initially ships all of his boxes, with himself as 'cargo' (Stoker, 2003: 90), to the port of Whitby, the progress of these boxes to

London hinges on the various real estate deals that Harker, acting for his employer, Mr. Hawkins, has set up. (Hawkins, presumably, has been paid for this service, so when he dies and leaves everything to Jonathan, he is in a sense 'infecting' Jonathan with Dracula's gold.) In bringing his own soil, repeatedly described as odiferous, to England, Dracula is turning his land and himself into commodities and thereby polluting – literally soiling – Britain via the purchase of real estate. It is no wonder that Jonathan Harker says of his dealings with Dracula, '[H]e certainly left me under the impression that he would have made a wonderful solicitor' (Stoker, 2003: 38): Dracula's invasion takes place in a highly systematic and businesslike manner, and is strictly, in the phrase Van Helsing uses in his anecdote about the house, 'en regle': 'according to rule' (Hindle, 2003: 451). Trained as a barrister himself, Stoker surely knew that the law or 'regle' offers little protection against those who, like Dracula, have worked out ways of making rules conform to their own needs.

However, if everything Dracula himself does is perfectly legal, the 'little band' (Stoker, 2003: 402) violates the law in one of the novel's several instances of breaking and entering: while planning what is essentially a burglary of the Count's house in Piccadilly, Lord Godalming warns Harker against joining him and Quincey in the effort: '"[Y]ou are a solicitor and the Incorporated Law Society might tell you that you should have known better."' However, he adds, '"My title will make it all right with the locksmith, and with any policeman that might come along"' (Stoker, 2003: 318). One of the 'rules' of British society is that aristocratic privilege overrides the law that Harker is bound to uphold. In this, Godalming mirrors the Count's sense of the power of his own nobility, manifested in his harangue to Harker about his Szekely background and its alleged descent from Attila the Hun: '"What devil or what witch was ever so great as Attila, whose blood is in these veins? ... Is it a wonder that we were a conquering race; that we were proud?"' (Stoker, 2003: 36). He adds that the Szekelys '"can boast a record that mushroom growths like the Hapsburgs and the Romanoffs can never reach"' and locates the greatness of his ancestry in his blood: '"Blood is too precious a thing in these days of dishonourable peace; and the glories of the great races are as a tale that is told"' (Stoker, 2003: 37). Dracula's 'glorious' race is, he alleges, as aristocratic as Godalming's British bloodline; his reverse colonization of Britain is the mirror image of the many invasions of his native land.

Harker's two trips to Transylvania serve as bookends to the Count's abortive attempt at immigration, and during each of these trips, a 'band of Szgany' (Stoker, 2003: 49), or Gypsies, materializes to serve as the Count's henchmen, fellow travelers in his vast project. Although the Szgany are clearly not vampires, since they are seen during the day, they serve him with ferocity that appears to stem from sympathy with his project. As Dracula works to colonize London, the Szgany remain behind in Transylvania, ready to do his bidding as one of the many ethnic groups that constitute the 'imaginative whirlpool' (Stoker, 3003: 8) of Transylvania's hybrid population. As the novel opens, this rampant hybridity, which Dracula threatens to export to England, is explained by Harker, whose journal notes the ethnic diversity of Dracula's homeland: 'In the population of Transylvania there are four distinct nationalities: Saxons in the south, and mixed with them the Wallachs, who are the descendents of the Dacians; Magyars in the west, and Szekelys in the east and north' (Stoker, 2003: 8); in addition, on his journey to Dracula's castle, Harker encounters 'Cszeks and Slovaks, all in picturesque attire' (Stoker, 2003: 14). Dracula explains this whirlpool to Harker by claiming that waves of invaders were drawn to the region by the search for hidden treasure: gold that has been buried in the ground. He adds that '"there is hardly a foot of soil in all this region that has not been enriched by the blood of men, patriots, or invaders"' (Stoker, 2003: 28). Here, blood and gold are conflated and located in the soil itself, allowing soil to become a synecdoche of the national identity that has been destabilized by all this co-mingling of the blood. While Dracula strongly identifies himself as a Szekely during his lecture to Harker, he alludes to his own hybridity: '"We Szekelys have a right to be proud, for in our veins flows the blood of many brave races who fought as the lion fights, for lordship"' (Stoker, 2003: 35–6). He goes on to describe his land as '"the whirlpool of European races"' that includes these waves of invaders (Stoker, 2003: 36). Here, Dracula explicitly connects blood to race, and to the complicated web of his vexed national identity; it is with this emblem of Transylvania's racial hybridity, of which the soil is a literal conduit, that he seeks to infect his victims.

Dracula's lecture echoes one of Stoker's sources, Emily Gerard, whose two-volume study/travelogue of Transylvania, *The Land Beyond the Forest*, informs the novel's view of that country's ethnicities. Harker's narrative begins as just such a travelogue in which he, like Gerard, painstakingly observes the culture and customs of the region from a perspective that Cannon Schmitt has noted 'Orientalizes Eastern Europe and Count Dracula from the outset,' characterizing 'the East' in a way that does not simply 'construct [it] as a uniformly retrograde anti-West' but also as 'cathected, invested with desire' (1997: 139). Harker's description of Transylvania is replete with what Edward Said characterizes in *Orientalism* as the way the West regards 'Orientalized' subjects: 'The Orient at large ... vacillates between the West's contempt for what is familiar and its shivers of delight – or fear of – novelty' (1979: 59). Harker expresses both this delight in novelty and contempt for the oddities of what he terms 'the East' (Stoker, 2003: 7): its slow trains, its superstitions, its grotesquery (for example, a propensity for goiter). Harker echoes Gerard's multiple chapters devoted to each of the various ethnic groups of Transylvania in which she both parses and exoticizes their customs, dress, food, and superstitions, as well as remarking just as Harker does upon problems with 'railway communications' (Gerard, 1888, Vol. I: 30), suggesting that the East has a different approach to time than the punctual West.

But in other ways, Stoker deviates considerably from Gerard's mostly sympathetic portrayal of Transylvania's ethnic diversity. In Volume II of *The Land Beyond the Forest*, Gerard devotes six chapters to the Gypsies or 'Tziganes' of Transylvania. Using what appears to be his own spelling, 'Szgany,' Stoker locates this group at the heart of Transylvania's ethnic whirlpool, encamped in the epicentre of Castle Dracula, its courtyard (Stoker, 2003: 49). However, while Gerard depicts the Tziganes appreciatively, quoting extensively from Liszt's sympathetic description of '[t]his singular race' (Gerard, 1888, Vol. II: 73), in *Dracula*, the Szgany are represented as sinister from the outset. They are clearly the Count's emissaries, thwarting Harker's attempts to be rescued, and Harker, who seems to know something about them, asserts that they are 'allied to the ordinary gipsies all the world over,' speaking 'only their own varieties of the Romany tongue' (Stoker, 2003: 49), implying that they are part of the international conspiracy to facilitate the global spread of vampirism. Not only do they refuse to help Harker escape, turning his letters immediately over to the Count, but their treachery is underscored by their pointing and laughing at him (Stoker, 2003: 51), then continuing to work in the castle where the sounds of a 'muffled mattock and spade' indicate that they are performing some 'ruthless villainy' (Stoker, 2003: 52) that turns out to be filling the boxes of soil the Count intends to import to England.

In the novel's climax, the Sygany reappear to mount a brave challenge to the British interlopers who invade the Count's stronghold. If the Count has functioned as the 'burglar' (Stoker, 2003: 313) in Van Helsing's story who has attempted to dismantle the British landscape and leave only a metaphorical empty hole, the 'little band of men' (Stoker, 2003: 402) who travel to Transylvania stage an incursion with a similar goal, and are successful: the vampire bodies they destroy leave nothing but empty boxes in their wake. In their campaign to dismantle the Count's material existence, the box that houses his body and then the body itself, these British invaders do battle with the Szgany, who try to prevent this invasion. In a sense, the entire novel is the story of various forms of breaking and entering: breaking into houses, tombs, and bodies and impregnating them with foreign matter that sustains a form of alien life. If the 'little band's' invasion of Dracula's stronghold mirrors the many earlier invasions of Transylvania described by the Count, Mina's pregnancy at the novel's end is their culmination. In playing a peripheral but crucial role in Dracula's project, acting as his emissaries, the Szgany manifest an essential sympathy with the Count: they, like him, are nomadic outsiders, though according to Harker, they exist 'outside the law' (Stoker, 2003: 49), unlike the scrupulously legal Count.

While Stoker has used the term 'Szgany' with which he may have hoped to avoid any positive and romantic connotations of the term 'Gypsy', Harker does make clear that the Szgany are in fact Gypsies ('These Szgany are gypsies' (Stoker, 2003: 49)). As Deborah Nord has pointed out in *Gypsies and the British Imagination 1807–1930*, 'Although British Gypsies were considered alien, they were, at the same time, imagined as longstanding features of English rural life and, in some nostalgic views of the English past, signify the very essence of true and ancient Britishness' (2006: 4). Much of nineteenth-century British literature reflects both trepidation at and admiration for Gypsies' perceived iconic, romantic nomadism. In his 1807 poem 'Gipsies,' William Wordsworth seems to admire them, exclaiming, 'In scorn I speak not' of these 'Wild outcasts of society!' (1969, line 28: 153). Sir Walter Scott's novel *Guy Mannering* (1815) represents the Gypsy Meg Merrilies as a strange, imposing figure who is ultimately sympathetic, and instead of enacting the stereotype of Gypsies as thieves, she is instrumental in restoring a disputed property to its rightful owner. *Lavengro* (1851) and *Romany Rye* (1857), George Borrow's widely read, somewhat fictionalized accounts of his life with British Gypsies, have long been accused of romanticizing Gypsy life: Emily Gerard herself opines that Borrow 'idealises his figures often beyond recognition' (1888, Vol. II: 71). Matthew Arnold's 1853 'The Scholar Gypsy' tells the romantic tale of an 'Oxford scholar poor' who 'roamed the world with that wild brotherhood' (1961, line 36: 148). George Eliot's *The Spanish Gypsy* (1868) represents the Spanish crypto-Gypsy Fedalma and her long-lost tribe as charming and tragic figures. The delightfully exotic, albeit strange figures of Gypsies in much of nineteenth-century literature are a far cry from Stoker's sinister Szgany.

It is worth asking here how this exoticized, eroticized, perhaps dangerous, but fundamentally appealing figure of the nineteenth-century Gypsy has transmuted in *Dracula* into something so repulsive. Mary Burke suggests that in his depiction of Gypsies in *Dracula*, Stoker was influenced by late eighteenth-century discourse, and she points to Heinrich Grellmann's *Dissertation on the Gypsies* (1783) which describes 'the heathenish, asocial Gypsy, whose appetites and customs were an inverse of, or in monstrous excess, of sedentary norms' (2005: 54) and contains 'many references' to Transylvanian Gypsies (2005: 56). In Grellmann's view, Gypsies were 'superstitious, unruly, animalistic, instinctive, lazy, dishonest, and possibly even cannibalistic' (Burke, 2005: 54), a description that represents them as excellent candidates for a vampire's henchmen. While Burke locates Stoker's sources in 'the vast post-Grellman scholarship on Gypsies,' (2005: 57) I would argue that in associating Gypsies with fears of disruption to property, Stoker may be drawing from even older British discourses. From the earliest appearance in Great Britain of the Romany people, whose name 'Gypsies' derived from their calling themselves 'Egyptians,' legislation was directed against them that manifested anxiety about their relationship to property. The 'Egyptians Act' of 1530 banned them from Britain and made the accusation that 'by crafte and subtyltie [they had] deceived the people of theyr money, and also hath comytted many and haynous felonyes and robberies ...' (*Statutes of the Realm* 22 Hen. VIII. c. 10. (1530–1). A 1547 statute passed under Edward VI entitled 'An Acte for the Punishment of Vagabondes and for the Relief of the Poore and Impotent Parsons' connected Gypsies' alleged itinerancy with crimes against property: 'Idlenes and Vagabundrye is the mother and roote of all thefts Robberyes and all evill actes and other mischief' (Statutes of the Realm1 Edw. VI. c. 3). The idea that Gypsies pose a threat to property was deeply entrenched in the traditional view of them from the very beginning, and ultimately, legislation was directed against them simply for being 'Egyptians' or even 'counterfeit Egyptians' (Mayall, *Gypsy Identities*, 2004: 61–2). The romantic view of Gypsies that arose in the early 1800s ran directly counter to these earlier representations of them as thieving vagabonds.

However, it is not just Stoker who seems to betoken a shift in this view at the century's end. At the same time that the Gypsiologists of the Gypsy Lore Society, founded in 1888, embraced the romantic view of the Gypsy, at times literally (Nord, 2006: 125–55), other forms of late nineteenth-century discourse offered more negative representations. While writers such as Scott, Wordsworth, and Arnold constructed the Gypsy figure as 'mythic beings' who appeared to be 'a remnant of prelapserian England,' as Nord has noted (2006: 45), Stoker's contemporary Sir Arthur Conan Doyle, whom Nord cites as an influence on Stoker's depictions of Gypsies (2006: 162), manifested a view closer to that of Grellman: 'Whereas [Jane] Austen undermines the myth of Gypsy criminality [in *Emma*], Conan Doyle [in 'The Adventure of the Speckled Band'] depends on ... the image of marauding Gypsies' to throw the reader off the scent of the mystery's true culprit (Nord, 2006: 16, 161–2). This movement away from the Gypsiologists' romantic view of Gypsies is mirrored in a concomitant change in the tenor of anti-Roma legislation in the latter part of the nineteenth century, due in part to the efforts of 'George Smith of Coalville,' who fought for 'reform' of canal boat dwellers and then turned his attention to Gypsies, railing in print against the conditions in which they lived and thus, according to David Mayall, 'succeed[ing] in awakening the general public to the seriousness of the Gypsy problem' (*Gypsy-Travellers*, 2004: 136). Partly due to Smith's efforts, attention began to be paid to these sanitation issues, which led to the Moveable Dwellings Bills (1885–1894) in which the legislation Smith had fostered regarding canal boats was applied to travelers, regulating the amount of living space and sleeping accommodations and giving the government the power to inspect dwellings (Mayall, *Gypsy-Travellers*, 2004: 138). This emphasis on controlling sanitary conditions, expressed in such legislation as the 'Infectious Diseases (Notification) Act' of 1889, and its association with Gypsies surely might have resonated with Stoker, who was evidently influenced by his mother's 1875 written account of 'The Cholera Horror.' The 'new and terrible plague which was desolating all lands' Charlotte Stoker writes about ('Appendix' in Stoker, 2003: 412) not only resembles the fears of vampire contagion at the heart of *Dracula* but also evokes the source of anxiety about infectious diseases that is manifested in the 1889 legislation. Thanks to George's Smith's polemics, although the romantic view of the Gypsy continued to exist in the minds of the post-Borrovian Gypsy-lorists, by the 1890s, British discourses on Gypsies had undoubtedly been 'infected' by the Smithian picture of 'indescribable ignorance, dirt, filth, and misery ... divested of the last tinge of romantical nonsense' (qtd. in Mayall, 2004: 134).

Still another possible impetus for *Dracula*'s negative characterization of Gypsies may have been the general air of anti-Jewish xenophobia at that time noted by Jules Zanger, which presumably arose in response to the waves of immigration that Britain was experiencing in the decades leading up to *Dracula*. Zanger points to the arrival of 'European Jews

[who] from 1880 on had begun to appear in England in increasing numbers.... Between 1881 and 1900, the number of foreign Jews in England increased by 600 percent. The response to their presence was both hostile and fearful' (1991: 34). Zanger suggests that the Count, while not necessarily 'specifically Jewish,' 'vibrated sympathetically to the generalized unease resulting from the highly visible presence of great numbers of these Jews from the East .... Beyond a miscellaneous xenophobia, the Jew evoked ... a cluster of associations concerning blood, the cross, and money, of antiquity and ancient wisdom, all of which Stoker, probably quite unconsciously, integrated into his Dracula myth' (1991: 43). Judith Halberstam, too, has noted that 'Dracula ... with his peculiar physique, his parasitical desires, his aversion to the cross and all the trappings of Christianity, his blood-sucking attacks, and his avaricious relation to money, resembled stereotypic anti-Semitic nineteenth-century representations of the Jew' (1993: 333). While it may be overreaching to regard the Count as literally Jewish, it is certainly useful to consider the xenophobia that pervades the novel in terms of the anti-immigration sentiment that informed Britain in this time period, much directed against the Jews who fled to London's East End from Russia and Prussia, and whose 'alien presence aroused strong feelings in London' (Englander, 2010: 33). While the Szgany, unlike Dracula, do not appear to threaten England with 'reverse colonization,' (Arata, 1990: 623) as they seem to be staying put, presumably their relatives 'the world over' (Stoker, 2003: 49), with whom they ostensibly share the 'Romany tongue' (49) are already in place, waiting to facilitate Dracula's invasion, acting if not as his doubles, then certainly as his co-conspirators.

What Stoker's Szgany have in common with the other Gypsies of nineteenth-century British literature is the power to disturb the status quo with their mere presence in a text; and the status quo in *Dracula* is disturbed in multiple registers. According to Elizabeth Miller the novel's *outré* eroticism has been discussed by critics so inexhaustibly that she has called for a reassessment of twentieth-century voyeuristic readings, noting that 'every imaginable sexual practice, fantasy and fear has been thrust upon the pages of the novel: rape (including gang rape), aggressive female sexuality, fellatio, homoeroticism, incest, bestiality, necrophilia, paedophilia, and sexually transmitted disease' (2006: 2). While it would perhaps be redundant to rehearse *Dracula*'s steamier moments, it is worth considering this rampant eroticism in the light of the novel's conflation of blood, gold, soil, and nationhood. When three of the main characters, Jonathan, Lucy, and Mina, are threatened by vampires, each experiences a sort of rape that is rendered in terms that Maurice Hindle refers to as 'soft-pornographic' (Introduction, Stoker, 2003: xxi). Each of these rapes constitutes a mini-incursion by Dracula into England; by infecting British subjects with the plague of vampirism (as he does successfully with Lucy and Mina, and on British soil), he is moving his 'treasure,' vampire blood, into England. At the same time, Dracula is importing fifty boxes of literal Transylvanian soil, mined by Szgany from his castle, that figuratively contains the blood of the 'men, patriots, or invaders' (Stoker, 2003: 28) of his hybrid nation. While it is only Mina who, forced to drink Dracula's blood, is literally 'invaded,' the condition he attempts to spread does indeed infect and then kill Lucy. This pollution with blood and soil is by inference a soft-core rape of England, facilitated by the international Gypsy conspiracy, as it were; rather than being eroticized themselves, the Szgany function as the Count's panderers, facilitating his rape of England via the importation of his soil: the transfer of property.

Harker's narrative in the opening section of the novel suggests a parallel between his own rape and that of England: while by night, Harker is in terror for his life as he is accosted by various vampires in highly charged erotic terms, by day, he is arranging for the Count's transfer of assets to Great Britain. Much of the interaction between Harker and Dracula has to do with the Count's acquisition of British property, for which he has planned thoroughly by acquainting himself with all manner of things English, including train schedules. '"Come,"' the Count says to Harker, '"tell me of London and of the house which you have procured for me"' (Stoker, 2003: 29). The term 'procured' suggests that Jonathan is unwittingly serving as a pimp, as one definition of 'procure,' dating from 1603, is 'To obtain (women) for the gratification of lust' (*OED*). Dracula's lust for blood, for both men and women, and for a house in England are part of the same colonizing impulse: he wishes to become one of the waves of invaders who have co-mingled the blood of so many 'races' in both his own country and, as Mina points out in her journal during her trip to Whitby, in the destination of Dracula's boxes, Britain: Whitby Abbey was, as Mina notes, 'sacked by the Danes' (Stoker, 2003: 71). Stoker appears to be aware that Englishness has been complicated by invasion – and of course, this hybridization of 'blood' and 'race' is purely the result of heterosexual intercourse; *Dracula*'s apparent eroticization of hybridity is really merely a logical conclusion of tracing hybridity to its source in human reproduction. At the novel's denouement, as the band of Englishmen succeed in reducing Dracula's box to an empty hole, the vampiric female bodies that presented such a formidable erotic threat to Harker proceed to, with Van Helsing's exertions, 'melt away and crumble into [their] native dust' (Stoker, 2003: 395). Not only does the novel's leitmotif of eroticized blood suggest anxiety about female bodies and sexuality, but also anxiety about the pollution of bloodlines that is a by-product of sexual reproduction, of which the Count's incursions into the blood of his victims are a simulacrum. Dracula's calculated assault on England and Englishness is an attempt to infect its already hybrid national identity with the even more complex hybridity.

In the end of his introductory narrative, after several nights of attempted vampire-rape so harrowing that he has 'sat down and simply cried' (Stoker, 2003: 53), Harker himself makes the connection between the transfer of property, which he has facilitated, and the transfer of 'blood,' or vampirism, to which he now realizes he has also been party. As Harker gazes on the smiling, blood-bloated face of the Count, who is lying in one of his shipping boxes, and contemplates the imminent invasion of his own body, which he realizes might soon become 'a banquet' for the three vampire women, he laments his part in the Count's invasion of Britain: 'This was the being I was helping to transfer to London, where, perhaps, for centuries to come he might, amongst its teeming millions, satiate his lust for blood, and create a new and ever-widening circle of semi-demons to batten on the helpless' (Stoker, 2003: 60). As he contemplates his next move, after giving the Count a glancing blow to the forehead with a shovel, 'in the distance,' in a moment that recalls the singing dwarves of Disney's *Snow White* (1937) and the burlesquing of Rumanian attitudes toward Gypsies in Sacha Baron Cohen's 2006 *Borat* (see Narcisz Fejes for an extended comparison of *Borat* and *Dracula*), he hears 'a gipsy song sung by merry voices' (Stoker, 2003: 60); the insensitive, brutal Szgany, along with some Slovaks, are coming to move the fifty boxes of earth so they may be transported to England, thus proving themselves to be essential to Dracula's project.

While much of the novel centers on the threatened rapes, near-rapes, and virtual rapes of the characters – Mina's run-in with Dracula in which he forces her to drink his blood is as close to actual rape as the novel comes, and Lucy's posthumous murder, so to speak, has been characterized as a 'gang rape' by Miller (2006: 2) – I would argue that equally significant and sinister is the systematic and perfectly legal rape/colonization of England. Stephen Arata has noted the 'double thrust – political and biological – of Dracula's invasion' which are 'conflat[ed] into a single threat': 'Dracula's twin status as vampire and Szekely warrior suggests that for Stoker the Count's aggressions against the body are also aggressions against the body politic' (1990: 630). I would add that this invasion is only able to occur, at either the political or biological level, through the transfer of property. Indeed, as if to illustrate that this sort of transfer has gone haywire, several inheritances in the novel are allocated peculiarly, not according to primogeniture: in addition to Hawkins having left everything to Jonathan, Lucy's mother leaves everything to Arthur, though he has not yet married Lucy. The novel's continual emphasis on the legality, indeed, legalism, of Dracula's scheme suggests that what Stoker asks us to object to is the misappropriation of property to non-British subjects.

The instability of inheritance and heredity and its effects on primogeniture find their culmination in the novel's last section, in which the birth of Jonathan and Mina's baby is announced. Jonathan states that the baby's 'bundle of names links all our little band of men together, but we call him Quincey' (Stoker, 2003: 402), after the American member of the little band, who gave his life in pursuit of Dracula. What Jonathan fails to note is that these men have been linked together before: they have all given transfusions to Lucy, thereby commingling their blood. As if this didn't render Harker *fils*'s parentage unstable enough, there is also the problem, noted by Hindle, of Dracula's forced 'transfusion' of Mina: thus while Harker celebrates the birth of his son and hopes that he embodies some of their 'brave friend's spirit,' he is 'conveniently forgetting that something *else* has "passed into" the body of little Quincey, too' (Introduction, Stoker, 2003: xxxvi). Dracula's utterance at the time of Mina's 'rape' suggests that a kind of marriage has taken place between them: '"And you, their best beloved one, are now to me, flesh of my flesh; blood of my blood; kin of my kin ..."' (Stoker, 2003: 306). Thus little Quincey is not only the heir of Harker and his band of brothers, but of Dracula himself, a perverse inheritance indeed.

*Dracula* conflates the 'property' of body, blood, race, and empire to construct an erotic connection between the biology of inheritance and that of national identity. All of these elements are embodied in Dracula's 'cargo', the boxes, which not only pollute the land with his soil (both his own personal soil and that of his land) under the auspices of the law, but which commodify 'reverse colonization,' turning it into a legal transaction in which national identity becomes a form of capital. It is fitting, then, that the final role of the Szgany, who function as a frame for the novel's transactions, is to attempt to deliver the Count's last box to his castle before sunset and to do battle with the band of vampire-slayers; it is they who deal the death blow to Quincey Morris. In a strange reversal of Dracula's 'reverse colonization,' Morris and Harker now become the colonizers: when Jonathan cuts Dracula's throat with his kukri (colonial-Indian) knife and Quincey stabs him in the heart with his (also colonial) bowie knife, the vampire's body 'crumble[s] into dust' and the Szgany – referred to as 'gypsies' now, as if rendered harmless – flee 'as if for their lives' (Stoker, 2003: 401), their job as conduits, as catalysts, having concluded. The British Empire, freed for the moment of all foreign influences, apart from that of Van Helsing and, perhaps, of Mina's baby, whose bloodline is questionable, has been saved.

# 6
# Invasions Real and Imagined: Stoker's Gothic Narratives

*Carol A. Senf*

When Stoker wrote *Dracula*, he had his master vampire invade England, near 'the ruin of Whitby Abbey, which was sacked by the Danes' (Leatherdale, 1998: 116) in AD 867. That reference as well as other frequent references to real and imagined invasions means that *Dracula* can be described as an invasion narrative, a type of plot that originated with George Chesney's *The Battle of Dorking* in 1871 and produced more familiar novels such as *The War of the Worlds* by H.G. Wells (1898). The invasion narrative remained popular during the period that Stoker was writing because the English feared invasion by other industrialized powers (especially Germany), reverse colonialism, and the encroachment of immigrants from Eastern Europe.[1] Although invasions are standard Gothic fare even today, Stoker's works, even those that are not Gothic, are unusually dominated by references to invasions. His most Gothic works – *Dracula* (1897), *The Jewel of Seven Stars* (1903), *The Lady of the Shroud* (1909), and *The Lair of the White Worm* (1911) – all centre on real or imagined invasions, and references to actual historical invasions loom in the background of *The Snake's Pass* (1890), *The Mystery of the Sea* (1902), *The Man* (1905), and 'The Squaw' (1893).

Because *Dracula* is familiar to all of us and because it provides some of the most dramatic examples of invasions in all of Stoker's fiction, it is useful to begin there so long as we remember that *Dracula* it is not necessarily typical of his productions, for Stoker was the creator of more romances than Gothic fiction as well as one Western, a book of children's stories, a work of historical fiction, a memoir of his employer, and several works of nonfiction. While Stoker is best known for *Dracula*, Christopher Frayling is correct to describe it as Stoker's 'uncharacteristic creation' (1991: 181).

The following scene in which Jonathan Harker finds Dracula's lair and fears him as a potential invader, is especially dramatic:

> This was the being I was helping to transfer to London, where, perhaps, for centuries to come he might ... satiate his lust for blood, and create a new and ever-widening circle of semi-demons to batten on the helpless. The very thought drove me mad. (1998: 100)

That Harker fears the foreigner as a bloodsucker bent on invasion is significant in a novel that is filled with references to historical invasions and to the rise and fall of nations. For example, even before Harker begins to fear for his life at Dracula's hands, he records Dracula's stories of the invasions of his homeland, 'ground fought over for centuries by the Wallachian, the Saxon, and the Turk,' battles when the very soil had been 'enriched by the blood of men, patriots or invaders' (1998: 57). Later, when Professor Van Helsing informs his English disciples about the historical Dracula, he describes heroic endeavours against those who had invaded his homeland. Telling his youthful followers of their opponent, Van Helsing shares some of Dracula's history:

> He must, indeed, have been that Voivode Dracula who won his name against the Turk, over the great river on the very frontier of Turkey-land. If it be so, then was he no common man; for in that time, and for centuries after, he was spoken of as the cleverest and the most cunning, as well as the bravest of the sons of the 'land beyond the forest'. (1998: 337)

And Harker is almost seduced by Dracula's tales of the heroic past:

> Why, there is hardly a foot of soil in all this region that has not been enriched by the blood of men, patriots or invaders. In old days, there were stirring times, when the Austrian and the Hungarian came up in hordes, and the patriots went out to meet them. (1998: 57)

He changes his mind when he realizes that he is enabling Dracula's invasion of England.

These references to foreign invasions are typical of Stoker's fiction, not just his Gothic works, and the following essay explores Stoker's use of invasion as a trope and demonstrates that this trope is more nuanced than is generally thought. Because Stoker was thinking of a complicated world where people travel easily from one culture to another and where people are acutely aware of cultural differences, we in 2015 would be wise to care about these invasion narratives and learn from them. Indeed Stoker spent his entire professional life travelling from place to place. As a civil servant working at Dublin Castle, he travelled the circuit of courts, eventually writing a book about those courts, *The Duties of Clerks of Petty Sessions in Ireland* (1878). As business manager of Henry Irving's Lyceum Theatre, Stoker was responsible for making arrangements whenever the company travelled, and he often wrote about his travel in works such as *Lady Athlyne* (1908), which relates his travels in Italy; *The Shoulder of Shasta* (1895); *Snowbound* (1908), a series of stories set during a snowstorm when an acting company waits for rescue; his two-volume memoir of Irving in 1905, and 'A Glimpse of America' (1886), which he wrote as a result of his first visit to the United States. All reveal his eye for details though the descriptions about Transylvania included in *Dracula* are taken from the accounts of other writers.

The threat of invasion is less obvious in Stoker's next Gothic tale, *The Jewel of Seven Stars*, which Bradley Deane describes in an interesting essay on mummy fiction and the 19th-century relationship between England and Egypt as 'the darkest mummy story of the occupation period, and the one which has proven most influential in the subsequent mummy film tradition' (2008: 404). Although Stoker or someone else revised the conclusion to transform horror into romance and make subsequent editions less terrifying (by ending in the marriage of the narrator to the object of his affection, the beautiful Margaret Trelawny), the original ending has the resurrected Queen Tera, a double for Margaret, destroy almost everyone who had facilitated her rebirth before presumably unleashing her power on England.[2] Stoker reinforces the invasion trope by setting that resurrection in Trelawny's ancestral home, which the archeologist describes as 'built by an ancestor of mine in the days when a great house far away from a centre had to be prepared to defend itself' (1996: 197). Such fortifications are inadequate against Tera's power, however, which is described in chilling detail by Malcolm Ross, the barrister narrator and the only person to survive Tera's resurrection:

> I found them all where they had stood. They had sunk down on the floor, and were gazing upward with fixed eyes of unspeakable terror.... I did what I could for my companions; but there was nothing that could avail. There, in that lonely house, far away from aid of man, naught could avail. (1996: 250)

The novel ends here, and readers are left to imagine Queen Tera's invasion of England and the devastation that will result. Since the mummy is less established as a Gothic character than the vampire, readers know only that she comes from a world much more foreign and more alien than Dracula's Transylvania. Stoker is also less clear about Tera's motivation though the two Egyptologists assume that she wants to re-establish the social and political control she had during her lifetime. Furthermore, although there is no evidence that she needs to kill to ensure her own survival, she is consistently associated with ruthless behaviour. She leaves a trail of dead bodies in her wake and destroys almost everyone associated with the discovery of her tomb and the movement of her body. Ross, having second thoughts when the two Egyptologists plan to assist her resurrection, recalls the deaths associated with her:

> In the history of the mummy ... the record of deaths that we knew of, presumably effected by her will and agency, was a startling one .... Nine dead men, one of them slain manifestly by the Queen's own hand! And beyond this again the several savage attacks on Mr. Trelawny in his own room, in which, aided by her Familiar, she had tried to open the safe and to extract the Talisman jewel. (1996: 216)

Thus *Dracula* and *The Jewel of Seven Stars* would seem to focus on two very similar Gothic invaders, creatures from an exotic past who invade the present and bring death and destruction in their wake.

There are some problems with this rather facile analogy, however. The first is that the reader knows that Dracula had been a military leader and had heard from his own lips that he had been planning for a long time 'to go through the crowded streets of your mighty London, to be in the midst of the whirl and rush of humanity, to share its life, its change, its death, and all that makes it what it is' (1998: 55). Thus Dracula is clearly an invader whereas readers of *The Jewel of Seven Stars* are left with the nagging question of who exactly is the invader. Indeed Stoker weaves in some subtle references that suggest that England is the invader here, having established *de facto* rule in Egypt under the control of Evelyn Baring, Lord Cromer, the British Consul General from 1883 to 1907, and an army of occupation. That Stoker is thinking about the political relationship between England and Egypt becomes clearer when Corbeck the archeologist mentions that he and Trelawney had gone to Egypt 'soon after Arabi Pasha' when 'Egypt was no safe place for travellers, especially if they were English' (1996: 131).

This reference allows readers to date the year of Tera's removal from Egypt to the year 1882, the year of Arabi Pasha's nationalist rebellion against European intervention in Egypt. Nominally under the control of the Ottoman Empire, Egypt was for all intents and purposes a British colony when Stoker wrote *Jewel*, and the detailed descriptions of Trelawny's home reveal him as one of the numerous archeologists who had plundered Egypt of its antiquities. Seeing Trelawny's home for the first time, Malcolm Ross reveals how much Trelawny had taken from Egypt:

> There were so many ancient relics that unconsciously one was taken back to strange lands and strange times. There were so many mummies or mummy objects, round which there seems to cling for ever the penetrating odours of bitumen, and spices and gums. (1996: 45)

He has plundered so much from Egypt that he must commission a special train to transport the materials from London to his ancestral home, where the attempt to revive Queen Tera will take place:

> We shall to-day begin our packing up; and I dare say that by tomorrow night we shall be ready. In the outhouses I have all the packing-cases which were used for bringing the things from Egypt, and I am satisfied that as they were sufficient for the journey across the desert and down the Nile to Alexandria and thence on to London, they will serve without fail between here and Kyllion. (1996: 198)

There are so many antiquities that it takes the crew of four men and Margaret an entire day simply to pack them up for transport.

Thus we have two Gothic works that use the invasion trope but use it very differently. *The Man* (1905) and *The Lair of the White Worm* (1911), like *Dracula*, remind readers that England was once subject to frequent invasions. In fact, Stephen Norman's name in *The Man* is reminiscent of those invasions. Her name echoes one major invasion of England while her beauty results from other waves of invaders:

> The firm-set jaw ... and the wide fine forehead and aquiline nose marked the high descent from Saxon through Norman. The glorious mass of red hair ... showed the blood of another ancient ancestor of Northern race.... The purple-black eyes, the raven eyebrows and eyelashes, and the fine curve of the nostrils spoke of the eastern blood of the far-back wife of the Crusader. (2007: 10)

Most of the details associated with Stoker's description of Stephen evoke the numerous invasions that England had experienced in the past, but the reference to the East is another reminder that England had also been an invader. However, *The Man* is mostly concerned with the romance of two largely Anglo Saxon characters, so Stoker does little more with the invasion trope than use it to provide the family backgrounds for his central characters.

A different story entirely, *The Lair of the White Worm* associates each of the central characters with a particular piece of property and a particular group of invaders, and the references to historical invasions are so dominant that they sometimes threaten to overwhelm the central plot line. Written in the final year of Stoker's life, *The Lair of the White Worm* has received relatively little scholarly treatment, perhaps because the central plot is so implausible. While no plot summary can do the novel justice, its title character is an aristocratic woman who can transform herself into an enormous white worm. The illustrations in the first edition by Pamela Colman Smith show it towering over the tree tops, and one of the characters refers to it as 'an antediluvian monster' and a 'diplodocus' (1991: 113). The novel also includes a student of Mesmer, an African practitioner of voodoo, the romance of hero and heroine, and multiple explosions.

Using Sir Nathaniel de Salis, 'President of the Mercian Archaeological Society' (13) to provide young Adam Salton with a history of the area and therefore Salton's family history, Stoker focuses on the numerous invasions that had taken place before England became a unified country. For example, Castra Regis, the family seat of the Caswall family and the chief building in the region, 'contains the whole history of early England' (1991: 20) going back to the days before the Romans. Subsequently 'each fresh wave of invasion – the Angles, the Saxons, the Danes, and the Normans – found it a desirable possession' (1991: 20). Home of Lady Arabella March (the White Worm) is Diana's Grove, which was built on what was 'once the location of a Roman temple, possibly founded on a pre-existing Druidical one' (1991: 19). Other dwellings in the area associated with the ancient Anglo Saxon kingdom of Mercia are Mercy Farm, Doom Tower, and Lesser Hill. One gets a sense of England's history stretching back many centuries, a history that is full of invasions.

While Stoker alludes to invasions in England's past, he also reminds readers that contemporary England is a colonial power, in other words, an invader of other lands. Mimi Watford, who marries Adam Salton at the end of *The Lair of the White Worm*, is the offspring of a Burmese woman and an English soldier who was killed in Burmah by Dacoits (Hindi for bandits). While Burmah is half a world away, however, Stoker also suggests that future invasions of England are possible by introducing immigrants from other cultures. Adam Salton returns to his family home from Australia, Edgar Caswall returns from Africa where he had been living, and brings with him his African servant Oolanga, a man associated with numerous primitive practices. It is evident that all the English characters are uncomfortable with Oolanga, so uncomfortable that no one mourns his death when Lady Arabella/the White Worm sweeps him into the well hole:

> She moved towards him with her hands extended ... [and drew] him, her white arms encircling him, down with her into the gaping aperture.
>
> Adam saw a medley of green and red lights blaze in a whirling circle, and as it sank down into the well, a pair of blazing green eyes became fixed, sank lower and lower .... As the light sank into the noisome depths, there came a shriek which chilled Adam's blood – a prolonged agony of pain and terror which seemed to have no end. (1991: 98)

Reading this scene, one might conclude that Lady Arabella is protecting either herself or her property against invasion, and it is certainly true that Oolanga had attempted to court her because he is attracted to what he perceives as her power and violence. Shortly after the scene in which Oolanga is killed, however, Adam, his uncle Richard, and Sir Nathaniel conspire to protect themselves against Lady Arabella in her guise of the gigantic White Worm. Their plot involves both real estate transactions and knowledge of explosives, and the novel concludes with the deaths of both Lady Arabella and Edgar Caswall. And with the obliteration of their ancestral homes:

> The only evidence of the once stately pile of Castra Regis and its inhabitants was a shapeless huddle of shattered architecture, dimly seen as the keen breeze swept aside the cloud of acrid smoke which marked the site of the once lordly Castle. As for Diana's Grove, they looked in vain for a sign which had a suggestion of permanence. (1991: 157)

Reading of such utter devastation reveals a scene that is markedly different from the conclusion to *Dracula*. At the last minute, Stoker apparently chose to eliminate the passage in which he razes Dracula's castle.[3] As a result, he leaves standing that memento of Transylvania's past while he chooses to obliterate these remnants of England's past. It is also curious why Stoker destroys one invader, Oolanga, but welcomes another, Mimi, who marries into Adam Salton's decidedly Anglo-Saxon family. One obvious difference may be that Mimi had already assimilated into Anglo Saxon culture, having been reared by her grandfather in England, while Oolanga remains a 'savage' (1991: 25) 'unreformed, unsoftened' (1991: 26).

At least two more of Stoker's works demonstrate civilized Europe being invaded by individuals who might be classified as 'savage', 'unreformed', or 'unsoftened': 'The Squaw' and *Dracula*'s Quincey Morris. Set in Nürnberg, 'The Squaw' features a young married couple on their honeymoon and an American, 'Elias P. Hutcheson, hailing from Isthmian City, Bleeding Gulch, Maple Tree County, Nebraska' (2006: 47). While the husband, who is also the narrator, opens the story by mentioning that Nürnberg had 'been happy in that it was never sacked' (2006: 48), it is certainly invaded by tourists, including an American frontiersman who describes horrific adventures of battles with American Indians on the frontier, of sleeping inside a dead bison to hide from the Comanches, and of being trapped inside a gold mine in New Mexico. The following adventure is the most unsettling because Hutcheson relates it in such a flat and unemotional way:

> Wall, I guess that am the savagest beast I ever see – 'cept once when an Apache squaw had an edge on a half-breed ... nicknamed "Splinters" 'cos of the way he fixed up her papoose which he stole on a raid just to show that he appreciated the way they had given his mother the fire torture .... She followed Splinters mor'n three year till at last the braves got him and handed him over to her. They did say that no man ... had ever been so long a-dying under the tortures of the Apaches. The only time I ever see her smile was when I wiped her out. I kem on the camp just in time to see Splinters pass in his checks .... I took a piece of his hide from one of his skinnin' posts an' had it made into a pocket-book. It's here now! and he slapped the breast pocket of his coat. (2006: 49–50)

Hutcheson's death parallels that of Splinters. If Splinters is killed by the Apache woman whose child he had kidnapped, Hutcheson is killed by a resident of Nürnberg, this time a mother cat whose kitten he had accidentally killed. When he steps into the Nürnberg virgin, one of the torture devices on display, the cat springs at the custodian who is holding it open. It thus springs closed, impaling Hutcheson. 'The

Squaw' is a rich story for interpretation, so it is surprising that it has not been studied more frequently. Andrew Maunder, Lillian Nayder, and Lisa Hopkins suggest that it reveals anxiety about powerful women. Hopkins, for example, describes it as 'a sustained portrayal of monstrous motherhood' (2007: 39) and focuses on both the 'cat's lust for revenge' as 'alarming and dangerous' (2007: 40) and on the Apache squaw's vindictive response to the man who had killed her child. Likewise, Maunder observes that the ' "savage" malevolent mother of the title is the starting point for interrogating the expected nurturing role of the mother' (2006: 127). Not only does it lend itself to the kind of feminist interpretation that Nayder and Hopkins have done, but it also lends itself to a discussion of the relationship between the United States and Europe. Because Stoker visited the United States on a number of occasions, he often interpreted the United States for people in England, as evidenced by *A Glimpse of America* (1886) and by the American characters in his works: Hutcheson, Grizzley Dick in *The Shoulder of Shasta* (the only Stoker work to be set entirely in the US), Quincey Morris, Marjory Anita Drake in *The Mystery of the Sea*, the Stonehouse family in *The Man*, and the Ogilvie family in *Lady Athlyne* (parts of which are set in the United States).

Dick and Quincey seem to be cut from the same cloth as Hutcheson, all three frontier characters manifesting the same kind of uncouth behaviour and penchant for knives and firearms. Unlike the others, however, Dick survives, perhaps because he is content to remain on the frontier where he belongs as he confesses at the conclusion:

> Let me get back to the b'ars an' the Injuns. I'm more to home with them than I am here. Be easy, Little Missy, an' ye too, all ye ladies and gentlemen; it'll be no pleasant thinkin' for me up yonder, away among the mountings, that when I kem down to 'Frisco, meanin' to do honour to a young lady that I'd give the best drop of my blood for ... I couldn't keep my blasted hands off my weppins in the midst of a crowd of women! ... I ain't fit to go heeled inter decent kempany! (2000: 124)

While very few critics have commented on *The Shoulder of Shasta*, William Hughes, Louis S. Warren, Lisa Hopkins, and Alan Johnson do comment on its American setting and characters. Both Johnson and Warren observe that Dick is probably modelled on Buffalo Bill Cody, whose Wild West Show Stoker had attended, and Warren also suggests that Stoker is mulling over imperialism, racial issues, and the growing power of the United States. In his introduction to his edition of *The Shoulder of Shasta* Johnson comments explicitly on its 'purportedly realistic Californian setting' (2000: 10) and indicates that Stoker may have based it on a railroad journey he took through California.

Quincey Morris is a different question entirely, and a number of critics, including Warren, Franco Moretti, Elizabeth Miller and Robert Eighteen-Bisang (in their *Notes for Dracula*), and James R. Simmons, remark on his uniquely American character. Not only does he use slang, which amuses Lucy, but he is also associated with the use of firearms and the Bowie knife. Miller and Eighteen-Bisang, who have studied Stoker's notes, observe that Quincey's name was changed a number of times as Stoker worked on *Dracula* and that one incarnation was Quincey P. Adams, a decidedly American name.[4] Meeting him for the first time, Renfield identifies him as both a representative Texan and as a representative American:

> Mr Morris, you should be proud of your great state. Its reception into the Union was a precedent which may have far-reaching effects hereafter, when the Pole and the Tropics may hold allegiance to the Stars and Stripes. The power of Treaty may yet prove a vast engine of enlargement, when the Monroe doctrine takes its true place as a political fable. (1998: 341)

Renfield thus refers to the growing power of the United States, suggesting that it would continue to gain control over the vast North American land mass. Mentioning the Monroe Doctrine, an American policy written by John Quincey Adams and introduced in 1823, also reinforces the American intent not to be further colonized (or in the language of the current paper, invaded) by European nations.

If the Monroe Doctrine emphasized North American autonomy from colonial aggression, it also noted that the United States would not involve itself in European affairs, neutral behaviour that is apparently foreign to Quincey. In fact, he seems bent on bringing his uncouth frontier behaviour to old Europe, introducing Lucy to American slang, shooting off guns and thereby endangering his fellow vampire hunters, and generally behaving in ways that are incomprehensible to his companions and to us. That mysterious behaviour causes Moretti and Simmons to link him with Dracula. Simmons questions whether Quincey might even be a vampire:

> When we consider that all actions, from his mysterious and sudden appearance in Lucy's house after her final attack, to his nocturnal

habits and often inexplicable behavior, point to his being in league with Dracula, why couldn't Morris, too, be a vampire? (2002: 434)

Following in this line of thinking, P. N. Elrod, who is best known for her series *Vampire Files*, wrote a novel *Quincey Morris, Vampire* (2001) that depicts Quincey as a vampire. An intriguing theory and certainly an idea that would explain why he must be killed off at the end of *Dracula*. Like Dracula, he is too primitive to exist in a Europe dominated by professional individuals like Harker, Seward, and Van Helsing. There is no place for him in the modern world.

Seeing Quincey as a vampire is a bit of a stretch for me, but seeing him as a primitive helps to explain Stoker's treatment of invaders. For example, a number of Stoker's invaders assimilate into the cultures that they invade, and Stoker, who knew his history, undoubtedly knew that the Viking invaders of Ireland had founded the coastal settlements of Dublin, Waterford, Cork, and Limerick and stimulated the Irish economy at the same time they contributed to its culture. Other invaders also make substantial contributions or assimilate into the cultures they invade. Among those are the Americans Marjory Drake in *The Mystery of the Sea*, the Stonehouse family in *The Man*, and the Ogilvie family in *Lady Athlyne*. Stoker is careful to let readers know something of the family backgrounds here. He reveals, for example, that Marjory is an heiress whose father had made a fortune though he never reveals how. He is more specific about the Stonehouse family, identifying Andrew Stonehouse as 'the great ironmaster and contractor' (2007: 175). Finally, he refers to the father of the Ogilvie family as Colonel Ogilvie and notes that the family, which is from Kentucky, raises horses. Regardless of the source of their fortunes, all are independently wealthy. While readers might argue that the Stonehouses and the Ogilvies are tourists who do not intend to settle in Europe, Stoker has several occasions when visitors/ invaders become permanent settlers, often altering the land for the good. Such is the case in *The Snake's Pass*, *The Lair of the White Worm*, and *The Lady of the Shroud*. Arthur Severn decides to settle in Ireland, having fallen in love with the land and with Norah Joyce. Despite his love, Arthur proceeds to remake both Norah, whom he sends off to school on the continent for two years, and her father's land, which his friend the engineer Dick Sutherland transforms into 'a fairy-land' (2006: 212) albeit a fairy-land with 'exquisite gardens,' which are irrigated by elaborate water-works. Adam Salton comes to England from Australia and sets about improving his ancestral property and the land he purchases from Lady Arabella. He uses dynamite to eliminate the White

Worm, but the explosion also reveals a vast source of china clay that he can use to increase his already substantial fortune. Rupert St Leger in *The Lady of the Shroud* helps the heroic mountaineers escape from the control of their Turkish oppressors. He eventually becomes king of the Land of the Blue Mountains and introduces a number of significant technological improvements, including an air force, a navy, and a hydro-electric plant for generating electricity. Invaders certainly, but Stoker implies that they are invaders who bring with them nothing but improvements.

Looking once again at Stoker's works as a whole, I find myself observing that his perspective is more complex than that of most of his critics. Monika Tomaszewska provides a helpful beginning to our understanding of Stoker's views on invasions. Arguing that *Dracula* reveals a 'characteristic fear of foreign invasion' (2004: 3), she reads *Dracula* according to late Victorian theories of degeneration: 'In late Victorian England the threatening degenerate was commonly identified as the racial Other, the alien intruder who invades the country to disrupt the domestic order and enfeeble the host race' (2004: 3). The assessment applies to Dracula and Oolanga, perhaps to Quincey and Elias P. Hutcheson. It does not, however, help us to understand Lady Arabella or Edgar Caswell. Both can boast English pedigrees that go back for centuries, their respective homes associated with the Druids in the case of Lady Arabella and the Romans in the case of Edgar. They do, however, look backward rather than to the kind of progressive and technological future that Stoker so often celebrates in his novels. In fact, the woman with whom Adam Salton falls in love and ultimately marries is the dark-skinned daughter of an English soldier and a Burmese mother. Like Dracula, she comes to England from the East and is clearly a representative of a different racial group. Stoker's final novel, however, suggests that he is moving toward a different reading of contemporary history. Whereas Quincey Morris and Elias P. Hutcheson suggest Stoker's concern over the increasing power of the United States, Marjory Anita Drake and Joy Ogilvie show the benefits of the English literally marrying their American lovers. The result of Stoker's later fiction provides yet one more piece of evidence that his novels are rarely as simple as they initially appear. Because Stoker so obviously wrote for the popular market and adapted many of the formulas available to him, it is tempting to read him simplistically as a writer of genre fiction. However, many of the conflicts that he depicts are not merely the conflict between Good and Evil, or even of good and evil. His novels are complex responses to what he saw going on in his own world, a world that he saw in shades of grey rather than as black and white. Although Stoker did frequently imply that the problems and the conflicts depicted in his fiction had either scientific or technological solutions, the presence of science and technology is a topic for an entirely different discussion.

## Notes

1. The concern about invasions is developed by Stephen Arata, who explores the fear that 'what has been represented as the "civilized" world is on the point of being colonized by "primitive" forces' (1993: 85) and by Matthew Gibson, who characterizes Eastern Europe as 'Shambolic, wild and primitive, but with a sinister, threatening edge which argues not for control so much as exclusion' (2004: 243). Taking a slightly different though no less threatening approach is Andrew Smith, who looks at the threat that America poses to England, a threat made concrete in *Dracula* by the character of Quincey Morris.
2. Bradley Deane describes the conclusion as follows: 'The hopelessness of the story's end might be understood as a vision of the veiled protectorate twisted into nightmare, one in which an incarnate Egypt repays those who have revived and protected her with destruction'(2008: 406). He adds that the revised version 'departs from the logic of the occupation: the space of adventure has been closed, and the profound allure of Egyptian power has been reduced to a curious detour on the way to a cheerful British wedding' (2008: 406).
3. Leatherdale mentions this omission in a footnote to his annotated edition, *Dracula Unearthed*: 'At this point in the final manuscript Stoker wrote that the castle was swallowed up by the earth in a cataclysmic convulsion – like Poe's *Fall of the House of Usher* – but Stoker later erased the whole passage' (1998: 510).
4. Miller and Eighteen-Bisang cite Clive Leatherdale and argue that the name is 'rather too close to John Quincy Adams, the sixth president of the United States' (2008: 91). Following Stoker's notes, the two suggest their belief that Morris 'once played a more significant part in the novel' (2008: 29). They observe in their overview of Stoker's characters that he had planned to 'include a "Texan" from the beginning' (2008: 283) but that he changed many other aspects of Quincey's character. At one point thinking of him as an inventor, he ultimately settles on making him a rough and uncouth frontiersman.

# 7
# 'Gay Motes that People the Sunbeams': Dust, Death and Degeneration in *Dracula*

Victoria Samantha Dawson

> Over the earth the shadows creep with deepening gloom, wrapping all objects in a mysterious dimness, in which all certainty is destroyed and any guess seems plausible. Forms lose their outlines, and are dissolved in floating mist. The day is over, the night draws on.
> (Nordau, 1895: 6)

Social critic and physician Max Nordau's vision of *fin-de-siècle* anxiety stealing about the world is the stuff of nightmares, but most importantly for this investigation, it is the stuff of *Gothic* nightmares. In the wake of Darwin's *Origin of Species* (1859), the prevailing anxiety creeping through the late Victorian period was one of intellectual, physical and moral decline. Britain was haunted by the fear of degeneration at a time when its economic dominance was confronted by a real and credible threat from both Germany and America. New socio-political movements and a 'fundamental rearrangement of intellectual authority ... sparked by scientific advances' (Kucich, 2002: 120) rattled the foundations of Victorian social structures, attacking the traditions, methods and theories considered by most to be the very fundamentals of civilization. All established systems were being scrutinised: imperialism, religion, patriarchy, the sanctity of marriage, the nuclear family, law and science. The fear of recidivism spread into every aspect of human existence, and according to Nordau, the horrific suggestion of a sickening collapse of social structures evoked 'even in the most inchoate and rudimentary human being a wondrous feeling of stir and upheaval' (Nordau, 1895: 7). Bram Stoker's *Dracula* transmuted this stress into forms that appeared fantastical, but was at the same time a distorted embodiment of real *fin-de-siècle* anxiety. This chapter will show how *Dracula* can be read in the context of the contemporary 19th century science of atmospheric dust. Dracula pushes the boundaries of scientific knowledge to their limits by having the ability to exist in the interstices between life and death. Yet, despite its minatory presence, dust ultimately has an important role in the eradication of anxieties within the text and within the *fin de siècle*.

## The fin de siècle and the rise of scientific knowledge

One of the most significant features of the period was the position of science within popular culture. Science became an increasingly specialized field over the course of the 19th century. With fragmentation into areas such as mathematics, physics, organic chemistry and electrochemistry the discipline lost some of its unity, but by the 1890s all types of scientific discourse had come to 'dominate the intellectual sphere of the late Victorian period' (Ledger and Luckhurst, 2000: 221). The publication of scientific articles alongside fiction and essays in many contemporary periodicals, such as *The Fortnightly Review* and *Cornhill Magazine*, was largely responsible for bringing science to the forefront of public consciousness. Increased scientific activity and taxonomic study meant that by the late 19th century a 'powerful conceptual reorganization of the knowable world' (Kucich, 2002: 119) had occurred. Science was unravelling the mysteries of the world through the process of classification, and by defining the order of living things was reinforcing humanity's mastery over other organisms. The resulting sense of control derived from the augmentation of humanity's superiority was the source of what scientist William Clifford identified as the 'pleasure we derive from an explanation' (Clifford, 1879: 148). His observation that for something to be 'capable of explanation, it must break up into simpler constituents which are already familiar' (148), resulted in the realisation that humanity unconsciously possessed knowledge of seemingly unfamiliar things. This increased the overall feeling of a secure future for the human race, as it opened up the possibility that everything unfamiliar could ultimately be deciphered and brought under human control, thus minimising the risk to humanity. Only through taxonomy could the human desire for control be fulfilled, as Mary Douglas would later articulate: '[i]t is only by exaggerating the difference between within and without, above and below, male and female, with and against, that a semblance of order can be created' (Douglas, 2004: 5).

Science's intention was to make the world and everything within it more knowable, but the more taxonomists strove to categorize the matter that formed the building blocks of life, the more the integrity of human physicality was rendered ambiguous. In the groundbreaking *Origin of Species*, Charles Darwin illustrated how 'from so simple a beginning endless forms most beautiful and most wonderful have been, and are being evolved' (670). Protoplasm was discovered to be '"*the* physical basis or matter of life" [the] one kind of matter which is common to all living beings' (Huxley, 1869: 129) and biologist Thomas Huxley summarised contemporary Victorian feeling when he said 'that [living things'] endless diversities are bound together by a physical, as well as an ideal unity ... appears almost shocking to common sense' (129). The indifferentiation of the human body from lower forms of life defamiliarized human identity and blurred the very boundaries that taxonomy sought to create and the notion that all living forms were 'fundamentally of one matter' (Huxley, 1869: 135) profoundly changed the notion of what it meant to be human. Although Darwin had suggested that the human race and life in general would 'tend to progress towards perfection' (Darwin, 1900: 669), his theory provided the basis for notions of degeneracy that prevailed in the latter part of the century by 'demolish[ing] the model of human centrality in the universe, and replac[ing] it with one of human ephemerality, relativity and potential "degradation"' (Hurley, 1996: 56). With scientific discoveries rapidly diminishing the chasm between humans and other, lesser organisms, the shadow of humanity's capacity for degeneration deepened the *fin de siècle* gloom.

After the French psychiatrist Bénédict Morel sparked this long-running discourse by putting forward his influential theory of human mental degeneration in 1857, the biological case for degeneration was stoutly put forth by E. Ray Lankester in 1880. His study showed how life forms could physically regress under certain conditions, yet his assertion that 'Degeneration may be defined as a gradual change of the structure in which the organism becomes adapted to *less* varied and *less* complex conditions of life' (Lankester, 1880: 32) had not just scientific, but cultural implications. The 'conditions of life' were changing rapidly throughout the 19th century for all classes of Briton. 'It is possible for us', Lankester warned, 'to reject the good gift of reason with which every child is born, and to degenerate into a contented life of material enjoyment accompanied by ignorance and superstition' (60–1). The rejection of reason and embracing of material enjoyment were among the chief concerns of many who were scathing of the amoral influences of radical thought and creeping aestheticism among the fashionable, aristocratic elite. Beginning in the art sphere, the emphasis on sexual freedom, beauty and the pursuit of pleasure percolated into the mainstream, challenging the ethics of conventional Victorian culture. Such frivolity was not only morally, but physically dangerous. Lankester had shown that '[i]n Degeneration there is a suppression of form, corresponding to the cessation of work' (32) which had wider implications for the upper-class, lost to idleness thanks to its inherited wealth and investment income.

Perhaps the most at risk of a 'suppression of form' were the men of the burgeoning middle-class, whose white-collar work inspired a sedentary lifestyle spent largely behind a desk. As educational reformer Hely Hutchinson Almond espoused in *Macmillan's Magazine*:

> Boys and men who do not live by hard manual labour require a large amount of exercise in pure air in order to keep them in the highest possible state of health and vigour .... Generally speaking, under the conditions of civilisation as it exists in modern Europe, most men and boys get nothing of the kind. (283)

The middle-classes valued the accumulation of wealth and status by hard work and individual labour, which put pressure on those within the social strata to succeed by any means. Almond felt that such pressure was detrimental and put the longevity and health of the nation at risk:

> the increased strain and competition of modern life, the calamitous change, by which business hours have begun and ended later, till crowds of sallow clerks are now released from offices after the expiry of daylight for many months in the year, are all causes antagonistic to this prime necessity of a nation which is to be long vigorous. (283)

This did not necessarily mean that the working-class was immune from the effects of degeneration by means of manual labour. For them the Industrial Revolution had vastly changed the labour landscape as the mechanisation of production had introduced long hours of less skilled and less varied work for the workforce in dangerous and unsanitary conditions. Rapid urbanisation and low wages meant that the working-class lived in squalor with little or no health provision to counteract the ill-effects of work. With their high infant mortality rates and low life expectancy, the working classes were also being worked into a degenerative unhealthy state by their monotonous, repetitive employment in hazardous environments.

Lankester issued a stark warning that would be a blow to the confidence of a Victorian society that was wedded to the idea of its own historic progression:

> it is well to remember that we are subject to the general laws of evolution, and are as likely to degenerate as to progress. As compared with the immediate forefathers of our civilisation – the ancient Greeks – we do not appear to have improved. (Lankester, 1880: 60)

Culturally, Victorian Britain appeared to be at its zenith, yet it faced real economic decline with the recession of the 1880s, and the feeling that Britain had reached its imperial epitome created fear among many. The advancement of the nation and its accumulation of wealth, lauded and exported by the Empire, were contributing to the regression of the lower- and middle-classes, whilst literary and artistic movements were threatening the country's morality. Lankester's science was not only theorizing humanity's biological degeneration, it was also theorizing the cultural degeneration of humankind.

However, there was hope. Edwin Lankester posited that degeneration was not a new phenomenon. He observed that '[t]he traditional history of mankind furnishes us with notable examples of degeneration. High states of civilisation have decayed and given place to low and degenerate states' (53). Yet despite the echoes of history he firmly believed that scientific knowledge would undermine 'traditional history' and safeguard the race from degeneration. He said:

> [f]or us it is possible to ascertain what will conduce to our higher development, what will favour our degeneration. To us has been given the power to *know the causes of things*, and by the use of this power it is possible for us to control our destinies. It is for us by ceaseless and ever hopeful labour to try to gain a knowledge of man's place in nature. When we have gained this fully and minutely, we shall be able by the light of the past to guide ourselves in the future .... The full and earnest cultivation of Science – the Knowledge of Causes – is that to which we have to look for the protection of our race – even of this English branch of it – from relapse and degeneration. (61–2)

Knowledge of history twinned with advances in science would be the saviour of humanity, and in literature, no one would illustrate this point more profoundly than Stoker.

## Molecular degeneration in *Dracula*

Taxonomic '[v]iews that have hitherto governed minds are dead or driven hence like disenthroned kings' (Nordau, 1895: 6), as Dracula exists across multiple categories of physical states but complies with none. Dracula explodes all notions of fixed human identity as he metamorphoses between human and animal, but more terrifyingly for the Victorian reader species integrity is undone to the point of collapse by the breaking down of his human physical structure to a molecular level, embodying the fear that degeneration will result in the devolution of humanity to its basic, atomic state. In order to demonstrate how Dracula pushes the boundaries of scientific knowledge to their absolute limits by having the ability to exist in the interstices between life and death, one must consider what for many was and is the most basic elemental substance of all: dust.

For Max Nordau, dust was nothing more than mere 'organic detritus' (35), but for some it was an uncomfortable reminder of man's first lapse into spiritual degeneracy. Its biblical connotations of God's decree to Adam – 'for dust thou art, and unto dust shalt thou return' (Genesis, 3: 19) – evoked the 'fear, that dust equals oblivion, a return to origins which we cannot transcend' (Flint, 2000: 51–2). In 1891, an article written by the scientist J.G. McPherson appeared in *Longman's Magazine*, which drew attention to the paradoxical nature of dust by asking the reader '[w]hat, in fact, is one of the most marvellous agents in producing beauty for the eye's gratification, refreshment to the arid soil, sickness and death to the frame of man and beast? That agent is dust' (49). In reference to dust particles in the atmosphere, McPherson commented that 'an æsthetic eye is charmed with their gorgeous transformation effects; yet some are more real emissaries of evil than poet or painter ever conceived' (49–50). However, in a break from standard artistic conceptions, Stoker utilized the science of atmospheric dust to create his own terrifying envoy of malevolence. Consequently, a number of important scientific facts about dust must be understood before one can comprehend its significance within the text. Firstly, dust is delightful to the eye because, as McPherson explained, it is the cause of a colourful sunset:

> some of the most beautiful and delicate rose tints are formed by the air cooling, and depositing its moisture on the particles of dust .... As the sun sinks further, the particles overhead become cooler, and attract the water-vapour; thus they increase in size, and thereby reflect the red rays. (55)

In *Dracula*, Harker first encounters such a sunset whilst journeying through the Carpathian Mountains, where the sun 'seemed to glow out with a delicate cool pink' (Stoker, 2003: 14). The cooling of water-vapour in the atmosphere causes condensation, and it is this condensation that is reflecting the red tones. One of Harker's fellow travellers, witnessing the array, becomes distinctly troubled by it, 'cross[ing] himself reverently' (14). The terrifying significance of the red sky for the passenger is never adequately explained, and for the reader to interpret his anxiety a second scientific principle must be understood in relation to the vampire.

The collection of water-vapour upon dust particles before it can be fully condensed causes the vapour to be held in suspension, and the ratio of dust to water-vapour in the air determines the form the suspended matter takes. If there are a greater number of dust particles in comparison to vapour, then the compounded particles are:

> closely packed, but light in form and small in size, taking the more flimsy appearance of fog. But if the dust-particles are fewer in proportion to the number of molecules of water-vapour, each particle soon gets weighted, becomes visible, and falls in mist or rain. (McPherson, 1891: 50–1)

In short, '[i]nvisible dust, then, is required in the air for the production of fog, cloud, mist, snow, sleet, hail, haze, and rain, according to the temperature and pressure of the air' (McPherson, 1891: 50). Dracula and his vampire women can assume the form of elemental dust, and they utilise the same principle of suspending matter in the air in order to traverse seemingly impossible boundaries. As mist or fog they can '"come out from anything or into anything, no matter how close it be bound or even fused up with fire"' (Stoker, 2003: 255). Harker's first experience of this technique comes whilst he is looking out of a window from Castle Dracula. He notices 'some quaint little specks floating in the rays of the moonlight. They were like the tiniest grains of dust, and they whirled round and gathered in clusters in a nebulous sort of way' (52). Although he enjoys the unusual 'aerial gambolling', he soon realizes the danger of the display:

> I watched them with a sense of soothing, and a sort of calm stole over me ... the floating motes of dust began to take new shapes ... as they danced in the moonlight. I felt myself struggling to awake to some call of my instincts; nay my very soul was struggling, and my

half-remembered sensibilities were striving to answer the call. I was becoming hypnotized! Quicker and quicker danced the dust .... More and more they gathered till they seemed to take dim phantom shapes. And then I started, broad awake and in full possession of my senses, and ran screaming from the place. The phantom shapes, which were becoming gradually materialized from the moonbeams, were those of the three ghostly women to whom I was doomed. (52–3)

In their suspended forms vampires negate structural and corporeal borders, covertly using their molecular state to influence their victims into an involuntary submissive state that aides their corporeal attacks. The vampire women use movement in order to hypnotize Jonathan, but their attempts to desensitize him fail. Dracula however, is more successful in his endeavour to violate Mina Harker. He gains entry to her bedchamber in the form of a mist, and his vaporous constitution induces her into a state of semi-narcosis as she is overcome by 'some leaden lethargy [that] seemed to chain my limbs and even my will' (275). The air becomes 'heavy, and dank, and cold', as Dracula manipulates the natural atmosphere, creating the cool conditions necessary for his solidification whilst combining the moisture from the air with his dust particles, growing 'thicker and thicker' (275) until his 'livid white face [materializes] out of the mist' (276). It is the knowledge that vampires can assume the form of dust, and that dust creates the redness of a sunset, that reveals the ominousness of the red sky to the passenger. Vampires are literally what McPherson described as the '"gay motes that people the sunbeams"' (McPherson, 1891: 51–2) and a blood-coloured sky signifies the forthcoming appearance of a vampire. It is a warning unrecognized not only by Harker, but also by Lucy and Mina, who see 'the setting sun [that] seemed to bathe everything in a rosy glow' (Stoker, 2003: 104) from the cliff-top in Whitby. That very same evening, Dracula is seen in the form of a bird at Lucy's window, and Lucy becomes 'drawn [and] haggard' (105) as a result. McPherson deduced that:

> if our atmosphere were perfectly void of dust-particles, the sun's light would simply pass through without being seen, and soon after the sun dipped below the horizon darkness would ensue. The length of our twilight ... depends on the amount of dust in one form or another in our atmosphere. (McPherson, 1891: 56)

The twilight is elicited as metaphor in Nordau's concept of *fin de siècle* anxiety, and similarly in *Dracula*, human stability is dissolved in the floating mist of the transmuted vampire and the security of the race fades into darkness with the setting of the sun. The length of humanity's twilight decline is dependent on the amount of vampiric dust ready to corrupt mankind and instigate its degeneracy into a bestial metastability.

Despite its minatory presence, dust has an important role in the eradication of the anxieties that *Dracula* creates. In the Victorian psyche, dust had been closely associated with dirt because, as Mrs Beeton told the nation, it contained 'among other things, innumerable epithelial scales from the skin of men and animals' (Beeton, 1888: 1563). The organic element of dust was classified as 'deleterious and dangerous' (1563), and much domestic attention was given to 'abolish[ing] the evil' (Tyndall, 1870: 308). 'People observed with their senses that the smallest living creatures – bugs, spiders and worms – were creatures of dust' (Amato, 2000: 20) and whilst biology showed that man and animal are all made of the same base materials, humanity sought to differentiate itself from the lower life forms:

> With taboos and rituals against the contaminated and the polluted, and with elevating and sublimating religious conceptions, they sought to transcend the biology that ruled their bodies. They insisted that they were not just the dust grovelers, dirt eaters, and excrement makers they knew themselves to be. (21)

Dust is to be found in the neglected rooms of Castle Dracula in copious amounts, and Harker's footsteps frequently disturb its 'long accumulation' (Stoker, 2003: 44), signifying the change in Harker's situation as he defies the Count's order to remain confined for his own safety. In forcing open a locked door and disturbing the dust within, Harker has allowed evil and terror into his life on an unprecedented scale.

Yet dust is not merely found in the form of dirt, or motes that 'swathe the earth as a light haze' (Tyndall, 1870: 310), but also as the degenerative dust of decayed bodies. The inhalation of effluvia from rotting material marked out the dead as a risk to the living and in 1841, the surgeon George Walker wrote of the 'contamination of the atmosphere' around grave yards 'from putrefying animal substances' (Walker, 1841: 4). Walker's account described how graveyards suffered from over-capacity, with 'the abode of the dead [being] openly violated – its deposits [being] sacrilegiously disturbed, and ejected' (3) as space was sought for the newly deceased. The result was 'unchristian' as coffins and bodies were 'exposed, mangled or mutilated' resulting in a 'gaseous profusion, contaminating, as it circulates, the habitations of the living' (3). Having studied official documents he calculated that a total of 2,105,112 bodies had been buried in London between 1741 and 1837, leaving a mass of rotting material whose exudations would be inhaled by the living. Walker was frank in his opinion: 'to the neighbourhood of the "Grave yard" may be attributed the violence, if not the origin, of some of the most destructive diseases which have depopulated the human race' (4). He documented his findings of visits to many neighbourhoods in the vicinity of cemeteries, recording the rates of illness and disease. He found it no coincidence that the residents of Clement's Lane suffered an excessively high mortality rate from typhus fever, and felt that those in Portugal Street, whose houses overlooked the open space of the cemetery had, he said, 'suffered most' as '[t]he exhalations of the grave yards in this neighbourhood, it may be reasonably inferred, have increased the malignancy and putridity of disease' (23). The smell of Castle Dracula is 'deathly, sickly' and gets 'closer and heavier' (Stoker, 2003: 56) as Harker searches his prison. When the men visited Carfax, they 'prepared for some unpleasantness, for as we were opening the door a faint, malodorous air seemed to exhale through the gaps, but none of us ever expected such an odour as we encountered' (267). Harker writes:

> here the place was small and close, and the long disuse had made the air stagnant and foul. There was an earthy smell, as of some dry miasma, which came through the fouler air. But as to the odour itself, how shall I describe it? It was not alone that it was composed of all the ills of mortality and with the pungent, acrid smell of blood, but it seemed as though corruption had become itself corrupt. Faugh! it sickens me to think of it. Every breath exhaled by that monster seemed to have clung to the place and intensified its loathsomeness. (267)

The vampire is a dead organism, living among the dead, exhaling the poisonous breath of death and evil. He has transported his own earth from Transylvania, for '"We Transylvanian nobles love not to think that our bones may be amongst the common dead"' (30). Yet even here, cross-contamination is a likely certainty. Everything in the known universe has the capability to be ground to dust, or turned to ash in fire, or made minutiae through decomposition and 'True cleanliness is a matter of minutiae, and admits of no subterfuge' (Bartlett, 1878: 153).

In religion and science, dust is inextricably linked with death and earth. For the scientist, earth is made through the process of ancient organisms composting over time. For the clergyman, that process is the will of God, who decreed that in death humans must 'all go unto one place; all are of the dust, and all turn to dust again' (Ecclesiastes, 3: 20). In a statement that melded both scientific and religious principles, the 19th century evangelical minister Edward Bickersteth told his congregation: '"[w]here are the bodies of all the millions that have peopled the earth? ... Mingled with the dust on which those now living are moving and treading ... they are mouldering in the dust, and they are mingled with the earth"' (Hamlin, 2005: 3). When understood from both the scientific and religious angles, Mary Douglas's theory regarding the taxonomy of dirt is useful, as it forms the basis of a complete understanding of dust's capacity for atonement:

> if we can abstract pathogenicity and hygiene from our notion of dirt, we are left with the old definition of dirt as matter out of place. This is a very suggestive approach. It implies two conditions: a set of ordered relations and a contravention of that order. Dirt then, is never a unique, isolated event. Where there is dirt there is system. Dirt is the by-product of a systematic ordering and classification of matter, in so far as ordering involves rejecting inappropriate elements. (Douglas, 2004: 44)

The notion of dust as dirt, and therefore the 'by-product of a systematic ordering and classification of matter', is crucial to the understanding of Stoker's text. As Harker searches for a way to escape the Castle, he encounters the 'deathly, sickly odour, the odour of earth newly turned' (Stoker, 2003: 56). He enters into an 'old, ruined chapel, which had evidently been used as a graveyard' (56), and discovers that large quantities of earth had been removed and put into large wooden boxes. He ventures further into the castle, and passes 'fragments of old coffins and piles of dust' (56), before he finds the Count inside one of the earth-filled boxes, ready for transportation to England. Dracula relies upon rejected particles for his existence, but although his 'earth-home' (255) amongst the dirt can similarly define the vampire as an 'inappropriate element', it is important to recognise that the vampire himself is *not* part of the 'systematic ordering' of which dust is a 'by-product'. He lives amongst the dust of the earth, and can assume the form of dust, but he is *not* dust itself. In a religious sense, to become dust is to return to the base elements prescribed by God, and the vampires' inability to become dust is to countermand the system of life as defined within Holy Scripture. To live amongst the dust signifies rejection, but to *become* dust signifies acceptance from God. In the eyes of God:

> hybrids and other confusions are abominated .... Holiness requires that individuals shall conform to the class to which they belong. And holiness requires that different classes of things shall not be confused .... Holiness means keeping distinct the categories of creation. It therefore involves correct definition, discrimination and order .... To be holy is to be whole, to be one; holiness is unity, integrity, perfection of the individual and of the kind. (Douglas, 2004: 66–7)

Holiness is impossible for vampires, because their amorphousness and undead state contravene God's hierarchy. They are taxonomically unstable, dismantling the boundaries of somatic structure that differentiate the human, the animal and the molecular, whilst existing in the interstice between life and death. The vampire can only re-enter the hierarchy of God by returning to a human, molecular stability, which is to be attained exclusively by becoming '"true dead"' (Stoker, 2003: 256), and returning to the base element from whence it came. The very reconciliation of Dracula into the taxonomic order of human life is considered one of divine Providence, as Mina Harker writes: 'It was like a miracle ... the whole body crumbled into dust and passed from our sight', and the joy of fomenting Dracula's true and spiritual death brings universal relief: 'I shall be glad as long as I live that even in that moment of final dissolution, there was in the face a look of peace' (401). In this religious context of Stoker's novel, the analogy of *fin de siècle* dusk employed by Nordau loses its sinister overtones with the recognition that dust is an intrinsic component in the process of reconciliation between man and God. With this knowledge, the twilight dust becomes a phenomenon of beauty, the evidence that people are dying within the spiritual order of the Creator. If the length of humanity's twilight is dependent on the volume of atmospheric dust, then a sustained twilight is a vision of comfort to a Christian believer.

Max Nordau declared that 'The clearest notion we can form of degeneracy is to regard it as *a morbid deviation from an original type*' (Nordau, 1895: 16). Dracula is especially terrifying as he is a 'morbid deviation' of the human type. Vampires push the boundaries of humanity to their absolute limits and as such are incarnations of degeneracy; predominantly human in form, but humans that have regressed into a more savage, animalistic state. Their amorphousness is an indicator that their human components are deteriorating, and they are so far into the process of devolution that they can regress to a molecular level. The 'especial terror ascribed to these monstrous nonhuman species lurking within the natural landscape is that they prey on human flesh' (Hurley, 1996: 61), corrupting their victims, rendering them physically or mentally unrecognisable as human beings, making them too dissolutions of a perfect form. These attacks on humans signify the threat degeneration is *not only* to individuals but to the entire human race.

As humanity is attacked by the vampires, representatives of humanity congregate to extirpate the threat, enacting Lankester's philosophy by acquiring the 'Knowledge of Causes ... to look for the protection of humanity from relapse and degeneration' (Lankester, 1880: 5). The vampires are classified as wayward human degenerates, and this allows the possibility of their re-admittance within both the taxonomic, scientific order and God's hierarchy, thereby eradicating the *fin de siècle* anxiety by dissolving it into the *true dust* of the twilight. Certainty is therefore regained, as the vampire 'forms lose their outlines, and are dissolved in floating mist' (Nordau, 1895: 6).

# 8
# The Imprint of the Mother: Bram Stoker's 'The Squaw' and *The Jewel of Seven Stars*

Sara Williams

Like the bite of the vampire, the theme of marking punctuates Stoker's work. Birthmarks, the indelible touch of the devouring mother, are seared into the skin of the child. Stoker's lesser-read Gothics express Victorian patriarchal gynaecological anxieties of maternal imprinting, the notion that the pregnant mother's sensory experiences and traumas would physically mark her unborn child *in utero*. *Dracula* (1897), of course, notoriously codifies the maternal as consuming through the figures of the Weird Sisters and the Bloofer Lady, whilst simultaneously exploring and repeating the idea of returning to the imprinting womb, whose bite begins at the vampiric *vagina dentata*. But *Dracula* is also surrounded by works in Stoker's oeuvre where the devouring mother is embodied by the act of maternal imprinting, and in *The Jewel of Seven Stars* (1903/1912) and the earlier short story 'The Squaw' (1893) the birthmark inflicted against the child in the womb functions as a symbol of territory and possession, of colonial and psychic conflicts between the devouring mother and the Symbolic father waged on the battleground of the child's body. Offering new ways to read the intersections of motherhood, superstition, science and anxiety in his work this chapter writes a new direction for the critical and cultural reception of Stoker's Gothic.

In *Dracula* anxiety and desire collide in the threat of the bite, evidenced acutely by Jonathan Harker's encounter with the Weird Sisters: 'Two were dark, and had high, aquiline noses like the Count's, and great dark, piercing eyes ... the other was fair, as fair as can be, with great, wavy masses of golden hair and eyes like pale sapphires' (1996: 37). Jonathan's reaction is a Gothic mix of the neurotic repulsion/attraction dynamic which saturates the novel, as he recalls in his journal 'there was something about them that made me uneasy, some longing and at the same time some deadly fear. I felt in my heart a wicked, burning desire that they would kiss me with those red lips' (1996 37). These red lips sheathing 'white sharp teeth' (1996: 38) are the *vagina dentata* which Joseph Bierman identifies in Stoker's works as 'organising the childhood fantasy of the ... *claustrum*, which represents the interior of the mother's body as an orally-regressive safe haven' (1972: 22). The sight of them ignites Jonathan's desire to be devoured by the womb, the fate of the baby which Dracula brings for the sisters to feed on, and later in the text of the children on Hampstead Heath the Bloofer Lady attacks. Both Bierman and Barbara Almond discuss Stoker's childhood invalidism and the attendant prolonged passivity in the care of his mother as a source of his oral fixation (Bierman, 1972; Almond, 2007) and Stoker was clearly troubled by these voracious women, as Robert Eighteen-Bisang and Elizabeth Miller comment about his notes for *Dracula* that 'this scene [with the sisters] must have been embedded in [his] imagination from the start, for it emerges again and again like a recurring dream' (2008: 280).

Saturated with orally aggressive symbolism and womb-spaces of crypts and coffins, *Dracula* compulsively codifies the maternal as monstrous whilst simultaneously being compelled to explore and repeat the idea of returning to the womb, a repetition which narrativises and perpetuates its uncanny effect. Stoker was similarly compelled to write the devouring maternal body into his less well-known texts, weaving elements of myth and superstition into his Gothic as well as drawing on socio-medical patriarchal discourses which, despite their scientific imperative, found their basis in old wives' tales and practices. Both *The Jewel of Seven Stars* and 'The Squaw' engage with the belief that the pregnant mother's sensory experiences, especially what she sees, could physically impact upon her unborn child's body. This belief betrayed a masculine medical anxiety about the power of the unquantifiable womb and evidenced the enduring influence of superstitions and old wives' tales. Stoker's narratives combined the folkloric and the medical, using superstitions and symbolism of the malevolent mother as well as drawing on scientific gynaecological theories which find their origins in the folklore.

In psychoanalytical terms, although entry into the Symbolic demands the child disavows the maternal body, its position within the paternal contract is always precarious and it is the birthmark, the shadow of the womb cast onto the skin, which seals its return to mother. For Slavoj Žižek, skin is the primer of subjectivity, as he explains that 'the true object of horror is not the shell without the slimy body in it

[but] the "naked" body without the shell' (1991: xvii); to disrupt the skin's integrity is to fracture these discrete boundaries and reawaken the abjection which characterised the subject's dyadic bond with the mother. In *Visual Perversity* (2004) Alina Luna argues that the mother who is marked or disfigured represents a rupture in the bodily integrity for which the paternal order stands by visually affronting those who behold her. The marked mother infects those around her through the spectacle of her mark, which tacitly signals towards the vulnerability of their own body. Stoker explores this through Mina Harker's scarring from the communion wafer, as while she is not a mother until the end of the text, Mina is figured as maternal through her assertion 'we women have something of the mother in us that makes us rise above smaller matters when the mother-spirit is invoked' (1996: 230). In the novel women and, by Mina's association, mothers are characterised as a direct threat to the perceived moral and genetic purity of the British race as the Count, himself a maternal figure surrounded by uncanny wombs of castles, crypts and coffins, has spawned a matrilineage of contamination: 'My revenge is just begun! I spread it over centuries, and time is on my side. Your girls that you all love are mine already; and through them others shall yet be mine' (1996: 306). Having communed with the womb-monster Dracula in his own breastfeeding ceremony of the 'Vampire's baptism of blood', Mina becomes infected and infectious, her body rejecting patriarchal medical and religious intervention from Van Helsing as her skin recoils from the touch of the wafer, nullifying the power of the (Holy) Father (1996: 284, 322): 'As he placed the Wafer on Mina's forehead, it had seared it – had burned into the flesh as though it had been a piece of white-hot metal .... Pulling her beautiful hair over her face, as the leper of his old mantle, she wailed out: – "Unclean! Unclean!"' (1996: 296).

Jonathan's perception of Mina as leprous specifies her contaminative potential and implicates her in the matrilineage of pollution the novel writes. As Julia Kristeva contends, the wounds of leprosy are particularly visually abject because they signal towards the rupturing maternal body, the wound of the vagina, as the origins of the self, and these wounds are the manifestations of the subject's attempts to ab-ject the mother from themselves, a 'fantasy of self-rebirth' where the devouring mother is herself devoured (1982: 102). Mina's wound is the manifestation of the conflict between the maternal and the (Holy) Father, waged on the battleground of the child's body. While *Dracula* considers the effects of the marked mother in the paternal order, in 'The Squaw' and *The Jewel of Seven Stars* Stoker's unease towards mothers is symbolised through the birthmark she imprints onto the child.

## Maternal impressions

For the psychoanalyst Helene Deutsch the trauma of birth was preceded by the 'abnormal psychic charge' of pregnancy (1945: 135), and this charge sears a mark onto the child which guarantees its mother's return. Such scars are the birthmarks and bitemarks which occupy Stoker's texts. Searing onto the child's flesh a brand of her ownership, the womb mutilates and scars it as a means by which to later identify and snatch it back into the maternal fold. The trauma of breaking away from the maternal body in birth is not only manifested as a psychological compulsion to return to her, but also more immediately through the bodily wound, with *trauma* being etymologically rooted to the Greek τρang, for wound. Thus the maternal body, on losing the child to the patriarchy, inscribes both the child's body and psyche with her gaze, a traumatisation which can only be allayed through return to, and repossession by, the mother, the fatal experience of a Lacanian maternal *jouissance*. With *The Jewel of Seven Stars* and 'The Squaw', the mark of the mother is created by the womb's gaze during pregnancy, ostensibly the effects of stress felt by the mother but symbolically a psychical imprinting upon the flesh of the foetus which renders it unable to break away from her grasp. Similarly, the punctures in the skin made by the vampire's bite are a birthmark, evidence of the jaws of the *vagina dentata*'s attempt to re-consume the child back into the womb, or to stop it from leaving. These maternal scars are imprints of the uncanny, what Freud termed 'that species of the frightening that goes back to what was once well known and had long been familiar' (2003: 124). The feeling of the uncanny is a phenomenological scar, branding the subject with eruptions of the repressed past and dis-locating them from the present. The uncanny is the shadow of the past shared with mother, the locus of which is the womb and after birth the maternal space of bedroom, nursery, the mother's arms, and so the strange and displacing feeling of the uncanny is a psychical recognition of the womb within one of its metonymic spaces. For Freud this occurs at the uncanny's most intense juncture of beholding female genitalia, 'the entrance to the man's "old home", the place where everyone once lived' (2003: 151). Freud elaborates that concomitantly if the neurotic man (Jonathan in *Dracula*) envisages a certain place or landscape that compels the uncanny then this is also a remnant feeling of the mother's genitals or womb (2003: ibid.). Thus, like the gaze the uncanny is born of the mother and stalks the child as it enters the paternal contract. The birthmarks which punctuate these Gothic texts are the uncanny womb's branding, a symbol of the mother's control over the child, an imprint of maternal ownership which warns of her return, the womb's gaze searing into the child.

The concept of maternal imprinting can be traced from classical and Biblical allegories (Jacob in Genesis: 30: 37–9), through the hoax of Mary Toft who in 1726 claimed to have given birth to a litter of rabbits (Wilson, 2002: 6), to sexological and medical studies in the 19th century, and betrays a patriarchal concern about maternal autonomy during pregnancy. The theory inhabits an uneasy space in the annals of medical discourse; long discredited as a legitimate diagnosis for birth defects and congenital disorders it remains a revered belief in individual communities, a maternal proverb passed down through generations which accords the pregnant mother great power, dictating that she can imprint the child through her emotional and sensory experiences, especially, as the womb's searing gaze testifies, through what she sees. As Ann Oakley explains, the theory of maternal impressions would now be translated as the effects of general stress on the pregnant body (1984: 24), but historically this stress had been attributed to sensory perception.

Havelock Ellis, Stoker's contemporary, discusses maternal impressions caused by the mother's gaze. In 'The Psychic State in Pregnancy' (1906) Ellis refers to examples found in 'medical journals of high repute' including *The Lancet*, which suggest that the child's deformity or birthmark is the result of the pregnant mother seeing something monstrous, the trauma of which mutilates the child:

> Early in pregnancy a woman found her pet rabbit killed by a cat which had gnawed off the two forepaws, leaving ragged stumps; she was for a long time constantly thinking of this. Her child was born with deformed feet, one foot with only two toes, the other three, the *os calcis* in both feet being either absent or little developed. (Lancet May 4, 1889, in Ellis, 1923: 218)

Here the mother's vision catalyses the imprinting while eidetic meditation upon the spectacle causes the child's deformity. In Stoker's work skin bears witness to the ravages of the maternal gaze through scars, birthmarks and bitemarks, which, along with the *vagina dentata*, form part of his iconography of the devouring mother.

### *The Jewel of Seven Stars*: The Hand that Rocks the Cradle is the Hand that Rules the World

Stoker articulates the maternal gaze through the motifs of the cat and the birthmark and the hand in his eighth novel *The Jewel of Seven Stars*, originally published in 1903, and re-issued in 1912 with a revised, ostensibly less ominous, ending which William Hughes describes as 'a deliberate act of self-censorship on Stoker's part' which 'thwart[s] epistemological doubt' written in the original (1994: 132, 139). A maternal spectre invades Stoker's London through the embodiment of Tera, an ancient Egyptian queen whose mummified form is plundered and probed by the Egyptologist Abel Trelawny, who wishes to perform the 'Great Experiment' of her resurrection.

During Trelawny's expedition, on which he embarked with his van Helsingesque friend Corbeck, Tera's mummified hand is torn from her body by a Bedouin guide, and this disturbance of her tomb precipitates the death of Trelawny's pregnant wife back in England, who dies giving birth to their daughter Margaret, perpetuating the puerperal narrative that pervaded 19th-century fiction. Wrenched from the mother at the most crucial moment, Margaret bears the scar of both Tera's dismemberment and her own traumatic birth in the form a birthmark on her wrist which serves to bind her indelibly to the mummy's body, and a vengeful Tera returns to reclaim her after several years when Trelawny performs the Great Experiment. Margaret is betrothed to a solicitor Malcolm Ross who narrates the text, and so Tera's return in the original ending in which all of the participants in the Experiment apart from Ross die, serves as the intervention of the maternal gaze before it loses the child to patriarchy through its mechanism of heteronormative marriage.

That Stoker rewrote the ending to include Margaret's and Ross' innocuous happily-ever-after attests to the nihilism of the original and the damage the maternal gaze can cause, and although *Jewel* is a text which attempts to reinforce discourses of the male gaze, articulated through the scrutiny of Sergeant Daw's criminal investigation and magnifying glass and Trelawny's fetishistic collection of artefacts, an act of archaeological voyeurism that climaxes at the unwrapping of Tera, it is the maternal gaze which triumphs, in the original ending at least, in re-possessing its object of desire, the child. Margaret is marked by the womb's gaze with the portentous birthmark made literally at the hand of the mother, and Tera's disembodied hand perpetuates her power by enacting her own strategies of fracturing, not only on the bodies of her victims but also the narrative structure itself.

These connections between hand and visual agency carry implications of the uncanny, castration and death. The device of the disembodied or severed hand mobilises the gaze throughout the Gothic, and like other carriers of the gaze, like the mother's breast and the familiar, the spectral hand punctures the Symbolic order and obstructs patriarchal agency, which is intensely manifested in the original 1903 ending of *Jewel* when Margaret dies during the Great Experiment, preventing Malcolm from taking her own hand in marriage. As Aviva Briefel demonstrates, hands in *Jewel* perform a (dis)possession of autonomy, and the actions of Tera's dismembered hand contests Trelawny's and Ross' attempts to objectify both her own body and that of Margaret. From their first interaction, Ross is obsessed with seizing her actual hand:

> 'Miss Trelawny's hand somehow became lost in my own'; 'There was a long pause, and I ventured to take her hand for an instant'; 'Margaret Trelawny's hand was a joy for me to see – and touch'; 'She put out her hand. I held it hard, and kissed it. Such moments as these, the opportunities of lovers, are gifts of the gods!' and so on. (2008: 269)

Ross's act of kissing Margaret's birthmark is not only symbolic of his acceptance of it but also his desired ownership within the Victorian heterosexual paradigm, and the tensions of possession and control implicit in the marital contract, of taking someone's hand in marriage, are initially demonstrated through the symbolism of the hand in the novel; like the artefacts of Tera's tomb, Margaret is something to be collected, owned and controlled by the masculine hand which is controlled by the sexual focus of the male gaze. Such attempts to own Margaret are swiftly challenged by Tera's own hand which haunts the text in an attempt to snatch Margaret back. Katherine Rowe argues that this invasion of the spectral hand in the Gothic presents 'a challenge [to] the concept of autonomous human agency' and symbolises the 'loss, theft or withering of the capacity to act with real personal or political affect' (1999: xi, 4); whereas the somatic, connected hand is culturally embedded with patriarchal ideological constructs of manual production, control and selfhood, the disembodied hand which pervades the genre violently dislocates and punctures these assumptions, rupturing the paternal order which seeks to rule Margaret through the institution of marriage, and succeeds in symbolically castrating Ross by denying him the opportunity to 'take' her hand. Thus, the maternal spectral hand as carrier of her gaze poses a threat to the ontological and phenomenological fabric of the Symbolic order; whereas the male architects of the Great Experiment are left helpless and unable to act, it is Tera who succeeds in snatching Margaret back into the maternal fold.

## From tomb to womb: The mummy returns

Margaret's traumatic entrance into the world correlates with the plundering of Tera's womb/tomb, a colonial rape which Tera avenges through the astral-murder of Trelawny's wife and the attack on Trelawny which opens the narrative, and eventually the murder of Margaret, in the 1903 ending. Tera's Egyptian tomb is repeatedly figured as an uncanny womby terrain inhospitable to patriarchy. The entrance to the tomb lies high up in a cliff face in the Valley of the Sorcerer, a 'narrow, deep valley' that 'showed a wide opening beyond the narrowing of the cliffs', covered in cabalistic signs including 'disjointed limbs and features, such as arms and legs, fingers, eyes noses ears and lips' (1996: 96–7), portents of castration against penetrating what lies within, which signal towards Tera's own disembodied and autonomous hand. Reached through the vaginal Valley of the Sorcerer, the tomb itself is comprised of a 'pit shaft' that must be descended to reach the inner chamber of the 'Mummy pit' where Tera's sarcophagus lies (1996: 116, 113), a chthonic grotto space which symbolically and etymologically implies the grotesque and 'cavernous anatomical female body' (Russo, 1995: 1). Mirroring the neck of the cervix as the entrance to the womb, and foreshadowing the secret and treacherous cavern beneath Trelawny's house in Cornwall where the Great Experiment takes place 'whose further end tapered away into blackness' (1996: 171), the treacherous maternal hinterland of the tomb is the devouring *vagina dentata,* which Trelawny and Corbeck fear (or fantasise as Freud would have it) would 'bury us there alive' (1996: 115).

The walls of the tomb/womb reveal that Tera was a formidable Queen who came to power after her father's death. Pictured wearing the White and Red crowns of Upper and Lower Egypt, which flouted gender codes and implied divinity and her resurrection 'for it was a rule, without exception in the records, that in ancient Egypt either crown was worn only by a king; though they are to be found on goddesses', Tera's history is written in terms of knowledge she possesses and that others desire. Tutored in magic 'she had won secrets in strange ways' and 'had power to compel the Gods' (1996: 111–2), a power which threatened the priesthood who subsequently tried to 'suppress her name', 'a terrible revenge ... for without a name no one can after death be introduced to the Gods, or have prayers said for him' (1996: 112), which is evidenced on the external cliff-face of the tomb in which the hostile priests had carved 'Hither the Gods come not at any summons. The "Nameless One" has insulted them and is forever alone. Go not nigh, lest their vengeance wither you away!' (1996: 107).

Tera is the Gothic unspeakable, a dangerous maternal body of knowledge which corresponds with Karen Macfarlane's contention that the mummy of *fin de siècle* fiction 'embodies fantasies of imperial immortality and anxieties about the extent of imperial control' and symbolises the conflict between 'the known and the unknowable' (2010: 4). Tera represents the desire to unearth female secrets, and so the colonial penetration of the tomb becomes an attempt to control the womb as the first body of knowledge the child experiences, establishing *Jewel* as a text which betrays the anxiety of a 'profoundly ignorant' patriarchal surveillance which fails to understand the depths of the archaic maternal body it once knew (1996: 145). As Trelawny attests, echoing Havelock Ellis:

> Men may find that what seemed like empiric deductions were in reality the results of a loftier intelligence and a learning greater than our own .... as yet we know nothing of what goes on to create or evoke the active spark of life. We have no knowledge of the methods of conception; of the laws which govern molecular or foetal growth, of the final influences which attend birth. (1996: 160)

Portending the climactic sublimity of the Great Experiment where the participants are blinded by the intra-uterine ambience of (re)birth, Trelawny explicitly links Tera's bodies of knowledge – what she knows and what she is – to the opacity of the womb and the unquantifiable and sublime machinations of the maternal body (Patricia Yaeger, 1993). Nodding towards Nathaniel Hawthorne's short story 'The Birthmark' (1843), in which a scientist experiments upon his wife to the point of her death in order to remove the tiny hand-shaped birthmark on her cheek, *Jewel* expresses masculine anxieties about the pursuit and possession of the female body of knowledge and reflects 19th-century medical concerns about the inability of the male gynaecological gaze to penetrate the womb. The anxiety about unknown maternal 'influences' over the foetus obsessively punctures the text through Margaret's birthmark, the scar of the womb's gaze which enacts a symbolic dismembering of her subjectivity and binds her back to the maternal body. Dismembering the child perversely functions to reconstruct it as part of the mother/child dyad, and this is what Margaret's birthmark, the shadow of Tera's disembodied hand, signals towards. Margaret is inextricably linked to Tera as the mother who precipitated her traumatic birth; she is both haunted by her mother(s) and a projection of her, as Trelawny 'could never forget that her birth had cost her mother's life' (1996: 117).

When Tera is unwrapped and revealed to be the mirror of Margaret the suspicion of their collusion is verified, and their 'dual existence' (1996: 186) confirmed. This phrase, borrowed from the frame narrative of J. Sheridan Le Fanu's vampire novella 'Carmilla' (1872) which describes Le Fanu's tale as involving 'some of the profoundest arcana of our dual existence and its intermediates' (1995: 207), and repeated several times throughout *Jewel*, expresses Ross and Trelawny's deepest fear for, and of, 'Margaret's strange condition': 'If it was indeed that she had in her own person a dual existence, what might happen when the two existences became one?' (1996: 186). The success of the Great Experiment in the original text answers this question: reintegration into the maternal dyad can only occur through the annihilation of the child's subjectivity, its existence.

Exploiting her unspeakable 'nameless' status which the priests hoped would quell her and adopting multiple identities Tera performs a strategy of parthenogenetic naming as hers and Margaret's oneness is galvanised through the matronymic reciprocity of their names, as Lisa Hopkins notes that 'the mirror-effect [of] "Tera" reverse[s] the latter half of *Margaret*' (1998: 136). Also a linguistic pun on 'terror' and 'terra', the Latin for Earth which grounds her in the mythology of the chthonic prehistoric maternal, Tera's and Margaret's names bind them together through a matrilineage of what Holly Tucker defines as 'onomastic marking' (2000: 38), an oral-linguistic maternal imprint which is manifested corporeally through Margaret's birthmark. While *Dracula*'s debt to Le Fanu requires little explication as Stoker carries on the intertextual weaving of the maternal vampire where 'Carmilla' left off, the similarities between *Jewel* and Le Fanu's tale are not so violently explicit but instead deeply embedded, making the (maternal) bond between the texts harder to tease out in the fabric of the Gothic. Like the story's relationship between vampire Carmilla and Laura, *Jewel* stages the reestablishment of the dyadic bond shared between the dead mother and the daughter she has lost to patriarchy, a subjectivity which absorbs the selfhood of the latter to the point that the two fold in and fall into one another. Like the linguistic cat's cradle of Tera's and Margaret's names echoing the uncanny repetition of Carmilla's reincarnations, this falling carries a sense of the maternal infinite which is acutely expressed through Tera's parthenogenetic ability to rebirth herself through resurrection; not only is her plundered tomb/womb the site of trauma which induces Margaret's birth, it is the place where she has lain – 'for these forty or fifty centuries she lay dormant in her tomb – waiting' (151) – gestating, waiting to give birth herself, *to herself*, through a union with the child which her gaze seeks through the metaphoric harbingers of the maternal.

The rape of Tera's tomb/womb is symbolised most intensely through the theft of her mummified hand which had protected the titular Jewel of Seven Stars. Her hand is an object of uncanny beauty for those who behold it, as Ross describes that 'in the embalming it had lost nothing of its beautiful shape', with skin 'of a rich creamy or old ivory colour; a dusky fair skin which suggested heat, but heat in the shadow' (1996: 81). The anatomical doubling of the seven fingers displayed by the hand, 'there being two middle and two index fingers' (1996: 81), should, but does not, warn its admirers of its uncanniness, and those who covet it inevitably meet a violent end at the spectral hand of the mother, whose clutches sear her mark into the skin of her victims' throats. Desired by 'covetous glances' (year: 100), Tera's hand is a colonial and sexual commodity stolen repeatedly throughout the novel. Its removal from her body replicates the trauma of separation during birth, and awakens Tera into vengeful desire for recompense in the form of Margaret, who bears the scar of her mother's wound, 'the shattered, bloodstained wrist' (1996: 204). Tera's hand invades the text through uncanny shadows and doublings; whilst reading van Huyn's original narrative of Tera's history which initially excited the colonial desire of Trelawny, Ross fancies 'I had seen across the pages streaks of the shade, which the weirdness of the subject had made to seem like the shadow of a hand' (1996: 102), a shadow then made flesh:

> There lay a real hand across the book! What was there to so overcome me; as was the case? I knew the hand that I saw on the book – and loved it. Margaret Trelawny's hand was a joy to me to see – to touch; and yet at that moment, coming after other marvellous things, it had a strangely moving effect on me. (1996: 103)

Ross is reticent to make this association between Margaret and Tera but the connection is sealed by the birthmark which is later revealed to him: 'On her wrist was a thin jagged red line, from which seemed to hang red stains like drops of blood!' (1996: 138).

Margaret's birthmark is doubly threatening, not only as a scar of the maternal gaze which inverts the logic of vision and pertains to Tera's ownership of her, but its shape and position forecast death, dismemberment and castration at the will of the vengeful mother. Tera's hand simultaneously taps into the theme of the spectral hand in the Gothic which Deborah Harter argues fractures the subjectivity of those who behold it as it forces 'a palpable confrontation with the human body itself' (1996: 27), and engages with the notion of the hand as the visual signifier of a portent, a belief upheld by the ancient Egyptian practice of chiromancy (palmistry).

The hand is a conduit for the malevolent maternal, as its mark, both that which it leaves on those who try to thwart her and the birthmark replicated on Margaret's wrist, is the imprint of the womb's gaze. In van Huyn's internal narrative which describes the dead Bedouin chief, one of whose men had taken Tera's hand during the plundering of her tomb, as 'staring horribly up at the sky, as though he saw there some dreadful vision' (year: 102). Murdered by Tera's disembodied hand, the chief is also left with the symbol of the womb's gaze burned into his skin, an imprint of her seven digits which functions as a (birth)mark of *repossession*, echoing Ellis's discussion of a case of maternal imprinting where 'a lady when pregnant was much interested in a story in which one of the characters had a supernumerary digit, and this often recurred in her mind. Her baby had a supernumerary digit on one hand' (1996: 220). Its ability to replicate itself upon other bodies makes Tera's hand multivalent and unconquerable, which is mirrored by the seven claws on Margaret's cat Silvio and the mummified cat's polydactyl paws, the 'hypnotic' quality of Margaret's own 'rare and beautiful' hand and the 'strange hand' in which she writes to Ross for help (1996: 103, 8, 7). Infecting the narrative through these acts of repetition, shadowing and doubling, modes of the uncanny which signal towards their maternal origins, Tera's hand re-members the maternal body and the first traumas of separation it represents.

Tera's final revenge is a visual one. In the 1903 ending, the group witnessing the resurrection of the queen show the recognition of their annihilation in their petrified faces, as Ross remembers that 'they had sunk down on the floor, and were gazing upward with fixed eyes of unspeakable terror', that 'Margaret had put her hands before her face, but the glassy stare of her eyes through her fingers was more terrible than an open glare' (1996: 211). This petrification is another mark of the maternal gaze, and here 'terror' and 'terrible' are pregnant with meaning; implicitly calling to Tera, it also recalls Burke's understanding of terror, that 'no passion so effectively robs the mind of all its powers of acting and reason as fear', that 'whatever therefore is terrible, with regard to sight, is sublime too' (1998: 53). Observed by the 'fixed eyes' and 'glassy stare' of her victims, like Medusa the vision of Tera, in both senses, inverts the gendered conventions of the masculine sublime and enthrals her victims' gaze, rendering them helpless to the fatal effects of her sublime maternal body.

With the completion of desire must come the end of existence in the paternal order upon which desire is founded, and Ross is the only survivor of the experiment in the original ending because his vision is mistaken when he believes he sees Margaret's white gown in the gloom of the cavern; to realise it was Tera would have been fatal. He sustains the pretence of lack while the others fall inexorably back into the maternal abyss, and he continues to generate this lack through his account of the event, as like the priests threatened by her power, he attempts to write Tera the Nameless One out of the narrative by not speaking her name. However, his Gothic phrasing of a *'terror* which has no name' and 'unspeakable *terror*' implicitly invokes the maternal which reaffirms her victorious position at the end of the text, and exposes the inability of the Symbolic to quantify and control the maternal through the structures and strictures of language. Tera exploits her nameless state to haunt the end of the text as a sublime being whose gaze has petrified her victims into objects to be fetishised, yet resists objectification herself.

## Pussycat, Pussycat

As we will also see 'The Squaw', in *Jewel* Stoker employs the trope of the cat as familiar to the maternal gaze through its symbolic associations with the mother's genitalia and the *vagina dentata*. Tera infiltrates the Trelawny household through two felines, her own mummified pet, 'an appeal to Bast' the Egyptian cat goddess which Trelawny foolishly keeps in his bedroom and which attacks him in his sleep, and Silvio, Margaret's cat who is linked to Tera through his polydactylism, as his seven claws, 'like razors!' on each paw, mirror her supernumerary digits (1996: 26, 90). The mummy cat with its impenetrable 'obsidian eyes' becomes the conduit for Tera's astral body and uses the 'fierce force of her familiar' (1996: 28, 152) to harm those who thwart her possession of both the Jewel and Margaret. This is demonstrated by the cuts on Ross' wrist, 'the same wound as Father's!' (1996: 45), again thought to be inflicted by Silvio during a shadowy tussle in which Margaret resists something unseen, which clearly has its sights set on her:

> [She], too, had stood up and was looking behind her, as though there were something close to her. Her eyes were wild, and her breast rose and fell as though she were fighting for air. When I touched her she did not seem to feel me; she worked her hands in front of her, as though she were fending off something. (1996: 44)

This tension of in/visibility is crucial to Tera's mobilisation in the novel, as it is her ability to see without being seen, via the medium of her familiar, which gives her maternal gaze power. Her astral and animal gaze 'mocks the very limits of the physical body' (54), manifesting a familiar presence (in both senses) which ensures that it is not she who is the spectacle but Margaret, her chosen object of desire, and Margaret's own vision is infected by Tera as Ross describes her as feline; her 'great, beautiful black eyes' (64) share a darkness with the mummy cat's and transform from being 'raised' to her male companions in a docile and submissive manner (1996: 11, 20) to becoming indecipherable as she is re-possessed by the maternal gaze: 'There was something in her voice so strange to me that I looked quickly into her eyes. They were bright as ever, but veiled to my seeing the inward thought behind them as are the eyes of a caged lion' (1996: 186).

Like the teeth of *Dracula*'s vamps, and as I discuss below those of the Iron Virgin in 'The Squaw', Stoker's obsession with the *vagina dentata* erupts into his narratives again, as the mark of the mummy-cat, like the imprinting of Tera's hand onto the Bedouin chief's neck and Margaret's wrist, inflicts a bloody memento of the victim's origins onto their own body. This mark of the cat weaves the image of the cat as manifestation of the female/maternal spectre who bites, wounds and marks the subject into their narratives. Tera's aggressive Egyptian feline is also later invoked in Sax Rohmer's *The Green Eyes of Bast* (1920), where the villainess Nahémah, described as a feline 'psycho-hybrid', is born after an evil spirit in cat form terrorises her mother, who imprints the trauma onto her unborn baby (1920: 274).

By its crudest interpretation, Stoker's obsessively codified tangle of cats, wounds, claws, jaws and teeth immediately symbolises the castrating power of the maternal body, but moving beyond this Freudian reading I contend that these images function as meta-symbols which hark back to the violence of being wrenched from the mother's body, a violence which awakens the womb's gaze in search of the child. Repeatedly woven into the Gothic, this symbology of castration veils a deeper, primal terror which remembers the trauma of separation and renders it a violent act, which in the original edition of *Jewel* is mirrored, that is, both replicated and inverted, by the Great Experiment and Tera's repossession of Margaret. While the text attempts to objectify Tera through the voyeuristic scenes of unwrapping, she takes the action in hand and manipulates it into a narrative of maternal violence. Luna contends 'the child will mutilate the mother to annihilate his own origin, to destroy the very link that binds them together' (102), and so Tera's disembodied hand points towards the trauma of severance, and equally that of absorption.

Stoker's repetition of these themes signifies a failed attempt to understand, control and disavow this trauma, as he never quite makes the final cut and these symbols uncannily resurface throughout his work. Hopkins comments on the formidable presence of Stoker's mother Charlotte, who would recount to her young invalided son gruesome tales about her childhood during the cholera epidemic in Sligo, including a familiar incident of dismembering where 'on one of the last, desperate days, [she] saw a hand reaching through the skylight [and] seizing an axe, she cut it off with one tremendous blow' (2007: 23). Catherine Wynne also notes that 'Stoker's Gothic imagination is generally attributed to his mother's story-telling' (2009: 50), and cementing the association he dedicated *The Watter's Mou'* (1895), a smuggling narrative which writes the amniotic seascape as the treacherous and devouring *vagina dentata*, to 'my Dear Mother, in her loneliness' (2009: 50). Like his fictional mummy, Charlotte Stoker is bound up in the knotted web of castration, fragmentation, violence and trauma that the disembodied hand carrying the gaze symbolises in the Gothic, a web her stories helped to spin, one in which she trapped her son into repeating.

### 'Her eyes look like positive murder': 'The Squaw'

Stoker's fiction betrays how he was haunted by his mummies, and 'The Squaw' is a typically lurid example of his writing, an unseasonal story of a disastrous honeymoon published in the 1893 issue of *Holly Leaves*, the Christmas edition of the *Illustrated Sporting and Dramatic News*. 'The Squaw' repeats the Gothic scenario of the return of the vengeful maternal gaze through the vessel of a cat, the birthmark and the maternal womb/tomb, this time in the form of the Iron Virgin, and Andrew Maunder uses Jane Gallop's (de)coding of the cat as symbolic of the vagina (1982) to argue that Stoker's wronged (pussy)cat with 'white, sharp teeth', mirroring those of Dracula's Weird sisters, that 'shine[d] through the blood which dabbled her mouth and whiskers' (1975: 53), embodies the 'coded language of the feline' which simultaneously implies the devouring *vagina dentata*, 'the vagina that kills', and disavows it as too vulgar and dangerous to be named outright within the context of a middle-class publication (Maunder, 2006: 130).

The story begins with a 'quarrelling' couple honeymooning in Nuremberg, who in the second week 'naturally wanted someone else to join [their] party' (1975: 51, 50), and so befriend the brash American Elias P. Hutcheson, hailing from 'Bleeding Gulch', Nebraska (50), the portentous motherland to which he will soon return. Hutcheson accidentally kills a kitten in an attempt to impress the couple, and it is the revenge of the kitten's mother that returns Hutcheson to the Bleeding

Gulch as the cat (implausibly) traps him inside an Iron Virgin. The cat is described as having 'eyes like green fire' that 'look like positive murder' (1975: 53, 55).

The unnamed husband's narrative in 'The Squaw' is densely populated by the womb in the form of the cat and the Iron Virgin. Furthermore after Hutcheson kills the kitten he tells the couple a story of how a Native American woman's baby had been executed, an act which she revenged by brutally killing her baby's slayer. Here Stoker returns to the colonist-as-rapist motif he explored in *Jewel* where the penetrated body of the mother/land is avenged through acts of maternal violence, and the racial frontiers of North America's colonisation becomes the backdrop for the controlling of the maternal body and its offspring. This subject of the colonial rape of virgin territory which Stoker revisited in *Jewel* feminises the geographical body of land invaded and oppressed by the male explorer and compounds the sense of maternal revenge which pervades the text; as Hutcheson, like van Huyn, Trelawny and Corbeck, represents the 'colonist-as-rapist' (Maunder, 2006: 129), so his punishment must reflect this sexual violence. In this sense, his symbolic, and most likely physical, castration is entirely appropriate.

The Iron Virgin in which Hutcheson meets his death is a femininely figured carnivorous torture device which devours and blinds – castrates – her victims:

> It was a crudely-shaped figure of a woman, something of a bell order, or to make a closer comparison, of the figure of Mrs. Noah in the children's Ark, but with the slimness of waist and perfect *rondeur* of hip .... It was only, however, when we came to look at the inside of the door that the diabolical intention was manifest to the full. Here were several long spikes, square and massive, broad at the base and sharp at the points, placed in such a position that when the door should close the upper ones would pierce the eyes of the victim, and the lower ones his heart and vitals. (1975: 59, 60)

The penetrating and orally aggressive Iron Virgin embodies the ambivalence of the sacred paradox of being simultaneously virginal and maternal, and Stoker's reference draws on a heritage of female violence and cruelty towards children, as the contraption was employed by the Hungarian 'blood countess' Erzsébet Báthory (1560–1614), who was tried and executed for the brutal deaths of 80 young girls she purportedly tortured for the rejuvenating property of their virgin blood (many sources claim she killed over 600 (see Raymond McNally, 1983). It is likely that Stoker would have been aware of Báthory's exploits from Reverend Sabine Baring-Gould's *The Book of Werewolves* (1865), which he read for his research for *Dracula* (Eighteen-Bisang and Miller, 2008: 129). Baring-Gould documented how 'when she was ill, and could not indulge her cruelty, she bit a person who came near her sick bed as though she were a wild beast' (2007: 141), and this vampiric behaviour, reminiscent of the Bloofer Lady, is also evoked in 'The Squaw' through the figure of the Iron Virgin.

Stoker explicitly codifies the Iron Virgin as vampiric and maternal; an oversized, monstrous, *vagina dentata*, the shape – the 'perfect *rondeur* of hip' – evokes the female body as inherently, expectantly, maternal, and draws associations with the wife Amelia who we learn has conceived on the honeymoon, while its name, evocative of the Virgin Mary, carries the possibility of conceiving without physical penetration. Stoker's reference to Noah's wife is also significant as it rewrites the biblical emphasis on patrilineage and 'the generations of Noah' (Genesis, 5: 32, 6: 9), and forges a place for her maternal agency. That the shapely Mrs Noah is mentioned in the same breath as the devouring spikes of the Iron Virgin cements the archetypal maternal as innately vicious through the invocation of previously innocuous and sacred figures of Noah's wife and the Virgin Mary, the ultimate yet impossible state of motherhood, 'the standard no woman can live up to but to whom Victorian women ... were compared' (McKnight, 1996: 14).

The spikes of the Iron Virgin which invoke the glistening teeth of the cat and the *vagina dentata*, foreshadows the 'jaws of hell' and the 'jaws of his death-trap' Stoker later writes into *Dracula* (1996: 314, 355) and dismembers the victim's body. Like a Venus Flytrap the Iron Virgin lures its prey in, and the irrepressible, fatal, desire felt on the part of the child to return to the *jouissance* of the womb is demonstrated by Hutcheson, who with idiotic bravado insists that he must experience the terror of the deathly contraption: 'Now, Judge, you jest begin to let this door down, slow, on me. I want to feel the same pleasure as the other jays had when those spikes began to move toward their eyes!' (1996: 63). Like Tera's wrapped form the shape of the Iron Virgin titillates the male spectator, and what is intriguing is Hutcheson's happiness at the prospect of (re)entrance into the maternal space, as his 'face was positively radiant as his eyes followed the movement of the spikes' and he insists 'don't you rush this business! I want a show for my money this game – I du!' (1975: 63–64). Here, recalling the blindness-as-castration myths of Oedipus and Medusa, the dynamics of the maternal gaze are played out through a torture which renders the victim/child blind and thus implicitly empowers the sight of the mother as a destructive and devouring force.

Hutcheson's return to the womb is a final and bloody one; the vengeful mother-cat reappears and blinds the operator of the Iron Virgin with her claws, causing him to let go of the (umbilical) cord which holds the door open and trap Hutcheson inside its jaws:

> And then the spikes did their work ... they had pierced so deep that they had locked in the bones of the skull through which they had crushed, and actually tore him – it – out of his prison till, bound as he was, he fell at full length with a sickly thud upon the floor, the face turning upward as he fell .... the custodian [was] moaning in pain whilst he held his reddening handkerchief to his eyes. And sitting on the head of the poor American was the cat, purring loudly as she licked the blood which trickled through the gashed sockets of his eyes. (1975: 65–6)

The maternal gaze in this horrific scene is foreshadowed by the interplay of vision observed by the narrator between his wife and the cat which immediately precedes Hutcheson's death. It is the pregnant Amelia who observes the animal first, as her husband notes:

> When I looked at her again [I] found that her eye had become fixed on the side of the Virgin. Following this direction I saw the black cat crouching out of sight. Her green eyes shone like danger lamps in the gloom of the place, and their colour was heightened by the blood which still smeared her coat and reddened her mouth. (1975: 64)

Invoking the rage of the squaw, the cat covered in the war paint of her kitten's blood is the essence of the orally aggressive *vagina dentata*, an image that portends the feasting on Hutcheson's blood at the close of the narrative. What is telling is the confluence of maternal gazes at play as the pregnant Amelia, who like the cat has fiery green eyes, is the first to notice the beast yet does not alert her companions, and it is her husband who cries 'the cat! Look out for the cat!' (1975: 64). Embedded within Amelia's silence is a complicity in the horrific violence of the vengeful pussycat, and her predecessor the squaw, enacted against the men who have wrenched their children away from their hold.

This maternal spectacle proved 'too much for poor Amelia', who faints and has to be removed from the torture chamber (1975: 60). Yet, beneath her delicate disposition lurks a similarly vengeful womb, which imprints upon her unborn baby the sign of the Iron Virgin that forever indebts the child to the mother: 'That she felt it to the quick was afterwards shown by the fact that my eldest son bears to this day a rude birthmark on his breast, which has, by family consent, been accepted as representing the Nurnberg Virgin' (1975: 61). Having sat accidentally on a 'torture chair' 'full of spikes which gave instant and excruciating pain' (1975: 59), Amelia is impregnated by the *vagina dentata*, eschewing the phallus of the paternal order and mimicking the parthenogenetic virgin womb which portends annihilation for the patriarchal order. Stoker's implication is clear; even the bodies of the most submissive women can mutate into vicious monsters if that which they treasure the most, the child and the narcissism it gives them, is taken away, and 'The Squaw' pathologises a biological inevitability of maternal monstrosity:

> Under the guise of portraying [her] as a sensitive and impressionable woman shocked 'to the quick' by the Virgin's inner spikes, [Stoker] suggests that [Amelia's] womb, like that of the Iron Virgin, is hostile to patriarchy – lined with teeth that leave their mark on the chest of her eldest son. (Nayder, 1997: 90)

Hutcheson's delight in entering the womb of the Iron Virgin, being suspended on the precipice of maternal abyss in an attempt to conquer/colonise it and experience it as safe and pleasurable, is soon thwarted. As the castrating jaws of the Iron Virgin snap shut under the force of the vengeful pussycat, the trauma of the death drive is realised as a spectacle which others are helpless but to witness. Consequently, what is expressed in 'The Squaw' and the original ending of *The Jewel of Seven Stars* is the notion of both characters and readers bearing witness to the effects of the devouring mother; through the narration of the survivors the climactic scenes in these texts reveal the fatal effects of the wombed-in existence upon the bodies of Hutcheson and the participants of the Great Experiment.

For the child marked by the womb, whether during pregnancy, its evacuation/escape or (re)entry, can never fully attain subjectivity, as the skin which designates bodily integrity has been indelibly inscribed with the mark of the mother. The birthmark is the focus of trauma enacted against the child's body by the maternal gaze, the evidence of the womb's attempts to keep the child inside. 'Evocation of the maternal body and childbirth induces the image of birth as a violent act of expulsion through which the nascent body tears itself away from the matter of maternal insides', Kristeva argues; 'now, the skin apparently never ceases to bear the traces of such matter' (1982: 101). The marked child occupies an ambivalent position in the Symbolic; it has managed to negotiate its way in but now, bearing the scar of the mother, it cannot be accepted because its birthmark 'points to the imperfection of the bodily surface and the opening of the maternal body during childbirth' (Creed, 1993: 70–1). The maternal imprint is the mark of ownership of the child.

## 9

# 'Empire of the Air': Ireland, Aerial Warfare and Futurist Gothic

Luke Gibbons

> First – oh! it's an old story now – there was those Wright Brothers out in America. They glided – they glided miles and miles. Finally they glided off stage. Why, it must be nineteen hundred and four, or five, *they* vanished! Then there was those people in Ireland – no, I forget their names. Everybody said they could fly. *They* went. They ain't dead that I've heard tell of; but you can't say they're alive. Not a feather of them do you see.
>
> H.G. Wells, *The War in the Air* (1908)[1]

At a critical point in the protracted Anglo–Irish Treaty debates in late 1921, Lloyd George threatened 'immediate and terrible war' within three days, should talks break down irretrievably between the negotiating parties.[2] That the threat of force lay behind the constitutional 'peace by ordeal' was never in doubt, but what exactly was meant by terrible and immediate war seems less clear. One likelihood is that it would have involved what was then the ultimate military weapon: aerial warfare, including the lethal use of aerial bombing to subdue enemy populations. British reluctance to use this last option in Ireland was motivated by many considerations but one underlying issue was that by winning the military battle, it might risk losing the rhetorical war. As Stephen Howe observes, aerial bombing of the new strategic kind was deployed to put down colonial revolts, as in the unmitigated terror used to quell 'tribal' insurgency in Iraq and elsewhere (2001: 230). To subject the 'white' population of Ireland to such treatment would have exposed the pretence that Ireland was an integral part of the Union, aligning it instead with subdued colonial peoples throughout the empire. But that is not to say aerial warfare was dismissed out of hand, or was not given serious consideration. In 1918, a cartoon protesting the possible introduction of conscription in Ireland, 'The First Irish Conscript', showed the roped captive being frog-matched under military escort, tanks pointed in his direction and, above all, a squadron of British aeroplanes overhead. The RAF initially stationed two squadrons in Ireland, 'to fly low over small villages and inspire considerable fear among the ignorant peasantry' (Morrow, 2013: 47). The power to instill 'fear' recurs in reports, as if aerial warfare was to become the new technological Gothic. On his appointment as military Commander in Chief in Ireland in 1918, Lord French advocated the imposition of martial law and the establishment of 'strongly entrenched "Air-Camps"' in the centre of each province in Ireland, doubling the number of squadrons. The range of distances involved would have allowed aircraft, in his words, 'to play about with either bombs or machine guns': in this real-life Gothic, either course of action 'ought to put the fear of God into these playful young Sinn Feiners' (Townshend, 2013: 11). Winston Churchill was of a like mind, stressing the value not only of intimidating but also of targeting insurgents from the air: 'I see no objection from a military point of view ... to aeroplanes being despatched with definite order in each particular case to disperse them by machine-gun fire or bombs, using of course no more force than is necessary to scatter and stampede them' (Qtd. in Ring, 1996: 223). Proposals of aerial bombing and machine-gunning were taken up again by General Macready in 1920 and were warmly received by the War Cabinet but were eventually challenged on tactical grounds by the Chief of Air Staff, Sir Hugh Trenchard, who had formerly flown in the RAF with Erskine Childers, now a leading figure in the Irish Republican movement (Townshend, 2013: 153–4). Nevertheless, as John L. Morrow notes, the lessons of airpower had been learned: 'Events in Ireland, Africa, and the Middle East demonstrated that the war had perfected the air weapon sufficiently to enable the realization of pre-war visions of imperial domination through aviation' (2013: 47).

What were these pre-war visions? In his history of early aerial warfare, Lee Kennett notes that on account of the uniqueness of this uncharted area of combat, 'there was very little realistic conception of how airpower might be used – what air forces like to call doctrine .... And if the airmen themselves could not read into the future, generals on the ground could scarcely be expected to' (Kennett, 1991: 21–2). But in fact there were people reading – and writing – into the future of aerial combat, in the genres of science fiction, adventure stories and imperial romance. Jules Verne was the most widely read of these utopian (or dystopian) writers, followed closely by H. G. Wells, and in 1908 the publication of Wells' *War in the Air* (as we shall see below) brought home the prospect of a new menace from the sky with an ominous immediacy. The Anglo-Irish inventor (and future philosopher of time) Lieutenant John William Dunne, a friend of H. G. Wells, was one of those who took fictional genres to heart and sought to implement them in practice, his 'tailless' flying machine taking off (but sadly not for too long) under the watch of the British military in 1907. In its successive variants, however, it attracted the attention of Orville Wright and within five years was capable of crossing the channel to France.[3] Dunne's tailless machine had already been anticipated in the pages of science fiction by another Irish visionary, the medical physician and Home Rule candidate, Tom Greer, whose *A Modern Daedalus* (1885) may also have foreshadowed the imaginative flights of another Dedalus a few decades later.[4]

Greer's novel is unusual in that it is an *anti*-imperial romance, an alternative vision of the Land Question and Home Rule politics in which the Irish possession of airpower overwhelms British military rule in Ireland, destroys Dublin Castle and breaks the grip of the Unionist stronghold on Belfast, all of which eclipses Home Rule and culminates in an Irish Republic. The first person narrator of the novel, John (Jack) O'Halloran, grows up on a farm on the north-west coast of Donegal, determined the master the mystery of flight and become the first human to perfect (or to become) a flying machine. Receiving a university education (denied to his siblings) at Trinity College, he eschews a career in the professions to pursue his single-minded obsession, and eventually builds the wings that carry him into the air. Though insistent at the outset that his invention is solely for the good of humanity, a birds-eye flight over the Donegal countryside awakens him to the full extent of the desolation and ruin wrought by the strong-arm tactics of Landlordism and the 'Crowbar-brigade'. But he also witnesses something he does not expect: the shooting of a notorious landlord's agent on his way to an eviction by a long-range rifle used by a hidden sniper, but who is not, of course, hidden from the all-seeing eye of the aviator. On returning to his family home, he notices one of his brothers is missing, and at this point realizes the full extent of his family's involvement in the agrarian fight for freedom. At first (given his well-meaning humanism), he refuses to take sides and absconds to London, giving a demonstration of his flying prowess that brings the city – and parliament – to a standstill. While the new marvel causes a sensation in the popular press, the political reaction is different as the Tory government responds solely in terms of national security, outlining the damage to railway and shipping interests, and other forms of 'Jingoism' (to use the narrator's term, motivated by disgust at the repudiation of his invention). Jack's disappointment soon turns to hostility when he realizes the Government has placed him under house arrest, and has begun to suppress Parnell's Irish Parliamentary Party, on the grounds (later to take effect in real-life in the Pigott forgery trial) that Parnell is a secret supporter of terrorism (though no aerial terror has yet manifested itself in the novel). Jack's escape is effected when his brother (the sharp-shooter who assassinated the Landlord's agent earlier) manages to smuggle a set of his wings to him, and Jack heads back to Ireland to lead a rebellion in concert with his brothers against colonial rule, spearheaded by the lethal use of his invention.

The possession of airpower at this early stage is considered to render an army invincible, even if it takes the rather makeshift form of wings that can be neatly folded and carried in a holdall without attracting any attention. The ease of mastering the technology is compared to learning to ride a bicycle (*Modern Daedalus*, 1975: xiv), and it is this control of the machine, which facilitates its pinpoint accuracy in dropping bombs (the cover of the first publication of the novel shows the hero carrying three such bombs strapped to his waist in mid-flight). In addition, the relative invisibility and impunity from gunfire on the ground adds a major element of surprise, increasing the vulnerability of enemy targets. Following the destruction of Dublin Castle at night, Jack (incognito) inspects the ruins and then visits Adelaide hospital reflecting ruefully on the destruction he has wrought, at which point he is addressed by one of the wounded soldiers describing the conflagration in the Castle:

> After the first shell burst', said he, 'it was simply like hell. There was such a lot of dust and smoke that everyone was blinded by it. We couldn't tell where it was coming from. We couldn't see anything, or tell where to turn to, or what to do. If there has been an enemy before us we would have charted through it all and thought nothing of it; but you might as well have tried to fight an earthquake.
> (*Modern Daedalus*, 1975: 223)

It is clear from this that the ground rules of war, and notions of a fair fight, courage, etc, have been altered fundamentally, as was later to transpire on a massive scale in the Great War.

The element of surprise as a weapon of the weak does not derive solely from the air: it derives, in the novel, from the stealth of the 'dynamite war' instigated by the Fenians in London but also, as noted above, from the subterfuge of guerilla warfare in the Irish countryside.⁵ The latter is facilitated in the novel by the more immediately available technology of the long-range rifle, used to deadly effect by Boer marksmen at the Battle of Majuba in 1881, in which a carefully planned attack overwhelmed British forces in a stunning Boer victory. The lesson of Majuba recurs in the novel, but one of the ironies here is that the very invisibility of guerilla warfare at ground level is jeopardized precisely by aerial reconnaissance of the kind, which alerts Jack to his brother's accuracy as a sniper at the outset. Surveillance was the main purpose for which aircraft were deployed during the Irish War of Independence, General Macready noting that the lack of anti-aircraft defences (unlike in France during the Great War) meant that planes could fly much lower, thus aiding target identification. But as noted earlier, The Chief of Air Staff, Sir Hugh Trenchard, warned against the deployment of aerial fire in Irish conditions, for the difference between combatants and civilians 'would not be obvious to a man in aeroplane', and would further alienate the public. The inaccuracy in dropping objects, even notices, would lead to 'a great popular outcry' and 'great bitterness will be engendered' (Townshend, 2013: 153–4).

According to Karl Marx, one of the welcome consequences of attaining Irish independence through revolution would be to spark off a socialist revolution in Britain, and this duly follows in *A Modern Daedalus*. The ruling classes – or, more accurately, the leisured classes – are alarmed into reconvening parliament, 'flocking in from the moors of Scotland, from the salmon streams of Norway, from yachting tours in the Mediterranean, from pic-nics on the Nile and shooting parties in the Rocky mountains' (*Modern Daedalus*, 1975: 249). The legislators were now target practice themselves in a world turned upside down, a shift in narrative voice both mimicking their outrage and ventriloquizing anti-colonial sentiment:

> In short, the Radical and Republican prints, which advocated such Utopian and Socialistic (and therefore wicked) dreams as universal peace and co-operation among working-men of all countries, irrespective of the Imperial schemes of sovereigns and statesmen, were found to be unexpectedly and disgustingly popular among the masses. Public opinion had undergone one of those revolutions to which it is so subject in England, having been helped to it by the discovery that the Irish for once had shown themselves able to fight, and proved their fitness for self-government by successfully kicking their would-be governors out of the country. (251)

The end of empire is also nigh: 'Are there ten thousand picked troops to be spared from holding down India and Egypt, watching Russia, and reconquering the Soudan, not to speak of another illustrious general and two more scions of royalty?' (251). While this may have seemed like utopian thinking in the 1880s, the perception that air power spelt the end of the central role of naval supremacy in international relations was to prove true. Brittannia might rule the waves, but it would no longer to rule the world, and it was with this in mind that another Irishman, Gerald Pierce de Lacy, from Forras (sic), County Westmeath, takes to the air in Luke Netterville's (aka Standish O'Grady) imperial romance, *The Queen of the World, or, Under the Tyranny* (1900).[6] This time, the aim is not to challenge but to save the British Empire from another menace, the Yellow Peril looming large in the East with the resurgence of Chinese civilization.

If the underground Fenian movement formed the subversive threat to Empire allegorized in Greer's republican fantasy, the rebellion launched in 1899–1900 by the martial arts inspired 'Boxer' secret society in China provided a backdrop to the futuristic World War imagined in *The Queen of the World*.[7] In its reputation for supplying the Chinese military and navy with its best recruits, but also with its equal notoriety for banditry and rebellion, the Shandong region that gave rise to the Boxers has affinities with Ireland's fractious relationship to the metropolitan centre (Esherick, 1987: 45). The Boxers' dedication to martial prowess was also invested with supernatural beliefs, not least in the ability to fly, and this is anticipated in the paranoid imagery of Chinese aerial 'dragons' ruling the world that informs the novel (Purcell, 2010: 238). British leadership of the eight-national alliance that eventually cut down the rebellion took control of Peking in August 1900, and this also has its parallels in the novel, in which an English alliance of European, African, and American powers eventually overthrows the tyranny of Chinese rule.

In *The Queen of the World*, the Irish adventurer, de Lacy, is transported 300 years into the future to the year 2176, in which he encounters a Mongolian world tyranny based on airpower, giant mechanical 'creatures' whose folding wings magnify Jack O'Halloran's portable version on a stupendous or 'sublime' (a favourite word in the novel) scale. Following his initial capture in South America, de Lacy prepares to meet his fate until 'a dark eyed- daughter of Erin,' the pride of the local tyrant's harem, intercedes for him on account of his national identity: '[I] often blessed that love of country which is such a characteristic of the far-wandering children of Erin' (*Queen of the* World, 1900: 77).

It turns out that much of the wandering of the Irish has been in the service of the British Empire rather than the Irish cause:

> The Irish having long taken a leading part in the vast expansion of the Iberno-English Empire felt acutest shame at the condition of subjection and slavery to which the whole race was reduced. They forced the rebellion and, when it was suppressed, were all but annihilated, The famous commander, Zerketch, son of Sarkhoff, with twenty ships sailed round and over Ireland raining fire .... Now, when the subject nations murmur about oppressive taxation and the Tyranny of the Imperial officers, the significant answer is ever, 'Remember Ireland.' (*Queen of the World*: 118)

The historical lesson to be learned from the Irish rebellion is indeed 'croppies lie down' all over the world, and – except, of course, for 'the dark eyes and very luxuriant hair' (*Queen of the World*, 91) of the daughter of Erin who saves de Lacy early in the novel. Intrigued as to the source of fuel of these airships, de Lacy discovers that they are not run by horse-power but more elusive reserves of *will*-power – a spiritual *vril-power* that infuses the sinews of empire and its weapons of mass destruction. The discovery of Vril is generously attributed to Lord Lytton in his *The Coming Race* (1871), and its 'motive-power' in driving both air and sea vessels exhilarates de Lacy:

> A light dawned upon me. The source of this power was metaphysical and spiritual, perhaps occult and magical in its character. The driving force of these swift and mighty cruisers of the deep was but a more perfect manifestation of subtle intellectual human power which was beginning to be recognized by a few in my own time. (*Queen of the World*: 190)

In keeping with its creative potential in human beings, the energy is appropriately transferred to air-borne vehicles through playing on the keyboard of a kind of piano. As de Lacy describes his friend's Elliot's 'filling' a machine at a Vril station:

> Elliot now stepped briskly to that little transparent chamber, and sat before a mahogany board, resembling a very small piano, but with keys variously coloured. On them he began to play with both hands exactly like a pianist. At the first touch our bird-like craft sprang from its berth as if powerful springs attached to her bottom and serving the same uses as the legs of a bird had suddenly been brought into

action. The little craft started some yards into the air. Simultaneously the wings, expanding gently, winnowed the air, edging themselves as they rose, and broadening out as they struck. Attaining a certain elevation, this bird-like being – Elliot still manipulating the little piano in front of him – curved round gracefully until her head was directed towards that parent craft, and presently was flying with a steady and very gentle motion above the numerous air-ships with which the piazza was thronged. (*Queen of the World*: 83–4)

The divination of 'will-power' does in fact point to some of the well-springs of imperial ideology. Physiognomy abounds in the racial pathologies that inform perceptions of character in the novel, the key consideration here that lesser or inferior types live only at a surface level, with little or no interior life, or psychological depth pulling against outer appearance. At one point, de Lacy suspects a spy amongst the crew of the airship on with he travels with his guard (but who has now become his friend) Elliot:

> While I moved to and fro I studied attentively the faces of the crew. Was it possible to discover the spy by any outward signs and tokens? Many of the crew were pure Caucasians; some showed traces of Semitic origin, some of Mongolian. There were three men who might have been Hindus, brown-complexioned with regular features, and five magnificent Africans of those noble Arabianized types which flourish on the east coast of the Dark Continent. Under the strong and comprehensive grasp of the great Tyranny, or owing to events and developments of which I knew nothing, race prejudices seemed to have disappeared. (*Queen of the World*: 101)

Racial types have certainly not disappeared, however, and one of the attributes of the 'Britannic' race is that though defeated by the Chinese at the Battle of Cacatanga, they did not accept their fate. Though dominated, they never became slavish: 'To be a slave is not so terrible, but to be willing slaves – no more, no more' (*Queen of the World*: 37). Britain's decline as a world power is, in fact, due to a fatal flaw in its character that emerged in the 19th century, leading to Napoleon's dismissive epithet of a military people becoming little more than a nation of shopkeepers. 'How did it happen' that the British became subject to a race of 'slant-eyed Celestials'?

> How did the glorious race from which I sprang, and which in my time, though in its infancy, promised so fair, sink so low? A thought flashed through my mind. I recalled the England of my experience,

the feverish greed of money, the sordid aims, the general low level of thought. Was this the punishment of that? Had the English race been doomed to pursue material wealth for ever, and therefore to fall under the yoke of people with higher ideals and thoughts not quite so grovelling? (*Queen of the World*: 90)

Hence the English (or perhaps Irish) precursor of the nation of 'Paudeens' 'fumbling in the greasy till' that O'Grady's friend W. B. Yeats feared would materialize in Ireland at the turn of the 20th century.[8]

The British no longer enjoyed world domination, but one scion of the ancient race, the appropriately named King Alfred, escaped from the overwhelming defeat and retreated to a secret lair in the Antarctic, biding his moment for a counter-revolution:

> He was, so I have heard, a youth of very quiet, unpronounced manner and bearing, whom a careless observer might not much regard. He was neither tall nor handsome, but his forehead was broad, compact, and intelligent, and his eyes like coals of fire. One who knew him, told me, that under a plain exterior he possessed qualities of a heroic character, infinite audacity, unsubduable purpose and a strength of will by which he could mould the minds of men as he pleased. (*Queen of the World*: 127-8)

The love interest in the novel derives from de Lacy's being smitten with the beautiful Leonore who comes to his aid when he is first captured in the Andes on being transported into the future. Leonore, it duly turns out, is King Alfred's missing daughter, and the scene is set for de Lacy's uniting all the lost causes to overthrow the Mongol tyranny. Central to this is his guard Elliott, whose British father went over to the Oriental cause and who is charged with dispatching de Lacy, as a prisoner, to an unknown destination in his flying fortress. With his eye for seeing beyond facial appearances, de Lacy discerns that Elliott is still a free-born Englishman and paying only lip-service to his masters: in this Elliot follows his father who, having second thoughts over his own defection, instills doubts in his son's loyalty. For this reason, Elliot is under surveillance by a spy on board, and a mysterious letter bequeathed by Elliot's father on condition that he not open it until his 23rd birthday (which is about to fall), finally seals his fate. As de Lacy soars through the clouds, ostensibly a prisoner, he ruminates:

> My new friend [Elliot] was not at heart devoted to the Tyranny. So much was plain. I entertained, too, a hope that the sealed document

which he bore on his person, would contain a specific command from his father to shun utterly all associations with the Tyranny. If that should turn out to be so, he would certainly carry over himself and his ship, which was his own, into the service of the man who alone [i.e. the outlaw King Alfred] on the Earth openly defied, resisted, and waged war upon the Tyranny. In such an event I would escape the death by torture which I perceived would certainly befall me when brought before the Imperial Criminal Court, unable as I was to furnish an even plausible account of my antecedents. (*Queen of the World*: 100)

Though *The Queen of the World* is an absurd and risible confection even by the standards of the day, the emphasis on 'will-power' suggests that where there is a will, there is a way to offset the dangers not only of slavish submission, but also the Gothic fear induced by the terror of despotic rule. O'Grady makes no secret of his dislike for democracy, and his preference for the kind of aristocratic leadership and chivalry designed to keep ungentleman-like Absolutism at bay. Codes of honour only obtain between civilized powers, and do not come into play with lesser – or 'ignorant' – breeds. That the gap between civilization and barbarism is closing, however, is clear from H. G. Wells' observation, in *The War in the Air,* that national borders would be among the first casualties of air power. In keeping with this, locally bounded notions of patriotism would no longer be satisfied with 'one's own mother speech and one's familiar land' (*War in the Air*, 2005: 73), but would inevitably cast eyes elsewhere: 'the old separations into nations and kingdoms were no longer possible, a newer, wider synthesis was not only needed but imperatively demanded' (*War in the Air*: 73). Hence 'the modernizations of patriotism produced by imperial and international politics' (72) and, as if in mind of this, the 'Aerial League of the British Empire' was founded in 1909, supported by key imperialists such as Lord Montagu, Lord Roberts, Rudyard Kipling and – notwithstanding his misgivings – H. G. Wells (Paris, 1992: 90). The prognostication was that airpower in future warfare would decrease reliance on old-fashioned ground wars, but would also induce, as a consequence, an enervation of metropolitan sensibilities akin to the supine nature of colonized peoples: 'the mass of their citizens was a teeming democracy as heedless of and unfitted for fighting, mentally, morally, physically as any population had even been ... people grew less and less warlike' (*War in the Air*: 77). One of the most shocking passages in Wells' novel notes the amoral detachment with which the German aerial fleet, operating at a distance through airship technology, wreak devastation on the civilian population of New York: 'men who were neither excited, nor expect for the remotest chance of a bullet, in any danger, poured death and destruction upon home and crowds below' (*War in the Air*: 149). But it is not only technology that is responsible: the new global order, as Hannah Arendt was later to argue, would bring colonial methods back home in wars of waste and extermination in the West (1973). As Wells outlines, indicting the German war machine in advance of both World Wars: 'Below they left ruins and blazing conflagrations and heaped and scattered dead, men, women and children mixed together as though they had been no more than Moors, or Zulus, or Chinese' (*War in the Air*: 150). It is not surprising that this dismal view of technological progress fuses the Gothic with dystopian science fiction, as a devastated Britain itself is bombed back into a haunted wasteland, with 'stories of moonlight nights and things walking about' (*War in the Air*: 169). Recounting the grim experience of a survivor wandering through the ruins, an old man relates:

> People, I say ... but they wasn't people. They was the ghosts of them that was overtook, the ghosts of them that used to crowd those streets. And they went past 'im and through 'im and never 'eeded 'im, went by like fogs and vapours .... One came very close .... And she 'adn't got a face to look with, only a painted skull, and then 'e see they was all painted skulls .... [A]nd straightaway the came a cock crowing and the street was empty from end to end. (*War in the Air*: 170)

The imperial underpinning of the 'aesthetics' of aviation was flaunted in Italian Futurism, and particularly in the art and writing of the technological visionary, F. T. Marinetti, whose novel *Mafarka le futuriste* (1910) glorified the role of aerial warfare in subjugating African barbarism. Marinetti's novel can be seen as a 'futurist' prelude to the first recorded use of aerial bombing in which Italian forces dropped bombs in successive operations on Arab encampments in North Africa, near Tripoli, in November 1911: 'The bombing,' an official communiqué reported, 'had wonderful moral effect upon the Arabs' (Paris: 108). In the same year, the French novelist (and colonial army officer) Emile Driant, following Marinetti's lead, published his second aviation novel, *Au-dessus du contenient noir*, advocating lighting airstrikes 'against dissident and evil natives' in the Tchad desert on North Africa who, in the novel, are too astounded to even shoot back at the planes (Wohl, 1994: 88–9). The emergence of precision bombing, however, had to await the Second Balkans War the following year in which Bulgaria, Greece, Serbia and Montenegro joined in the Balkan League against the Turkish Empire. 'The modern aerial bomb, with its distinctive elongated shape, stabilizing fins and nose-fitted detonator' was dropped on a Turkish railway station in October 1912, 'the design, or something like it, soon [becoming] standard issue in all the world's first airforces' (Overy, 2013: 1). The fateful theatre of war in the Balkans already had a fictional precedent in another imperial romance, Bram Stoker's *The Lady of the Shroud*, published in 1909. Stoker is rightly acclaimed as the author of *Dracula* (1897), a masterpiece of Gothic fiction that deals with the 'undead' and the power of the past to throw a shadow over the present, but in futurist Gothic, shadows are also thrown by things to come. When Bert Smallways, the 'anti-hero' of Well's *War in the Air*, is taken captive by German military guards following the crash-landing of his balloon near the German air fleet's secret aerodrome, he is overawed at the impending spectacle of destruction:

> A peculiar strangeness was produced by the lowness of the electric light, which lay on the ground, casting all shadows upwards, and making a grotesque shadow figure of himself and his bearers on the airship sides, fusing all three of them into a monstrous animal with attenuated legs and an immense fan-like humped belly. (*War in the Air*: 83)

In this prefiguring of the German Expressionist style of *Nosferatu* (1923), it is indeed possible to see the shadow of Dracula, and it is this uncanny combination of the vampire tale and science fiction that marks Stoker's *The Lady of the Shroud*.

Modern technology was already a feature of *Dracula*, the telephone, typewriter, phonograph, and the Kodak camera (mentioned by name) being enlisted in the fight against the spectre from Eastern Europe. Interestingly, it is not electric lamps that vanquish the prince of darkness but the spiritual light of the Crucifix and Christianity. The vampire was also an aerial creature: though it is played down in film adaptations of *Dracula*, the Count's magical properties include that of shape-shifter, and it is as a large vampire bat that he hovers outside the window of Lucy Westerna – the winged creature, clinging to the wall, depicted in the illustration on the dust-cover of the first edition. It is striking that the protean nature of the vampire, its capacity to deceive by appearances, also features in *The Queen of the World*, the father of de Lacy's guard, Elliott, warning his son in his secret letter about his own regrettable decision to side with the triumphant forces of tyranny:

> My dear father [Elliot's grandfather] warned me, as I do you, to suffer any extremity rather than enter the service of the Tyranny, 'which,' he said – I use his own words – 'is, however glorious in outward form, the great Vampire of the earth ... No one can ever know the pangs of remorse which I have endured in the knowledge that I disobeyed my father's commands, that I was supporting a most vile and destructive form of government ... when it was by no means clear to which of the peoples struggling for the mastery of the world a good mans allegiance was due. (*Queen of the World*: 153)

In part, Stoker's interest in the future and new 'masters of the world' was bound up with his admiration for the United States, prompted by his early adulation of Walt Whitman, the Allen Ginsberg of the 19th century. As manager of Henry Irving's world-famous Lyceum Theatre, Stoker arranged several tours of the United States and published his views on the new world as *A Glimpse of America* (1886). He added Buffalo Bill Cody and Abraham Lincoln to his pantheon of American heroes, taking time out, while working on *Dracula*, to write a romance based on Buffalo Bill, *The Shoulder of Shasta* (1895), set in the mountains of the Californian wilderness.

The fusion of the Gothic genre – in particular the demonizing of the 'medieval' or Gothic threat presented by the terror of the Spanish Inquisition in the classical Gothic genre – with advanced modernity is also found in Stoker's *The Mystery of the Sea* (1902), a story set on the Aberdeenshire coast of Scotland but taking place against the global backdrop of the closing of the Wild West in the 1890s, and the opening of a new frontier in the Spanish–American–Cuban war (1898–1901). In this novel, references to *reconcentrados*, the concentration camps introduced by the Spanish into Cuba, and technological advances in warships, provide dystopian glimpses of the mechanized violence of 20th-century warfare (Gibbons, 2014: 188–205). At the turn of the 20th century, the frontier for European powers was not in the West but in the East, the contested borders of the Balkans and the perceived threat of the Turkish Ottoman Empire. Count Dracula is a frontier hero of sorts, and 'won his name,' as the vampire hunter Van Helsing relates, defending Transylvania against the Turks (Stoker, *Dracula*, 1997: 212).

Set in the 'Land of the Blue Mountains' (resembling Montenegro), *The Lady of the Shroud* deals with the attempts of an Anglo-Irish hero, Rupert

Sent Leger, to act as a Lawrence of the Adriatic, defending a 'gallant little nation' against Turkish – and, more ominously – Austrian expansion. In the Victorian period, Britain initially supported the Ottoman Empire as a bulwark against Russian supremacy in Eastern Europe, but the Turkish massacre of Christians in Bulgaria in 1876 was a turning point, leading Gladstone in particular to oppose Turkish interests. Ireland and the Balkans were thus conjoined in an unlikely pairing in British foreign policy: 'The Eastern Question and Home Rule together constituted for Gladstone the main issues for national debate in the last quarter of the nineteenth century' (Coundouriotis, 2000: 152). In the first half of the novel, the young hero, St Leger, discovers that he has inherited not only an estate but also virtually a whole territory in the Balkans, due to a deal made between his financially astute millionaire uncle Roger Melton, and the Voivode (Chief) of the Vissarion race in the kingdom. In what reads like a continuation of – or an outtake from – *Dracula*, St Leger's sleep in his palatial new surroundings in the Castle of Vissarion is continually interrupted by a mysterious night-time femme fatale, barely clothed in a wet shroud, whom he can only conclude is a vampire (the books he has read in his aunt's library perhaps included Stoker's previous work):

> In that moment came to my mind all that had been, which bore on the knowledge of my Lady; and the general tendency was to prove or convince that she was indeed a Vampire. Much that had happened, or become known to me, seemed to justify the resolving of doubt into belief. Even my own reading of the books in Aunt Janet's little library, and the dear lady's comments on them, mingled with her own uncanny beliefs, left little opening for doubt. My having to help my Lady over the threshold of my house on her first entry was in accord with Vampire tradition; so, too, her flying at cock-crow from the warmth in which she revelled on that strange first night of our meeting; so, too, her swift departure at midnight on the second. Into the same category came the facts of her constant wearing of her Shroud, even her pledging herself, and me also, on the fragment torn from it, which she had given to me as a souvenir; her lying still in the glass-covered tomb; her coming alone to the most secret places in a fortified Castle where every aperture was secured by unopened locks and bolts; her very movements, though all of grace, as she flitted noiselessly through the gloom of night. All these things, and a thousand others of lesser import, seemed, for the moment, to have consolidated an initial belief. (*Lady of the Shroud*, [1909]: 173)

Though he does not even know her name, Sent Leger falls in love with the dark lady and marries her in a secret ceremony in an underground crypt of the church of St Sava. The Lady of the Shroud turns out to be Princess Teuta, the daughter of the Voivode deposed by a Turkish invasion, and it is her kidnapping by Turkish marauders that emboldens Sent Leger on his mission to free the Land of the Blue Mountains from Turkish despotism. At this point, the novel seems to switch genres to the futuristic world of science fiction, as St Leger pulls out all the stops, and his considerable private wealth, to equip his insurgent force with all the latest military technology. The nation is distinctively premodern, with 'neither roads nor railways nor telegraphs', but to make up for lost time, the intrepid hero brings the most striking advances in armaments to bear on the conflict, not least submarines and airpower. The submarine and the torpedo had already made their presence felt in military warfare, notably through the efforts of the Irish inventor John Philip Holland. Even at that, the warship procured by St Leger is state of the art, equipped with 'electric guns and the latest Massillon waterguns, and Reinhardt electro-pneumatic 'deliverers' for pyroxiline shells. She is even equipped with war-balloons easy of expansion, and with compressible Kitson aeroplanes' (*Lady of the Shroud*: 192). Air power was still a thing of the future, since Louis Blériot's epochal crossing of the Channel only took place when the novel was completed, but inspired perhaps by Wells (or his Irish precursors), the aeroplane takes off in a chapter entitled 'The Empire of the Air'. It allows St Leger and Princess Teuta to rescue her father, the captured Voivode, from a seemingly impregnable tower high up in the mountains (St Leger's plane had the advantage of being noiseless, an innovation which would be welcome for people living near airports today). When the crew eventually arrives in England, Stoker writes, perhaps tongue in cheek, that a new plane 'twice as big' (*Lady of the Shroud*: 291) awaits delivery from Whitby (where Dracula first sets foot on British soil).

Aviation sets the pace for the rapid modernization of the beleaguered kingdom, hydraulic power and the boring of tunnels through mountains facilitating roads and railways. This regeneration culminates in a grand scheme for a Federation of the Balkans to bring peace to the region, but this is secured by an arms race: 'We can have, in chosen spots amongst the clouds, depots of war aeroplanes, with which we can descend and smite our enemies quickly on land or sea. We shall hope to live for Peace; but woe to those who drive us to War!'(*Lady of the Shroud*: 296). One of the most remarkable shifts in the novel, akin to its shape-shifting genres, is the sudden replacement of the Turks as Britain's main foe in the region to the newer threat presented by the Austro-Hungarian annexation of Bosnia-Herzegovina in 1908–9 as the novel was being written. This coincided with a rapprochement with Turkey, prompted by the overthrow of the despotic Sultan, Abdul Hamid, by the 'Young Turks' movement, which was more amenable to British models of parliamentary democracy (Sage, 1998). It is in this light that we might read the almost journalistic topicality of the Voivode's speech on regaining his kingdom (with the 'independent' British help of Sent Leger):

> Brothers, we are entering on stirring times. I can see the signs of their coming all around us. North and South – the Old Order and the New, are about to clash, and we lie between the opposing forces. True it is that the Turk, after warring for a thousand years, is fading into insignificance. But from the North where conquests spring, have crept towards our Balkans the men of a mightier composite Power .... Now they are hard upon us, and are already beginning to swallow up the regions that we have helped to win from the dominion of Mahound. The Austrian is at our very gates. Beaten back by the Irredentists of Italy, she has so enmeshed herself with the Great Powers of Europe that she seems for the moment to be impregnable to a foe of our stature. There is but one hope for us – the uniting of the Balkan forces to turn a masterly front to North and West as well as to South and East.
> (*Lady of the Shroud*: 304–5)

As subsequent events were tragically to show, it was the assassination of Archduke Franz Ferdinand, the heir to Austro-Hungarian empire, by a Serbian committed to an independent Balkan state which sparked off the Great War – and, indeed, Britain's going to war against the 'mightier composite power' from the North.

Stoker's 'prophetic' powers extended even further into the future, in keeping with the gift of 'second-sight' possessed by Sent Leger's Scottish aunt, Janet McAlpie, an occult force that remains unresolved, despite the Mrs Radcliffe-type secular explanation of the superstitious 'apparitions' of the vampire.[9] H.G. Wells is rightly acclaimed for predicting the rise of nuclear weapons in *The World Set Free* (1914), but they are already envisaged in Sent Leger's high-energy utopia: 'The factories for explosives are, of course, far away in bare valleys, where accidental effects are minimized. So, too, are the radium works, wherein unknown dangers may lurk' (*Lady of the Shroud*: 328).[10] The novel ends with an air display celebrating the federation of the

Balkans, attended by the King and Queen of 'the greatest nation of the earth' (Britain). When an aircraft drops letters, which flutter down on a battleship containing the dignitaries, the 'Western' King remarks to the Admiral: '"It must need some skill to drop a letter with such accuracy." With [an] imperturbable face the Admiral replied: "It is easier to drop bombs, Your Majesty"' (*Lady of the Shroud*: 354). The moral of the story is clear: 'the flight of aeroplanes was a memorable sight. It helped to make history. Henceforth no nation with an eye for either defence or attack can hope for success without the mastery of the air' (*Lady of the Shroud*: 354–5). In this case, life indeed imitated art. Adept at charting the terrors of the past in the traditional Gothic, Stoker was also among the few who sensed that the future, often welcomed in the name of peace and liberty, presented its own airborne chambers of horrors.

The Gothic, in the strict sense, entails the persistence, if not the resurrection, of the medieval, with all its putative terrors and superstition on the one hand, and codes of honour and gallantry on the other. Not least of the ironies of aerial warfare is that while heralded as a showcase of chivalry in a modern, anonymous age, it marked the ultimate reversal of the illusory return to Camelot, and the re-emergence of Gothic fear and violence on a global scale. At a time when Victorian values lay in tatters on the battlefields of the Great War, 'heroic air fighters', Michael Paris reminds us, 'were an attractive alternative to the squalor of the trenches ... the "ace" provided an heroic national image' of one-to-one combat between knights in the sky, with aircraft instead of steeds and lances leading the charge. Hence Lloyd George's references in 1917 to the 'Cavalry of the Clouds' and the 'Chivalry of the Air,' imbuing the flying corps with the derring-do of romance and adventure that became the staple of the popular press, comics and cinema (1992: 6–7, 13). Codes of chivalry permeate the fictions of *A Modern Daedalus, Queen of the World*, and *The Lady of the Shroud*, with O'Grady's novel literally building Castles in the Air ('aircastles,' 183) to defend home territories, and featuring spacecraft designed like 'Titanic swords' to engage in slashing duels in the sky. Yet the terrors unleashed were closer to visitations of the horseman of the apocalypse emerging from the clouds: not only national borders but victims were also invisible from high altitudes, as Wells noted, and face to face combat gave way to detached, mechanical destruction. Courage there certainly was given the high rate of casualties among pilots (up to 50 percent in the Great War), but this was offset by stealth and lack of warnings (already noted in *A Modern Daedalus*). For the first time, civilians became targets on a mass scale, Lord Weir instructing Sir Hugh Trenchard in 1918, two decades before Dresden, to

> start up a really big fire on one of the German towns. If I were you I would not be too exacting as regards accuracy in bombing railway stations in the middle of towns, The German is susceptible to bloodiness and I would not mind a few accidents due to inaccuracy. (Strachan, 2014: 306–7)

Following the Great War, 'recalcitrant natives' in the colonies were singled out for attrition using gas bombs, Winston Churchill explaining: 'I do not understand this squeamishness about the use of gas. I am strongly in favour of using poison gas against uncivilised tribes' (Gilbert, 2005).

If aerial bombing was not adopted to counter Irish insurgency, it was due to strategic reasons rather than moral scruples, but the power to instill panic and fear in crowds, Gothic fashion, was exploited. Sir Henry Wilson noted in his diary:

> They gave Macready permission to do a little aeroplane bombing. I think he ought to do more than just show the natives it can be done, at present they don't care a button for aeroplanes because they know they are not allowed to shoot or bomb. (Cited in Jeffrey, 1984: 67)

By 1920, however, military reports noted that 'the aeroplane inspired a fearsome dread in the rebels,' and if republicans on hunger strike inside Mountjoy feared an Amritsar-style attack on the crowds supporting them outside, it is not too difficult to see why (Gallagher, 1967: 79). Demonstrations of up to 20,000 led by keening women were gathering in the streets and aircraft armed with Lewis machine guns were called on for crowd control:

> [M]atters looked very black at one time, and it seemed that bloodshed could not be avoided. Intrepid work was done by the Air Force on the 13th with low-flying planes, in spite of a 50-mile [per hour] gale of wind, and the proximity of the houses. In one case an aeroplane flew along a broad street below the eaves of houses. This clearly demonstrated that aeroplanes could be used for clearing streets by dropping warning notes and if necessary, using Lewis gunfire. (Sheehan, 2007: 12–13)

In July, 1920, Winston Churchill, as Minister for Munitions, authorized the bombardment of Irish rebels, with or without arms, if they could be identified from the air:

> I see no objection from a military point of view, and subject of course to the discretion of the Irish government and of the authorities on the spot, to aeroplanes being dispatched with definite orders in each particular case to disperse them by machine-gun fire or bombs, using of course no more force than is necessary to scatter and stampede them. (Gilbert, 2005)

To have opened fire on the crowd in the streets, not to mention initiating aerial bombing of Irish targets, would have exploded the myth that Ireland as integral to the Union as the Home Counties, and to this extent the authorities were constrained by their own rhetoric. Military discussions pointed out the difficulties in targeting of combatants from the air when insurgents were not clearly distinguishable from 'people going about their everyday business': 'To operate this scheme the civilian population would have to be removed, as in South Africa. And placed in concentration camps. This would then would have left a free-fire zone, making a target of anyone within the cleared areas' (McKenna, 2011: 120). But rugged terrain and the far from open countryside still posed problems, even to widespread aerial reconnaissance: 'It is doubtful whether an airman can see much in a country of this nature, but he should, I think, be able to reconnoiter roads and report whether they are trenched or blacked' (122).

The importance of airpower featured in the Treaty debates when the retention of aerodromes in Ireland, in addition to control of seaports, became an issue of contention. As noted at the outset, recourse to more lethal forms of aerial destruction was perhaps implied in the veiled threat of 'immediate and terrible warfare' should negotiations break down, but the Irish delegation also had plans for their own 'flying column' in this eventuality. The introduction of two former RAF pilots to Commandants Emmet Dalton and Sean Dowling in Dublin led to plans to secretly purchase an aeroplane (under the guise of a Canadian forestry acquisition) to enable Michael Collins to make a speedy getaway to Ireland, given the likelihood of his arrest should the talks fail. The aeroplane, a Martinsyde, was parked at Croydon, then the main airport in Britain. As it happened, Collins did not need its services but the plane, nicknamed 'The Big Fella,' was immediately appropriated by the new Irish Free State, and became the first plane in the fledgling Irish airforce.[11]

## Notes

1. H.G. Wells, *The War in the Air* (2005: 17). The reference to 'feathers' is not explained in the Penguin edition, but it is possibly a sly allusion to one of the Wells' Irish precursors in aerial science-fiction, Tom Greer's *A Modern Daedalus* (1885), discussed below.
2. Michael Collins, *The Path to Freedom* (1922: 34). Collins regarded the threat as a bluff and, linking Ireland with other colonies, wrote: 'I am not impressed by talk of duress or by threats of a declaration of immediate and terrible war. Britain has not made a declaration of war upon Egypt, neither has she made a declaration of war upon India' (35). Nevertheless, the fact that Collins secretly purchased an aeroplane, as we shall see below, to make a quick getaway should negotiations fail, shows that she was not sanguine about possible British recriminations.
3. For Dunne's aviation experiments, see Hugh Driver, *The Birth of Military Aviation: Britain, 1903–1914* (1997). Dunne's later fame as an idiosyncratic theorist of time, promoting the idea of 'prevision' or clairvoyance, may have been more relevant to the uncanny 'prophecies' of fictional treatments of aviation than to aeronautics. John William Dunne, *An Experiment with Time* (1927).
4. Tom Greer, *A Modern Daedalus* (1975).
5. For critical discussions of Greer's fantasy, see the perceptive account relating it to other depictions of Irish subversion in Deaglán Ó Donghaile, *Blasted Literature: Victorian Political Literature and the Shock of Modernism* (2011: 79–88) and Stephen Morton's situating of Greer's novel in a wider colonial context, *States of Emergency: Colonialism, Literature and Law* (2013: 40–1).
6. The Netterville family in Ireland (which included the judge Luke Netterville (1510–1560) among its forbears) were based primarily in County Meath, but also had substantial holdings in County Westmeath.
7. For the alarmist and racist overtones of O'Grady's novel, see Christopher Frayling, *The Yellow Peril: Dr. Fu Manchu and the Rise of Chinaphobia* (2014: 263–5). Nicholas Allen discusses the Irish context of *Queen of the World* in relation to George Russell's fantasy, *The Interpreters* (1922), which also imagines a future ruled by airpower. *George Russell (AE) and the New Ireland, 1905–30* (2003: 116–43).
8. W. B. Yeats, 'To a Wealthy Man' and 'September 1913', *The Collected Poems of W. B. Yeats, Vol. 1 The Poems* (1997: 106–7).
9. Victor Sage, for example, rightly notes that 'by discrediting a vampire tale, and producing finally the explained supernatural, the text adjusts its readers to the "reality" of its external political plot' (126). This fails to account for the accuracy of Aunt Janet's 'second-sight', which constitutes an abiding Gothic (and 'Celtic') remainder in the shift to a more realist science-fiction plot.
10. Radium as a source of power is introduced earlier in Princess Teuta's account of Sent Leger's giant plane from Whitby, travelling on a gothic path via 'Otranto': 'When he heard that the aero was coming from Whitby, where it was sent from Leeds, he directed by cable that it should be unshipped at Otranto, whence he took it here all by himself. I wanted to come with him,

but he thought it better not. He says that Brindisi is too busy a place to keep anything quiet – if not secret – and he wants to be very dark indeed about this, as it is worked by the new radium engine. Ever since they found radium in our own hills he has been obsessed by the idea of an aerial navy for our protection. And after to-day's experiences I think he is right' (*Lady of the Shroud:* 291).

11. See Irish Military Archive, Bureau of Military History, Witness Statement 641, Emmet Dalton: IMA, BMH, WS327, Patrick Egan.

# 10
# Bram Stoker, Ellen Terry, Pamela Colman Smith and the Art of Devilry

*Katharine Cockin*

When Oscar Wilde designated Ellen Terry 'Our Lady of the Lyceum' (Robertson, 1931: 149), the Marian terminology positioned the Lyceum Theatre itself as a sacred space or seat of worship. It was Henry Irving's temple, with Bram Stoker as his trusted business manager, where he gained a reputation for playing both saints and sinners: the fiendish Mephistopheles in *Faust* (1885) and guilt-ridden murderer, Mathias, in *The Bells* (1871) as well as Oliver Goldsmith's well-meaning Vicar and Tennyson's martyred Becket. Matters of faith and morality were respected by Irving and Terry, although in somewhat unorthodox fashion. They unexpectedly gained the respect of Henry Ward Beecher (1813–87), who preached love and questioned the existence of hell (Hatton, 1884, pp. 155–61) but they found they shared similar values and a belief in the redemptive power of doing good. This was the age of exploration into new ways of thinking and living and the nature of the spiritual world was a central concern. Philip Holden (2001) has described this period as one in which mesmerism and the occult were so familiar that they had attained a certain banality. Mesmer himself features in Stoker's *Famous Impostors* (1910) and a mysterious artefact attributed to him appears in Chapter XIII (entitled 'Mesmer's Chest') of Stoker's novel, *The Lair of the White Worm* (1911). The circle of friends, colleagues and acquaintances at the Lyceum Theatre included two young women characterised as 'the devils'[1]: Terry's daughter, Edith Craig (1869–1947) and the young artist, Pamela Colman Smith (1878–1951), whom Ellen Terry informally adopted.[2] Many of Terry's letters have survived from this period and, although Bram Stoker himself features only fleetingly, they provide some intriguing insights into the prevailing concerns of these Lyceum associates.

This essay explores the extent to which the nexus of aesthetic and other interests at the Lyceum Theatre provided a suitably heady atmosphere for Stoker in the period when he was writing *Dracula* and after 1899, when Terry introduced the Lyceum Company to the industrious and highly unusual young artist, whom she named 'Pixie'. Terry had a sense of her own alignment with the stars, her place in the universe. She often transcribed her favourite lines from Shakespeare to accompany her autograph: 'There was a star danced, and under that was I born' (*Much Ado About Nothing*, Act 2 sc. 1). The reiteration served to create a sense of her own destiny and to convince her autograph hunters of the authenticity of her charmed life. Graham Robertson recalled her delight in nocturnal wanderings with unconscious echoes of Dracula: 'Ellen Terry was a daughter of the night, happy in its shadow and mystery and loving the moon with a strange ecstasy which I have never met with in another' (Robertson, 1931: 143). Terry reported to Robertson that she had instilled a similar sense of wonder in one of her young grandsons, who made her 'promise to wake him up once a month to see the sight' (letter 1807 [16 December 1915], *The Collected Letters of Ellen Terry Vol. 6*, 2015: 93). In Stoker's novel, Dracula remarks proudly on the vocalization of other nocturnal predators:

> There seemed a strange stillness over everything; but as I listened I heard as if from down below in the valley the howling of many wolves. The Count's eyes gleamed, and he said:
>
> 'Listen to them – the children of the night. What music they make!' Seeing, I suppose, some expression in my face strange to him, he added:
>
> 'Ah, sir, you dwellers in the city cannot enter into the feelings of the hunter.' (Stoker, 1993: 29)

Thus after the appreciative attribution of 'music' to those with whom he had affiliations as a fellow nocturnal 'hunter', Dracula articulates his perceptual difference from Harker spatially in terms of the country and the city.

A rural setting is evident in W. Graham Robertson's depiction, emphasising Terry's affinity with the moon. It recalls Lilith, who haunts the imagination of the Pre-Raphaelites as a powerful figure of female desire. A woman's freedom of movement defied the convention of gendered separate spheres. Terry claimed the right to roam wherever she pleased – the East End of London or a wood in the countryside – making herself available for new encounters, new experiences. This kind of independence typified the New Woman but Terry had anticipated it by several decades, relishing the novelty of the bicycle and the motor car as well as the toboggan and the hammock. The confidence appears to have been under-written by her financial security and autonomy and partly informed by the outlaw status that George Bernard Shaw had recognised in her (St John, 1932: xvii). Irrepressibly generous towards those who found themselves outcast or marginalized, she was determined to leave the world in a better state than she found it.

This kind of charitable act provides the context for Ellen Terry's anecdote, reported to George Bernard Shaw, about her chance encounter with a destitute woman in the woods. Terry casts herself at first in the role of rescuer but, in her fanciful story, she rapidly mutates into something slightly predatory; perhaps as Shaw's avatar, blending his name mischievously together with that of her second husband, she seems to construct Shaw's gaze on the destitute woman:

> A woman spoke to me [p. 2] to day in the woods at Coombe where I had been wandering wandering for an hour with a book, & where she had slept all night, & her voice – the misery in it – ! I can never forget it – I gave her a drive in my Shandererday! – & she thought it so fine = but my stars! She was dirty = tears & dust, made a pretty mess of her poor face! She looked quite nice when she'd had a nice 'wash & brush up' – her *voice* [p. 3]
> 
> however needed no washing – it was too – too – too beautiful = I tried to make her sing to me in the wood – but she thought I was cracked & was almost frightened to drive with me = She asked me my name & I said it was Nelly Shaw Wardell She has indigestion by now – She *did* eat!! – & so did I!! ——Where were we? At 'Throbs' wasn't it? I only feel sort of misty-kind about you – & a gently warming warming-all-over-sensations-of-pleasure when I see your writing, & know that by & bye – up stairs – I'm going to enjoy you – all to myself – lingeringly – & word by word = The womans voice made my heart [p. 4]
> 
> Throb! – or rather stand still – & so would the touch of – but I fly from 'throbs' in these days – It is not becoming – it's absurd =. (3 July 1897; Cockin, 2012: 277)

Terry presents herself as patrolling the countryside and bringing under her wing those who were lost but her response to the woman is rendered with exquisite emotion. The description of excessive eating recalls Christina Rossetti's *Goblin Market* (1862),[3] and the topic abruptly shifts to the verb 'throbs', to Shaw specifically and the potential for physical pleasure at a distance. It is not unusual for the object of attention to be highly mobile in Terry's letters but in this instance, in the recounting of the anecdote, there is a further layer of dramatization and fantasy which facilitates the uncertainty concerning both the object of desire and also the desiring subject. The ambiguities of Terry's position in this anecdote perhaps align her with the *rural* predator Dracula as much as both Mina Harker and Lucy Westenra. Having discovered Lucy missing from the house at night, Mina hunts her down to the West Cliff across the harbour where she is visible in the light of the full moon. The previous day they had enjoyed a liberating walk across fields by the lighthouse before tea at Robin Hood's Bay where they unleashed appetites to exceed that of even the New Woman (Ch. VIII).

In *Dracula*, Terry is instead explicitly cited in reference to the 'winningly attractive' children in their 'favourite game' in 'luring each other away by wiles' on Hampstead Heath as they mimic the as yet unidentified vampiric Lucy whom they have described as a 'Bloofer Lady' (Stoker, 1993: 229). Here the *Westminster Gazette* report provides a little distance from the comparison,[4] but the emphasis is on the acting skills of the children: 'Our correspondent naively says that even Ellen Terry could not be so winningly attractive as some of these grubby-faced little children pretend – and even imagine themselves – to be' (229). This may allude to Ellen Terry the child actor who had made such a profound impression on Charles Dodgson. The poignancy of innocent children engaging in a performance, described in the *Westminster Gazette* newspaper report in terms of the 'irony of grotesque', restaging the horrific activities of the vampire, is at work in the uneasy word 'attractive'. It constructs a vampiric gaze in the narrative at this point as well as alerting the reader to the contagious performances of the vampire, extending even to little children. The novel omits any explicit link between Terry and Lucy but the association offers itself metonymically through the publicity photograph of Terry in her gown as Margaret in *Faust* and its congener, of Henry Irving, as Mephistopheles.[5]

In the year of *Dracula*'s publication Terry had magical powers of invisibility as well as flight on her mind. She wrote to George Bernard Shaw, imagining how she would implement these powers and he was intimately involved in this fantasy:

> Off on a bit of Magic Carpet wd I go if I could & wave my hands over your blessed head touch your cerise Cerise <?> hair gently with my lips – whisper to you I was there, although invisible – that I loved you tho' I cd not show you how much (one never does!) & then skip

back again on my Carpet to —— this place. Tho' I'd rather go to Edy – (Friday 24 September [1897]; Cockin, 2012: 292)

Terry fantasises about intimacy with Shaw but ensures that the brief and tantalising vision ends with her safe return and their separation. This anecdote lacks detail as to what kinds of 'magic' were in Terry's imagination at this time and whether her 'Magic Carpet' was in the manner of an Orientalist Gilbert and Sullivan device, conveniently moving the plot forward, however implausibly, and freed from the mundanities of everyday reality. Indeed it is precisely the kind of business matters for which Stoker was responsible at the Lyceum Theatre, that Ellen Terry sometimes negotiated and repressed in her correspondence in favour of fairytales: she is Red Riding Hood (or maybe the wolf) roaming the wood but the problem of destitution remains a hard fact resistant to defeat even by her *dea ex machina*.

Relationships were subject to playful reinvention in the theatre, where loyalties and confidences were powerful ties, so it is not surprising to find them articulated in familial discourse. Stoker, trusted guardian of the Lyceum Theatre fortunes, was one of the available father figures when Terry had difficulties with her troublesome son. Terry's understanding of her own place in the world, of her own family of touring actors (her parents Ben and Sarah and siblings, especially Marion, Fred and Kate) and the family she created herself, was shaped by the complexity and unorthodox nature of these relationships. Lacking the reassurance of role models, Terry adapted and applied what she knew and understood in order to make sense of her pioneering way of living. In this context, in a letter in 1889, Ellen Terry refers to 'Bram-mama' (Cockin, 2011: 3). The nature of the humour is uncertain in its feminisation but I want to suggest that it playfully disconnects gender from essentialism. Kate Thomas has suggested that Stoker's correspondence with Walt Whitman demonstrates the generationally and 'relationally composite' male object of desire. Thus Stoker wrote to Whitman about desire for a man 'who can be, if he wishes father, and brother and wife to his soul' (Stoker quoted in Thomas, 2012: 182). If Stoker is the maternal to Irving's paternal, this left Terry perhaps the opportunity to flit posthumanly between other roles so diverse that they made the 'New Woman' seem rather inspid: an Ariel figure; a snake-like Lilith; a glittering beetle-clad diva; 'a wearied machine' (Cockin, 2013: 79) in another state of being, in a different realm. Roles and relationships are opened up for reinvention. The global reach of Dracula, his shape-shifting and powerful influence on others, are all features not just of the

Mephistophelian Henry Irving as a possible model but more abstractly the Lyceum Company itself and Ellen Terry within it, offering an alternative family structure which roams across the ocean to spread its message and collect others along the way. In 'Postal Dracula', a section in *Postal Pleasures* (2012), Kate Thomas has attributed the mastery of communication systems to Dracula, whom she sees as pre-eminently a correspondent (181). Terry is the prolific correspondent at the Lyceum and it is her intervention which leads to Colman Smith's addition to the Lyceum fold, two years after the publication of *Dracula*.

Some years before Colman Smith joined the Lyceum, the topic of mesmerism was dominating the London theatre. In 1894 the publishing sensation surrounding George du Maurier's *Trilby*, in which Svengali transformed the voice of Trilby making her a brilliant singer, had captivated Henry Irving. Irving retaliated competitively with Beerbohm Tree, who played Svengali in the dramatization, by staging the ultimately unsuccessful play, *The Medicine Man*. However, the use of hypnotism was reportedly a practice disapproved of by Irving and Terry warned her son against its practice (19 August [1891]; Cockin, 2011: 105, Vol. 2). Yet in a later letter in 1894 she uses 'mesmerism' positively and presumably metaphorically as a means of describing what happens in the magical, un(self)conscious moment when a performance works:

> My first Portia scene (on the sofa – with Nerissa) is <u>charming</u> comedy, & when I force it, it goes for nothing but when one is <u>very quiet</u> & <u>subtly</u> <u>enjoys it</u> <u>oneself</u> it goes with mesmerism between Actress & Audience = <u>Twinkle</u> over it & don't be <u>set</u> – if <u>it seems to happen</u> *<u>then</u>* it's right = You always force your gaiety too much – I noticed it in Harry Ashton = & <u>keep stiller</u> = You'll be alright if you don't <u>worry</u> or <u>over act</u> – (22 October 1894; Cockin, 2012: 42, Vol. 3)

She urged her son to keep working: only through regular practice would his art improve. Nevertheless Terry's own relationship with work was often hanging in the balance between success and ill health. One fleeting description of such a moment may be reminiscent of the vampirism of *Dracula*. In a letter in March 1897 she says to George Bernard Shaw: 'I'm back from Margate – Still not well = Isn't it maddening? – & I'm longing to get my work by the throat –' (Saturday 13 March [1897]; Cockin, 2012: 253, Vol. 3). The throat becomes a highly resonant bodily zone in the context of *Dracula* but for Terry there were further personal associations. Her throat was like the heel to Achilles. Often losing her voice at times of exhaustion, she talks about her overwork in terms of being drained of life; work is compelling but it is also a predatory force to be kept in check and she therefore fantasises about retaliation in a similar fashion. When she criticises her son for indolence she describes her overwork not only as directly caused by his idleness but as a beastly and homicidal mechanism:

> The months go by & you, a man now, all doing no work & it makes me very unhappy, & therefore it's best I see little of you – at least until my work ceases to drag the life out of me . (29 [August? 1894]; Cockin, 2012: 60, Vol. 3)

Both Terry and her son had faced serious health problems involving the blood. It is widely known that Terry was saved from blood poisoning by Stoker's medically trained brother, George, but less so that her son, Edward Gordon Craig, had had jaundice in December 1890 (Cockin, 2011: 86, Vol. 2).

In the 1890s, towards the century's end, Ellen Terry's letters are often preoccupied with survival, life and death, heaven and hell, God and the Devil. She was highly supportive of a controversial play about leprosy by Henry Irving's son Laurence, entitled *Godefroi and Yolande* and fascinated by Shaw's *The Devil's Disciple*. The Lyceum productions of *Faust* beginning in 1885 brought the Devil's helper onstage in the form of Mephistopheles/Henry Irving. Although characteristic of her fantasising and dramatising discourse, this theological landscape also helped her to engage with the traumatic effects of bereavement following the deaths of her parents and her sister Florence. In symbolist art and literature at this time the dream or vision was ubiquitous as a means of engaging with the spiritual or other dimensions, and they feature regularly in the occult practices and rituals that attracted individuals such as the artist, Pamela Colman Smith, the actor Florence Farr, theatre entrepreneur Annie Horniman and the poet W. B. Yeats. I want now to set the exploration of Ellen Terry's epistolary (day)dreaming and the possible correspondences with vampiric discourse alongside other kinds of seriously prophetic dreams and visions in order to propose some continuities and lines of influence.

Pamela Colman Smith was active in the Order of the Golden Dawn, a Rosicrucian society which included W. B. Yeats, Florence Farr and Annie Horniman in its membership. It is her association with Yeats and her involvement in this society that have led to Smith featuring at all in studies of the period and details about her life and career have yet to be fully documented.[6] In *Women of the Golden Dawn: Rebels and*

*Priestesses* (1995), Mary K. Greer dates Smith's membership of the Order of the Golden Dawn as likely to be from November 1901. In November 1903 she followed A. E. Waite when the society split and it was at this time that she founded her own little magazine, *The Green Sheaf*, which included work by Yeats. It was also 1903 when Yeats, Pamela Colman Smith and Edith Craig were all involved in The Masquers theatre society, and Smith and Craig collaborated on scene designs for Yeats.[7]

Smith and Craig had already collaborated on costume design for an extraordinary theatrical production in 1901 featuring a serpent-like demonic woman, Nicandra.[8] The names of A. E. Waite and the publisher William Rider are associated with the set of Tarot cards that Smith designed in 1909. The designs are unusual apparently in the subtlety of facial expressions of the characters depicted. At least two of the cards have possible links to the Lyceum Theatre. The Queen of Wands is said to resemble Ellen Terry.[9] The Devil is depicted in various ways in Tarot cards and although wings are not unique to the Smith design, she draws the bat wings in a fairly realistic and distinctive manner. The anatomically correct depiction of the bat's thumb, the hook-like structure halfway along the wing, is reminiscent of Smith's caricature of Stoker in evening dress and bat-like cloak, with the caption 'Bramy Joker'.[10]

Pamela Colman Smith's technical style was influenced by Arthur Wesley Dow (1857–1922). Dow taught at the Pratt Institute, Boston from 1896–1903, his students including Georgia O'Keefe as well as Colman Smith. His methods, published as *Composition: A Series of Exercises in Art Structure for the Use of Students and Teachers* (1899), involved attention to line, notan (universal beauty) and colour. This spatial balancing of white and black and hand-coloured printing, shared affinities with the work of Walter Crane, the 'Beggarstaffs' (James Pryde and William Nicholson) and Jack B. Yeats. The symbolist concerns of *The Green Sheaf* were most apparent in the numerous short stories it published about dreams. W. B. Yeats's only written contribution was a short story, 'Dream of the World's End', in issue No. 2. It is an account of the narrator attempting to control the dream state by meditating on an image, something which Yeats practised. After dreaming of the chaos of the crowds of workers in Paris and the patent medicine seller as a thief in the night, the narrator wakes in terror. Roy Foster locates the origins of this story in 1899 and interprets its publication, in the context of the recent news of Maud Gonne's marriage, as aligning the charlatan with Gonne's new husband, MacBride:

> He now chose to publish the vision of four years before, when her symbol of apple-blossom brought on a dream of the World's End

(set in her city, Paris), with visions of wickedness, unworthiness and cant; his fear when he awoke, that an armed thief was hidden in his bedroom, must have seemed like a rueful prescience of MacBride. (Foster, 1997: 290)

For Yeats, visions and dreams, in particular, were obviously integral to his belief system and his art. His essay, 'Magic' (1901), begins with a testament:

> I believe in the practice and philosophy of what we have agreed to call magic, in what I must call the evocation of spirits, though I do not know what they are, in the power of creating magical illusions, in the visions of truth in the depth of the mind when the eyes are closed. (Yeats, 1961: 28)

He accepts at once the necessity of pursuing the spirits in a leap of faith, 'though I do not know what they are'. To make them explicit would be perhaps to render them unattainable, to change their nature or to invalidate them. Such mysticism may explain Yeats' artistic contribution to *The Green Sheaf*, not mentioned by Foster. A very indistinct drawing, 'The Lake at Coole', reproduced as a supplement to issue No. 4 held a special significance for Yeats. In 1937, half a lifetime after its publication in *The Green Sheaf* and reflecting on the context of his writing, Yeats arrives at some sort of conclusion. He describes it as a kind of place where the senses have registered an impossible presence:

> I think I now know why the gamekeeper at Coole heard the footsteps of a deer on the edge of the lake where no deer had passed for a hundred years [...] I am convinced that in two or three generations it will become generally known that the mechanical theory has no reality, that the natural and supernatural are knit together, that to escape a dangerous fanaticism we must study a new science; at that moment Europeans may find something attractive in a Christ posed against a background not of Judaism but of Druidism, not shut off in dead history, but flowing, concrete, phenomenal. (Yeats 1961: 518)

The site depicted in Yeats's drawing in *The Green Sheaf* is where the gamekeeper heard footsteps of deer from ancient times. The place reminded him of that knowledge available only through the effort of spiritual pursuit.

Colman Smith, who shared with W. B. Yeats a serious interest in the workings of magic and membership in the Order of the Golden Dawn, was also known for her visionary powers. In her work as a visual artist she depicted music, based on synaesthesia, and in this practice she was apparently respected by Claude Debussy (Greer, 1995: 408). Colman Smith also performed as a story teller, under the name 'Galukiezanger', enchanting her audiences with Jamaican tales that she published as *Annancy Stories* (1899). This book was a very early example of the transcription and publication of Jamaican oral stories, but according to Hyacinth Simpson, Colman Smith 'discarded the Jamaican dialect almost entirely and muted the tales' subversive tones, opting instead to represent these trickster texts as tamed moral stories for the nursery' (Simpson, 2004: 7). Although the perceived inadequacies in rendering the dialect were problematic, the childlike discourse that Simpson refers to may have been misinterpreted. It was intrinsic to Colman Smith's symbolist aesthetic and her spiritual values, giving it a wider force and frame of reference than the genre of children's literature. Several of her illustrated books and stories, such as *Susan and the Mermaid* (1912), featuring apparently harmless serpentine women, adopt a challengingly childlike discourse and take the reader into a fantastic world in which dreams and myths unfold. Colman Smith herself was described as childlike and it was this aspect of her aesthetic and her demeanour that was favoured by Alfred Stieglitz (1864–1946). Her artwork had been exhibited in London between 1902 and 1908 but most significantly in New York in January 1907, when her work was chosen in preference to that of Rodin by Stieglitz for his non-photographic exhibition at the Little Gallery of the Photo-Secession. Stieglitz is known for his promotion of photography as an art form. In 1907 Colman Smith was honoured with the first one-woman and non-photographic exhibition at the gallery. Colman Smith's aesthetic has been given serious critical attention by Kathleen Pyne (2007), in a study which reassesses the Stieglitz circle in a modernist context and focuses on the female artists involved such as Gertrude Kasebier, Anne Brigman, Katharine Nash Rhoades and Georgia O'Keefe. Colman Smith was actively involved in producing posters for the women's suffrage organization, the Suffrage Atelier, and was a prominent member of the Pioneer Players theatre society, illustrating play programmes and designing their distinctive logo. Colman Smith's place in the history of visual arts, literary and theatre studies has yet to be established, partly because her work was often ephemeral and her strange and childlike presentation has led to her being overshadowed by the more famous figures with whom she worked.

The Lyceum Theatre and its journeys were particularly inspiring for Colman Smith. Stoker had commissioned her, instead of Edward Gordon Craig, in 1899 to design a souvenir brochure for the company (Cockin, 2013: 95). In her characteristic perspective as an onlooker, she depicted the effects on the company of a broken down train in a densely populated and witty drawing, published in 1901 and reproduced in Ellen Terry's *The Story of My Life* (1908). An apparently unpublished series of drawings record the transatlantic voyage of the Lyceum Company, some of which are reproduced in Barbara Belford's biography of Bram Stoker (1996), and depict the main players with cryptic names and the two marginal pixie-like onlookers are the 'two devils', otherwise Pixie and 'Puck'. The caricatures are particularly illuminating in seizing on a particular aspect of the individual's character.

Some of the collaborations continued after the Lyceum Theatre had changed direction.[11] Colman Smith produced the illustrations for Stoker's novel *In the Lair of the White Worm* (1911). Colman Smith chooses a striking red for the depiction of the hawk-shaped kite, somewhat reminiscent of Henry Irving's Mephistopheles' costume in *Faust*. The illustration of Arabella March's dress and her sinuous body with upstretched hands, 'dancing in a fantastic sort of way' against a lilac background, recalls of Colman Smith's sketch of a costume design for Cora Brown Potter who played the protagonist in a 'mystic farce', *Nicandra* (1901) by Russell Vaun. This play had originally been licensed for production at the New Cambridge Theatre on 16 June 1898. Nicandra is described in the 1898 play text as 'the name of an Egyptian Priestess – famous for her wickedness – she worshipped serpents' (20). She has been transformed by Isis into a snake as a punishment and finds herself in London, accidentally returned to her female form and wreaks havoc until a black pigeon magically restores the snake.[12] The play involves Nicandra dancing in flames as a bewitching Carmen figure and episodes of disguise, crossing gender and class boundaries, in order to manipulate the outcome of several relationships. During the magical episodes, chanting is a striking feature. Nicandra's predatory arrogance is expressed in cross-species terms similar to Dracula or possibly Renfield: 'Tell a man he's good looking & he's your slave for life – oh these flies – these human flies – how willingly they are caught' (65–6). I have suggested elsewhere that Nicandra's dress, described in a review as shimmering and transparent violet, green and silver fabric with chiffon scarves and a trailing black net with black beads to imply scales, resembled Ellen Terry's Lady Macbeth costume.[13] The colours used in the costume appear to have been a matter of interpretation, since the stage directions in the 1898 play text describe Nicandra as 'in a dress composed entirely of sequins to represent the scales of a snake with a long train covered in jewels' (116). The involvement of Colman Smith in the design for the 1901 production raises a question about the extent to which the production of this 'mystical farce' may have mocked the rituals of the Order of the Golden Dawn and Florence Farr's experiments with the psaltery. Florence Farr had been a member of the Order of the Golden Dawn from 1890 to 1902 and had already established her knowledge and interest in Egyptian culture and history, publishing *Egyptian Magic: An Essay on the Nature and Applications of Magical Practices in Pharaonic and Ptolemaic Egypt*, (1896), in which she described Egyptian mummification and beliefs about vampires. On 16 November 1901 Florence Farr performed the Priestess Hathor, using chanting to the psaltery in *The Beloved of Hathor* at the Victoria Hall, Archer Street for the first meeting of the Egyptian Society (Schuchard, 2008: 54–5). Farr's play was reviewed in the *Daily Chronicle* by Henry Wood Nevinson (An Egyptian Play, *Daily Chronicle*, 18 November 1901, p. 6). In the wake of these experiments in magical practices and Egyptian cultural history, some serious and others faddish, Bram Stoker published his novel *The Jewel of the Seven Stars* (1903).

The new insights presented here highlight perhaps that although the Lyceum Theatre and Dracula are extremely well-known and many of these individuals were highly successful in various ways, for some of them there were missed opportunities and only posthumous acknowledgement. During his lifetime, Stoker did not receive the overwhelming response to *Dracula* that it has drawn in recent years. Irving saw some value in *The Medicine Man* but missed the opportunity to embody the bat on the Lyceum stage. Edward Gordon Craig and Edith Craig dreamt of artistic control in their own theatres but were both frustrated in different ways. In 1909 Pamela Colman Smith designed what has become the most famous deck of Tarot cards in the world but it is often labelled with two male names (Rider-Waite) while her artistry has been obscured. However, each card bears her devilish mark – a monogram that resembles a caduceus with snake-entwined staff formed by the etiolated letter P overlaid with a C and an S – and some of them show traces of her Lyceum days.

## Notes

1. Some unpublished sketches and an illustrated manuscript of a narrative poem (song or dramatic script) depict Edith Craig and Pamela Colman

Smith as the 'two devils'; held in the Ellen Terry archive at Smallhythe Place, Tenterden, England. These relate to the transatlantic Lyceum Tour of 1899 and may be part of the 'shipboard entertainment' cited by Belford, 1996, p. 285. Colman Smith depicts herself and Edith Craig devilishly miniaturized in the margins, watching Terry as Nance Oldfield on stage but in the exhibition catalogue these have been cropped from the photographic illustration of 'Ellen Terry as Nance Oldfield'; *Ellen Terry: The Painter's Actress*, Watts Gallery, 2014, p. 10.
2. Ellen Terry described the situation of the orphaned young woman, whom she describes as 'the Japanese Toy', in a letter to her friend Audrey Campbell [4 June 1900]; Cockin, 2013, p. 119. The infantilizing and Orientalizing terminology suggests that Colman Smith was being positioned as different in terms of ethnicity as well as her unorthodox aesthetic and spiritual values.
3. In 1893 Macmillan published a new edition of *Goblin Market*, illustrated by Laurence Housman (1865-1959), whose play, *Bethlehem*, Edward Gordon Craig was to produce in 1902.
4. See Catherine Wynne for analysis of the obfuscation in this scene; C. Wynne, *Bram Stoker, Dracula and the Victorian Gothic Stage*, Basingstoke: Palgrave, 2013, p. 97.
5. This image of Henry Irving was used to illustrate the cover of the Penguin edition (1993).
6. See Melinda Boyd Parsons, who organised an exhibition of her work in 1975. This sketch is reproduced in Cockin, 1998, p. 123. Greer (1995) has detailed Colman Smith's involvement in the Order of the Golden Dawn and Stuart R. Kaplan (2009) has recently published a highly illustrated booklet to accompany the commemorative edition of the Smith-Waite Tarot cards that collates reproductions of many of her visual artworks.
7. For further information on the short-lived Masquers theatre society, see Cockin, 1998, pp. 73–5.
8. This sketch is reproduced in Cockin, 1998, p. 123.
9. See Melinda Boyd Parsons' catalogue for exhibition at Delaware Art Museum, 1975, 'To All Believers: The Art of Pamela Colman Smith Kaplan. A detailed account of the various versions of the Smith-Waite tarot cards is provided in Janson, 2005.
10. This sketch is reproduced in Wynne, 2011, p. 31.
11. See Cockin 2001; and Tickner 1987.
12. 'Nicandra', *Illustrated Sporting and Dramatic News*, 20 April 1901, p. 289.
13. An account of Craig's costume design work, and *Nicandra* is given in Cockin, 1998, pp. 45-6, where Colman Smith's sketch of the Nicandra costume is reproduced as an illustration.

# 11
# Beyond 'Hommy-Beg': Hall Caine's Place in *Dracula*

*Richard Storer*

On 23 February 1897 (in a letter now in the Manx National Heritage Library) Bram Stoker wrote to his friend Hall Caine proposing to dedicate *Dracula* to him and suggesting the obscure wording which all readers now encounter at the beginning of the novel: 'To my dear friend Hommy-Beg'. Stoker floated the alternative of naming Caine more formally but evidently preferred the idea of using his joke name for his friend, reassuring him that 'if the book is ever worth remembering it will be well understood what is meant'.[1]

Everyone does understand that 'Hommy-Beg' is Hall Caine. This identity has become one of the few things for which Caine is still remembered. But how fully has 'what is meant' by Caine's liminal presence in *Dracula* been explored? It is often observed how intensively the text of *Dracula* has been worked over during the last 50 years and how many different meanings it has been made to produce. This one little bit of the text seems to remain rather under-developed, however, and in this essay I want to suggest some ways in which more can be known about it, and made of it, as another way of contextualising *Dracula*. To do this I am going to draw on some of Caine's writings, and also some more of the letters of Stoker to Caine, about 60 of which survive as part of the Hall Caine archive.

The centenary of Stoker's death was also the centenary of the one text by Hall Caine which does get quoted from time to time in connection with Stoker. This is his obituary, 'Bram Stoker: The Story of a Great Friendship', published in *The Daily Telegraph* on 24 April 1912, the day of Stoker's funeral. Caine's essay (reprinted in Dalby, 2011: 45–7) is notable for its belittling of 'our poor Bram' who had 'no other claim to greatness' besides his big heart and genius for friendship, and for its casual dismissal of Stoker's writings as shallow and written only 'to sell'.

Several details in the essay suggest that Caine had paid little attention to Stoker's literary output during their long friendship. He regrets that Stoker never wrote memoirs of the 'multitude of interesting persons' (including Tennyson, Gladstone and Whitman) he had met during his career, even though this is exactly what Stoker had done in numerous chapters of *Personal Reminiscences of Henry Irving*. He obliquely acknowledges his association with *Dracula*, but seems to want to distance himself from it by claiming that the 'disguise' used in the dedication (i.e. the 'Hommy-beg' identity) was 'impenetrable' to all except himself – as I suggest below, the opposite was true and Caine had actively used the name for undisguised self-promotion before Stoker borrowed it. Above all, Caine seems to have forgotten that he had the evidence of his old friend's own letter to refute his assertion that as a novelist Stoker had 'no higher aims' and 'I cannot truly say that this deeper side of the man ever expressed itself in his writings .... Frankly, he wrote his books to sell'. In 1890 Stoker had fervently thanked Caine for some positive comments on his first novel *The Snake's Pass*, in terms which suggest that, far from being a mere speculative sideline, his literary ambitions were as important to his sense of self (the 'deeper side of the man') as his athletic prowess had been in his Dublin days:

> I shall try to do better work and believe me old fellow that if it be better it will in great part at all events be due to you. Your letter has left me in a tumult and you must pardon my seeming incoherence – I have not felt the same way since I won my first race – twenty-three years ago and whilst I enjoyed the triumph did not quite understand it. It will be a keener pleasure to me still tomorrow.[2]

If Caine was dismissive of Stoker's literary achievements, Stoker scholarship has tended to return the compliment; Caine's identity as 'Hommy-Beg' and his friendship with Stoker are acknowledged, but there has been little interest in the novels by Caine which Stoker claimed to admire so much, and the same basic facts and assumptions about Caine's life and relations with Stoker tend to be re-circulated. The need to improvise a minor role for Caine has led to some odd exaggerations and even mistakes. Some time ago McNally and Radescu speculated that Hall Caine might have been the 'ghost' writer or editor posited by H. P. Lovecraft who was needed to bring order to Stoker's material before the narrative reached its final form (Miller, 2006: 60). The idea that there was such an editor now seems discredited, but in any case it must strike anyone who has ever read a Hall Caine novel as quite unimaginable that he could have performed this role: Caine's novels are generally longer and more self-indulgent than Stoker's, he never attempted anything like the 'papers ... placed in sequence' technique used to such effect in *Dracula*, and he later relied heavily on Stoker to edit his autobiography. More recently, in the new (2011) Oxford World's Classics edition of *Dracula*, a note on possible sources for the Hampstead graveyard scenes implies that Caine assisted Dante Gabriel Rossetti in the exhumation of his wife's body (383). Caine did become Rossetti's personal assistant at the very end of his life, but he did not meet Rossetti until ten years after the notorious exhumation incident, and even Rossetti himself was not present when the coffin was opened, so neither can be cast as a real-life Seward or Van Helsing. Lisa Hopkins's recent biography perpetuates another questionable story about Caine's input when she repeats Peter Haining's claim that in 1902 Caine furnished Stoker with 'a considerable amount of esoteric and occult knowledge' that he used in *The Jewel of Seven Stars* (Haining, 1990: 152; Hopkins, 2007: 24). Haining does not provide any source for this claim, and his brief overview of Caine's career includes several other quite serious factual inaccuracies.[3] In the absence of any other evidence it seems implausible that Caine had a private interest in Egyptology. If it had been so, he would have used the knowledge in a novel of his own, as he used all his other research, whereas in fact he did not write his Egyptian novel, *The White Prophet* (1909), until some years after *The Jewel of Seven Stars*, and when he did his subject was colonial politics rather than mummies. *The White Prophet* even contains a disparaging remark about Egyptology as 'vandalism' (Caine, 1909, Vol 2: 154).

In all these cases, the tendency is the same. As Caine has no established profile, being now so little read or known, he is set up as a shadowy figure who intensifies the 'Gothic' profile of Stoker. A sensational variation on this theme is Neil Storey's *The Dracula Secrets: Jack the Ripper and the Darkest Sources of Bram Stoker* (2012), which suggests that through Stoker's friendship with Caine a metonymic connection can be made between *Dracula* and the Whitechapel murders of 1888. The idea of a *metaphorical* connection between *Dracula* and these murders, that the novel somehow retells the news story, is a familiar one: it has been explored in detail by Nicholas Rance and others; and it is now well known that Stoker himself included a teasing suggestion along these lines in his preface to the Icelandic edition of the novel.[4] What Hall Caine brings to the table, however, is a personal relationship with a recognised leading suspect in the murders: the Irish-American quack doctor, Francis Tumblety, whom Caine briefly worked for and corresponded with as a young man in Liverpool (one or two passages in Tumblety's letters to Caine even suggest they may have had a more intimate relationship). These letters were discovered by Vivien Allen, who was the first scholar to have access to Caine's papers, and their possible implications are also the subject of a 2008 novel, James Reese's *The Dracula Dossier*. But whereas Reese's treatment is explicitly fictional (he only goes so far as to say that the events he describes are not impossible), Neil Storey's book does put quite a lot of effort into making a historical case, based on a chain of either documented or possible associations: Tumblety knew Caine; Caine knew Stoker; Tumblety was the Whitechapel murderer; Caine suspected this; Caine obliquely articulated his suspicions in his story 'The Last Confession', in *Capt'n Davy's Honeymoon*, a volume dedicated to Stoker; Stoker met Tumblety at the Beefsteak Room and shared Caine's suspicions; Stoker encoded his suspicions in *Dracula*, dedicated to Caine. If every link in this chain (rather than just the first two) could be convincingly documented, it would fashion a powerful tool indeed for interpreting *Dracula* and other texts – starting for example with one of Stoker's first notes for his novel, 'some terrible fear … man knows secret' (Eighteen-Bisang and Miller, 2008: 15). But of course Neil Storey is not able to do this. Who could? *The Dracula Secrets* should probably be valued by Stoker scholars for exposing the impossibility of such a project, while also demonstrating that it is likely to remain a tantalising distraction – generating thrilling questions even though these can almost certainly never be answered.

As interest grows in contextualising Bram Stoker as a man of Victorian letters and the theatre, rather than just the author of *Dracula*, a different kind of understanding of Hall Caine's place in his life and work needs to be developed – one which explores what can be known of the dynamics of their relationship as two close friends who were both prolific writers, rather than hurrying past Caine to access more Gothic figures like Tumblety. Two recent collections of relevant documents (Dalby, 2011; Browning, 2012) certainly help to redress the balance along these lines, although it could be argued that they go to the opposite extreme from the sensational, and rather too uncritically accept Stoker's dedication and Caine's obituary as cues simply for a commemoration of 'great friendship'. *Dracula* itself provides a pretty clear hint that affirmations of 'friend'-ship are not always to be taken at face value. In the text the first declaration of friendship is in the dedication but the next is in the letter which greets Jonathan Harker as 'My friend' and is signed 'Your friend, Dracula' (Stoker, 2011: 7).

To explore the significance of this friendship further, I want to revisit three elements of the context for the dedication to *Dracula* which are known and often mentioned in connection with it: the 'Hommy-beg' name itself; the loan which Stoker asked Caine for the year before *Dracula* was published; and the fact that Caine had previously dedicated one of his books to Stoker. To begin (as *Dracula* does) with 'Hommy-Beg', all modern editions gloss this as Manx for 'Little Tommy' and explain that Caine's full name was Thomas Henry Hall Caine. Some add that this was the name that Caine's grandmother gave him when as a child he stayed with her on the Isle of Man. But none that I have seen address the question *why* Bram Stoker would use this name for his friend. The implication of the story when it is glossed in terms of Caine's grandmother is that the name was a personal secret ('impenetrable' as Caine later claimed) that Caine disclosed to Stoker as a seal of their close friendship. Yet the opposite seems to be the case. The grandmother / 'Hommy-Beg' story was one which had already been publicly disclosed, *before* 1897, as part of Hall Caine's rebranding of himself as an authentic 'Manxman'. And if it was a purely private name, it came into the friendship rather late. Stoker's surviving letters to Caine up to 1890 (they met in 1878) address him as 'My dear Hall Caine'; there is a gap of six years in the surviving correspondence; then all the letters from 1896 onwards are addressed to 'My dear Hommy-Beg'. The most likely scenario is that Stoker started using the name – not at Caine's suggestion but as an affectionate joke at his expense – after the publication in 1895 of a profile of Caine in *The Windsor Magazine* in which Caine rather blatantly, with accompanying photos of 'Genuine old Manx kitchen' and 'A glimpse of Manx fisherfolk at work', talked up his Manx pedigree. As a journalist himself, Caine was adept at controlling the content of such articles and using them for self-promotion. At the start of his career, he had had no interest in exploiting his Manx connections and had presented himself as a metropolitan critic and a novelist with Cumbrian roots. Now he was described as more or less having grown up on the Isle of Man and as having acquired all his interest in narrative (and an interest in the supernatural) from his picturesque grandmother: 'Hommybeg – it was a pet name she had given to him – Hommybeg, she would say, I will tell you of the fairies …' (Sherard, 1895: 565). It is easy to imagine Bram Stoker being amused by this; and an extra element may have been added to the joke by the fact that Caine seemed to have forgotten that he had actually used the name 'Hommy-Beg' in his first successful Manx novel, *The Deemster* – not for the hero, but for a minor comic character, the deaf and illiterate old gardener.[5]

The second bit of context that is fairly well known is that in 1896 Stoker asked Caine for a loan of £600, assuring him that he would be repaid from the proceeds 'if the new book comes out well at all'.[6] In this sense *Dracula* as a source of income was literally dedicated to Caine. Richard Dalby quotes extensively from the letter in which Stoker made this request, including Stoker's comment that he had approached Caine because 'you are closer to me than any man I know'. But Dalby omits what I think is the most interesting part of this sentence: 'you are closer to me than any man I know, *and I prefer to ask my own kind who are workers like myself rather than rich men who do not understand*'.[7] It is interesting to note the phrase 'my own kind' there, similar to the phrase 'my kind' which Stoker had used in his letter to Whitman 20 years earlier – and which Talia Schaffer interprets in terms of sexuality (Schaffer, 1994: 383). But here Stoker glosses 'my own kind' in professional terms – 'workers like myself rather than rich men'. This elides the fact that Caine was actually quite a rich man by this time, due to the success of his novels, serialisations and adaptations – so rich, in fact, that he had recently bought a castle and other property on the Isle of Man. Implicit in this exchange is an acknowledgment of Caine's greater success as a writer since the early days of their friendship in the 1880s. In a later letter, written in 1898, Stoker notes ruefully that Caine had a much better publisher for his 1897 novel, *The Christian*, than he had for *Dracula*: 'There is no-one like Heinemann to push a book. I wish to goodness *Dracula* had been with him and it would have sold at least five or six times as many'.[8] Heinemann, ironically, was the business partner with whom Stoker had lost money earlier in the decade. There is a version of the Cain and Abel story shaping up here, except of course with Caine as the Abel figure. Or perhaps we could see the difference between the two writers, and the commercial success of Caine's old-fashioned romances, as figured in the pile of antique gold which Harker finds in Dracula's castle and plans to take some coins from when he escapes.

Recent bibliographical and critical work has raised awareness of Stoker's numerous short stories, and one story in particular seems to corroborate the idea that Stoker had mixed feelings, of both loyalty and jealousy, about his friend's literary success. As Catherine Wynne has pointed out (2009: xxxiii), 'The Coming of Abel Behenna', written during the period of composition of *Dracula*, is of interest partly because it rehearses a scenario used again in *The Watter's Mou* – the body washed ashore, signifying a fatal sexual entanglement.[9] The surname Behenna also initially suggests the story has something to do with Irving, as this was his mother's family name. But the name 'Abel' of course conjures Cain(e) and the story does retell the Bible story – at the dramatic climax it even includes the ambiguous phrase 'hatred of Cain', which figuratively refers to the biblical Cain's hatred of the successful Abel, but could also be heard literally as someone's hatred of the successful Caine. Reworking biblical myths was a signature technique of Caine, who based at least two of his bestsellers, *The Deemster* (1887) and *The Bondman* (1890), on the story of Cain and Abel. The plot of 'The Coming of Abel Behenna' is a kind of pastiche of devices from both novels. Thus we have the woman waiting for a letter from her lover, who has gone abroad, and gradually surrendering to the attentions of his rival (the situation of Greeba in *The Bondman*); the shipwreck watched from the cliffs and the decision of one of the watchers to take perilous steps to rescue someone (Red Jason's action in *The Bondman*); the fatal lone encounter between the two rivals on a cliff edge (Dan and Ewan in *The Deemster*); the body of the murdered man being washed ashore to incriminate the murderer (*The Deemster*). In all three narratives there is also a similar physical contrast between the two rivals – one Viking (and Stoker-like), one 'Phoenician' (Caine). Caine of course did not have a monopoly on any of these melodramatic devices, but another detail in the narrative suggests Stoker did have Caine's novels and their success in mind when putting this story together. One minor character in 'The Coming of Abel Behenna' is named as 'Michael Heavens' – an unnecessary detail which would seem to be added just to provide an allusion to Michael Sunlocks, the main character in *The Bondman*. This was a name particularly associated with Caine's success: as Stoker would have known, William Heinemann was so pleased with the sales of *The Bondman*, one of his first ventures as a publisher, that he adopted the name 'Sunlocks' as the telegraphic address for his company's London office.

The third element in the received wisdom about the 'Hommy-Beg' dedication is that by dedicating *Dracula* to Caine, Stoker was repaying a debt of another kind, inasmuch as Caine had already dedicated – at embarrassing length – his 1892 book *Capt'n Davy's Honeymoon* to Stoker. This is certainly true, but again no-one seems to have considered in more detail the dynamics of this exchange. Caine's dedication to Stoker anticipates the obituary he would write 20 years later, emphasising his friend's simple virtues. But, more interestingly, Caine explicitly identifies Stoker with Captain Davy Quiggin, the main character in the first of the three stories which make up the book. The final sentence of this two-page dedication, which also serves as a preface to the three stories, reads:

Of Capt'n Davy's Honeymoon,' ... I prefer to confess that I publish it because I know that if anyone should smile at my rough Manx

## Hall Caine's Place in Dracula 179

comrade, doubting if such a man is in nature and now found among men, I can always answer him and say 'Ah, then, I am richer than you are by one friend at least, – Capt'n Davy without his ruggedness and without his folly, but with his simplicity, his unselfishness and his honour – Bram Stoker!

This is a useful clue, as Capt'n Davy is really just a (rather feeble) comic variation on a recurring character type in Caine's novels. An equivalent but often more tragic Stoker-like character can be identified in most of Caine's successful novels from *The Deemster* (1887) – at least up to *The Eternal City* (1901) in which the Bram Stoker character is Bruno Rocco, the big-hearted revolutionary and self-sacrificing follower of the hero, David Rossi. One of Bruno's identifying characteristics is to make frequent references to the villain of the novel, the corrupt politician Bonelli, as 'Old Vampire'. The clearest example of Caine using Stoker as a model is 'Red Jason' in *The Bondman* (1890), the Icelander who exactly fulfils Caine's obituary description of Stoker as 'a massive and muscular and almost volcanic personality' – Stoker was sometimes described by contemporaries as red-haired, and even the name Red Jason is a syllabic analogue of Bram Stoker (like a later name, 'Black Zogal', in *The White Prophet*). After 1895 the Stoker character's role is usually reduced to that of faithful sidekick to the hero but in *The Deemster* (1887), *The Bondman* (1890) and *The Manxman* (1894) the antagonistic bond between this character and the other main male character provides the basic narrative structure. This other main character is also consistently typed, to contrast with the Stoker character: he is always slighter and weaker, easily exhausted, more sensitive, more visionary, and higher-achieving. This character conforms in many ways to Stoker's own descriptions of Caine in *Personal Reminiscences of Henry Irving*: 'his face is pale ... the head so like to Shakespeare's ... His hands have a natural eloquence – something like Irving's ... when he had finished a novel he used to seem as exhausted as a woman after childbirth' (Stoker, 1906, Vol 2: 119–20).

Some of the scenarios that Caine imagined for his Stoker-Caine antagonists have a noticeable homoerotic element to them. In one of the most dramatic scenes in *The Deemster*, they fight to the death on a cliff-edge, but before they start they fasten their belts together so that they fight 'breast to breast' with 'thighs entwined'. In *The Bondman* the two characters are shackled together in an Icelandic prison camp, and the homoerotic element is taken even further when they escape. The Stoker character, Red Jason, has to carry the Caine character, Michael Sunlocks, who is exhausted and blinded, through a landscape feature called 'The Chasm of All Men'. But Michael is unconscious and, at a crucial moment, when the two are hiding and Michael seems to be about to reveal their hiding place by involuntarily crying out, Red Jason has to silence him by kissing him on the lips. Jason and Michael are half-brothers who have actually sworn to kill each other, but by the end of the novel Jason has submitted to Michael so totally that he sacrifices his life to ensure Michael's final escape from imprisonment and his reunion with the woman they both love. Similarly in *The Manxman* Pete, the Stoker character, gives up his wife and child to Philip, the Caine character, and actually emigrates from the Isle of Man so he is out of their way. All the novels which have this pairing in them carry a subtext of the ultimate submission of Stoker to Caine – a fantasy fulfilled in 1905 when Stoker was co-opted by Heinemann to write short introductions to a deluxe special edition of Caine's novels. 'I feel very diffident on the subject' Stoker wrote to Caine: 'It is to me ridiculous that *I* should write a preface for *your* work'. He added: 'I have read nearly all the books again and more than ever old chap *admire your greatness*'.[10]

The following year, after the interval of Irving's death, Stoker took the opportunity to write at more length about Caine in *Personal Reminiscences of Henry Irving*. If one trawls through the two volumes of this text looking for traces of the creation of *Dracula*, it is quite striking how many of these are clustered in the chapter on Caine (Stoker, 1906, Vol 2: 115–130). Here we have the reference to 'seeing a reflection not his own' in the mirror – a story attributed to Caine although it perhaps also belongs to a longer tradition of Gothic mirror-business. In the chapter on Caine we also have the story of the visit to London Zoo where an animal suddenly turns violent ('a veritable, red-eyed, restrainless demon') – echoing not just the London Zoo narrative in *Dracula* but also some of the scenes in the asylum with Renfield. A few pages further on Stoker describes how Caine seemed to have the power to draw a large crowd behind him as he walked down a street in New York (141–2), an incident which recalls Dracula's power to fill his castle courtyard with wolves or the Carfax chapel with rats. I am not suggesting that these incidents, if they really happened, *were* sources for *Dracula* – only that in thinking about him later Stoker seems to have associated Caine, more than most of his other subjects in *Personal Reminiscences*, with echoes of *Dracula*. Throughout the whole chapter, in fact, he seems to be trying to project a 'Gothic' profile for Caine, transferring his own Gothic imaginings onto Caine: 'Irving had a great opinion of Caine's imagination and always said that he would write a great work of weirdness some day' (123).

This brings us back to Hall Caine's liminal place at the beginning of *Dracula* – in the text but also kept out of it, confined in a five-word dedication which pointedly contrasts with Caine's 400 words. Given Caine's acknowledged figuring of Stoker in his novels, and the numerous instances of transformation and escape from confinement in the rest of Stoker's novels – not to mention the coded form of the dedication itself, which inaugurates the hermeneutic process which the rest of the novel has been so successful in drawing modern critics into – it doesn't seem unreasonable to look for other places in *Dracula*, beyond 'Hommy-beg', where Hall Caine may be figured. This might begin with Jonathan Harker's journey: Caine also made a difficult journey across Eastern Europe, in 1892, and he used this as a source for the nightmarish journey in 'The Last Confession' which is the second story in the volume he dedicated to Stoker.[11] We could also note that, like Dracula, Caine lived in a castle in a remote location. Caine would, as Stoker makes a point of telling us in *Personal Reminiscences*, always do a lot of research before committing himself to a project – not unlike Dracula preparing for his move to London. We might even note the similarities between the numerous portraits and cartoons of the red-haired Caine, with his distinctive high forehead that he liked to think resembled Shakespeare's, and Mina's description of Van Helsing: 'such a forehead that the reddish hair cannot possibly tumble over it' (Stoker, 2011: 170).

What would it mean, though, to add Hall Caine to the ever-expanding sum of 'what is meant' by the novel? It does seem that, once we get past the clichés of 'great friendship', Caine could play a part in a psycho-biographical reading of *Dracula* - along with all the other dominant individuals Stoker may have had a close but conflicted relationship with. But I think a more fruitful approach could be developed from reading 'Hommy-beg', as I've suggested, as an allusion to Caine's activity in the literary marketplace – specifically to what Conan Doyle in 1897, in a public letter protesting against Caine, called Caine's 'wire-pulling' and 'self-heralding' (the practice also known as 'booming' – hence the lampooning of Caine, author of *The Deemster*, as 'the boomster'). In this letter there is quite a suggestive match between what Conan Doyle is saying – gentlemanly authors need to band together to stop Hall Caine degrading literature – and Stoker's vampire hunters combining forces to defend their values against Dracula:

> What he [Caine] has never seemed to realise is that in every high profession – be it law, medicine, the Army or literature – there are certain unwritten laws – a gentlemanly etiquette which is binding upon all ... All these wire-pullings and personalities tend to degrade

literature, and it is high time that every self-respecting man should protest against them ... [12]

Conan Doyle's was not a lone voice, and his complaint was not a new one. Despite some grudging critical acknowledgment, in the 1890s Caine was increasingly unpopular with other writers – not so much for his work as for the way his phenomenal financial success seemed to be based on the kind of PR exercise typified by the 'Hommy-beg' profile. Philip Waller quotes H. G. Wells writing (with a cartoon) to George Gissing: 'Have you seen something like this about? If so – shoot it! It's not human. It's Hall Caine' (Waller, 2006: 759). This public demonising of Caine is, I would suggest, the context in which for Stoker the imagining of *Dracula* would have entailed the imagining of Hall Caine. The dedication, in its coded form, signals Stoker's private loyalty to his friend. But the rest of the novel enacts the collective resistance to him.

A curious postscript to *Dracula* can be found in a letter which Stoker wrote to Caine, a few months after publication, congratulating him on the success of his own new novel *The Christian* (which would become Caine's first million-seller). As I have suggested elsewhere (Storer, 2014), some interesting parallels can be drawn between *Dracula* and *The Christian*; and Stoker seems to have recognised this, singling out for special mention not John Storm, the tragic hero, who after a troubled quest for religious fulfilment in London dies at the hands of a mob of his own followers, but a more minor character. 'I like Drake' Stoker told Caine: 'He is a *gentleman*! Man of the world but still gentleman ... I am inclined to hope that later on he and Glory [the heroine] will marry ...'[13] Drake, a government official, evidently represents by his survival (like Harker, Seward and Lord Godalming in *Dracula*) the return to social and sexual order after a turbulent episode, and this may be one reason why Stoker identified with him. But one can't help wondering whether Stoker had not also anticipated later writers of *Dracula* sequels, such as *Tomb of Dracula* or *Blade: Trinity*, and noticed that 'Drake' can be imagined as a modern alias of 'Dracula'. That Caine's gentlemanly establishment figure should thus acquire the ultimate Gothic secret identity, unsuspected even by his author, might just have been one more subversive joke over names that Stoker privately enjoyed at the expense of his more successful friend.

## Notes

1. Bram Stoker to Hall Caine, 23 February 1897; unpublished letter in MNH MS 09542, Manx National Heritage Library (MNHL). Quoted courtesy of Manx

National Heritage. Published courtesy of the Bram Stoker Estate Collection. © Noel Dobbs 2015. On this letter the date is written in ink as 3.2.97 but the number 2 seems to have been pencilled in before the 3.
2. Bram Stoker to Hall Caine, 20 [May?] 1890 (MNHL).
3. Haining quotes the passage from *Personal Reminiscences of Henry Irving* in which Stoker describes Caine's powerful storytelling, but he mistakenly refers to this as a description of how Caine 'enraptured other dinner guests' at the Beefsteak Room, when in fact Stoker sets the scene in his own house, with just himself and Florence Stoker as Caine's audience – a point worth noting because there are so few references to Florence, or home life, in the book. Haining also says that Caine was born on the Isle of Man (he was born in Runcorn – it was his father who was Manx-born) and refers to *The Demon Lover* as one of Caine's 'exotic best-sellers' (in fact *The Demon Lover* was an unpublished play script).
4. See Rance (2002); also Miller (2006: 34–5) for an overview of the question of *Dracula*'s relation to the Whitechapel murders. In his Icelandic Preface, which is dated 1898 though it was published in 1901, Stoker refers to the events of the novel as 'a series of crimes which appear to have originated from the same source, and which at the time created as much repugnance in people everywhere as the notorious murders of Jack the Ripper, which came into the story a little later' (quoted in Miller, 2006: 34).
5. Clive Leatherdale, acknowledging Clive Bloom as source, suggests that another reason the name appealed to Stoker was that it reminded him of an article on Theosophy that had appeared in *Punch* in September 1891, where the Mahatma Koot Hoomi was lampooned as 'Hoomi-Boog' (Leatherdale, 1998: 26). The similarity of the names is certainly worth noting, but, as Caine was not especially interested in or associated with Theosophy, using the name for this reason does not seem as good a joke as the reasons to do with his self-publicising that I have suggested.
6. Bram Stoker to Hall Caine, 3 June 1896 (MNHL).
7. Bram Stoker to Hall Caine, 3 June 1896 (MNHL) [my italics]; see also Dalby (2011: 5).
8. Bram Stoker to Hall Caine, 25 August 1898 (MNHL).
9. Another recently rediscovered Stoker story which could be considered cognate with both 'The Coming of Abel Behenna' and *The Watter's Mou'* is 'Old Hoggen: A Mystery' (1893) in Browning (2012). This also turns on a man's body washed ashore (though in this case freighted with economic rather than sexual symbolism – his pockets are full of money). 'Hoggen', the surname of the drowned man, is an old Dublin place name, but can also be thought of as 'Hall Caine' spoken quickly.
10. Bram Stoker to Hall Caine, 20 June 1905 (MNHL). The special edition of Caine's novels, with Stoker's prefaces, was published by Heinemann in 1907, although the prefaces are dated 1905. All the prefaces are reprinted in Dalby (2011).
11. 'The Last Confession', as Stoker points out in his 1905 preface to *Capt'n Davy's Honeymoon*, is based on the apocryphal story told by Sir Richard Burton of how he committed a murder in order to prevent discovery while travelling to Mecca in disguise. Burton is often associated with *Dracula* because of Stoker's description of him, and pointed reference to his canine

tooth, in *Personal Reminiscences* (Stoker, 1906: Vol 1, 200). Stoker's Preface indicates that in his mind Burton was also associated with Caine.
12. 'Literary Etiquette', letter to *The Daily Chronicle*, 7 August 1897; the letter is signed 'An English Novelist' (Doyle's card was enclosed with the letter) and addressed from 'Authors' Club'; it is reprinted in Gibson and Green (1986) 52–3. A private letter from Doyle to Caine, dated 13 September 1897, assuring him that 'my feelings on the subject are absolutely impersonal and if it had been my own brother I should have written the same', is among Caine's papers (MNHL).
13. Bram Stoker to Hall Caine, 20 August 1897 (MNHL).

# 12
## The Du Mauriers and Stoker: Gothic Transformations of Whitby and Cornwall

*Catherine Wynne*

It was surely a mistake to go to Whitby for a holiday; he might have realized that every corner held a ghost, and every twist and turning of the narrow cobbled streets was haunted by memories. There was an echo in the cry of the gulls, and other footsteps followed his upon the quay. The skies were grey, and the sea wind-blown and cold; the waves broke upon the beach and against the pier with a shudder and a cry of lament.

There were shadows everywhere, and voices from another world, voices from the past now dead and gone.... Down the streets ran the phantoms of children who had played there long ago. Papa walked with Chang in the fish-market; if Gerald listened carefully he could hear the echo of his song around the corner.... And there was a pause as Papa lit a cigarette, and threw away the match; and then away went his footsteps once more tap-tap with his stick, echoing down the street until it was lost in the shout of some passer-by and the high thin cry of the fisherwomen, 'A-ny fresh herrings.' Papa was gone, vanished with his song, and, however quickly Gerald walked to the corner, he could not find him.

When he passed the house in St Hilda's Terrace and glanced up instinctively at the window, he saw Mummie outlined for a moment against the blind; she waved and beckoned, and called out something that he could not hear; and then she was gone, as though she had never been, and there was no figure by the open window, only a blind that swung backwards and forwards in the north wind. (Du Maurier, *Gerald*, 2004: 148–9)

In this extract from the memoir of her father, *Gerald: A Portrait* (1934), Daphne du Maurier resurrects the actor-manager Gerald du Maurier and places him in Whitby in 1917. This port town of North Yorkshire had been a favourite holiday retreat of Gerald's father, the cartoonist and writer, George du Maurier. In the 1880s and 1890s George and his wife Emma frequented Whitby with their five children, the youngest of whom was Gerald. But by 1917, Gerald's only brother, Guy, a soldier, had been killed in the First World War; his sisters Beatrix (Trixie) and Sylvia (whose sons inspired J. M. Barrie's *Peter Pan*) as well as his parents, were all dead and only one sister, May, remained. Daphne's account of her father's life is certainly a portrait – as much a creation as a reflection of a person. It is both actual and imaginative: Gerald did visit Whitby in 1917 but Daphne inhabits her father's mind to create a Whitby of ghostly forms and shadows: George du Maurier singing in the fish-market while walking his dog, Chang, and Emma at the window of a house on St Hilda's Terrace, one of the houses which the family rented for those Whitby late Augusts and Septembers. The ghosts of holidays past appear and dissipate and the 'cobbled streets' of Whitby haunt as the gulls cry and the sea is 'wind-blown and cold'. Whitby is infused with loss and becomes, at this moment, a Gothic place.

In fictional terms, Whitby as a Gothic place, is more firmly, of course, associated with *Dracula*, while Daphne's preferred English Gothic setting is Cornwall. Her Whitby is mostly a place 'inherited' from the grandfather she never knew; her Cornwall a place she discovered and claimed in her own right. George du Maurier, Stoker's contemporary, died in 1896, and the Whitby illustrations he produced for *Punch* magazine adopt a light tone, celebrating, even sentimentalizing Whitby's fishing community and middle-class holidaymakers. Nonetheless, there is, as this chapter explores, a melancholic aspect to George's Whitby sojourns, captured, not by George himself, but in the memories of him by his friend Henry James. This chapter examines the transformation of Whitby from the tourist site of George du Maurier to the Gothic place of Bram Stoker before examining Daphne's 'Cornish Gothic'[1] as well as Stoker's use of that county to stage some of his lesser-known Gothic fictions. It forges new connections between Stoker and the Du Mauriers in their touristic and Gothic predilections.

## Gerald in Whitby

*Gerald: A Portrait*, which Daphne started writing just eight days after her father's death, is also a working out of her own loss. Nina Auerbach describes how Daphne 'nestles in her father's mind and makes him experience his own story' and that 'her apparent emotional withdrawal' – she did not attend her father's funeral – 'facilitated an audaciously dramatic resurrection of a theatrical man' (2002: 36). In this rebirthing the talented and highly successful actor-manager becomes a permanent child – a type of Peter Pan figure, although Gerald, as an actor, was famously associated with the dual role of Mr Darling and Captain Hook.[2] The Whitby memories in *Gerald* focus on childhood. In the early part of the memoir, Whitby plays its part in perpetuating an image of a safe and cosseted childhood. Here Daphne creates the thoughts of her father as a child:

> Of course, Mummie's fussiness could bring its annoyances as well. When he was thoroughly enjoying himself on the sands at Whitby she would make a dash at him with a wretched muffler ... or she would pursue him and May, as they went from the rooms in St Hilda's Terrace to the tennis courts, with jerseys and overcoats over her arm ... What fun Whitby was though! What an unending delight and discovery, with the big seas that broke over the end of the pier, and the slime and smell of herrings and cod in the fish market; and bathing and cricket on the sands, tennis tournaments, picnics on the moors, with Mummie clinging to her hat and her skirt, and Trixie, too, while Papa smoked and sketched, and Guy read, and Gerald and Sylvia and May scampered about in the heather with Chang padding slowly at their heels. (*Gerald*, 2004: 24)

A relaxed family holiday is undercut by 'Mummie's fussiness', a feature of Du Maurier family life. This anxiety about illness, though not an unusual one for middle-class Victorian families, is connected to a traumatic moment in George du Maurier's life. As a young man George's training in fine art at the Antwerp Academy of Fine Arts came to an abrupt end when he suddenly became blind in one eye, forcing him to relinquish fine art for illustration. In her second hybrid fiction-biography of her family, *The Du Mauriers* (1937), Daphne describes this event in 1857 as a moment of sudden blindness:

> He sat with the other students that morning, painting the head of an old man from life, and he found suddenly that he could not focus

properly; the man's head dwindled to the size of a pin ... when he shut his right eye and looked towards the model with his left eye only, he could not see anything at all. (*The Du Mauriers*, 2004: 251–52)

George had grown up in Paris and London in near poverty. With a feckless father, his family relied on his maternal grandmother's allowance which was extracted through blackmailing her former lover, the Duke of York. Tragedy and melodrama intermingle in the Du Maurier history. Daphne describes how 'they pass out of memory ... the figures of fifty, of a hundred years ago. Some of them were comic, and some a little tragic' (*The Du Mauriers*, 2004: 314). However, they return as 'Ghosts ... not phantoms with pale faces trailing their chains into eternity, not headless horrors creaking on the boards of lonely houses, but the happy shadow-ghosts of what has been, no more fearful than the blurred photographs in the family album' (314). A domesticated Gothic suffuses Daphne's account of her family past.

Gerald, too, is a ghost, just as he is surrounded by the phantoms of his own past in Whitby. In the third Whitby episode in *Gerald* the protagonist finds himself on honeymoon with the actress Muriel Beaumont, Daphne's mother, in April 1903:

> He took her to Whitby for their honeymoon. He wanted her to know the old rooms where they used to go every year, and the harbour where Papa had strolled with Chang padding at his heels and the broad-hipped fisherwomen had paused to smile at him, the red roofs and the cobbled stones, the salty, fishy spray-laden Whitby air, with its tang of cutch and rope yarn, nets and herrings. (*Gerald*, 2004: 78)

All three Whitby episodes occurring at crucial moments in Gerald's life replay aspects of his juvenile past with the recurrent imagery of parents, the family's St Bernard, and siblings blended into the backdrop of the fish market, red roofs and cobbled stones. For Daphne's Gerald, Whitby is ultimately re-lived as bereavement.

A review of *Gerald*, which appeared in *The Saturday Review* on 17 November 1934, describes it as a 'novel' rather than a memoir, remarking that Daphne 'has allowed herself so much latitude that there is apparently little distinction between fact and fiction. She never hesitates to put thoughts into Gerald's mind when she thinks it right to do so' (403). What she produces is 'a strange, contradictory, capricious, spoilt, and frequently childish person ... yet at the same time lovable' (*Saturday Review*, 403). The review focuses on the sense of 'moments of deep despondency' (403) located in Gerald's loss of family, reinforcing the image of him as a Peter Pan figure:

> His mind went back often to all his own family, his father Kicky, the famous artist and novelist, his mother who had spoilt him from childhood, his sisters, Trixie, Sylvia, and May, and beyond all to Guy. He anguished himself by returning to the haunts of his boyhood as though to seek them. (403)

By the time Daphne produced *Gerald* she was already a successful novelist after the publication of *The Loving Spirit* (1931), a Cornish family saga which commences in the 19th century. Written when Daphne was newly settled in Cornwall, the novel is presided over by the matriarchal Janet Coombe. In this fictional transformation that draws heavily on ideas about family and lineage Janet is a type of George du Maurier figure. Daphne also uses the theme of time travel which George explored in his first novel, *Peter Ibbetson* (1891). Janet has the ability to see beyond physical time and, as a young woman, crosses over the barriers of time to meet her middle-aged son, who in her timeline has not yet been conceived. This occurs one Christmas Eve when Janet is drawn to her favourite Gothic locale:

> She leant against the castle ruins with the sea at her feet, and the light of the moon on her face ... she was possessed with the strange power and clarity of the moon itself. When she opened her eyes for a moment there was a mist about her, and when it dissolved she saw kneeling beside the cliff with his head bowed in his hands, the figure of a man .... And she knew him to belong to the future, when she was dead and in her grave, but she recognized him as her own. (*The Loving Spirit*, 2004: 32–3)

He is her son, Joseph, but they see each other in this moment 'as they never would on earth. She saw a man, bent and worn, with wild unkempt hair and weary eyes; he saw a girl, young and fearless, with the moonlight on her face' (34).

In *The Loving Spirit* Daphne embeds her literary legacy in Cornwall and in family tradition but absorbs another Gothic place: Emily Brontë's Yorkshire moors in *Wuthering Heights* (1847). Both novels focus on family lines and on intense, quasi-incestuous relationships. Daphne's novel also takes its title from a line in Brontë's 'Self-Interrogation' (1846) – a poem on death. Again focusing on ideas of heredity and place, Daphne argues in *Vanishing Cornwall* (1967) that the 'seed of imagination' in the

Brontës was fired by 'hereditary factors' (1967: 156). Having a Cornish mother and an aunt who lived with the children after their mother's death fostered Emily's imagination in her 'formative years' (1967: 157). She argues:

> This heritage played an undoubted part in the development of later genius, and if Emily Brontë, and *Wuthering Heights*, will always be associated with the Yorkshire moors it must not be forgotten that both her mother and her aunt had on their doorstep, through childhood and adolescence, the wild moorland scenery, the stories and legends, of West Penrith. (1967: 157)

For Daphne Yorkshire is transposed to Cornwall:

> The rocks and stones of those Yorkshire moors, which became famous as Penistone Crags, in *Wuthering Heights*, have the same austerity, the same remote splendour as those of West Penrith; to a walker who knows both the only difference is that in Cornwall the sea wind blows upon him on all sides. (1967: 161)

To emphasize heritage, Daphne argues that Emily's 'vision, nurtured by personal knowledge and observation of the Yorkshire landscape, was drawn from within, part of the heritage bequeathed to Brontë from the Cornwall she had never seen or known' (1967: 162). As Avril Horner and Sue Zlosnik note, '[i]t was, of course, only one step from this assertion to the implication that du Maurier, writing from within Cornwall, had access to the narrative power of the Brontës' (1998: 69). *Vanishing Cornwall* – Daphne's reflection on the literary and cultural landscape of Cornwall – works out notions of heritage which emerge in her first novel.

Towards the close of *The Loving Spirit*, Daphne fictionally reinvents herself as Jennifer which brings the novel up to the post First World War period. Jennifer, who is a physical embodiment of her great-grandmother, Janet, is born in Cornwall, but grows up in London only to return to settle in Cornwall as a young woman. Here she lays the family ghosts to rest but narrowly escapes an accidental fire in the house of her great uncle. He is, however, engulfed in flames in a Miss Havisham-like manner, a punishment at last for destroying the life of Janet's son and Jennifer's grandfather, Joseph. Rescued from the burning house by her distant cousin, the novel closes with the union between them which signals, like Cathy and Hareton's relationship in *Wuthering Heights*, a more peaceful future.

In an interview shortly before her death, Daphne observed: 'I have a strong sense of the things that lie beyond our day-to-day perception and experience. It is, perhaps, an extension of this feeling that makes me live through the characters that I create' (Shallcross, 1987: 111). Daphne certainly lives through and creates her father in *Gerald* and resurrects him again in a fictional form in her novel of the theatre, *The Parasites* (1949), where three siblings remember the adulation their parents received on stage. Their father's mesmeric singing drove the audience wild: 'They would scream, and wave handkerchiefs, and stamp with their feet – just because he did nothing at all but stand perfectly still on stage and sing a little simple song that everybody had learnt in their cradle' (2005: 51). After the loss of his wife in a tragic accident Delaney selfishly leans on his youngest daughter Celia, 'spoil[ing] her life' (82). Her talent as an artist is put aside to take care of her father. In old age he becomes more exacting but Celia trained in self-sacrifice reasons: 'However demanding Pappy may have been, however tiring, however petulant, he was in the true and deepest sense, her refuge. He shielded her from action .... She need not go out into the world ... because she looked after Pappy' (276). Here in fictional form is a portrait of a demanding Gerald.

Daphne's repossession of her father in *Gerald* and recreation of him in *The Parasites* also evokes her grandfather's famous novel, *Trilby* (1894), in which a young artist's model is mesmerically possessed by an older man who transforms her into a concert singer. The *Trilby* inheritance was also channelled through Gerald who played a small role in the actor-manager Henry Beerbohm Tree's first adaptation of *Trilby* for the stage. Perceived as a 'naturally gifted' (Harding, 1989: 184) performer Gerald had undergone no formal training but his 'quieter, more realistic' (45) style of acting was a departure from his predecessors, notably, Henry Irving, for whom Stoker worked as business manager, and Tree. Indeed, Gerald liked caricaturing Irving, before he gained his own place in a new generation of actor-managers. In *Dracula* Stoker produces a type of Svengali-figure, but his mesmeric possessor has, unlike George's human creation, supernatural abilities. Both are, of course, Gothic creations of a particular *fin-de-siècle* mindset of racial and psychological anxiety. More importantly, both George and Stoker were drawn to Whitby.

### George in Whitby

George du Maurier's acquaintance with Whitby began in illustration when he was commissioned to illustrate Smith Elder's one-volume edition of Elizabeth Gaskell's Whitby-based novel, *Sylvia's Lovers* (1863). Gaskell had renamed the town Monkshaven. At this point George had never visited Whitby but Bill Ruddick notes that George used the Whitby sketches of Henry Keene (brother of the *Punch* illustrator, Charles Keene) 'without knowing that he had hit on Mrs Gaskell's very choice of town' (1987: 49). George's only outdoor illustration for the novel was the frontispiece showing the town's bridge in the distance with fishing tackle and an anchor in the foreground.

In August 1864 George and Emma visited Whitby for the first time and writing to his mother from their lodgings on the West Pier, he describes how:

> We are now settled for a month or six weeks in the most beautiful place I ever saw ... Whitby has been most beautifully described by Mrs Gaskell in *Sylvia's Lovers* ... old red houses rise above each other against the side of the cliff, and above is the splendid old church and ruins of a magnificent abbey, founded in the sixth century etc. I can't tell you how we are enchanted with the place'. (*The Young George du Maurier*, 1952: 237)

In her introduction to her collection of her grandfather's letters, *The Young George Du Maurier*, Daphne emphasizes the significance of Whitby in George's life: 'He had no wish to travel, except to France, or to the Yorkshire port of Whitby' (1952: xii). In September 1864 he writes to his mother that he is 'delighted with Whitby' (1952: 240). During this holiday he also met the *Punch* illustrator John Leech, getting 'quite intimate' (1952: 241) with him. At that point Leech was in 'desperate bad state of health' (1952: 242). In her notes to the collected letters Daphne quotes from a lecture which George gave on Leech in 1892, providing an insight into George's activities in Whitby in the Autumn of 1864: 'I used to foregather with him every day and have long walks, and talks with him – and dined with him once or twice at the lodgings' (1952: 300). Whitby was a place for family holidays, artistic discussion and artistic endeavour. When Leech died on the 30 October 1864, George immediately assumed his position on *Punch*, the pressing need for an artist to undertake Leech's unfinished work accounted for the swift appointment (Ormond, 1969: 160).

In his subsequent holidays to the Yorkshire port in the 1880s, George produced numerous illustrations. As well as directly drawing on Whitby for his illustrations, T. Martin-Wood argues that George nearly always used Whitby as the backdrop for his seaside illustrations (1913: 146).

John K. Walton argues that 'The narrow streets, yards and stairways of the "old town" on either side of the harbour, particularly the East Side, where (in favoured metaphors) warrens and honeycombs of houses were built up the valley sides, piled one on top of each other ... [gave] visitors a strong sense of a living history' (2011: 130). Herring was 'an important aspect of the fishing port's contribution to the distinctiveness of Whitby as a tourist destination' as the herring season coincided with the holiday season (130). From at least the 1880s the 'irregularity and informality of layout, with the activity of fishing and commercial ports, was central to Whitby's attractions ... reinforced by artistic representations of Old Whitby' (132). In George's Whitby illustrations these two worlds – middle-class holiday makers and herring workers – collide. In 'Honi Soit' two middle-class governesses pushing babies in prams encounter fisherwomen in knee length skirts, prompting the remark: 'Clothed *that* indelicate that you might have knocked them down with a feather!' (*Punch*, 29 September 1866, 132). In 'Seaside Sports: Toboganning at Whitby' a young middle-class girl points to local boys toboganning down the boat ramp on the quay and asks her governess if she and her sister 'can play it too'. Her governess replies: 'Sir Pomprey would consider such a proceeding most unladylike' (*Punch*, 16 September 1882, 121). Another illustration – 'The Vikings of Whitby' – depicts the fishermen at ease upon the quayside (*Punch*, 23 September 1882, 138).

In his final novel, *The Martian* (1898), George provides a nostalgic description of Whitby's fish market:

[W]e never tired of watching the miraculous draughts of silver herring being disentangled from the nets and counted into baskets, which were carried on the heads of the stalwart, scaly fishwomen, and packed with salt and ice in innumerable barrels for Billingsgate and other great markets. (455)

In 'A Powerful Quartet' (Figure 12.1) George pays tribute to these 'stalwart, scaly fisherwomen' as two figures face each other, hands on hips and baskets of herring balanced on their heads (*Punch*, 24 September 1881: 134).

*The Martian* continues with a description of the town:

Then over that restless little bridge to the picturesque old town, and through its long, narrow street, and up the many stone steps to the ruined abbey and the old church on the East Cliff; and the old churchyard, where there are so many stones in memory of those who were lost at sea.(456)

*Figure 12.1* George du Maurier, 'A Powerful Quartet', *Punch*, 24 September 1881

Despite a final image of death, which evokes Lucy and Mina's discussion with Mr Swales of the tombs with no corpses in St Mary's Churchyard in *Dracula*, Whitby, George observes, 'is an ideal place for young people; it almost makes old people feel young themselves there when the young are about; there is so much to do.' (458)

Both a touristic and a Gothic quality emerges in Henry James' depiction of George in Whitby in his review of *The Martian* and concomitant obituary of his friend for *Harper's Monthly Magazine* in September 1897. James, who had spent holidays with the Du Mauriers in Whitby, perceived a melancholic aspect in George's personality and infuses George's Whitby with a sense of loss:

> I have ... no friendlier notes ... than sundry remembrances of that deeply delectable Whitby to which [George] returned with a frequency that was half a cry of fondness and half a confession of despair, until, in that last summer of his life, he found himself braving once too often, on a pious theory of its perfection, its interminable hills and immitigable blasts. (1897: 602)

It is, James affirms, impossible to resist a 'sketcher's or the storyteller's impulse to circle and hover' in this place with its 'great cold cliffs and its great cold sea, its great warm moors and its big brown fishing-quarter, all clustered and huddled at its brave river-mouth' (1897: 602). In his article James resurrects George in Whitby:

> I see Du Maurier still on the big, bleak breakwater that he loved, the long, wide, sea-wall, with its twinkling light-house at the end, which, late in the afternoon, offered so attaching a view of a drama never overdone, the stage that had as back-scene the ruddy, smoky, smelly mass of the old water-side town, and as foreground the channel egress to the windy waters, under canvas as rich in tone as the battered bronze of faces and 'hands,' for the long procession of fishing-boats – each, as it met the bar and the coming night, thorough master of its part. (602)

For George this scene 'was a play in many acts, that he never wearied of watching, that always gave a chance for wonder if the effect were greater of the start or of the return, and that he was quite willing to rest upon regarding as the most beautiful thing he knew' (602). James argues that this was a 'patient renunciation ... begotten in him by the need, through long years, to do his work at home' and James 'wish[ed] for him ... a glimpse of argosies with golden sails, an hour of sunset, say, in Venetian waters, an exposure to the great composition such hours and such waters unroll' (602). James imbues George's life with the sense of loss, the loss of other vistas and possibilities in his dogged Whitby routines.[3]

Drawn into the circle of Whitby friendships in the 1880s was James's close friend, the American poet, James Russell Lowell. Both 'devoted' to James, Lowell and George's 'intimacy', Leonée Ormond notes, 'developed at Whitby' (1969: 409). James had holidayed in Whitby with the Du Mauriers in 1887 and returned to visit Lowell in 1889. George's death, like Lowell's earlier death in 1891, left James with 'an agonizing sense of loss. He never forgot Du Maurier nor lost the consciousness that his had been a tragic and unsatisfied life' (1969: 399). Remembering Lowell in 1905, James recalls how Whitby rushes into his memory: 'I don't know why, but there rises from it, with a rush that is like a sob, a sudden vividness of the old *Whitby* days, Whitby walks and lounges and evenings, with George Du M. – bathed, bathed in a bitter-sweet of ghostliness too' (Qtd in Ormond, 1969: 412).

Like Daphne's various fictional and quasi-biographical resurrections of her father and grandfather and James's resurrection of George in Whitby, David Lodge's bio-novel *Author, Author* (2004) reimagines the relationship between James and George du Maurier. On his 1893 visit to Whitby, Lodge imagines James's 'ambivalence' about the place: 'Seen at a distance, on a sunny day ... the huddled red and brown buildings of the port, the graceful skeletal ruins of the abbey on the grassy clifftop ... made a delightful picture' (2005: 187). However, 'bitterly cold winds blew off the North Sea on to this rugged stretch of Yorkshire coast even in September' (187). Lodge reimagines the Du Maurier family at play in scenes reminiscent of *Gerald*: 'They bathed in the freezing sea ... and played cricket on the sand at low-tide. They rowed up the river Esk' (188). Lodge has Henry James and George walk to Staithes, discussing enroute George's illustrations for *Trilby* which was to commence serialization in *Harper's Monthly* in 1894. George, enamoured with the views

> wanted to stay on until the evening to watch from the end of the long harbour wall the flotilla of boats going out to sea for the night's fishing, so frail the craft seemed, setting sail towards the coming darkness under the ominous bulging brow of the great cliff. (193)

Another boat, of course, gets into difficulties on that coastline: the *Demeter* in *Dracula*.

## Bram and Daphne: From Whitby to Cornwall

Stoker arrived in Whitby and lodged at 7 Royal Crescent in August 1890 with his wife Florence and son Noel for what became, like George's Whitby sojourns, a working holiday as he researched his vampire novel. Stoker's holiday overlapped with George's who was staying that year at 1 St. Hilda's Crescent.[4] Some years earlier the Stoker family were the subject of George's gentle satire in a *Punch* illustration entitled 'A Filial Reproof' (11 September 1886). Here the Stokers are in the grounds of country house and Florence, occupied with sewing, chastises the young Noel who is standing behind her wicker chair: '*Mamma to Noel (who is inclined to be talkative).* "Hush Noel! Haven't I told you often that young boys should be seen and not heard!" To which Noel replies: '"Yes, Mamma! But you don't look at me!"' (126) The silent Bram sits opposite Florence and looks directly at his son. George's illustration confirms that Stoker was famous enough through his role as business manager to the period's leading actor-manager, Henry Irving, to appear in *Punch*. It also reveals a certain intimacy with the Stoker family.

The product of Stoker's 1890 holiday to Whitby was published in 1897. Whitby, like the Transylvania Stoker never visited, becomes central to the novel's Gothic atmosphere. Stoker's visit to Whitby Museum on 19 August provided him with the *Principalities of Wallachia and Moldovia* which shaped the Transylvanian part of his narrative. In the novel Stoker introduces Whitby as a tourist destination. Mina arrives in Whitby to join her friend, recording the event in her journal: '24 July. Whitby. – Lucy met me at the station, looking sweeter and lovelier than ever, and we drove up to the house at the Crescent, in which they have rooms' (1997: 63). In *The North Riding of Yorkshire* (1904) Joseph E. Morris describes Whitby as a 'picturesque town on the Yorkshire coast – the most picturesque even in England' (400). For Mina, Whitby is also conceived as picturesque place:

> This is a lovely place. The little river, the Esk, runs through a deep valley, which broadens out as it comes near the harbour. A great viaduct runs across, with high piers, through which the view seems somehow further away than it really is. The valley is beautifully green, and it is so steep that when you are on the high land on either side you look right across it, unless you are near enough to see down. (1997: 63)

Mina continues with a description of the town: 'The houses of the old town – the side away from us – are all red-roofed, and seem piled up one over the other anyhow, like the pictures we see of Nuremberg' (1997: 63). The reference to Nuremberg recalls Irving's trip to Nuremberg in 1885 with members of his Lyceum company in order to research his forthcoming production of *Faust* (Wynne, 2013: 50). There is no evidence to suggest that Stoker accompanied Irving on the trip and Mina's comment that Whitby reminded her of the 'pictures' of Nuremberg would suggest that for Stoker Nuremberg was a place seen in pictures.

As if to prepare the reader for the arrival of the invading Count Mina recounts the history of the town with its 'ruin of Whitby Abbey, which was sacked by the Danes', and which 'is also the scene of part of 'Marmion,' where the girl was built up in a wall' (1997: 63). The abbey was sacked by the Danes in 867–70 (Morris, 1904: 402) but Mina's literary reference to Walter Scott's 'Marmion' is incorrect. Although St Hilda, Whitby Abbey's founder, features in the poem, the 'girl' was 'built up' in a wall in Lindisfarne Abbey. Literary inaccuracies aside, Mina depicts the Abbey as a 'noble ruin, of immense size, and full of beautiful and romantic bits' (1997: 63). She is also intrigued by the legend of a 'white lady who is seen in one of the windows' (63) but is drawn to the neighbouring church, St Mary's, 'round which is a big graveyard, all full of tombstones' (63). Here there are 'walks, with seats beside them, through the churchyard; and people go and sit there all day long looking at the beautiful view and enjoying the breeze' (63).

However, the pleasant tourist experience quickly becomes ominous when Mina and Lucy encounter Mr Swales. Swales initially rails against the local folklore including the 'White Lady at the Abbey' which services the day trippers (64): '"Them feet-folks from York and Leeds that be always eatin' cured herrin's an' drinkin' tea an' lookin' out to buy cheap jet would creed aught"' (64). The newspapers, he declares, are '"full of fooltalk"' – a comment on the unnamed *Whitby Gazette* which regularly featured local folklore on its pages. What becomes frightening in Swales's narrative is his description of the empty graves – memorials on land for those lost at sea. Lucy discovers that her favourite seat in the churchyard is over the grave of a suicide but Swales reassures her that he has '"sat here off an' on for nigh twenty years past, an' it hasn't done me no harm"' (68). It harms them both. Dracula occupies the suicide's grave and on 10 August Swales is found dead on the seat with a broken neck. Mina records how the 'doctor said [he] had fallen back in his seat in some sort of fright, for there was a look of fear and horror on his face that men said made them shudder' (85). On 11 August Lucy sleepwalks to her favourite seat and becomes the vampire's easy prey.

In the days preceding Lucy's attack, Whitby transforms into a place of unease. Mina pastes a cutting from the *Dailygraph* in her diary on 8 August, recording an atmospheric change:

> Saturday evening was as fine as ever known, and the great body of holiday-makers laid out yesterday for visits to Mulgrave Woods, Robin Hood's Bay, Rig Mill, Runswick, Staithes and the various trips in the neighbourhood of Whitby ... some of the gossips who frequent the East Cliff churchyard ... called attention to a sudden show of 'mares'-tails high in the sky to the north-west. (75)

The sky is transformed as the sun's 'downward way was marked by a myriad clouds of every sunset-colour – flame, purple, pink, green, violet and all the tints of gold' with 'masses' of 'seemingly absolute blackness, in all sorts of shapes, as well outlined as colossal silhouettes' (75). The newspaper records how the scene was 'not lost on the painters and doubtless some of the sketches of the "Prelude to the Great Storm" will grace the R. A. and R. I. walls in May next' (75) – a tribute, perhaps, to artists like George du Maurier who frequented Whitby. The tempest grows and boats rush to port with the exception a 'foreign schooner' (76). Meanwhile 'masses of sea-fog ... swept by in ghostly fashion' and it required 'but little effort of the imagination to think that the spirits of those lost at sea were touching their living brethren with the clammy hands of death' (76). When the *Demeter* lands ashore only the dead captain remains on board, found with his hands tied to the 'spoke of the wheel' and '[b]etween the inner hand and the wood was a crucifix' (78–9). But just as the boat lands an 'immense dog' (78) bounds ashore and makes its way towards the churchyard. Later a coal-merchant's 'half-bred mastiff' (80) is found dead: '[i]t's throat was torn away' (80). The tourist town suddenly becomes menacing.

To distract Lucy from the disturbing events, Mina takes her for a walk to Robin Hood's Bay 'which seemed to wipe the slate clean' (86). The friends have a tea there 'in a sweet, old-fashioned inn' (86) and Mina observes how they would have 'shocked the "New Woman" with [their] appetites' (86). Lucy returns refreshed but exhausted and Mina admires the loveliness of her sleeping figure, wondering what Lucy's fiancé Arthur 'would say if he saw her now' (86). She further conjectures that '[s]ome of the "New Women" writers will some day start an idea that men and women should be allowed to see each other sleeping before proposing or accepting' (87). She continues: 'But I suppose the New Woman won't condescend in future to accept; she will do the proposing herself. And a nice job she will make of it, too!' (87). George du Maurier produced an illustration on a similar topic on his 1894 holiday in Whitby where he stayed at 1 Terrace Crescent.[5] In 'A Little "New Woman" (Figure 12.2) a boy and a girl, walking along a beach discuss marital proposals:

> *He.* "What a shame it is that men may ask women to marry them, and women mayn't ask men!" *She.* "Oh, well, you know, I suppose

Figure 12.2  George du Maurier, 'A Little "New Woman"', *Punch*, 1 September 1894

they can always give a sort of *hint!*" *He.* "What do you mean by a *hint?*" *She.* "Well – they can always say, "Oh, I do love you, so!". (1 September, 1894: 107)

Both Mina's thoughts and the George's illustrations on the New Woman take place in Whitby.

Lucy's sleepwalking on 11 August finally turns the Whitby vacation into an 'agonizing experience' (87). Finding Lucy absent from the house, Mina searches for her outside and looking across the harbour from the West Cliff to the East Cliff she spies Lucy at her favourite seat with 'something dark' standing behind her 'half-reclining figure' (88). When she finds pricks on Lucy's neck next morning, she attributes them to the safety pin she used to fasten her cloak on Lucy. From this point onwards Lucy continues to be drawn to her favourite seat and on one occasion as she glances back at the seat from the West pier as they make their way home, she remarks: '"His red eyes again! They are just the same"' (91).When Mina follows the direction of her gaze she sees 'a dark figure' who was 'seated alone' (91). Later she sees Lucy hanging out of her window, fast asleep, with something that seemed like a 'good-sized bird' seated on the sill (91). By 17 August Lucy is 'fading away' but on 18 August (by this time Dracula has departed for London), she is better and is able to recall her sleep-walking experience which is conveyed as a type of aerial projection over Whitby: '"I have a vague memory of something long and dark with red eyes ... my soul seemed to go out from my body .... I seem to remember that once the West Lighthouse was right under me"' (94). Whitby's topography is drawn into this Gothic nightmare. This is the last time that Mina will see Lucy alive because on 19 August Mina is summoned to Budapest to tend to her sick fiancé, Jonathan Harker.

Harker's journey to Transylvania, which occupies the opening sections of the novel, is a working visit but his journal accounts simultaneously convey it as a tourist experience. At the Hotel Royale in Klausenburg, Harker notes how enjoys a chicken dinner. The train becomes more unpunctual as it 'dawdles through a country which was full of beauty of every kind' (11). The women 'looked pretty, except when you got near them' (11) and the Slovaks had 'big cowboy hats, great baggy dirty-white trousers ... long black hair and heavy black moustaches' (11). His welcome at the Golden Krone Hotel, however, takes a mysterious turn when the landlord who has had a letter from Dracula directing him to secure a place on the coach for Harker, pretends not to understand Harker's German and he and his wife look at each other in a 'frightened' way (12). When Harker questions them about the Count they cross themselves and refuse to speak. Before his departure the landlady implores Harker not to leave: '"Do you know where you are going, and what you are going to?"' (12). Finally, after her pleas have no effect, she gives him a crucifix. As Harker boards the coach he picks up the words '"Ordog" – Satan' and similar variations (13). His last image of the inn is both quaint and mysterious with 'its crowd of picturesque figures, all crossing themselves, as they stood round the wide archway' (14). As nightfall approaches on their journey to the Borgo Pass the passengers get more restless and urge the driver to speed and they force gifts on Harker. When Dracula's coach is not at the designated spot the driver urges Harker to proceed to Bukovina, just as a caleche pulls up 'amongst a chorus of screams from the peasants and universal crossing of themselves' (17). On his journey on Dracula's caleche, Harker hears howling wolves and sees blue lights. On one occasion Harker fears that he may have been dreaming when he experiences a 'strange optical effect' when the driver who leaves the coach when he sees these blue flames stands in front of one of the flames but does not 'obstruct it' (19). Eventually, Harker finds himself at a 'great door, old and studded with large iron nails' (21). It all seems 'like a horrible nightmare' (21) when Dracula opens the door. The tourist experience transforms into supernatural horror.

Daphne's *Jamaica Inn* (1936) – the Cornish-based novel she published before *Gerald* – recreates such Gothic journeys. Like Harker's journey to Castle Dracula the newly orphaned Mary Yellan finds herself on a coach to her uncle's inn, 12 miles from Bodmin on the road to Launceton. In flashbacks Mary recalls her farming life with her widowed mother in rural Helford with its 'green hills' and 'sloping valleys' (2003: 3). Before she dies, Mary's mother makes her promise that she will live with her Aunt Patience although she has never met the man whom Patience married. The coach ride is through a hostile landscape: 'No trees here, save one or two that stretched bare branches to the four winds, bent and twisted from centuries of storm' (3). When Mary does not descend the coach at Bodmin, the driver questions whether she is going to Launceton as '"There'll be none in this coach going on but you"' (9). When he discovers that her destination is Jamaica Inn, he 'looked at her curiously' (10) commenting that Jamaica Inn is '"no place for a girl"' (10). When Mary replies that she is not frightened of the loneliness he corrects her: '"I never said nothing about loneliness .... It's not the twenty-odd mile of moor I'm thinking of, though that'd scare most women"' (10). He calls to a woman in the porch of the inn for assistance who confirms that '"[i]t's a wild, rough place up there"'

(10) but when Mary tells them that her uncle is the landlord of Jamaica Inn, 'there was a long silence. In the grey light of the coach Mary could see that the woman and the man were staring at her. She felt chilled and suddenly anxious' (10) and the woman refuses to speak any more. The driver avoids her eyes: '"Jamaica's got a bad name ... queer tales get about .... Respectable folk don't go to Jamaica anymore" because they are "afraid"' (11). As Mary progresses on her journey she describes a 'bleak moorland, dark and untraversed' where 'No human being could live ... and remain like other people; the very children would be born twisted, like the blackened shrubs of broom' (13). The inhabitants of this place would be a 'strange stock' who 'would have something of the Devil left in them' (13). Finally, on the crest of a hill Mary sees 'some sort of building standing back from the road' with tall chimneys, murky dim in the darkness' (14). The inn 'stood alone in glory, foursquare to the wind' (14). The driver hurries her from the coach and whips up his horses in a 'fever of anxiety' (14) to depart the place.

Like Harker's trip to Castle Dracula, Mary's journey to Jamaica Inn assumes aspects of danger, isolation and mystery. While the Transylvanian peasants cross themselves and speak of devils, Mary's conversations with the driver and the woman from the inn, convey that Jamaica Inn is also a place of fear. Despite the remarkable similarities of these Gothic journeys, *Jamaica Inn* is not a supernatural novel and as Mary encounters her uncle Joss Merlyn at the door of the inn, the text moves into the terrain of *Wuthering Heights* (it is set in the same period as Brontë's novel), where a cruel and drunken Merlyn subordinates and brutalizes his wife who was like 'a whimpering dog that has been trained by constant cruelty to implicit obedience' (19). Mary, unable to leave her aunt alone, discovers that 'Jamaica Inn was a nest of thieves and poachers, who, with their uncle, as leader apparently, worked a profitable smuggling trade between the coast and Devon' (51). They are also, as Mary later discovers, wreckers.

'As with traditional Gothic tales, the house as a place of threat, is central to the story' (Horner and Zlosnik, 1998: 72). Mary overhears a fracas in the bar when one of Joss's associates tries to break with the group and Joss with an unknown figure secreted in an upstairs bedroom, hangs him and Mary, though friendless in this hostile place, plans to 'have the better of her uncle in the long run, and expose him and his confederates to the law' (62). The moor, by contrast to the inn, seems to 'offer physical and psychic freedom' but this is 'illusory' (Horner and Zlosnik: 75). Like Conan Doyle's *The Hound of the Baskervilles* (1902), where the Devon moors yield up a murderer in the shape of disguised Baskerville intent on killing off the heirs to the estate, the moor in *Jamaica Inn* is a source of danger and duplicity. One of Joss Merlyn's brothers had been drowned in a marsh, a story which Joss tells her on her first evening at the inn. In this landscape no one is quite who they seem to be. When Mary discovers a local vicar on the moor and seeks his confidence, she later discovers that Francis Davey is the smugglers' ringleader, and Joss Meryln is his puppet. It is Jem Merlyn, Joss's brother, whom she mistakenly believes to be involved with his brother, who saves her from the vicar who kidnapped her and took her onto the moors after he had killed Joss and Patience.

In *Vanishing Cornwall* Daphne describes how the germination of her novel occurred on an excursion on horseback over the moors with a friend. Leaving the inn in the afternoon they discover that 'tors and boulders inaccessible on horseback, even perhaps on foot, barred our passage' (1967: 143). Then the 'track leading us on descended to a slippery path that disappeared' (143) and the day 'darkened', descending into fog. (144). Disorientated they let their horses guide them but they are led by them towards a disused quarry: 'Bogs, quarries, brooks, boulders, hell on every side' (145). Finally, the horses brought them to Jamaica Inn by eight o'clock where 'the landlord and his wife had only then begun to think of us, and here was the turf fire for which we had longed, brown and smoky sweet, a supper of eggs and bacon ready to be served with a pot of scalding tea' (146). But 'out of that November evening long ago came a novel which proved popular, passing, as fiction does, into the folklore of the district' (146). Daphne takes some responsibility for the tourism that has affected Jamaica Inn: 'Today all is changed .... Motor-coaches, cars, electric light, a bar dinner of river trout, baths for the travel-stained instead of a cream jug of hot water. As a motorist I pass by with some embarrassment, feeling myself to blame' (146). Just as Whitby is indelibly associated with *Dracula*, Daphne's novel continues to bring the tourist to Jamaica Inn, although the inn of Daphne's fiction bears no resemblance to the inn she encountered after she returned from being lost over the moors.

Although not as well known as his Whitby creation, Stoker also produced some Cornish-based fictions, products of his holiday in Boscastle. In 'The Coming of Abel Behenna' (1893) a frivolous young woman cannot decide between two suitors. But when Abel Behenna wins her hand by casting lots, he goes to sea to acquire money to marry her but makes a pact with his rival in love that if he fails to return within a year he must relinquish his claim. His rival Eric claims Sarah just as the year is expiring. Then a ship is wrecked off the coast and Eric attempts to rescue a drowning man but when he discovers that it is Abel he lets go of the rope, flinging him back into the sea. Eric marries Sarah but as they return to their cottage they discover the body of Abel washed up on the river bank, his dead hand outstretched as if to receive Sarah's. The rugged landscape of Pencastle takes on a Gothic atmosphere and the story ends with Eric realising that he has sold his soul to the devil. Cornwall is also the location to which an Egyptologist takes the mummy of an Egyptian queen in order to resurrect her in *The Jewel of Seven Stars* (1903). In the original ending to the 1903 novel (the novel's ending was changed in the 1912 edition), only the narrator remains alive in this cave under a Gothic mansion as the queen take her revenge on all who watch her resurrection and strikes them dead. Left alone in this grim place, the narrator observes how he finds his companions 'sunk down on the floor ... gazing upward with fixed eyes of unspeakable terror .... I did what I could for my companions; but there was nothing that could avail. There, in that lonely house, far away from the aid of man, naught could avail' (1996: 178). For Stoker, like Daphne du Maurier, Cornwall is transformed into a Gothic place.

Shelley Trower argues that Cornwall as a tourist location was perceived as a place 'of adventure, with its primitive traditions and folklore, its superstitious natives and dramatic landscapes' (2012: 202) in the 19th century. As an 'otherworldly' (202) space it is, Trower argues, 'comparable' to Whitby which is 'similarly distant from the urban centre with its own landscapes and legends and dialects' (207), providing an 'escape for tourists' (207). Daphne also gothicizes Cornwall in *Vanishing Cornwall* focusing on its prehistoric past and superstitions which are reminiscent of Swales's stories of the bodies lost at sea in *Dracula*: 'A drowned father, brother, son became a menace in the night, eternally reproaching, and changed in a fearful way from the loved one he had been' (1967: 71). For Daphne the family ghosts of Gerald and George return to Whitby to be laid to rest, while she forges her own creative and Gothic landscape in Cornwall. Stoker turns Whitby from a tourist town to Gothic place in *Dracula* and, just as Daphne's influence continues to shape a tourist perception of Cornwall, Stoker has transformed the Whitby of today into a place of Gothic tourism.

## Notes

1. Avril Horner and Sue Zlosnik coined the term 'Cornish Gothic' to describe Daphne's Gothic productions (1998: 64–98).
2. Barrie had conceived separate actors for the roles but Gerald conceived the idea of playing both roles. Auerbach argues that he excelled in portraying dual figures (Auerbach, 2002: 33). James Harding argues that 'Gerald, with his

actor's egoism, saw a magnificent part in Hook but was greedy as well to show off his virtuosity by playing Mr Darling' (1989: 58–9). The play premiered on the 27 December 1904 at the Duke of Yorks's Theatre.

3. The Du Mauriers alternated between Whitby and Dieppe in Normandy. In his *Punch* cartoon of 2 October 1880, 'Farewell to Fair Normandy' George portrays his children (called the Browns) leaving the beach for the last time. Chang is accompanying the children.

4. A letter to Henry James from George du Maurier confirms that the Du Mauriers were in Whitby at the end of August. Letter from George du Maurier to Henry James, 25 August 1890. *James, Henry, 1843–1916. Correspondence and journals of Henry James Jr., 1855–1916. MS Am 1094 (142–182)*. Houghton Library, Harvard University, Cambridge, Mass.

5. George writes in a letter to Henry James on 11 September that 'Whitby has not been kind this year' as Emma had fallen ill which required a protracted stay in the resort. George du Maurier, Letter to Henry James, 11 September 1884. *James, Henry, 1843–1916. Correspondence and journals of Henry James Jr., 1855–1916. MS Am 1094 (142–182)*. Houghton Library, Harvard University, Cambridge, Mass.

# 13
# The Un-Death of the Author: The Fictional Afterlife of Bram Stoker

*William Hughes*

As an author, Bram Stoker has long been the subject of an intense process of fictionalisation. This process is, arguably, almost totally a consequence of the critical drive to interpret *Dracula* through the biography of its author, to trace its origins in what have been conventionally interpreted as the significant but traumatic incidents of Stoker's life, from his mysterious childhood illness to the alleged syphilis which supposedly hastened his death. As Barbara Belford asserts in the Introduction to her *Bram Stoker: A Biography of the Author of Dracula* (1996),

> Calumnies have been spawned to justify the premise that no genial Irishman could have written such a perversely sexual novel. In biography and fiction, Stoker variously has been given a frigid wife, a penchant for prostitutes (particularly during their menstrual period), a sexually transmitted disease, and inherited insanity. (1996: x)

If this were not enough, Stoker has additionally been configured as a repressed homosexual in a queer triangular relationship with Oscar Wilde and his literary reputation; a sentimental hero-worshipper; and the victim – or witness – of child sexual abuse.[1] Implicitly, then, Stoker can be 'no genial Irishman', because he wrote such a work as *Dracula*. In common with all eminent, notorious or representative Victorians, Stoker *must* be something other than what he actually said he was. In other words, he cannot, in modern critical and biographical discourse, be anything other than an evocative repository of secrets, repressed desires and abiding guilt.

In the perception of his 19th-century counterparts, however, Stoker was, indeed, *explicitly* 'the genial acting manager' (175), 'a mild, gentle Irishman' (216) whose 'ruddy face, bright eyes and beaming smile are sufficient to placate even the most cross-grained visitor' (210) to the Lyceum Theatre.[2] Stoker's visual presence, whether recorded in the sober formality of evening dress or the dishevelled aftermath of attempting to save a drowning man in the Thames, is likewise bluff, guileless, chivalric – and, if not genial, at least courteous and urbane.[3] This is very much the impression, it might be added, which might be gleaned from the author's own essays into the field of autobiography. Stoker's *Personal Reminiscences of Henry Irving* (1906) is sporadically its author's autobiography, also, and the source of a corpus of potentially conflicting material that configures the writer of *Dracula* as being open in his spontaneous professions of emotion, the very presence of which hint of a darker, repressed and possibly effeminate self to counterpart the stridently manly exterior.

The short intimation which accompanies the epiphanic moment on 3 December 1876 when Stoker effectively cemented his friendship with Irving is the pivot upon which so many accounts of the author's life and assumed character are forced to revolve (Stoker, *Personal Reminiscences*, vol. 1, 1906: 32–3). The author's retrospective account of himself, which is associated with an apparently unfeigned emotional outburst in Irving's presence, contains the core of much that has been rendered significant in subsequent attempts to fictionalise a troubled and complex character truly worthy of the author of *Dracula*. Stoker recalls his demeanour in the silence that followed Irving's closing words thus:

> As to its effect I had no adequate words. I can only say that after a few seconds of stony silence following his collapse I burst out into something like a violent fit of hysterics. (*Personal Reminiscences*, vol. 1, 1906: 31)

Such extraordinary behaviour in the company of even theatrical gentlemen must surely demand an explanation – and Stoker is quick to contextualise his outburst. The account continues with Stoker explaining:

> I was no hysterical subject. I was no green youth; no weak individual, yielding to a superior emotional force. I was as men go a strong man, strong in many ways. If autobiography is allowable in a work of reminiscence let me here say what I was:

> I was a very strong man. It is true that I had known weakness. In my babyhood I used, I understand to be, often at the point of death. Certainly, till I was about seven years old I never knew what it was to stand upright. (*Personal Reminiscences*, vol. 1, 1906: 31)

Stoker's pointed emphasis upon his current strength – he later goes on to recount his success as a college athlete and proclaim himself an exemplar of 'that aim of university education *mens sana in corpore sano*' – is here explicitly deployed as the rhetorical foil to his apparently hysterical collapse at the climax of Irving's dramatic reading of Thomas Hood's *The Dream of Eugene Aram* (*Personal Reminiscences*, vol. 1, 1906: 32). It is Irving's dramatic presence that has – temporarily – unmanned Stoker, by matching his character with an equivalent in idealised, manly strength at the point at which, Stoker contends, 'Soul had looked into soul!' (*Personal Reminiscences*, vol. 1, 1906: 33).

Stoker's Edwardian readers, quite possibly, did not read any particular significance into his admission that his twice-named 'hysterical' breakdown 'was distinctly a surprise to my friends' (*Personal Reminiscences*, vol. 1, 1906: 32). For later critics and biographers, however, the sparse intimations of the author's youthful and early adolescent life vouchsafed by the *Personal Reminiscences of Henry Irving* are the building blocks of literary legend. Lisa Hopkins, in her *Bram Stoker: A Literary Life* (2007), for example, makes much of Stoker's 'insistent troubling of the borderline between life and death', which she suggests 'seems to be traceable back to his childhood' (2007: 25). That childhood, no doubt, necessarily implicates Stoker in a gendered submission: Belford suggests of the author that 'his mother haunts his writing' (1996: 25), where Andrew Maunder is more emphatic in his suggestion that the self-fictionalisation of the *Personal Reminiscences* encodes and expresses 'the matriarchal restraints embodied in Charlotte Stoker' (2006: 132). Such insecurities may be perpetuated into later life. Hopkins is persuasive in her association of Stoker's hysterical seizure with his inglorious existence as a clerk in government service, incarcerated in sickly and unmanly servitude (2007: 17). Stoker's emotional collapse is elsewhere suggested as both significant and indicative in Harry Ludlam's *A Biography of Dracula* (1962), the earliest sustained study of Stoker's life, as it is in Belford's 1996 biography and in Andrew Maunder's *Bram Stoker* (2006); in Daniel Farson's *The Man Who Wrote Dracula* (1975), again, the occasion represents 'a turning-point' for the author.[4] The sickly child and the vulnerable adult, it is thus consistently argued, somehow meet and express their common liminality and insecurity in the emotional honesty prompted by Irving's mesmeric performance. This oft-cited scene has become central to the reconstructed persona of Stoker as envisaged by 20th-century biography: its implications, though, far exceed the biographical commentary upon the author.

To this basic compound image of an infant Stoker, sickly, thoughtful and dominated by his mother, and the adult male who rejoices in the bulky virility of his athletic body, is customarily conjoined another, apparently revealing, portrait of the Victorian artist as a young man. This latter was not readily accessible to Stoker's contemporaries, other than in its consequences – a letter from the then-controversial American poet Walt Whitman praising the 24-year-old Irishman's candour, reprinted in facsimile and transcribed in the *Personal Reminiscences of Henry Irving*. Stoker's letter to Whitman of 18 February 1872, which was written 'so unconventionally, so fresh, so manly, and so affectionately' that the poet encouraged further correspondence, is a rather naïve piece of almost-adolescent hero-worship (*Personal Reminiscences*, vol. 2: 97). Its content, which rather emphatically describes its author as being 'six feet two inches high and twelve stone weight naked', prompted Whitman to interpolate this image as 'a mighty graphic picture' – this acutely homoerotic response not being readily available to neither the young athlete's Victorian contemporaries nor the elder writer's Edwardian readers (Traubel, 1953: 183).

Stoker's letter has variously been interpreted as evidence of the author's recurrent tendency to engage in uncritical hero-worship as well as a tacit admission of his otherwise-repressed homoerotic tendencies.[5] Perhaps more significant in the letter, though, are those elements which anticipate Stoker's later *public* pronouncements regarding the standards appropriate to contemporary masculinity. Critics have been almost universal in their association of the heroic masculinity of Stoker's heroes with his own behaviour: Jeffrey Richards, for example, sees the author's heroes as 'frequently projections of himself, big, burly, athletic manly men who act according to chivalric ideas' (1995: 146-7), just as Lisa Hopkins contends that 'Stoker seems to have invested considerable emotional energy in the creation of his heroes' (2007: 9). This is tenable, and quite in keeping with some of the uncompromising sentiments regarding manliness voiced in Stoker's *A Glimpse of America* (1885).[6] To Whitman in 1872, however, Stoker confided:

> I am equal in temper and cool in disposition and have a large amount of self control and am naturally secretive to the world. I take a delight in letting people I don't like – people of mean or cruel or sneaking or cowardly disposition – see the worst side of me. (Traubel, 1953: 183)

Stoker here, as it were, proclaims himself to be the diametric opposite of those people he doesn't like, appointing himself their judge and their scourge: indeed, Harry Ludlam recounts – without substantiation – one such episode of male cowardliness in a New York theatre, thwarted by a defiant Stoker (1962: 76). Such episodes and attributes – physical, gentlemanly, consistent – constitute the public face of a man who has subsequently been fictionalised into quite another character. In biography, Stoker has become a man who may only be truly comprehended through the occluded hints ostensibly embedded not merely in the *Personal Reminiscences* but also in *Dracula* and the author's other fictions.

The Bram Stoker projected in biography and affirmed through the criticism of his writings is thus many things. On the surface he is manly, chivalric, and brusque in a manner which to some may suggest a personal simplicity quite cognizant with a hero-worshipper scarcely in control of his sycophancy. His red-tinged hair and beard, and possibly his accent also, hint of Hibernian origins, and implicitly proclaim him an outsider in the English milieu. He is overshadowed by a powerful Other, Irving, with whom he enjoys an ambiguous relationship, and his declining health in later years – a stroke, debilitating exhaustion and fading eyesight – is associated with that relationship, and comes eerily to echo his earliest years in the hands of a domineering mother. He is courteous to women, yet perversely fearful of his wife or else reluctant to engage in intimacy with her. He is a *bricolage* of implications and motivations, some of them undoubtedly true – but he has become, through the attention of biographers and literary critics alike, a fiction rather than a reality, a character rather than an author.

Belford, though, it might be recalled, was sufficiently astute to consider the contested depiction of a Stoker accessed through 'biography *and* fiction', and though the former of these, in its critically applied as well as strictly biographical incarnation, has formed the subject of critical scrutiny, the latter has received relatively little attention (1997: x; italics mine). The Bram Stoker encountered as a character in 20th-century fiction is highly dependent upon the biographical depiction of the author, but characteristically draws also upon the perceived relationships explicated in criticism between *Dracula* and the life experiences of its writer. The fictional Stoker, who moves in a Victorian world redolent as much with clichés as with actual historical accuracy, is thus a curious hybrid which embodies implications that go far beyond those delivered speculatively in criticism. In fiction, Stoker acts, reacts, thinks and talks. He meets with – and sometimes exceeds – the expectations of the reader, gleaned as these are from biography and criticism, and provides a temporary (though seldom ultimately convincing) explanation for his own writings and behaviour and, on occasions, for those of his contemporaries also. He is, in this respect, a literary phenomenon as worthy of study as his avatars in biography and those masculine figures critically associated with the perceived demeanour of the author in the pages of his own fiction. This is the un-death of the author.

Stoker has long been a minor participant in fictions which feature a historical Count – or Prince – Dracula, and in such works this latter figure is characteristically keen to redress the perceived injustice to his historical reputation and current vampiric state committed in the pages of Stoker's 1897 novel. In Dan Simmons's pointedly titled *Children of the Night* (1992), for example, an embittered and enfeebled Count contemplates both *Dracula* and its author in one of the interpolated 'Dreams of Blood and Iron', historical reminiscences that punctuate the contemporary action of the novel, which is set in post-Ceauşescu Romania. The ageing vampire complains:

> I have read Stoker. I read his silly novel when it was first published in 1897 and saw the first stage production in London. Thirty-three years later I watched that bungling Hungarian ham his way through one of the most inept motion pictures I have ever had the misfortune to attend. Yes, I have read and seen Stoker's abominable, awkwardly written melodrama, that compendium of confusions which did nothing but blacken and trivialize the noble name of Dracula. (1992: 297; original italics)

If such sentiments regarding the historical liberties taken by the plot of *Dracula* might be regarded as being typical in evoking Stoker's reputation in vampire-narrated works, a *slightly* more positive acknowledgement is to be found in 'O Captain, My Captain' (1987) by Katherine V. Forrest, a lesbian-inflected science-fiction story which terms Stoker not a novelist but 'A nineteenth-century historian' (215). On being reproached with the contention that Stoker is *not* a historian but 'A nineteenth-century novelist ... Author of a novel popular well into the twenty-first century', the vampire, star-ship Captain Drake, is not deterred:

> 'A historian,' Drake countered with cool emphasis. 'And a most limited one at that. He recorded in fictional form what glimmerings he knew of an entire species.' She added, 'I possess extensive knowledge in this area.' (1987: 215)

The penultimate point here is oddly significant. In later writings Stoker is frequently portrayed as a mortal who has encountered 'true' vampirism, and who has 'recorded in fictional form' a reality otherwise unacknowledged and unacknowledgeable.

It is in works such as this, where vampires walk the earth and apparently meet with the author of *Dracula*, that Stoker functions most fully as a character in fiction. Such works blur the boundaries between fiction and history, transplanting known individuals – the reputations and clichés of authors long dead – into imaginative revisions of the worlds they themselves depicted. Such fictionalisations are seldom a structured *mise en abyme* or a metafiction, however. The fictionalised author may here function on occasions as a form of authority for the text's intricacies – the actions of the postmodern novel are referred backwards to its Victorian forebear, rather in the manner of the spurious documents so frequently referenced in earlier Gothic works. Elsewhere, he may be featured in such a way as to cast fictional light upon the motivations for writing, and possible sources, of the work with which he is best associated. It is a common form of fictional autobiography: the deployment of Stoker as a subject in fiction is paralleled by that of many other authors in the Gothic tradition, among them John Polidori, Lord Byron and H. G. Wells.[7] Stoker, though, with his vast critical heritage and ongoing topicality as a subject in popular biography as well as academic criticism, holds perhaps the greatest potential for exploitation by an author familiar with the conventions accorded to his life and writings.

Among the many works which deploy Stoker as a character to a greater or lesser extent, *The List of Seven* (1993) by Mark Frost is particularly intriguing in its depiction of the author of *Dracula* at large in late-Victorian Whitby. *The List of Seven* revolves around the secret cabal of the title, a group of powerful public figures engaged in an occult plot to dominate British and Imperial political culture. Drawing in part upon the 20th-century mythologies surrounding the Whitechapel Murders popularised by Stephen Knight and others, the narrative deploys stock Victorian locations such as the séance room, the country house and the streets of London, interconnecting these with rail and cab journeys. The central plot to introduce an implicitly satanic heir into the Royal bloodline via the dissolute and degenerate Duke of Clarence is uncovered by another sporadically fictionalised author, Arthur Conan Doyle, who – the logic of the novel suggests – comes eventually to cast his own Sherlock Holmes in the mould of Jack Sparks, the heroic agent of the Crown who enlists the good doctor in the cause of right and civilisation (Frost, 1994: 405).

Doyle and Sparks arrive in a snowbound Whitby in pursuit of the truth behind certain fatal events in London, and encounter Stoker outside the parish church which features prominently in the second phase of *Dracula*.[8] The first encounter is with a physical presence that matches utterly the volume of a voice which is, none the less, tinged with 'the musical lilt of Erin':

> 'There's no one here,' said a deep and resonant voice behind them.
>
> They turned: a giant of a man stood before them, six and a half feet tall if he was an inch, cloaked against the cold as they were, but he wore no hat; a leonine shock of red hair crowned his massive head and his face was framed by a thick red beard encrusted with icicles. (Frost, 1994: 298)

There is a moment of partial recognition on the part of Sparks, not truly uncanny, but certainly hesitant, and this is solved when the bearded man introduces himself as 'Abraham Stoker, manager to Henry Irving and his theatrical company. Bram to my friends.' Even here, Stoker is an apostrophe to the actor's greatness; for the Doctor's thoughts immediately turn from the stranger he faces to 'the legendary Irving', so that 'Doyle felt dumbstruck in proximity to someone even remotely connected to the man' (Frost, 1994: 298). Stoker's famous employer, as is the case in the biographies and in those critical works which see Irving as the motivation for the Count, effectively eclipses the novelist and manager, even in the actor's absence.

Stoker's sojourn in Whitby, though, is here given a relevance to the plot of *The List of Seven* which has no parallel in the author's biography. Whitby was a preferred holiday destination of the Stoker family in the 19th century (Farson, 1975: 151). Frost, though, envisages Stoker travelling to the resort in pursuit of information regarding the same fatal theatrical performance – styled as a séance – witnessed by Doyle at the novel's inception (Frost, 1994: 303, 305). The account of Stoker's delivery of his narrative is telling, considering the action explicitly precedes the author's first novel, which was published six years later in 1890:

> Stoker had not spent his years around the stage in vain; his delivery was practised to wring maximum dramatic effect from every pause or inflection, but the result was so spontaneous and laden with import that the listener was effortlessly persuaded to deliver himself into this storyteller's crafty hands. (Frost, 1994: 300)

Stoker's narrative, though, is ponderous, in places pompous, even, and fractured by pregnant pauses and hearsay testimony, with paperwork being produced in evidence in much the same way as in *Dracula*

(Frost, 1994: 300). Doyle is notably (and ironically, it might appear) irritated: 'Damn the man's vanity and his orderly unfolding of information' (Frost, 1994: 302, cf. 305). It is when the issue of a gentleman's relationship to women is raised in *The List of Seven*, though, that the fictional Stoker emerges more clearly as a character cast in the mould of his own heroes. Two people were murdered during the fatal séance, and this is the point that Stoker's frequently stressed chivalry and deference to women is deployed. He confirms the fatalities: '"Man and wife. And the woman six months pregnant," said Stoker, his repugnance at the atrocity surfacing for the first time from under the polish of his delivery' (Frost, 1994: 304). If this is an ambiguous indignation, more straightforward is Stoker's tracking of Eileen Temple, the one female survivor of the séance, to Whitby and his protective attitude towards her. Unlike Sparks, Stoker does not question her ostensible guilelessness. The actress is, though, self-consciously literary and theatrical, given that she abides in Whitby 'like some haunted, heartbroken lover. Some poor lost soul out of Brontë' (Frost, 1994: 314).

The fictionalised origins of *Dracula*, however, are made evident from this point, for the beleaguered Eileen has encountered an occult being in her rooms whose presence suggests a vampire undoubtedly familiar to Frost's 20th-century readership and a scenario that will be familiar from events enacted in the violated bedroom of Mina Harker:

'I was awakened in the middle of the night. Gently. I don't know why, I didn't move, I just opened my eyes. I wasn't sure, I'm not sure now, if I wasn't dreaming. A shape was standing in the shadows in the corner of my room. I looked at it for a long time before I could be sure what I was seeing. A man. He didn't move. He looked ... unnatural'.

'Describe him for me,' said Sparks.

'A pale face. Long. All in black. His eyes – it's hard to describe – his eyes burned. They absorbed light. They never blinked. I was so terrified I couldn't move. I could hardly breathe. I felt as if I were being watched by something less than human. There was hunger. Like an insect.' (Frost, 1994: 315)

Stoker, gallantly, has acted to prevent a recurrence of such night terrors, much as the Van Helsing circle do on the evenings following Mina's violation by the Count, having 'sat up all night' in her room, armed with a shotgun (Frost, 1994: 315). He is, though, none the less concerned for his moral reputation, and swears Doyle to secrecy regarding his presence in Temple's room (Frost, 1994: 319–20).

Stoker, though, reveals more of his discoveries in Whitby to Doyle and Sparks, and these again fictionally anticipate *Dracula*. A garrulous sailor reports a near shipwreck at Tate Hill Pier, the depositing of crates, a mysterious black dog and the apparent 'arrival of our Lord' (Frost, 1994: 317). The great secret of both the Sherlock Holmes stories and of *Dracula*, as propounded in *The List of Seven*, is that the authors – who were acquaintances in documented life – based their fictions upon a shared experience in which the mysterious and the horrible were juxtaposed in their sight. The fantasy is that the satanic Count and the invasion motif involving Whitby are ostensibly as factual as the Holmes and Moriarity which Doyle is supposed to have fabricated out of his observations of Jack and Alexander Sparks. Stoker is, again, a sort of historian.

A more profound encounter with the fictionalised author is to be found in a sequel to *Dracula* partially written by his great nephew Dacre Stoker. In *Dracula, The Un-Dead* (2009) the genesis of *Dracula* is effectively imbricated into an imaginative continuation of that novel, via the conceit that Stoker adopted the story from a tale told to him by an intoxicated Jonathan Harker, one of the scarred survivors of an incursion into Britain which took place in 1888 rather than 1897: 'How' the narrator queries, 'could Bram have known that some of the people in the madman's tale were real?' (Stoker and Holt, 2009: 204, 207). Stoker thus becomes a momentary pivot at the centre of an ongoing narrative which is suspended at the point at which *Dracula* concludes, but which is revived as the vampire returns to London to both castigate the author for his fictive inaccuracies and be revenged upon those opponents whose behaviour has been exonerated in the 1897 novel (Stoker and Holt, 2009: 91).

Stoker, who has been fictionally gifted the Lyceum by Irving in *Dracula, The Un-Dead*, is a far less hearty – though still utterly recognisable – character, heavily reliant upon the clichés of his appearance and aspirations. He is 'Bram Stoker, a husky old Irishman with greying reddish hair and a beard', reliant now upon a cane to support his hobbling gait, and who 'did not want to be remembered as a faded footnote in Irving's illustrious biography' (Stoker and Holt, 2009: 79, 84). If this were not enough to locate the man as a fiction founded upon biography, a touch of bio-critical speculation is interleaved in the suggestions that the author's wife, Florence, was unsympathetic to *Dracula* and 'thought Bram was wasting his time trying to write horror, and she considered this newest endeavor quite beneath them' (Stoker and Holt,

2009: 86). Wilde, and his apparently successful *Dorian Gray* are a constant presence in the work also, with a reminder of the dramatist's failed relationship with Florence indexed more than once (Stoker and Holt, 2009: 84–6). Most pointed, though, are the references to Stoker's allegedly troubled sex-life, and the critically endorsed connection between the novel and inexpressible personal sexual trauma:

> *Dracula* was Bram Stoker's last chance. One last chance to prove himself as a writer; one last chance to live his dream; one last chance to keep his theatre. Now that his son was grown and had left the house, Stoker had nothing waiting at home. Even his beautiful wife made him feel quite unwelcome, and it no longer mattered to Bram if his bed was loveless. (Stoker and Holt, 2009: 83–4)

Stoker and Holt here stress carefully the family motto, '*Quid verum atque decens* ... Whatever is true and honorable', and it is this element of an evident familial loyalty which in *Dracula, The Un-Dead*, deflects the allegations made in 1975 by Daniel Farson, another member of the family, that the author consorted with prostitutes and contracted syphilis on account of his wife's sexual reluctance (Farson, 1975: 233–34).

Farson's sensationalistic account casts doubt even upon Stoker's paralytic stroke, which apparently interfered with the author's eyesight as well as his mobility (Farson, 1975: 234). This, again, is addressed in *Dracula, The Un-Dead*, as the stroke becomes associated not with Irving's death but with the anger of an enraged Prince Dracula who, in the guise of the actor Basarab, berates the ageing author for his literary inconsistencies:

> Stoker could retreat no more. He was backed into a corner. The room seemed to grow darker. Basarab was so close that he completely filled Stoker's vision. Those eyes! Those black eyes! Stoker could feel his left arm growing numb and cold. He was on the verge of tears. (Stoker and Holt, 2009: 208)

There is something here that recalls both Harker's frustration in Transylvania and the menacing presence in Mina's London bedroom. The strong man is feminised, and the vampire adopts a stance familiar from fiction and cinema even where it is evident that he will not bite. The account continues:

> Sweat poured down Stoker's face. He leaned against the wall for support, rubbing his dead arm. The room seemed to spin and tilt. Stoker

averted his eyes to avoid Basarab's soul-piercing stare. Pain seared through his arm and into his neck as he struggled to breathe. Stoker forced himself to meet Basarab's gaze, even as he sensed himself sliding to the floor. 'Who are you?' he gasped. (Stoker and Holt, 2009: 208)[9]

The touch of the vampire is not immediately fatal, but certainly debilitates:

> It was as if Basarab's grip had been the dam holding back the flood of pain. Searing agony shot up Stoker's neck, along the side of his jaw and into his brain. He grabbed his skull. It felt as if a hot poker had been thrust into his eye. Stoker collapsed to the floor. Basarab turned away from him. Stoker reached out for help, but was paralyzed. His pleas came out as dry wheezes.
>
> He could only watch helplessly as Basarab took hold of his most prized possession: the *Dracula* playbook.
>
> Then, blackness. (Stoker and Holt, 2009: 209)

This is a complex gesture. The fictional character has taken possession, quite literally, of the text in its next incarnation – the Hamilton Deane *Dracula* stage play. Stoker, though, is the victim of his own creation, and if he has a vice at all, it is to have not been original, to have perpetuated the self-justificatory mythology of Harker and Van Helsing. Much of the imagery of 'searing' grief and 'black numbness', though, recalls Ludlam's account of the stroke which robbed 'his robust frame of much of its boundless vitality ... leaving his eyesight impaired' (Stoker and Holt, 2009: 134).

Though Stoker and Holt avoid the sensationalism of sexual intrigue in the author-character's demise, they still draw heavily on the biographical tradition associated with the author of *Dracula*. Still worrying on his deathbed about being an ephemeral appendix to the successful Irving and the literary Wilde, Stoker is not unaware of the symmetry of his closing life:

> The bitter irony was not lost upon him. He had begun his life as a bedridden child and would spend his last days as a bedridden old man. He had become a prisoner in his own body, paralyzed on his left side, unable to move, or even feed himself. He had to suffer the indignity of having to be bathed and changed as if he were a helpless infant. (Stoker and Holt, 2009: 287)

This description, again, echoes biographical consensus. Ludlam depicts the dying Stoker as being 'as helpless and near to death as he had been in the first years after his birth' (*A Biography of Dracula:* 149). Farson, likewise, envisages an author bedridden, 'as feeble as when he had begun his life in Clontarf Crescent' (1975: 233).[10]

In *Dracula, The Un-Dead*, however, Stoker's death gains a final, literary symmetry not cognizant with the tragedy of a man who possibly *did* die of simple physical exhaustion – the poignant phrase which terminates the writer's formal death certificate.[11] A long passage here begins with a scene reminiscent of that in Mina's bedroom, when 'the shadows that now shrouded the room, created by the moonlight spilling past the shade, began to move':

> A shadow detached itself from the wall, blocking out the moonlight as it passed the window, and crept to the foot of his bed ... He watched in helpless disbelief as the shadow began to take on the outline of a human form, certain he was having a terrible nightmare. (Stoker and Holt, 2009: 288)

Of course, this is not nightmare but the familiar evocation of a vampire's attack, albeit reproduced with the graphic frankness of the 20th rather than the 19th century:

> The shadow's black mass lunged forward, enveloping him. It had weight, like another human being pressed down on him, pinning him to his bed. Using what little strength he had, Stoker tried to fight back.
>
> He screamed as something punctured his neck. He felt no pain, but he knew his blood was being drained from his body. The shadow was alive and he would soon be dead. (Stoker and Holt, 2009: 288–9)

There is nothing of the erotic here, and if the death of the author appears to be a somewhat gratuitous (and, for some, possibly inappropriate) detail in a work penned by a relative, it provides a necessary and justified closure to the extended narrative of *Dracula* – assuming, that is, Bram Stoker does not himself join the ranks of the un-dead. Most significant, though, is the final affirmation of how biographically inflected fiction blurs not merely the boundaries of narrative genre but of perceived reality also. The narrator intones, by way of a coda to Stoker's fictional death:

> He had made a terrible mistake. The madman he had met all those years ago in the pub had not merely told him an amusing story.

That man had tried to warn him that vampires did exist. (Stoker and Holt, 2009: 289)

If this is the case, then Stoker's last moment of lucid vision, in which he perceives the cover of his personal copy of *Dracula*, defaced with the single word '*LIES!*', (Stoker and Holt, 2009: 289) seems quite appropriate.

The author of *Dracula* has thus become, for better or worse, a character in a mythology which has long exceeded the boundaries of the 1897 novel, and which has now also extruded itself far beyond academic debate. Stoker's sporadic appearances in fiction are often derivative of pre-existent critical or biographical writings, and almost always serve to show the dependence of the reputation of the author upon a creation that is not always capable of easy containment. The overwhelming trend within such novels, it might be argued, is to utilise fiction as a form of criticism, to force Stoker to voice, demonstrate or reveal his sources and motivations for the novel with which he still remains associated. This may well be a sort of critical biography for the masses, a dissemination of academic consensus (or at least of prevailing debate) for those who might never attend an undergraduate class or read an article in a refereed journal. That being the case, it is a telling index of the quality and consistency of works such as *The List of Seven* and *Dracula, The Un-Dead*, which fictionalise Stoker and his research and writing processes, that they can themselves be subjected to critical scrutiny 100 years after the death of the author.

## Notes

1. See, for instance, Talia Schaffer, '"A Wilde Desire Took Me": The Homoerotic History of Dracula', *ELH*, 61 (1994), 381–425; Laurence Irving, *Henry Irving: The Actor and His World* (1989); Daniel Lapin, *The Vampire, Dracula and Incest* (1995).
2. See *The Era*, 11 October, 1890, p. 10; *Cleveland Plain Dealer*, 25 April 1912, p. 8; *Boston Sunday Herald*, 6 April 1902, p. 36: reprinted in John Edgar Browning, ed., *The Forgotten Writings of Bram Stoker* (2012: 175, 216, 210).
3. See, for example, the illustration in Belford, *Bram Stoker* (1997: 287); A. B. [pseud.], 'Bravo, Stoker' [cartoon], *The Entr'acte*, 23 September 1882 (4).
4. Harry Ludlam, *A Biography of Dracula: The Life Story of Bram Stoker* (1962: 44); Belford, *Bram Stoker*, (1997: 74); Daniel Farson, *The Man Who Wrote Dracula: A Biography of Bram Stoker* (1975: 31); Maunder, *Bram Stoker* (2004: 6–7).
5. Hopkins, *Bram Stoker* (2007: 4); Clive Leatherdale, *Dracula: The Novel and the Legend*, Third Edition (2001: 66).
6. Bram Stoker, *A Glimpse of America* in *A Glimpse of America and other Lectures, Interviews and Essays*, ed. Richard Dalby (2002: 11–30 at p. 19).

7. See, for example, Tom Holland, *The Vampyre* (1995) and Karl Alexander, *Time After Time* (1979).
8. Frost departs from historical accuracy here by re-naming St Mary's Church Goresthorpe Abbey (the name alludes to a ghost story written by Doyle), and granting Whitby in 1884 a bishopric it did not actually receive until 1923.
9. Stoker's words, it might be added, teasingly recall those uttered by Mina Harker when she encounters Dracula, in the guise of Prince Vlad, in a London cinema in Coppola's 1992 film *Bram Stoker's Dracula*.
10. Other similar attributions include Belford, *Bram Stoker* (1997: 311).
11. Reproduced in Elizabeth Miller, ed., *Bram Stoker's Dracula: A Documentary Volume* (2005: 27).

# 14
# Gallants, Ghosts, and Gargoyles: Illustrating the Gothic Tale

*Jef Murray*

Gothic literature consists of many elements that have evolved over the centuries. From the first recognized Gothic romance, Horace Walpole's *The Castle of Otranto* in 1764, through to American writer Flannery O'Connor's "Southern Gothic" short stories of the 1950s and '60s, many features have changed. But, a few have remained largely untouched, and these are important to recognize when developing visual images for Gothic tales. My perspective is as an illustrator rather than as a Gothic scholar. In that capacity my chapter discusses the features of Gothic literature that I find important as an artist, including the themes of romance, the themes of horror and the grotesque, and the importance of religious settings and symbolism, followed by case studies of Gothic works including my illustrations for a 2012 edition of Stoker's *The Lady of the Shroud* (1909). I begin by explaining how I conceive the processes of illustration; I will include example images from my own work in graphite and oil later in the chapter.

The process of illustrating any story might be described differently by each artist, but I would like to suggest perhaps the most obvious but powerful analogy, that of illustration as a quest, or a journey. As a quest, it seems clear that illustration involves delving into a twilight realm – a realm composed both of the natural world and of the imagination. And travels through such lands may take us through unpremeditated twists and turns, the outcome of which is rarely known in advance. The mementos of such odysseys are the end products: the sketches or paintings – the things that we "bring back with us" from our artistic travels. With illustration, as with any artistic endeavor, it is the journey itself which is of paramount importance; without these there would be no stories to tell, no insights to share, no images to ponder. Without the journeys, we would have no new things to delight us – we would only have carbon copies of what we already know. And, more importantly, without the journeys, we would have no opportunities for enriching and transforming ourselves.

## Observation and attention

Every journey has a starting point. And the starting point of all illustration is with what we can observe in the world around us. J. R. R. Tolkien makes this case plainly in his essay "On Fairy Stories":

> Fantasy is a natural human activity. It certainly does not destroy or even insult Reason; and it does not either blunt the appetite for, nor obscure the perception of, scientific verity. On the contrary. The keener and the clearer is the reason, the better fantasy will it make. (1997: 370)

And I would add to that, the better illustration it will make. So, if we begin our journey by observing and being attentive, to what must we attend? There are two fundamental starting points, I would suggest, for most artists to concentrate upon, and these are, learning to truly *see* nature, and second, to truly *see* mankind.

## Observing nature and the built environment

So, let's look first at observing nature, or more specifically, the natural *and* the built environments. How many of us really know what a tree looks like? Or what the ocean looks like? Or a moor? Or a castle? I would suggest very few. We all have notions of what a castle looks like, for example (Figure 14.1, Bram Stoker Conference Image), and we all have different capacities for describing castles, drawing castles, sculpting castles. But without looking closely at the real thing, we are likely not to know enough about them to be able to "capture" that truth, that reality that is a castle. The same is true of mountains, of lakes and streams, of insects and fish, of birds and beasts. I've often quipped that my own progression as an artist might be likened to a climb up the evolutionary ladder, because when I first started to paint seriously, I began with insects. From there I moved on to crustaceans and mollusks, then to fish, then birds, then mammals. It was only at that point that I finally began to tackle human beings. But at each step of the way, I was forced to spend a lot of time looking at the actual things that I hoped to better render – to learn how leaves joined branches; how antennae bristled;

*Figure 14.1*  Bram Stoker Conference Image

what moods are captured in the play of light and wind on waves; the gestures of fish swimming and fowl in flight. Much of this has to do with form and shading. We only see splotches of light and darkness in our field of vision and it is from these that we intuit what is genuinely

*Figure 14.2* The Human Figure

before us. So the job of an artist is to seek the exact form of the natural world around us so that it can be re-cast in two-dimensions.

## Observing people

But just as I believe most of us do not know what a cathedral truly looks like, we emphatically do not know what other people look like (Figure 14.2, The Human Figure). We perceive as much variation in the human form as in all the rest of nature combined; this is simply because we *are* human and therefore we take great interest in what can be understood from the human form and human features. We have learned to "read" stories about people from very limited visual and/or behavioral and/or verbal clues. However, from a visual perspective, we are multiply vexed when it comes to rendering human beings because, although we may not be able to tell when a tree or a squirrel looks wrong, we almost always know when a person looks wrong in a painting or a sketch. The slightest extra length of a limb or an awkward angle of the head might never be noticed in a bat, but in Homo sapiens, it screams out for correction.

## Firing up the imagination

I said before that the starting point of illustration has to be what we already know. But this is only a portion of what is required. The other half (or more!) comes from our own imaginations. Illustration involves honing our understanding of the world around us, as well as tapping into our "capacity to conjure". Let's talk for a moment about "conjuring" or, to use a more familiar term that children use all the time – "making believe." "Make believe" is something that we do naturally – or at least it's something that we once did naturally, and with a facility that we as adults may find amazing. Yet, that ability is not lost; it merely needs to be rediscovered and nurtured. The participant has to imagine himself present at a very specific scene. When you do that, you immediately have a number of problems you have to solve. For example, you have to choose where you are. Within a building? Or outdoors? You have to determine what you can see from where you are standing. That means you have to know where the light is coming from, who is holding the lamp or lamps, or perhaps whether there is a moon outside that is providing all of the light. In other words, the very attempt to imagine ourselves present at any event, real or feigned, forces us to incarnate that event – forces us to define its specifics.

*Figure 14.3* The Magic Ring – Sir Otto

*Figure 14.4* The Magic Ring – Bertha and the Mirror

Illustrating the Gothic Tale 229

In the autumn of 2009, I developed illustrations for a book that was published in the US by Valancourt Classics. It was the first fully illustrated edition of Baron Friedrich Heinrich Karl de La Motte-Fouque's masterpiece of Gothic chivalry, epic battle, and horror, *Der Zauberring* (*The Magic Ring*). (Figure 14.3, The Magic Ring – Sir Otto) The story, written in the 19th century Germany, is filled with great scenes: squires praying over their armor in overnight vigils as they seek the title of Knight; unrequited love between an almost Marian protagonist and her chivalric hero; a magic mirror that is inhabited by spirits; battles with demons on the fir tree-filled slopes of Norway; castles and watchtowers wherein are kept many secrets.

However, when I attempted to capture the "look and feel" of such an epic, I had to make some very practical decisions: (Figure 14.4, The Magic Ring – Bertha & the Mirror) what color hair does Bertha, the protagonist, have? How is it cut? The author didn't provide the details! What sort of clothing would she wear during the time of the 3rd crusade? What sort of armor and livery would accompany Sir Otto, the hero of the tale, on his travels and his adventures?

Researching some of these issues and then imagining others ultimately leaves a trail of sketches in its wake, to say nothing of stacks of books and reference photos and prints around my chair at home. I personally "think" by rendering pencil sketches, but then I'll proceed to more detailed color images or full paintings. But you can readily see the nature of this augmentation of the known (the historical facts) with the unknown (the physical appearance of people who have never actually lived). This sort of process is a prototype for all of my own illustration work.

## Applying creativity to the Gothic

### Romance

One consistent element across most of the incarnations of Gothic literature, is the romantic (Figure 14.5, Romance). The more traditional Gothic tales follow the trials and tribulations of a particular star-crossed or star-destined pair of lovers, or in some cases multiple pairs of the same, over the course of the tale. And whether or not the romance is consummated, ultimately, the formula of "boy meets girl, boy loses girl, boy regains girl" lies at the heart of at least as many Gothic tales as it does "true" romance stories. There are, of course, exceptions, but these generally serve to prove rather than disprove the rule. Couples classically consist of a heroine and a hero. And there are some intriguing characteristics of both heroines and heroes that are worth exploring, visually.

*Figure 14.5* Romance

## Heroines

Many Gothic stories focus on what might best be described as the "perils of Pauline". They track the movements of a female protagonist either directly, as in *Jane Eyre*, or indirectly, as with figures like Elizabeth in Mary Shelley's *Frankenstein*. The heroine will be proactive in defining her own fate, as is Bertha in *The Magic Ring*, or Emily in *The Mysteries of Udolpho*, or she will be somewhat more passive, as is Lucy Westenra in *Dracula*. What visual elements become important when rendering heroines? Well, clearly, they are typically beautiful, or at least not unattractive. They call out, often, for classical treatments in clothing, in hair styles, in features, but with a further emphasis on "spooky" qualities such as garments (Figure 14.6, The Heroine) that suggest funereal shrouds and that have less ornamentation and color. In addition, the heroine's features may be haunted and gaunt, she may have raven hair,

*Figure 14.6* The Heroine

etc. Visually, there can be considerable overlap between treatment of Gothic heroines and heroines of other styles of literature, notably medieval chivalric tales, mythology, and fairy tales. And illustrators who have focused on these latter genres can often readily have their styles translate well into the Gothic (e.g., artists like Arthur Rackham and the PreRaphaelite painters).

*Figure 14.7* The Byronic Figure

## Heroes/protagonists and Byronic figures

Heroines are important in Gothic illustration, but so are heroes. This is particularly true because of the prevalence of the Byronic Figure in the Gothic. The Byronic Figure is the foundation of many male archetypes, from Victor Frankenstein, to Heathcliff, to the Man with No Name from the Clint Eastwood spaghetti westerns (Figure 14.7, The Byronic Figure). So, how to render the "Strong, silent type"? Again, as with heroines from chivalric, mythological, and fairy tales, Gothic heroes are often stern knights or aristocrats with strong moral fiber, but who also possess a brooding or melancholic air. As with heroines, there are treatments of clothing and accessories that can be compelling to the illustrator. These might include the use of capes, armor, medieval styles of hair, etc. Features might include a strong brow line, plus unusual height and physical presence, etc.

## Horror & the grotesque

But in addition to the romantic aspects of the Gothic, there is a second element that is of extreme importance to the illustrator, and that is the presence of horror and/or the grotesque. I'll mention three aspects of this: the landscape or setting, supernatural elements, and the existence of characters that are deformed, grotesque, or horrible to gaze upon.

## Setting (e.g., castle, moor, graveyard) as character

The visual setting of many Gothic tales is crucial to the story (Figure 14.8, The Gothic Setting). Whether that setting is the Castle Brockenheim, Carfax Abbey, the frozen polar seas, or the crags of the Blue Mountains, setting helps create the atmosphere, and it is the job of the illustrator to capture such moods and tones as they suggest. In Gothic tales, I find that the ancient estate, the castle, the ruined Abbey, or haunted tower, has more power to instill the right mood in an illustration than does a more natural setting, so these are the things that I often concentrate on when rendering Gothic images. As an example, there are strange castles, crypts, and graveyards in *The Magic Ring* that reek of sorcery. Likewise, in *The Demon of Brockenheim*, much of the action takes place in the seemingly deserted tower of the castle, wherein the Baron Von Brockenheim is practicing his alchemy. In *The Lady of the Shroud*, too, one of the most visually intriguing settings is an ancient church and the crypt beneath it. It is here that a coffin lies (Figure 14.9, The Coffin) the resident of which can only be seen through a glass cover, apparently dead but uncorrupted, during daylight hours.

*Figure 14.8* The Gothic Setting

*Figure 14.9* The Coffin

## Supernatural vs natural

Gothic tales vary regarding the use of the supernatural. Many of the earliest works, notably by Ann Radcliffe, contain the element of the "explained supernatural". That is, they hint strongly at supernatural activity, but in the end, all such activity is shown to be due to natural causes. This was a hallmark of Gothic tales for quite some time, and continues to be a regular element in them even today (Figure 14.10, The

*Figure 14.10* The Supernatural

Supernatural). But, as with so many other aspects of Gothic literature, there is no fixed *requirement* for all events to be due to natural phenomena; *Dracula* is, of course, a classic contrary example. But witness also the voice of Mr. Rochester that Jane Eyre "hears", calling her back to him, just at the crucial moment before she is about to agree to marry her cousin, St. John. That was clearly a supernatural event.

From the perspective of the artist, however, it is entirely unimportant whether the supernatural hinted at in Gothic tales is real or imagined; we get to have fun drawing supernatural motifs into our work, regardless. We can make great hay with dark and ghostly shapes, demonic faces, flickering candles and the like, without ever having to be too scrupulous about the nature of their origin.

## The grotesque

The Grotesque is also a fixture in Gothic tales. Much of the horror we encounter in Gothic tales comes from the deviant aspects of certain characters. Gothic tales exploit our repulsion toward those who differ from us (Figure 14.11, The Grotesque). But, unlike in fairy tales and Walt Disney productions, where those differences often are shown to mask underlying beauty (e.g., in *Beauty and the Beast*), Gothic tales often revel in deformity, showing it to be an outward sign of true evil and depravity.

What does this mean to the illustrator? That depends on the individual to be depicted. There are certain artists who render evil well, and who can capture horrid countenances magnificently; here I'm thinking of many of those who work in the film industry, and specifically on such creatures as the Orcs in Peter Jackson's *Lord of the Rings* films. But other artists prefer to leave ugliness "offstage," and hidden, thus relying on the imagination of the reader. I tend to be one of the latter.

## Religious elements

Just as Romance and Horror are important visual elements in Gothic illustration, so too are religious elements (Figure 14.12, The Religious Element). Gothic literature draws very heavily from medieval Christian culture. Since medieval Europe was nearly uniformly Catholic and/or Orthodox, it should not be surprising that Gothic tales are a kind of palimpsest, the "erased portion" of which is often the universal cultural religious beliefs of Christian Europe. So, let's discuss some of these elements, and how they figure in Gothic illustration.

238  Jef Murray

*Figure 14.11*  The Grotesque

## Medieval and Victorian trappings

First, it should be noted that medieval symbols, architecture, and ornamentation are quite prevalent in Gothic literature (Figure 14.13 Medieval Trappings). So, what specific images can artists tap for Gothic illustration? Well, there are quite a few. Gothic architecture, for one.

*Figure 14.12* The Religious Element

*Figure 14.13* Medieval Trappings

Without cathedrals like Notre Dame and Chartres, we would not be able to create the interplay of light and shadow, the use of ornaments like gargoyles and grotesques, the allusions to scriptural themes that lie deep within westerners' collective subconscious. Medieval cultural horrors, too, figure prominently, such as the plague, the constant warfare and treachery that occurred among the many kingdoms of Europe, and the intrigue of the Italian courts.

Likewise, visually, artists can incorporate heraldic images, the shapes and styles of armor, of weapons, of furniture, of manners and modes of transportation. From Victorian times artists can tap images of the coming industrialization, of murky cityscapes and the horrors of poverty and squalor amidst great wealth and disparity between classes, and between aristocracy and commoners. Visually, the Victorian gives the artist great iron-gated manors, country estates, gaslights, darkened alleys and grimy, smoke- and soot-filled shops, factories, and garrets. But it also gives us missions and hospitals, charitable schools and poor houses. It gives us religious institutions that are sometimes Satanic and sometimes Saintly.

## Clerics & conjurors

And this brings us to the representatives of religion itself, who often figure prominently in Gothic tales (Figure 14.14, Clerics and Conjurors). Whether they are Matthew Gregory Lewis' *The Monk*, the ecclesial commission from *The Demon of Brockenheim*, the Pope himself and Zelotes in *The Magic Ring*, or the prophet Tarwater in Flannery O'Connor's *The Violent Bear it Away*, explicitly religious figures appear in Gothic tales both as signs of grace and of the worst abuses of authority. Along with specifically *Christian* religious, Gothic tales often feature Muslim characters, usually as antagonists or as devious and treacherous malefactors. This reflects, again, the medieval mindset as well that of Victorian times.

Sorcerers, whether feigned or real, also appear in Gothic literature, although not with the regularity of religious figures. These are usually but not necessarily antagonistic, such as the witch Gerda, the sorceress in *The Magic Ring*, the counterfeit sorcerer, Hassan, in *The Demon of Brockenheim*, as well as Count Dracula himself. All of these figures, along with the devils that they often command, or appear to, give great visual flavor to Gothic tales.

In the Gothic, "what's missing" can be as important as what is present. And often the heart and soul of a story is a person or place or action that is "offstage." The final section of this essay focuses on my

*Figure 14.14* Clerics and Conjurors

illustrations of four different works, all of which are either truly Gothic, or have many elements of the Gothic within them. And all of these incorporate elements of storytelling and illustration that concentrate on things unseen or unknown.

## Case studies

### *The Magic Ring* (1813)

*The Magic Ring* is a fascinating work, and is situated in the early days of Gothic literature (Figure 14.15, *The Magic Ring*). So, it should come as no

*Figure 14.15* The Magic Ring

244  Jef Murray

surprise that it also contains elements that don't quite fit the standard Gothic mold. It is, at once, intensely romantic and filled with intrigue. But, it also includes truly supernatural events, chivalry, straight adventure, and mythological subplots. As an early example of Germanic Romantic fiction, it was a forerunner of what we know today as fantasy literature. Fouque influenced such writers as William Morris and George MacDonald. He also was a major influence on Edgar Allan Poe. And there is evidence to suggest his works were known by admirers of George MacDonald's fantasy tales, notably C. S. Lewis and J. R. R. Tolkien. *The Magic Ring* is an extremely elaborate weaving of multiple storylines. At the start, we meet many characters who subsequently go their separate ways until the very end, and we appear to be following entirely unrelated stories.

However, much of the reason for the appearance of chaos in *The Magic Ring* is the fact that the central character, in this case Sir Hugh, is largely offscreen. As with so many Gothic tales (e.g. *Frankenstein*), the prime mover of all that happens is actually a character we only encounter on occasion. In the case of *Frankenstein*, the character is the monster; in the case of *The Magic Ring*, the character is Sir Hugh, the aged knight who sits at home alone waiting for news of his son, Sir Otto. The Baron de la Motte plays a trick on modern readers, since understanding the nature of the book involves the slow process of puzzling out just who Sir Hugh is and why he is so important.

The climax of the book comes when this aged knight is confronted, by virtue of the conjuring power of the magic ring mentioned in the title, by the ghosts of his past lovers (Figure 14.16, Zelotes and Sir Hugh). He then must account for the seeming treachery he has committed against each of them. In this instance, he is protected against evil not only by his sons, Sir Otto and the monk Zelotes, but also by the Marian figure of Bertha (Figure 14.17, The Crowning of Bertha), who destroys the magic ring and is crowned as the ultimate hero of the tale by the historical figure of Blondel, the minstrel of King Richard the Lionhearted.

### *The Demon of Brockenheim* (1877)

Let's look now at a more classic Gothic tale which I illustrated for Udolpho Press in 2010 (Figure 14.18, *The Demon of Brockenheim*). *The Demon of Brockenheim*, the author of whom is unknown, was serialized between April and October of 1877 in *The Australian Journal*. It recounts the story of the Baron Von Brockenheim, who has frittered away his fortune and is desperately attempting to learn the secrets of alchemy

*Figure 14.16* Zelotes and Sir Hugh

*Figure 14.17* The Crowning of Bertha

*Figure 14.18* The Demon of Brockenheim

in order to restore his wealth. He knows that the Church is onto his attempts to use black magic, and so counterfeits his own murder so as avoid prosecution and imprisonment.

A young foreigner is hanged for the apparent murder of the Baron, and the Baron does nothing to stop the injustice. The young foreigner's father, unbeknownst to the Baron, comes to seek revenge, and he passes himself off as a sorcerer who can aid the Baron in his search for the Philosopher's Stone that will turn base metal into gold. But his real plan is to destroy the Baron.

The tale features standard Gothic features: a heroine (the Baron's daughter), a hero (largely offstage, but crucial in the end), suggestions of the supernatural that are largely feigned, the setting of a brooding castle in Mayence, Germany, the horror of the gallows and of the innocent youth hanged, and finally, the concluding crisis, as it appears that the Baron will actually sacrifice his own daughter rather than relinquish his desire for wealth.

### Seer: A Wizard's Journal (2012)

The book is *Seer: A Wizard's Journal*, which I wrote and illustrated has elements of the Gothic, while overlapping with the fantasy genre (Figure 14.19, *Seer, A Wizard's Journal*). It is a contemporary collection of short stories, poems, and essays. It was published by Oloris Publishing, an imprint for works of fantasy, and specifically for works that resonate with the writings of Charles Williams, C. S. Lewis, J. R. R. Tolkien, and George MacDonald. *Seer* includes short stories that deal with ghostly apparitions, visitations from tortured spirits, and mystifying objects that seem to possess unearthly powers. It also includes a character threaded throughout the tales who fulfills many of the requirements of a Byronic hero, but who also seemingly possesses the powers of a sorcerer. Illustrations for such a book do not need to conform to a fixed style or format, and as a result, they are not as formally rendered as with *The Magic Ring* and *The Demon of Brockenheim*. Rather, images are scattered throughout the tales, some in full page format and others nestled within the text.

### The Lady of the Shroud (1909)

Finally, *The Lady of the Shroud* (Figure 14.20, *The Lady of the Shroud*) brings me to my work on a tale by Bram Stoker. Ultimately, this novel turns out *not* to be a classic Gothic tale, nor is it a supernatural horror story like *Dracula*, but, nevertheless, it has many of the trappings of both of these. I developed the cover image for this book which was

*Figure 14.19* Seer: A Wizard's Journal

*Figure 14.20*  The Lady of the Shroud

published by Valancourt Books in the centenary of Stoker's death. And the image itself is of the "Lady of the Shroud," whom we meet at the onset of the tale. In the text she is described as wearing a funereal shroud and floating in a coffin off the coast of the land of the Blue Mountains. She is seen by the passengers and crew of a steamer. And, as with the superstitious peasants in Dracula's Carpathian Mountains, those who see the lady immediately believe her to be a horrific vision from the grave and promptly veer off course so as to avoid her.

> It was eleven minutes before twelve midnight on Saturday, the 9th day of January, 1907, when I saw the strange sight off the headland known as the Spear of Ivan on the coast of the Land of the Blue Mountains .... Captain Mirolani, the Master, is a very careful seaman, and gives on his journeys a wide berth to the bay which is tabooed by Lloyd's. But when he saw in the moonlight, though far off, a tiny white figure of a woman drifting on some strange current in a small boat, on the prow of which rested a faint light (to me it looked like a corpse-candle!), he thought it might be some person in distress, and began to cautiously edge towards it .... Presently I made out that the boat, which had all along seemed to be of a queer shape, was none other than a Coffin, and that the woman standing up in it was clothed in a shroud. Her back was towards us, and she had evidently not heard our approach. As we were creeping along slowly, the engines were almost noiseless, and there was hardly a ripple as our fore-foot cut the dark water. Suddenly there was a wild cry from the bridge – Italians are certainly very excitable; hoarse commands were given to the Quartermaster at the wheel; the engine-room bell clanged. On the instant, as it seemed, the ship's head began to swing round to starboard; full steam ahead was in action, and before one could understand, the Apparition was fading in the distance. The last thing I saw was the flash of a white face with dark, burning eyes as the figure sank down into the coffin – just as mist or smoke disappears under a breeze. (1909: 1–3)

In the tale, we learn of this apparition through the exploits of the hero, Rupert, who comes to the Land of the Blue Mountains as his uncle's heir. He falls in love with this enigmatic and seemingly supernatural creature in his subsequent adventures. Again, this story satisfies the one aspect of the Gothic that I was seeking to highlight with these case studies; that of the "missing person" or "missing truth" that is only revealed over time. In this case, that missing person is the Lady of the Shroud herself: who is she? More importantly, *what* is she? But, there are a few other observations one might make about the illustration I developed for this book. I did, in fact, diverge from the text by making the seas stormy, and by choosing a gown that more resembles a wedding dress than a typical funereal shroud. These seemed to better fit the overall theme of the book, and to, in a way, "Gothicize" it. The storminess and the wedding dress both anticipate further developments in the story, but also, as at least one observer has noted, the latter might be acknowledged as a subconscious nod to the character of Lucy Westenra in Stoker's *Dracula*.

It is the artist's job to explore, and in the context of illustration, to be both true to the written word and to suggest narratives that might not be explicit in the text – to explore the interstitial boundaries of the world presented to us by the author. Gothic tales have particular characteristics that we've noted, but all of these contribute to a sense of the strange, the heroic, and the transformative. These are the elements that an artist must evoke if he is to successfully capture, in image, what the Gothic artist has presented in prose.

# Works Cited

## Unpublished Letters

Du Maurier, George. Letter to Henry James, 25 August 1890. James, Henry, 1843–1916. Correspondence and Journals of Henry James Jr., 1855–1916. MS Am 1094 (142–182). Houghton Library, Harvard University, Cambridge, Mass. [Online]
——— Letter to Henry James, 11 September 1884. James, Henry, 1843–1916. Correspondence and Journals of Henry James Jr., 1855–1916. MS Am 1094 (142–182). Houghton Library, Harvard University, Cambridge, Mass. [Online]
Stoker, Bram. Letter to Hall Caine, 23 February 1897; unpublished letter in MNH MS 09542, Manx National Heritage Library (MNHL).
——— Letter to Hall Caine, 20 [May?] 1890 (MNHL).
——— Letter to Hall Caine, 3 June 1896 (MNHL).
——— Letter to Hall Caine, 20 August 1897 (MNHL).
——— Letter to Hall Caine, 25 August 1898 (MNHL).
——— Letter to Hall Caine, 20 June 1905 (MNHL).

## Illustrations

Du Maurier, George. 1880. 'Farewell to Fair Normandy,' 2 October. *Punch*.
——— 1881. 'A Powerful Quartet,' 24 September. *Punch*.
——— 1882. 'Seaside Sports: Toboganning in Whitby,' 16 September. *Punch*.
——— 1882. 'The Vikings of Whitby,' 23 September. *Punch*.
——— 1886. 'A Filial Reproof,' 11 September. *Punch*.
——— 1894. 'A Little "New Woman," ' 1 September. *Punch*.
——— 1866. 'Honi Soit,' 29 September. *Punch*.

## Website

Eyam Museum Website. http://www.eyam-museum.org.uk. Accessed 1 April 2012.

## Stoker Texts

Stoker, Bram, 1991. *The Lair of the White Worm*. Dingle, Kerry: Brandon, 1991.
——— 1994. *Dracula*. London: Penguin.
——— 1996. *Dracula*, intro. Maud Ellmann. Oxford: Oxford University Press.
——— 1997. *Dracula*. Ed. Nina Auerbach and David J. Skal. New York and London: W. W. Norton.
——— 2000, *Dracula*. Ed. Glennis Byron. Peterborough, Ontario: Broadview.
——— 1998. *Dracula Unearthed*. Ed. Clive Leatherdale. Westcliff-on-Sea, Essex: Desert Island Books.

―――― 1998. *Dracula*. New York: Norton.
―――― 1906. *Personal Reminiscences of Henry Irving*. 2 vols. London: William Heinemann.
―――― [1909]. *The Lady of the Shroud*. London: Rider and Co.
―――― 1909. *The Lady of the Shroud*. London: William Heinemann.
―――― 1911. *The Lair of the White Worm*. London: Rider.
―――― 1975. 'The Squaw.' *Dracula's Guest*. London: Arrow, 50–66.
―――― 1996. *The Jewel of Seven Stars*. Ed. Clive Leatherdale. Westcliff-on-Sea, Essex: Desert Island Books, 1996.
―――― 1996. *The Jewel of Seven Stars*. Stroud: Alan Sutton.
―――― 1996. *The Jewel of Seven Stars*. Intro. David Glover. Oxford: Oxford University Press.
―――― 2000. *The Shoulder of Shasta*. Ed. Alan Johnson. Westcliff-on-Sea, Essex: Desert Island Books, 2000.
―――― 2000. *Dracula*. Ed. Glennis Byron. Peterborough, Ontario: Broadview Press.
―――― 2001. *The Lady of the Shroud*. Ed. William Hughes. Westcliff-on-Sea, Essex: Desert Island Books.
―――― 2002. *A Glimpse of America* in *A Glimpse of America and other Lectures, Interviews and Essays*. Ed. Richard Dalby. Westcliff-on-Sea: Desert Island Books.
―――― 2003. *Dracula*. Ed. Maurice Hindle. London: Penguin.
―――― 2006. *Dracula's Guest and Other Weird Stories*. London: Penguin.
―――― 2006. 'The Squaw.' In: David Stuart Davies (ed.) *Dracula's Guest and Other Stories*. Ware, Hertfordshire: Wordsworth, 47–58.
―――― 2006. *The Snake's Pass*. Chicago: Valancourt Books.
―――― 2007. *Lady Athlyne*. Ed. Carol Senf. Southend-on-Sea, Essex: Desert Island Books.
―――― 2007. *The Man*. Charleston, SC: Bibliobazaar.
―――― 2007. *The Mystery of the Sea*. Ed. Carol A. Senf. Kansas City: Valancourt Books.
―――― 2009. The Watter's Mou.' In: Catherine Wynne (ed.) *The Parasite by Arthur Conan Doyle and The Watter's Mou' by Bram Stoker.'* Kansas City: Valancourt, 49–109.
―――― 2011. *Dracula*. Ed. Roger Luckhurst. London: Oxford World's Classics.
―――― 2012. 'The Coming of Abel Behenna'. In: Catherine Wynne (ed.) *The Parasite, by Arthur Conan Doyle, The Watter's Mou, by Bram Stoker*. Kansas City: Valancourt Books, 135–152.
―――― 2012. *The Forgotten Writings of Bram Stoker*. Ed. John Edgar Browning. Basingstoke: Palgrave.

## Other

A. B. [pseud.], 1882. 'Bravo, Stoker.' *The Entr'acte*, 23 September, 4.
Allen, Nicholas, 2003. *George Russell (AE) and the New Ireland, 1905–30*. Dublin: Four Courts Press.
Allen, Vivien, 1997. *Hall Caine: Portrait of a Victorian Romancer*. Sheffield: Sheffield Academic Press.
Almond, Barbara R., 2007. 'Monstrous Infants and Vampyric Mothers in Bram Stoker's *Dracula*.' *International Journal of Psychoanalysis* 88: 219–35.

Almond, Hely Hutchinson, 1881. 'Athletics and Education.' *Macmillan's Magazine* 43 (256) (February): 283–94.

Amato, Joseph A., 2000. *Dust: A History of the Small and Invisible.* Berkeley: University of California Press.

Andreescu, Ştefan, 1998. *Vlad Ţepeş (Dracula). Între legendă şi adevăr istoric* [*Vlad Ţepeş (Dracula). Between Legend and Historical Truth*]. Bucureşti: Editura Enciclopedică.

Anon., 1881. Review of '*Under the Sunset.* By Bram Stoker.' *The Academy* (10 December) 20 (501): 431–2.

Anon. Rev. of *Posthumous Works of the Author of The Vindication of the Rights of Woman. In Four Volumes.* 12 mo. 14s. Johnson. 1798. *The British Critic,* vol. 12 (1798): 234–35. Reprinted. in: Cynthia Richards (ed.), 2004. *The Wrongs of Woman; or Maria.* 1798. Glen Allen, Virginia: College Publishing.

Anon. Rev. of *The Posthumous Works of the Author of The Vindication of the Rights of Woman.* In 4 Vols. 8 vo. Abour 800 pa. Prince 14s. in boards. Johnson. 1798. *The Analytic Review,* vol. 27 (1798): 240–45. Reprinted in: Cynthia Richards (ed.), 2004. *The Wrongs of Woman; or Maria.* 1798. Virginia: College Publishing.

Anon., 1869. 'The Plague at Eyam.' *All the Year Round.* (17 July) 2 (33): 161–64. [Online] British Periodicals Online. Accessed 15 March 2015.

Anon., 1893. Famous Torture Instruments: The Earl of Shrewsbury's Collection Soon to be Exhibited Here. *New York Times,* 26 November. [Online] Http://query.nytimes.com/mem/archive-free/pdf?res=9805EEDB153EEF33A25755C2 A9679D94629ED7CF. Accessed 1 September 2014

Applegate, Debbie, 2006. *The Most Famous Man in America: The Biography of Henry Ward Beecher.* New York: Three Leaves Press.

Arata, Stephen D., 1993. 'The Occidental Tourist: *Dracula* and the Anxiety of Reverse Colonization.' In: Carol A. Senf (ed.) *The Critical Response to Bram Stoker.* Westport, CT: Greenwood Press, 84–104.

Arata, Stephen D., 1990. 'The Occidental Tourist: *Dracula* and the Anxiety of Reverse Colonization.' *Victorian Studies.* (Summer) 33 (4): 621–45.

Arendt, Hannah, 1973. 'Imperialism,' Part Two of *The Origins of Totalitarianism* [1951]. New York: Harcourt, Brace, Jovanovich.

Armstrong, Nancy, 2005. 'Feminism, Fiction, and the Utopian Promise of *Dracula.*' *Differences: A Journal of Feminist Cultural Studies* 16 (1): 1–23. MLA International Bibliography. [Online] www.galegroup.com. Accessed: 24 May 2012.

Arnold, Matthew, 1961. 'The Scholar-Gipsy.' 1853. In: A. Dwight Culler (ed.) *Poetry and Criticism of Matthew Arnold.* Boston: Houghton Mifflin, 1961, p. 148.

Auerbach, Nina, 2002. *Daphne du Maurier: Haunted Heiress.* Philadelphia, PA: University of Pennsylvania Press.

Barbauld, Anna Letitia, 1996. 'From The British Novelists: From On the Origin and Progress of Novel-Writing' (1810).' In: Anne K. Mellor and Richard E. Matlak (eds.) *British Literature 1780–1830.* Boston: Heinle & Heinle, Thomson Learning, 171–80.

Baring-Gould, Sabine, 2007. *The Book of Werewolves.* Stroud: The History Press.

Barnes, Geraldine, 2001. *Viking America: The First Millennium.* Cambridge: D. S. Brewer.

Bartholin, Thomas, 1689. *Antiquitatum Danicarum de Causis Contemptae a Danis adhuc Gentilibus Mortis.* Heidelberg: Joh. Phil. Bockenhoffer. [Online] http://books.google.com/books?id=2l8PAAAAQAAJ&printsec=frontcover&source=gbs_ge_summary_r&cad=0#v=onepage&q&f=false. Accessed 1 June 2014.

Bartlett, H.C., 1878. 'The Chemistry of Dirt.' *The British Architect and Northern Engineer* 10(18th October): 152–54.

Baum, L. Frank, December 20, 1890. Editorial. *Aberdeen Saturday Pioneer*. Cited in A. Waller Hastings. L. *Frank Baum's Editorials on the Sioux Nation*. [Online] http://hsmt.history.ox.ac.uk//courses_reading/undergraduate/authority_of_nature/week_7/baum.pdf. Accessed 1 September 2014.

——— January 3, 1891. Editorial. *Aberdeen Saturday Pioneer*. Cited in A. Waller Hastings. L. *Frank Baum's Editorials on the Sioux Nation*. [Online] http://hsmt.history.ox.ac.uk//courses_reading/undergraduate/authority_of_nature/week_7/baum.pdf. Accessed 1 September 2014.

Beeton, Isabella, 1888. *Mrs. Beeton's Book of Household Management*. Ed. S. O. Beeton. London: Ward, Lock and Co.

Belford, Barbara, 1996. *Bram Stoker: A Biography of the Author of Dracula*. London: Weidenfeld and Nicolson.

Bell, Gertrude, 2005. *Persian Pictures*. Intro. Liora Lukitz. London: Anthem Press.

Bierman, Joseph, 1972. '*Dracula*: Prolonged Childhood Illness and the Oral Triad.' *American Imago* 29: 186–98.

Blanning, Tim, 2010. *The Romantic Revolution*. London: Weidenfeld and Nicholson.

Bloom, Clive (ed.), 2007. *Gothic Horror: A Guide for Students and Readers*. Basingstoke: Palgrave Macmillan.

Boner, Charles, 1865. *Transylvania: Its Products and Its People*. London: Longmans.

Briefel, Aviva, 2008. 'Hands of Beauty, Hands of Horror: Fear and Egyptian Art at the Fin de Siècle', *Victorian Studies* Winter 50 (2): 263–71.

'[British Army] Dublin District Historical Record: January 1920 to May 1920 (Inclusive).' 2007. In: William Sheehan (ed.) *Fighting for Dublin: The British Battle for Dublin 1919–1921*. Cork: The Collins Press.

Brock, Marilyn, 2009. 'Desire and Fear: Feminine Abjection in the Gothic Fiction of Mary Wollstonecraft.' In: Marilyn Brock (ed.) *From Wollstonecraft to Stoker: Essays on Gothic and Victorian Sensation Fiction*. Jefferson, North Carolina and London: McFarland, 17–29.

Burke, Edmund, 1756. *A Philosophical Enquiry into the Origin of Our Ideas of the Sublime and Beautiful*. London: R. and J. Dodsley.

——— 1998. *A Philosophical Enquiry into the Origin of our Ideas of the Sublime and the Beautiful*. Oxford: Oxford University Press.

Burke, Mary, 2005. 'Eighteenth- and Nineteenth-Century Sources for Bram Stoker's Gypsies.' *ANQ* 18 (1): 54–9. [Online] www.literature.proquest.com. Accessed 12 December 2014.

C. B., 1934. 'Sir Gerald du Maurier's Life Story.' *The Saturday Review*, 17 November, 403–4.

Caine, Hall, 1887. *The Deemster*. London: Chatto and Windus.

——— 1890. *The Bondman*. London: William Heinemann.

——— 1892. *Capt'n Davy's Honeymoon, The Last Confession, The Blind Mother*. London: William Heinemann.

——— 1894. *The Manxman*. London: William Heinemann.

——— 1897. *The Christian*. London: William Heinemann.

——— 1908. *My Story*. London: William Heinemann.

——— 1909. *The White Prophet*. London: William Heinemann.

Carroll, Jordan S. 2012. 'The Aesthetics of Risk in *Dawn of the Dead* and *28 Days Later*.' *Journal of the Fantastic in the Arts* 23 (1): 40–9. [Online] Literature. proquest.com. Accessed 2 April 2015.

Charleton, Walter, 1663. *Chorea Gigantum: Or, the Most Famous Antiquity of Great Britan* [sic], *Vulgarly Called Stone-heng*. London: Henry Herringham.

Clifford, William Kingdon, 1879. 'On the Aims and Instruments of Scientific Thought.' In: Leslie Stephen and Frederick Pollock (eds.) *Lectures and Essays: Volume One*. London: Macmillan, 124–157.

Clunies Ross, Margaret and Lars Lönnroth, 1999. 'The Norse Muse: Report from an International Research Project.' *alvíssmál* 9: 2–28.

Cockin, Katharine, 1998. *Edith Craig (1869–1947): Dramatic Lives*. London: Cassell.

——— 2001. *Women and Theatre in the Age of Suffrage: The Pioneer Players 1911–25*. Basingstoke: Palgrave.

——— (ed.), 2011. *The Collected Letters of Ellen Terry, Volume 2 1889–1893*. London: Pickering & Chatto.

——— (ed.), 2012. *The Collected Letters of Ellen Terry, Volume 3 1894–1898*. London: Pickering & Chatto.

Collins, Michael, 1922. *The Path to Freedom*. Dublin: Talbot Press.

Colman Smith, Pamela, 1899a. *Annancy Stories*. New York: R. H. Russell.

——— 1899b. *The Golden Vanity and the Green Bed*. New York: Doubleday and McClure.

——— 1899c. *Widdicombe Fair*. New York: Doubleday and McClure.

——— 1908. 'Should the Art Student Think?' *The Craftsman* (July) 14 (4): 417–19.

——— 1912. 'Susan and the Mermaid', *The Delineator*. Republished with notes by Corinne Kenner, 2010.

Conan Doyle, Arthur, 1908. *Through the Magic Door*. New York: McClure.

Coundouriotis, Eleni, 2000. 'Dracula and the Idea of Europe.' *Connotations*, Society for Critical Debate, vol. 9. Universität Münster, North Rhine-Westphalia: Waxman.

Creed, Barbara, 1993. *The Monstrous Feminine: Film, Feminism and Psychoanalysis*. London: Routledge.

Crişan, Marius, 2008. 'The Models for Castle Dracula in Stoker's Sources on Transylvania.' *Journal of Dracula Studies* 10: 10–19. [Online] www. http://dractravel.com/drc/. Accessed 15 March 2014.

——— 2013a. *The Birth of the Dracula Myth: Bram Stoker's Transylvania*. Bucureşti: Editura Pro Universitaria.

——— 2013b. *Impactul unui mit: Dracula şi reprezentarea ficţională a spaţiului românesc*. (*The Impact of a Myth: Dracula and the Fictional Representation of the Romanian Space*). Bucureşti: Editura Pro Universitaria.

Crosse, Andrew F., 1878. *Round About the Carpathians*. Edinburgh and London: Blackwood.

Dalby, Richard (ed.), 2011. *To My Dear Friend Hommy-Beg: The Great Friendship of Bram Stoker and Hall Caine*. Dublin: Swan River Press.

Darwin, Charles, 1900. *The Origin of Species by Means of Natural Selection or the Preservation of Favoured Races in the Struggle for Life*. London: John Murray.

Davies, Gill, 2004. 'London in *Dracula*; Dracula in London.' *Literary London: Interdisciplinary Studies in the Representation of London* (March) 2.1 [Online] http://www.literarylondon.org/. Accessed 12 December 2014.

Dayan, Joan, 1999. 'Poe, Persons, and Property.' *American Literary History* 11 (3): 405–25.
Deane, Bradley, 2008. 'Mummy Fiction and the Occupation of Egypt: Imperial Striptease.' *ELT* 4: 381–410.
Demetrakopoulos, Stephanie, 1977. 'Feminism, Sex Role Exchanges, and Other Subliminal Fantasies in Bram Stoker's *Dracula*.' *Frontiers: A Journal of Women Studies* 2 (3): 104–13. *MLA International Bibliography*. [online] www.galegroup.com. Accessed 24 May 2012.
Deutsch, Helene, 1945. 'Pregnancy.' In: Helene Deutsch (ed.) *The Psychology of Women: A Psychoanalytic Interpretation; Volume Two: Motherhood*. New York: Grune and Stratton, 126–201.
Donno, Elizabeth Story (ed.), 1983. *Andrew Marvell: The Complete Poems*. Harmondsworth: Penguin.
Douglas, Mary, 2004. *Purity and Danger: An Analysis of Concept of Pollution and Taboo*. London: Routledge.
Driver, Hugh, 1997. *The Birth of Military Aviation: Britain, 1903–1914*. London: Royal Historical Society.
Du Maurier, Daphne, 1952. *The Young George du Maurier: A Selection of His Letters, 1860–67*. New York: Doubleday.
―――― 1967. *Vanishing Cornwall: The Spirit and History of Cornwall*. London: Victor Gollancz.
―――― 2003. *Jamaica Inn*. Intro. Sarah Dunnant. London: Virago.
―――― 2004a. *The Du Mauriers*. Intro. Michael Holroyd. London: Virago.
―――― 2004b. *Gerald: A Portrait*. Intro. Margaret Forster. London: Virago.
―――― 2004c. *The Loving Spirit*. Intro. Michèle Roberts. London: Virago.
―――― 2005. *The Parasites*. Intro. Julie Myerson. London: Virago.
Du Maurier, George, 1898. *The Martian*. London and New York: Harper Brothers.
Dunne, John William, 1927. *An Experiment with Time*. London: A&C Black.
Eighteen-Bisang, Robert, and Miller, Elizabeth (eds.), 2008. *Bram Stoker's Notes for Dracula: A Facsimile Edition*. Jefferson, NC: McFarland.
Elbert, Monika, and Marshall, Bridget M. (eds.), 2013. *Transnational Gothic: Literary and Social Exchanges in the Long Nineteenth Century*. Surrey & Burlington: Ashgate.
Ellis, Havelock, 1923. 'The Psychic State in Pregnancy.' In: Havelock Ellis (ed.) *Studies in the Psychology of Sex, Volume V: Erotic Symbolism; The Mechanism of Detumescence; The Psychic State in Pregnancy*. Philadelphia: F.A. Davis, 201–30.
Elrod, P.N., *Quincey Morris, Vampire*. Riverdale, NY: Baen, 2001.
Englander, David, 2010. 'Policing the Ghetto: Jewish East London, 1880–1920.' *Crime, History & Societies* 14.1: 29–50. [Online] http://chs.revues.org/. Accessed 28 December 2014.
Esherick, Joseph W., 1987. *The Origins of the Boxer Uprising*. Berkeley: University of California Press.
Farson, Daniel, 1975. *The Man Who Wrote Dracula: A Biography of Bram Stoker*. London: Michael Joseph.
Faulkes, Anthony (ed.), 1977–79. *Two Versions of the* Snorra Edda *from the Seventeenth Century*. Vol. 2, *Edda Islandorum. Völuspá. Hávamál: P. H. Resen's Editions of 1665*. Rit 13–14. Reykjavík: Stofnun Árna Magnússonar.
Fejes, Narcisz, 2011. 'Feared Intrusions: A Comparative Reading of *Borat* and *Dracula*.' *The Journal of Popular Culture* 44.5 (October): 992–1009. [Online] Wiley.com. Accessed 20 December 2014.

Fell, Christine, 1993. 'Norse Studies: Then, Now and Hereafter.' In: Anthony Faulkes and Richard Perkins (eds.) *Viking Revaluations. Viking Society Centenary Symposium 14–15 May, 1992*. Viking Society for Northern Research, University College London, 85–99.

——— 1996. 'The First Publication of Old Norse Literature in England and its Relation to its Sources.' In: Else Roesdahl and Preben Meulengracht Sörensen (eds.) *The Waking of Angantyr: The Scandinavian Past in European Culture*. Acta Jutlandica LXXI: I. Aarhus University Press, 27–57.

Fiedler, Leslie, 1960. *Love and Death in the American Novel*. Champaign, IL: Dalkey Archive Press, 2008.

Finlay, Alison, 2007. 'Thomas Gray's Translations of Old Norse Poetry.' In: David Clark and Carl Phelpstead (eds.) *Old Norse Made New: Essays on the Postmedieval Reception of Old Norse Literature and Culture*. London: Viking Society for Northern Research, University of London, 1–20.

Flint, Kate, 2000. *The Victorians and the Visual Imagination*. Cambridge: Cambridge University Press.

Ford, Thomas H, 2009. 'Mary Wollstonecraft and the Motherhood of Feminism.' *WSQ: Women's Studies Quarterly*. (Fall/Winter) 37 (3&4): 189–205.

Forrest, Katherine V., 1993. 'O Captain, My Captain' (1987). In: Pam Keesey (ed.) *Daughters of Darkness: Lesbian Vampire Stories*. Pittsburgh: Cleis Press, 185–228.

Foster, Roy, 1997. *W. B. Yeats: A Life Vol 1, The Apprentice Mage*. Oxford: Oxford University Press.

Frayling, Christopher, 1991. *Vampyres: Lord Byron to Count Dracula*. London: Faber and Faber.

——— 2014a. 'Mr Stoker's Holiday.' In: Jarlath Killeen (ed.) *Bram Stoker: Centenary Essays*. Dublin: Four Courts Press, 179–200.

——— 2014b. *The Yellow Peril: Dr. Fu Manchu and the Rise of Chinaphobia*. London: Thames and Hudson.

Freud, Sigmund, 2003. *The Uncanny*. Translated by David McClintock. London: Penguin.

Frost, Mark, 1994. *The List of Seven*. London: Arrow.

Gallagher, Frank, 1967. *Days of Fear: A Diary of Hunger Strike* [1928]. Cork: Mercier Press.

Gaskill, Howard, 2003. 'Ossian, Herder and the Idea of Folk Song.' In: David Hill (ed.) *The Camden House History of German Literature, Volume 6: Literature of the Sturm and Drang*. Woodbridge, Suffolk: Camden House, 95–116.

Gerard, Emily, 1885. 'Transylvanian Superstitions.' *The Nineteenth Century* (July) 101: 130–50.

——— 1888. *The Land Beyond the Forest*. New York: Harper & Brothers.

Getz, Faye, 1991. 'Death and the Silver Lining: Meaning, Continuity, and Revolutionary Change in Histories of Medieval Plague.' *Journal of the History of Biology* 24 (3): 265–89.

Gibbons, Luke, 2014. '"The Old Far West and the New": Bram Stoker, Race, and Manifest Destiny.' In Neil Gillespie and Christina Morin (eds.) *Irish Gothics*. London: Palgrave Macmillan, 188–205.

Gibson, John Michael, and Green, Richard Lancelyn (eds.) 1986. *The Unknown Conan Doyle: Letters to the Press*. London: Secker & Warburg.

Gibson, Matthew, 2004. 'Bram Stoker and the Treaty of Berlin (1878).' *Gothic Studies* 6: 236–51. Hopkins, Lisa. *Bram Stoker: A Literary Life*. New York: Palgrave Macmillan, 2007. Print.

Gilbert, Martin, 2005. 'Churchill and Bombing Policy,' The Fifth Churchill Lecture: The George Washington University, Washington D.C. 18 October. [Online]
Goddu, Teresa A., 1997. *Gothic America: Narrative, History and Nation.* New York: Columbia University Press.
Goldsworthy, Vesna, 1998. *Inventing Ruritania. The Imperialism of the Imagination.* New Haven and London: Yale UP.
Gordon, E.V., 1981. *An Introduction to Old Norse.* Oxford: Clarendon Press.
Graham, Robertson W., 1931. *Time Was: The Reminiscences of W. Graham Robertson.* London: Hamish Hamilton.
Greer, Mary K., 1995. *Women of the Golden Dawn: Rebels and Priestesses.* Rochester: Park Street Press.
Greer, Tom, 1975. *A Modern Daedalus.* New York: Arno Press.
Haining, Peter (ed.), 1990. *Bram Stoker's Midnight Tales.* London: Peter Owen.
Halberstam, Judith, 1993. 'Technologies of Monstrosity: Bram Stoker's *Dracula.*' *Victorian Studies* (Spring) 36 (3): 333–52.
Hall, Stephan Thomas, 2007. 'James Macpherson's Ossian: Forging Ancient Highland Identity for Scotland.' In: Andrew Wawn (ed.) *Constructing Nations, Reconstructing Myth: Essays in Honour of T. A. Shippey.* Turnhout: Brepols, 3–26.
Hamlin, Christopher, 2005. 'Good and Intimate Filth.' In: William A. Cohen and Ryan Johnson (eds.) *Filth: Dirt, Disgust and Modern Life.* Minneapolis: University of Minnesota Press, 3–29.
Hammond, Paul (ed.), 1995. *The Poems of John Dryden, Vol. 1, 1649–81 and Vol. 2, 1682–85.* London: Longman.
Harding, James, 1989. *Gerald du Maurier: The Last Actor Manager.* London: Hodder & Stoughton.
Harter, Deborah A., 1996. *Bodies in Pieces: Fantastic Narrative and the Poetics of the Fragment.* Stanford: Stanford University Press.
Hatton, Joseph, 1884. *Henry Irving's Impressions of America.* Boston: James R. Osgood.
Hawthorne, Nathaniel, 1973. 'The Birthmark.' *Hawthorne's Short Stories.* New York: Knopf, 177–93.
Hebblethwaite, Kate, 2006. 'Introduction.' *Dracula's Guest and Other Weird Stories.* London: Penguin, xi–xlii.
Hedeșan, Otilia, 'Romanian Vampiric Complex. Mythology and Geography.' *The International Microconference of the Research Project: The Impact of a Myth: Dracula and the Image of Romanian in British and American Literatures,* Timișoara, 18 July 2013. http://www.themythoftransylvania.ro/events_en.htm#events2013.
Hickes, George, 1703–05. *Linguarum vett. septentrionalium thesaurus grammaticocriticus et archæologicus.* Oxford: Sheldonian Theatre, Typis Junianis.
Hindle, Maurice, 2003. 'Introduction.' *Dracula.* London: Penguin.
Hoeveler, Diane Long, 1999. 'Reading the Wound: Wollstonecraft's Wrongs of Woman, or Maria and Trauma Theory.' *Studies in the Novel* (Winter) 31 (4): 387–408. *Literature Resource Center* [online] www.galegroup.com. Accessed 7 March 2012.
—— 2008. 'In Dracula, a Metaphor for Faith and Rebirth.' *All Things Considered* (21 March) *Literature Resource Center* [Online]. www.galegroup.com. Accessed 6 March 2012.
Holden, Philip, 2001. 'Castle, Coffin, Stomach: "Dracula" and the Banality of the Occult', *Victorian Literature and Culture,* Vol. 29, No. 2, 469–485.
Holland, Tom, 1995. *The Vampyre.* London: Little, Brown and Company.

*Holy Bible: King James Version (Standard Text Edition)*, Cambridge: Cambridge University Press.
Hopkins, Lisa, 2007. *Bram Stoker: A Literary Life*. Basingstoke: Palgrave Macmillan.
Horner, Avril and Zlosnik, Sue, 1998. *Daphne du Maurier: Writing, Identity and the Gothic Imagination*. Basingstoke: Palgrave.
Howe, Stephen, 2001. *Ireland and Empire; Colonial Legacies in Irish History and Culture*. Oxford: Oxford University Press. [Online] http://www.winstonchurchill.org/publications/finest-hour/finest-hour-137/churchill-proceedings-churchill-and-bombing-policy. Accessed 10 January 2015.
Hughes, William, 1994. 'Profane Resurrections: Bram Stoker's Self-Censorship in *The Jewel of Seven Stars*.' In: Allan Lloyd Smith and Victor Sage (eds.) *Gothick Origins and Innovations*. Amsterdam: Rodopi, 132–9.
—— 2004. '"*Dracula* and Other Novels": Reviewing Stoker's Fiction, 1882–1912.' In: Richard Dalby and William Hughes (eds.) *Bram Stoker: A Bibliography*. Southend on Sea, Essex: Desert Island Books, 13–31.
Hurley, Kelly, 1996. *The Gothic Body: Sexuality, Materialism and Degeneration at the Fin de Siècle*. Cambridge: Cambridge University Press.
Hutcherson, Dudley R., 1942. 'Poe's Reputation in England and America, 1850–1909.' *American Literature* 14 (3): 211–33.
Huxley, T. H., 1869. 'On the Physical Basis of Life.' *The Fortnightly Review* V (XXVI): 129–45.
Irish Military Archive, Bureau of Military History, Witness Statement 641, Emmet Dalton: IMA, BMH, WS327, Patrick Egan.
Irving, Laurence, 1989. *Henry Irving: The Actor and His World*. London: Columbus.
Ispas, Sabina. 'Dracula, o mască occidentală' [Dracula, an Occidental Mask], in *Anuarul Muzeului Etnografic al Moldovei*, X. In honorem Prof. univ. dr. Ion H. Ciubotaru, Iaşi, 2010, 411–28.
James, Henry, 1897. 'George du Maurier.' *Harper's Monthly Magazine* (September), 95: 594–609. [Online] digitallibrarycornell.edu. Accessed 1 January 2015.
Jansen, K. Frank, 2005. 'The Early Waite-Smith Tarot Editions.' *The Playing Card: The International Journal of the Playing Card Society* 34 (1): 26–50.
Jeffery, Keith, 1984. *The British Army and the Crisis of Empire, 1918–22*. Manchester: Manchester University Press.
Johannesson, Kurt, 1991. *The Renaissance of the Goths in Sixteenth-Century Sweden: Johannes and Olaus Magnus as Politicians and Historians*. Berkeley, CA: University of California Press.
Johnson, Claudia, 2002. 'Mary Wollstonecraft's Novels.' In: Claudia Johnson (ed.) *The Cambridge Companion to Mary Wollstonecraft*. Cambridge: Cambridge University Press, 189–208.
Johnson, Major E.C., 1885. *On the Track of the Crescent: Erratic Notes from the Piraeus to Pesth*. London: Hurst and Blackett.
Kaplan, Stuart, 2009. *The Artwork & Times of Pamela Colman Smith Artist of the Rider-Waite Tarot Deck*. Stamford: U.S. Games Systems.
Karl Alexander, Karl, 1979. *Time After Time*. New York: Delacorte Press.
Kennett, Lee, 1991. *The First Airwar: 1918–1918*. New York: The Free Press.
Kenton, Edna, 1914. 'The Pap We Have Been Fed On: The First Freewoman in Fiction.' *The Bookman* (June) 39 (4): 467–71. Rpt. in *Literature Resource Center*. [online] www.galegroup.com. Accessed 6 March 2012.

Kristeva, Julia, 1982. *Powers of Horror: An Essay on Abjection*. Translated by Leon S. Roudiez. New York: Columbia University Press.
Kucich, John, 2002. 'Scientific Ascendancy.' In: Patrick Brantlinger and William B. Thesing (eds.) *A Companion to the Victorian Novel*. Oxford: Blackwell, 119–36.
Lankester, Edwin Ray, 1880. *Degeneration. A Chapter in Darwinism*. London: Macmillan.
Lapin, Daniel, 1995. *The Vampire, Dracula and Incest*. San Francisco: Gargoyle.
Le Fanu, Joseph Sheridan, 1995. 'Carmilla.'*In a Glass Darkly*. Ware: Wordsworth, 207–72.
Leatherdale, Clive, 1987. *The Origins of Dracula*. London: William Kimber, 1987.
—— 1993. *Dracula: The Novel and the Legend*. Revised Edition. Westcliff-on-Sea: Desert Island Books.
—— 2001. *Dracula: The Novel and the Legend*. 3rd Edn. Westcliff-on-Sea: Desert Island Books.
Ledger, Sally & Luckhurst, Roger, 2000. 'Scientific Naturalism.' In: Sally Ledger and Roger Luckhurst (eds.) *The Fin de Siècle: A Reader in Cultural History, c. 1880–1900*. Oxford: Oxford University Press, 221–3.
Letter to Bram Stoker.' In: Maurice Hindle (ed.) *Dracula*: Appendix II. London:
Lodge, David, 2005. *Author, Author*. London: Penguin.
Lonsdale, Roger (ed.), 1969. *The Poems of Thomas Gray, William Collins and Oliver Goldsmith*. London and New York: Longmans.
Ludlam, Harry, 1962. *A Biography of Dracula: The Life Story of Bram Stoker*. London: Foulsham.
Luna, Alina M., 2004. *Visual Perversity: A Re-Articulation of Maternal Instinct*. Lanham, Maryland: Lexington Books.
MacFarlane, Karen E., 2010. 'Mummy Knows Best: Knowledge and the Unknowable in Turn of the Century Mummy Fiction.' *Horror Studies* 1 (1): 5–24.
Mallet, Paul Henri, 1755. *Introduction à l'histoire de Dannemarc, où l'on traite de la religion, des loix, des moeurs et des usages des anciens Danois*. Copenhagen: Berling.
—— 1756. *Monumens de la mythologie et de la poésie des Celtes, et particulièrement des anciens Scandinave*. Copenhagen: Philibert.
—— 1763. *Histoire de Dannemarc*. Geneva.
Malm, Mats, 1994. Olaus Rudbeck's *Atlantica* and Old Norse Poetics. In: Andrew Wawn (ed.) *Northern Antiquity: The Post-Medieval Reception of Edda and Saga*. Enfield Lock: Hisarlik Press, 1–25.
—— 1996. *Minervas äpple: Om diktsyn, tolkning och bildspråk inom nordisk göticism*. Doctoral dissertation, University of Gothenburg.
Mandell, Laura, 2008. 'Bad Marriages, Bad Novels: The "Philosophical Romance." ' In: Jillian Heydt-Stevenson and Charlotte Susman (eds.) *Recognizing the Romantic Novel: New Histories of British Fiction, 1780–1830*. Liverpool: Liverpool University Press, 49–76.
Martin, Robert K., and Savoy, Eric, eds. 1998. *American Gothic: New Interventions in a National Narrative*. Iowa City: University of Iowa Press.
Matheson, Richard, 2001. *I Am Legend*. London: Gollancz.
Matthews, S. Leigh, 2001. '(Un)Confinements: The Madness of Motherhood in Mary Wollstonecraft's *The Wrongs of Woman*.' In: Helen C. Buss, D. L. Macdonald and Anne McWhir (eds.) *Mary Wollstonecraft and Mary Shelley: Writing Lives*. Waterloo, ON: Wilfrid Laurier University Press, 85–97.

Maunder, Andrew, 2006. *Bram Stoker*. Tavistock: Northcote House.
Mayall, David, 1988. *Gypsy-travellers in Nineteenth-Century Society*. Cambridge: Cambridge University Press.
——— 2004. *Gypsy Identities 1500–2000: From Egipcyans and Moon-men to the Ethnic Romany*. London: Routledge.
[Mazuchelli, Nina Elizabeth], 1881. *'Magyarland': Being the Narrative of Our Travels Through the Highlands and Lowlands of Hungary*. Vol. 2. London: Sampson Low, Marston, Searle and Rivington.
McKenna, Joseph, 2011. *Guerilla Warfare in the Irish War of Independence, 1919–1921*. Jefferson, NC: McFarland & Company.
McKnight, Natalie J., 1996. *Suffering Mothers in the Mid-Victorian Novel*. Basingstoke: Palgrave Macmillan.
McNally, Raymond T., 1983. *Dracula was a Woman: In Search of the Blood Countess of Transylvania*. Maidenhead: McGraw-Hill.
McPherson, J.G., 1891. 'Dust.' *Longman's Magazine* XVIII: 49–49.
Mellor, Anne, 1996. 'Righting the Wrongs of Woman: Mary Wollstonecraft's Maria.' *Nineteenth-Century Contexts* 19 (4): 413–24.
Miles, Robert, 2007. 'Eighteenth-Century Gothic.' In: Catherine Spooner and Emma McEvoy (eds.) *The Routledge Companion to Gothic*. London and New York: Routledge, 10–18.
Millburn, Diane, 1998. '"For the Dead Travel Fast": Dracula in Anglo-German Context.' In: Elizabeth Miller (ed.) *Dracula: The Shade and the Shadow*. Westcliff-on-Sea: Desert Island Books, 41–53.
Miller, Elizabeth (ed.), 2005. *Bram Stoker's Dracula: A Documentary Volume*. Detroit: Thomson Gale, 2005.
——— 2006a. 'Coitus Interruptus: Sex, Bram Stoker, and *Dracula*.' *Romanticism on the Net*. 44. [Online] http://www.erudit.org/. Accessed 15 November 2014.
——— 2006b. *Dracula: Sense and Nonsense*. Westcliff-on-Sea: Desert Island Books.
Miller, Elizabeth, and Stoker, Dacre (eds.), 2012. *The Dublin Years: The Lost Journal of Bram Stoker*. London: Robson Press.
Mitford, John (ed.), 1835. *The Works of Thomas Gray. Vol. III: Letters*. London: William Pickering.
Moretti, Franco, 1988. *Signs Taken for Wonders*. Trans. S. Fischer, D. Forgacs and D. Miller. New York: Verso.
Morris, Joseph E., 1904. *North Riding of Yorkshire*. London: Methuen.
Morrow, John H., 2013. 'States and Strategic Airpower: Continuity and Change, 1906–1939.' In Robin Higham and Mark Parillo (eds.) *The Influence of Airpower upon History: Statesmanship, Diplomacy and Foreign Policy Since 1903*. Lexington, KY: University Press of Kentucky, 37–60.
Morton, Stephen, 2013. *States of Emergency: Colonialism, Literature and Law*. Liverpool: Liverpool University Press.
Murray, Paul, 2004. *From the Shadow of Dracula: A Life of Bram Stoker*. London: Jonathan Cape.
Nayder, Lillian, 1997. 'Virgin Territory and the Iron Virgin: Engendering the Empire in Bram Stoker's "The Squaw." ' In: Claudia Nelson and Ann Sumner Holmes (eds.) *Maternal Instincts: Visions of Motherhood and Sexuality in Britain, 1875–1925*. Basingstoke: Macmillan, 75–97.
Netterville, Luke, 1900. *The Queen of the World, or, Under the Tyranny*. London: Lawrence and Bullen.

Nord, Deborah, 2006. *Gypsies and the British Imagination 1807–1930*. New York: Columbia

Nordau, Max, 1895. *Degeneration*. London: William Heinemann.

Nyquist, Mary, 1997. 'Wanting Protection: Fair Ladies, Sensibility and Romance.' In: Eileen Janes Yeo (ed.) *Mary Wollstonecraft and 200 Years of Feminisms*. London and New York: Rivers Oram Press, 61–85.

Ó Donghaile, Deaglán, 2011. *Blasted Literature: Victorian Political Literature and the Shock of Modernism*. Edinburgh: Edinburgh University Press.

O'Donoghue, Heather, 2007. *From Asgard to Valhalla: The Remarkable History of the Norse Myths*. London and New York: I. B. Taurus.

Oakley, Ann, 1984. *The Captured Womb: A History of the Medical Care of Pregnant Women*. Oxford: Basil Blackwell.

Omberg, Margaret, 1976. *Scandinavian Themes in English Poetry, 1760–1800*. Doctoral dissertation, Uppsala: Borgströms Trykeri.

Ormond, Leonee, 1969. *George du Maurier*. London: Routledge & Kegan Paul.

Overy, Richard, 2013. *The Bombing War: Europe 1939–1945*. London: Allen Lane.

Paris, Michael, 1992. *Winged Warfare: The Literature and Theory of Aerial Warfare in Britain, 1859–1917*. Manchester: Manchester University Press.

Parsons, Melinda Boyd, 1987. 'Mysticism in London: The "Golden Dawn": Synaesthesia and "Psychic Automatism.' In: Kathleen J. Reiger (ed.) *The Spiritual Image in Modern Art*. London: The Theosophical Publishing House, 73–101.

Pearsall, Derek, 2001. *Gothic Europe 1200–1450*. London and New York: Routledge.

Percy, Thomas, 1763. *Five Pieces of Runic Poetry Translated from the Icelandic Language*. London: R. and J. Dodsley. [Online] http://books.google.co.uk/books?id=fFMJAAAAQAAJ&pg=PA3&source=gbs_toc_r&cad=3#v=onepage&q&f=false. Accessed 5 June 2014

Percy, Thomas (trans.) 1809. *Northern Antiquities: Or, A Description of the Manners, Customs, Religion and Laws of the Ancient Danes, including those of Our Own Saxon Ancestors, with a Translation of the Edda, or System of Runic Mythology, and Other Pieces, from the Ancient Islandic Tongue. Translated from Mons. Mallet's Introduction à l'histoire de Dannemarc, Etc.*, 2 vols. Edinburgh: C. Stewart.

Poe, Edgar Allan, 1982. *The Complete Tales and Poems of Edgar Allan Poe*. London: Penguin.

―― 2000. *Tales of Mystery and Imagination*. 1902. London: Wordsworth Classics.

―― 2009. *Tales of the Grotesque and Arabesque*. 1840. Royston: Worth Library Classics.

'Procurer.' *Oxford English Dictionary*. Second Edition, 1989. OED [Online] www.oed.com/. Accessed 1 January 2015.

Purcell, Victor, 2010. *The Boxer Uprising: A Background Study*. Cambridge: Cambridge University Press.

Pyne, Kathleen, 2007. *Modernism and the Feminine Voice: O'Keefe and the Women of the Stieglitz Circle*. Berkeley: University of California Press.

Quinn, Judy and Margaret Clunies Rosss, 1994. 'Images of Norse Poetry and Myth in Seventeenth-Century England.' In: Andrew Wawn (ed.) *Northern Antiquity: The Post-Medieval Reception of Edda and Saga*. Enfield Lock: Hisarlik Press, 189–210.

Rarignac, Noël Montague-Étienne, 2012. *The Theology of Dracula : Reading the Book of Stoker as a Sacred Text*. Jefferson, North Carolina: McFarland.

Reese, James, 2008. *The Dracula Dossier*. New York: Harper Collins.
Reeve, Clara, 1996. 'From *The Progress of Romance, through Times, Countries, and Manners, with Remarks on the Good and Bad Effects of It, on Them Respectively, in a Course of Evening Conversations* (1785). In: Anne K. Mellor and Richard E. Matlak (eds.) *British Literature 1780–1830*. Boston: Heinle & Heinle, Thomson Learning, 152–56.
Reijnders, Stijn, 2011. 'Stalking the Count: Dracula, Fandom and Tourism.' *Annals of Tourism Research* 38 (1): 231–48.
Rezachevici, Constantin, 2006. 'Punishments with Vlad Țepeș – Punishments in Europe. Common and Differentiating Traits.' *Journal of Dracula Studies* 8. [Online] www. http://dractravel.com/drc/. Accessed 15 March 2014.
Richards, Cynthia, 2004. 'Introduction.' In: Cynthia Richards (ed.) *The Wrongs of Woman; or Maria by Mary Wollstonecraft and Memoirs of the Author of A Vindication of the Rights of Woman by William Godwin*. Glen Allen, Virginia: College Publishing, 1–34.
Richards, Jeffrey, 1995. 'Gender, Race, and Sexuality in Bram Stoker's Other Novels.' In: Christopher Parker (ed.) *Gender Roles and Sexuality in Victorian Literature*. Aldershot: Scolar Press, 143–71.
Richardson, Angelique and Chris Willis, 2002. 'Introduction.' In: Angelique Richardson and Chris Willis (eds.) *The New Woman in Fiction and in Fact: Fin-de-Siècle Feminisms*. Basingstoke and New York: Palgrave, 1–38.
Ridenhour, Jamieson, 2013. *In Darkest London: The Gothic Cityscape in Victorian Literature*. Lanham: Scarecrow Press.
Ring, Jim, 1996. *Erskine Childers*. London: John Murray.
Rix, Robert W., 2011. 'Gothic Gothicism: Norse Terror in the Late Eighteenth to Early Nineteenth Centuries.' *Gothic Studies* 13 (1): 1–20.
Rohmer, Sax, 1920. *The Green Eyes of Bast*. New York: McKinley, Stone and Mackenzie.
Rousseau, Jean-Jacques, 1754. *Discours sur l'origine et les fondements de l'inégalité parmi les hommes* (Discourse on the Origin and Basis of Inequality Among Men). Amsterdam: Marc Michel Rey.
Rowe, Katherine, 1999. *Dead Hands: Fictions of Agency, Renaissance to Modern*. Stanford: Stanford University Press.
Ruddick, Bill, 1987. 'George du Maurier: Illustrator and Interpreter of Mrs Gaskell.' *Gaskell Society Journal* 1: 48–60.
Rumbold, Valerie (ed.), 1999. *Alexander Pope: The Dunciad in Four Books*. Harlow, Essex: Longman.
Russo, Mary, 1995. *The Female Grotesque: Risk, Excess and Modernity*. New York: Routledge.
Safford, Anson P.K., 1871. *Resources of Arizona Territory: With a Description of the Indian Tribes, Ancient Ruins, Cochise, Apache Chief, Antonio, Pima Chief, Stage and Wagon Roads, Trade and Commerce, etc*. San Francisco: Francis & Valentine.
Sage, Victor, 1998. 'Exchanging fantasies: Sex and the Serbian Crisis in The Lady of the Shroud.' In: William Hughes and Andrew Smith (eds.) *Bram Stoker: History, Psychoanalysis and the Gothic*. London: Macmillan, 116–33.
Said, Edward, 1979. *Orientalism*. New York: Vintage.
Sammes, Aylett, 1676. *Britannia Antiqua Illustrata: Or, The Antiquities of Ancient Britain*. London: Thomas Roycroft. [Online] http://books.google.co.uk/books?id=fdZUAAAAcAAJ&q=Ragnar#v=onepage&q=Bartholin&f=false Accessed 6 June 2014.

Sánchez-Verdejo Pérez, Francisco Javier, 2014. 'Gothic Literature: A Brief Outline.' In: Dana Percec (ed.) *Reading the Fantastic Imagination: The Avatars of a Literary Genre*. Cambridge Scholars, 39–56.

Schaffer, Talia, 1994. '"A Wilde Desire Took Me": The Homoerotic History of *Dracula*.' *ELH* (Summer) 61 (2): 381–425.

Schmitt, Cannon, 1997. *Alien Nation*. Philadelphia: University of Pennsylvania Press.

Schuchard, Ronald, 2012. *The Last Minstrels*, Oxford: Oxford University Press.

Senf, Carol, 1998. *Dracula, between Tradition and Modernism*. New York: Twayne.

—— 2000–2001. 'A Response to 'Dracula and the Idea of Europe by Eleni Coundouriotis.' *Connotations: A Journal for Critical Debate* 10 (1): 47–58.

Shanley, Mary Lyndon, 1988a. 'Divorce.' In: Sally Mitchell (ed.) *Victorian Britain: An Encyclopedia*. New York & London: Garland, 223–24.

—— 1988b. 'Marriage Law.' In: Sally Mitchell (ed.) *Victorian Britain: An Encyclopedia*. New York & London: Garland, 477–78.

Sherard, Robert Harborough, 1895. 'Hall Caine: A Biographical Study.' *The Windsor Magazine* (July), 562–77.

Shuttle, Penelope, and Redgrove, Peter, 1990. *The Wise Wound: Myths, Realities, and Meanings*. New York: Bantam Dell.

Simmons, Dan, 1992. *Children of the Night*. London: Headline.

Simmons, James R., 2002. '"If America Goes on Breeding Men Like That": *Dracula*'s Quincey Morris Problematized.' *Journal of the Fantastic in the Arts* 12 (4): 425–36.

Simpson, Hyacinth, 2004. 'Patterns and Periods: Oral Aesthetics and a Century of Jamaican Short Story Writing.' *Journal of West Indian Literature* 12 (1 & 2): 1–219.

Smith, Andrew, 2003. 'Demonising the Americans: Bram Stoker's Postcolonial Gothic.' *Gothic Studies* 5: 20–31.

Sowerby, Robin, 2000. 'The Goths in History and Pre-Gothic Gothic.' In: David Punter (ed.) *A Companion to the Gothic*. Oxford: Blackwell, 15–26.

Spooner, S., 1853. *Anecdotes of Painters, Engravers, Sculptors and Architects, and Curiosities of Art*. Vol. 2. New York: R. Worthington.

St John, Christopher (ed.), 1931a. *Ellen Terry and Bernard Shaw: A Correspondence*. London: Constable.

—— 1913b. *The Russian Ballet*. London: Sidgwick & Jackson.

Starrs, Bruno D., 2004. 'Keeping the Faith: Catholicism in Dracula and Its Adaptations.' *Journal of Dracula Studies* 6: 13–18. [Online] www. http://dractravel.com/drc/. Accessed 15 March 2014.

Stoddard, Jane, 2009. 'Mr. Bram Stoker. A Chat with the Author of *Dracula*.' In: Elizabeth Miller (ed.) *Bram Stoker's Dracula: A Documentary Journey into Vampire Country and the Dracula Phenomenon*. New York: Pegasus, 275–8.

Stoker, Charlotte, 2003. 'Charlotte Stoker's Account of 'The Cholera Horror' in a

Stoker, Dacre and Holt, Ian, 2009. *Dracula, The Un-Dead*. London: Harper.

Storer, Richard, 2014. 'Taking the City by Storm: Bram Stoker's *Dracula* (1897) and Hall Caine's *The Christian* (1897)'. In: Rosemary Mitchell (ed.) *Towards the Metropolis? Approaches to the Modern City*, Leeds Working Papers in Victorian Studies Vol 14. Leeds: LCVS, 26–36.

Storey, Neil R., 2011. *The Dracula Secrets: Jack the Ripper and the Darkest Sources of Bram Stoker*. Stroud: The History Press.

Strachan, Hew, 2014. *The First World War*. New York: Simon & Schuster.

Taylor, Barbara, 1997. 'For the Love of God: Religion and the Erotic Imagination in Wollstonecraft's Feminism.' In: Eileen Janes Yeo (ed.) *Mary Wollstonecraft and 200 Years of Feminisms*. New York: Rivers Oram Press, 15–35.

Terry, Ellen, 1908. *The Story of My Life*, London: Hutchinson.

Thomas, Kate, 2012. *Postal Pleasures: Sex, Scandal, and Victorian Letters*. Oxford: Oxford University Press.

Tickner, Lisa, 1987. *Spectacle of Women: Imagery of the Suffrage Campaign 1907–1914*. London: Chatto & Windus.

Tindall, George Brown, and Shi, David Emory, 1997. *America: A Narrative History*. Brief Fourth Edition. New York & London: Norton.

Tolkien, J.R.R., 1997. *Tales from the Perilous Realm*. London: HarperCollins, 1997.

Tomaszewska, Monika, 2004. 'Vampirism and the Degeneration of the Imperial Race – Stoker's Dracula as the Invasive Degenerate Other.' *Journal of Dracula Studies* 6: 1–8.

Townshend, Charles, 2013. *The Republic: The Fight for Irish Independence, 1918–1923*. London: Allen Lane.

Traubel, Horace, 1953. *With Walt Whitman in Camden: January 21 to April 7, 1889*. Ed. Sculley Bradley. Philadelphia: University of Pennsylvania Press.

Treptow, Kurt W., 2000. *Vlad III Dracula. The Life and Times of the Historical Dracula*. Iaşi, Oxford, Portland: The Center for Romanian Studies.

Trower, Shelley, 2012. 'On the Cliff Edge of England: Tourism and Imperial Gothic in Cornwall.' *Victorian Literature and Culture* (March) 40 (1): 199–214. [Online] literature.proquest.com. Accessed 10 February 2015.

Tucker, Holly, 2000. 'Like Mother, Like Daughter: Maternal Cravings and Birthmarks in the Tales of Mme d'Aulnoy and Mlle de la Force.' In: Buford Norman (eds) *The Mother in/and French Literature*. Amsterdam: Rodopi, 33–50.

Tyndall, William, 1870. 'On Dust and Disease.' *Frazer's Magazine*, 302–310.

Vora, Setu K. and Ramanan, Sundaram V., 2002. 'Ebola-Poe: A Modern Day Parallel of the Red Death.' *Emerging Infectious Diseases* (December) 8 (2): 1521–23. [Online] www.ncbi.nim.nih.gov/pmc/articles. Accessed 1 March 2014.

Walker, George Alfred, 1841. *The Grave Yards of London: Being an Exposition of the Physical and Moral Consequences, Inseparably Connected with our Unchristian and Pestilential Custom of Depositing the Dead in the Midst of the Living*. London: Longman.

Wallace, Alfred Russel, 1870. 'Are Humans One Race or Many?' In: Paul B. Armstrong (ed.) *Joseph Conrad, Heart of Darkness*. New York & London: Norton, 2006, 218–224.

Wallis, Patrick, 2005. 'A Dreadful Heritage: Interpreting Epidemic Disease at Eyam, 1666–2000.' Working Papers on the Nature of Evidence. 'How Well do 'Facts' Travel? Department of Economic History, London School of Economics (May) 2: 1–37. [Online] www.lse.ac.uk/collection/economichistory/

Walpole, Horace, 1996. *The Castle of Otranto*. W. S. Lewis (ed.) Oxford University Press.

——— 2011. *Horace Walpole's Correspondence*, The Lewis Walpole Library, Yale University Library. [Online site] http://images.library.yale.edu/hwcorrespondence/

Walsh, Thomas P., 1979. 'Dracula: Logos and Myth.' *Research Studies* 47: 229–37.

Walton, John K., 2011. 'Port and Resort: Symbiosis and Conflict in "Old Whitby", England Since 1880.' In: Peter Borsay and John K. Walton (eds)

*Resorts and Ports: European Seaside Towns Since 1700*. Bristol: Channel View Publications, 126–46.

Warren, Louis S., 2002. 'Buffalo Bill Meets Dracula: William F. Cody, Bram Stoker, and the Frontiers of Racial Decay.' *American Historical Review*, 107 (October): 1124–57.

Wawn, Andrew, 2005. 'The Post-Medieval Reception of Old Norse and Old Icelandic Literature.' In: Rory McTurk (ed.) *A Companion to Old Norse-Icelandic Literature*. Oxford: Blackwell, 320–37.

Wells, H.G., 2005. *The War in the Air*. London: Penguin.

Wilkinson, William, 1820. *An Account of the Principalities of Wallachia & Moldavia. Including Various Political Observations Relating to Them*. London: Longman, Hurst, Rees, Orme, and Brown.

Williams, Christopher G., 2007. 'Birthing and Undead Family: Reification of the Mother's Role in the Gothic Landscape of *28 Days Later*.' *Gothic Studies* 9 (2): 33–44. [Online] literature.proquest.com. Accessed 2 April 2015.

Willis, Martin, 2007. '"The Invisible Giant," *Dracula* and Disease.' *Studies in the Novel* (Fall) 39 (3): 301–35.

Wilson, Philip K., Spring 2002. 'Eighteenth-Century "Monsters" and Nineteenth-Century "Freaks": Reading the Maternally Marked Child', *Literature and Medicine* (Spring) 21 (1): 1–25.

Wohl, Robert, 1994. *A Passion for Wings: Aviation and the Western Imagination 1908–1918*. New Haven: Yale University Press.

Wollstonecraft, Mary, 2004. *The Wrongs of Woman; or Maria* (1798). Ed. Cynthia Richards. Glen Allen, Virginia: College Publishing.

Wood, T. Martin. 1913. *George du Maurier: The Satirist of the Victorians*. London: Chatto & Windus.

Wordsworth, William, 1969. 'Gipsies.' 1807. In: Thomas Hutchinson (ed.) *Wordsworth Poetical Works*. London: Oxford University Press, 153.

Worm, Ole, 1636. *RUNIR seu Danica literatura antiquissima*. Copenhagen: Martzan; Copenhagen: Holst; Amsterdam: Janson.

Wynne, Catherine (ed.), 2009. 'Introduction.' In *Arthur Conan Doyle's* The Parasite *and Bram Stoker's* The Watter's Mou'. Kansas City: Valancourt, vii–xxxviii.

——— 2011. 'Ellen Terry, Bram Stoker and the Lyceums Vampires.' In: Katharine Cockin (ed.) *Ellen Terry, Spheres of Influence*. London: Pickering & Chatto, 17–32.

——— (ed.), 2012. *Bram Stoker and the Stage*, 2 vols. London: Pickering & Chatto.

——— 2013. *Bram Stoker, Dracula and the Victorian Gothic Stage*. Basingstoke: Palgrave.

Yaeger, Patricia, 1993. 'The "Language of Blood": Towards a Maternal Sublime.' In: Shirley Neuman and Glennis Stephenson (eds) *Reimagining Women: Representations of Women in Culture*. Toronto: University of Toronto Press, 87–110.

Yeats, W. B. 1937 (1961). 'A General Introduction for my Work' in *Essays and Introductions*, London: Macmillan, pp. 509–26.

——— 1901 (1961) 'Magic', in *Essays and Introductions*, London: Macmillan, pp. 28–52.

——— 1903. 'The Lake at Coole.' *The Green Sheaf*, No. 4. Supplement.

——— 1903. 'A Dream of the World's End.' *The Green Sheaf*, No. 2.

―――― 1997. 'To a Wealthy Man' and 'September 1913.' In: Richard J. Finneran (ed.) *The Collected Works of W. B. Yeats, Vol. 1 The Poems*. New York: Simon and Schuster, 106. 107.

Zanger, Jules, 1991. 'A Sympathetic Vibration: Dracula and the Jews.' *English Literature in Transition* 34 (1991): 33–44.

Žižek, Slavoj, 1991. *For They Know Not What they Do: Enjoyment As a Political Factor*. London: Verso.

# Index

Barbauld, Anna, 30–32
   'On the Origins and Progress of Novel Writing', 31–32
Baring-Gould, Sabine, 134
   *The Book of Werewolves*, 134
Báthory, Erzsébet, 133–4
Belford, Barbara, 169, 209, 224
   *Bram Stoker: A Biography of the Author of Dracula*, 169, 209, 211, 220n
Bell, Gertrude, 3, 5
   *Persian Pictures*, 3, 5
Blair, Hugh, 24
   *Critical Dissertation on the Poems of Ossian*, 24
Boner, Charles, 63, 65, 69, 73
   *Transylvania: Its Products and Its People*, 63, 65, 69, 73
Boyle, Danny (dir.) 7, 9
   *28 Days Later*, 7–10, 11
Brontë, Emily, 189–90
   *Wuthering Heights*, 189, 190, 203
   'Self-Interrogation', 189
Bubonic Plague, 1–3
   see also Eyam Plague Village
Buffalo Bill, 49, 100, 150

Caine, Hall, 12, 172–83
   *The Bondman*, 178, 179
   *Capt'n Davy's Honeymoon*, 175, 178–9, 183n
   *The Christian*, 177
   *The Deemster*, 176, 178, 179, 181
   *The Eternal City*, 179
   *The Manxman*, 179, 180
   *The White Prophet*, 174, 179
Chesney, George, 92
   *The Battle of Dorking*, 92
Cholera, 3, 5–6
   see also Stoker, Charlotte
Churchill, Winston, 50–2, 139, 155, 156
Clifford, William, 106

Cornish Gothic, 186, 205n
Cornwall, 13, 125, 186, 189–90, 202–5
Craig, Edith, 159, 166, 170, 170–1n
Craig, Edward Gordon, 165, 169, 170, 171n
Cromer, Lord, 95
Crosse, Andrew, F, 63
   *Round About the Carpathians*, 63

Darwin, Charles, 56, 105, 107
   *Origin of Species*, 56, 105, 107
   *The Demon of Brockenheim*, 233, 241, 244–5, 248
   Illustrations of, 247
Doyle, Arthur Conan, 50, 86, 203
   *Hound of the Baskervilles*, 203–4
   'The Adventure of the Speckled Band', 86
   Fictionalized, 213–6
Dryden, John, 21
   'To the Earl of Roscommon', 21
   'Epistle to Dr Charleton', 21
Du Maurier, Daphne, 13, 186–91, 192, 196, 202–4, 205
   *The Du Mauriers*, 187–8
   *Gerald: A Portrait*, 185–6, 187, 188–9, 191, 196, 202
   *Jamaica Inn*, 202–4
   *The Loving Spirit*, 189–90
   *The Parasites*, 191
   *Vanishing Cornwall*, 189–90, 204, 205
   *The Young George du Maurier*, 192
Du Maurier, George, 12–3, 164, 186–9, 191–6, 199, 201, 205, 206n
   Illustrations, 193, 194, 196, 199, 200–1
   *The Martian*, 193, 195
   *Trilby*, 164, 191
Du Maurier, Gerald, 185–9, 191, 205, 205–6n

Ebola, 2
Ellis, Havelock, 122, 126, 129
Elrod, P. N., 102
  *Quincey Morris, Vampire*, 102
  *Vampire Files*, 102
Eyam Plague Village, 1- 3, 6, 10
  see also 'The Plague at Eyam'

Farr, Florence, 165, 170
Farson, Daniel, 209, 214, 217, 219, 220n
  *The Man Who Wrote Dracula*, 209, 214, 217, 219, 220n
Forrest, Katherine V., 212
  'O Captain, My Captain', 212
Frost, Mark, 213–6, 221n
  *The List of Seven*, 213–6, 220, 221n
Fuseli, Henry, 27

Gaskell, Elizabeth, 191–2
  *Sylvia's Lovers*, 191–2
Gerard, Madame, 63, 66–8, 82–3, 84
  *The Land Beyond the Forest*, 63, 67, 82–3, 84
  'Transylvanian Superstitions', 63, 66–8
*Gesta Danorum*, 15, 16
*Gesta Hammaburgensis Ecclesiae Pontificum*, 15
Gray, Thomas, 11, 14, 24–5, 26, 27
  'The Descent of Odin', 25, 26
  'The Fatal Sisters', 24–5, 26
Greer, Tom, 140–3, 157n
  *A Modern Daedalus*, 140–3, 157n
Godwin, William, 34, 36

Hawthorne, Nathaniel, 126
  'The Birth Mark', 126
Hecker, Justin, 3
  *History of the Black Death*, 3
Home Rule (Irish), 53, 140, 151
Horniman, Annie, 165
Huxley, Thomas, 107

Iron Virgin, 55, 56, 58–9, 61, 131, 132–6
Irving, Henry, 12, 48, 49, 53, 55, 61, 94, 150, 159, 162, 163, 164, 165, 169, 170, 171n, 177, 179, 180, 191, 197, 208–9, 211
  Fictionalized, 214, 216, 217–8

James, Henry, 50, 186, 195–6, 206n
  Fictionalized, 196
Johnson, Major E. C., 63, 69, 73
  *On the Track of the Crescent*, 63, 69, 73
Jónsson, Arngrímur, 16
  *Brevis commentarius de Islandia*, 16

Lankester, E. Ray, 107–8, 109, 117
Leech, John, 192
Le Fanu, J. Sheridan, 66, 126–7
  'Carmilla', 66, 126–7
Lewis, Matthew, 28, 55, 241
  *The Monk*, 28, 241
  *Tales of Wonder*, 28
Lodge, David, 196
  *Author, Author*, 196
Lowell, James Russell, 196
Ludlam, Harry, 4–6, 209–10, 211, 218–9, 220n
  *A Biography of Dracula*, 4–6, 209–10, 211, 218–9, 220n

Macpherson, James, 22, 23–4, 27
  *Fingal*, 23–4
  *Fragments of Ancient Poetry*, 23–4
  *Temora*, 23–4
Magnus, Johannes, 16–17, 18
  *Historia de omnibus Gothorum Sveonumque regibus*, 16–17
Magnus, Olaus, 16–17, 18
Mallet, Paul Henri, 22–4, 25, 26
  *Introduction à L'Historie Dannemarc*, 22–4, 26
Marvell, Andrew, 21
  'A Letter to Doctor Ingelo', 21
Matheson, Richard, 6
  *I am Legend*, 6–7, 10
Mazuchelli, Nina Elizabeth, 63, 64, 69
  *Magyarland*, 63, 64–5, 69
Mompesson, William, 1–2
Monroe Doctrine, 102
Morel, Bénédict, 107

New Woman, 4, 11, 37, 44–45, 47, 160, 162, 163, 199–201
  Illustration of, 200

272  *Index*

Nordau, Max, 53, 105, 110, 116–7
*Nosferatu* (film), 149
Nosferatu, 67–8
Nuremberg, 54–5, 132, 197–8

O'Grady, Standish [Luke Netterville], 143–7, 157n
  *The Queen of the World*, 143–7, 149–50, 154, 157n
Order of the Golden Dawn, 165–6, 168, 170, 171n

Pasha, Arabi, 95–6
Percy, Thomas, 23, 24, 35
  *Five Pieces of Runic Poetry*, 25
  *Northern Antiquities*, 23
  *Reliques of Ancient English Poetry*
'The Plague at Eyam', 1, 2–3, 6
Planché, J. R, 66
  *The Vampire, or the Bride of the Isles*, 66
Poe, Edgar Allan, 2, 11, 48, 49–50, 53, 54, 59, 60, 62
  'The Black Cat', 54, 59, 60–1
  'The Fall of the House of Usher', 49, 51–2, 53–4, 104n
  'The Masque of Red Death', 2
  'Murders in the Rue Morgue', 56
  'The Pit and the Pendulum', 55
  'The Tell-Tale Heart', 59
*Poetic Edda*, 15, 17–8
Polidori, John, 66, 213
  'The Vampire', 66
Pope, Alexander, 21–2
  'The Dunciad', 21–2
*Prose Edda*, 15, 18, 23
*Punch* Magazine, 37, 183n, 186, 192, 193, 197
  Illustrations, 194, 200

Radcliffe, Ann, 30, 55, 153, 236
  *The Mysteries of Udolpho*, 9, 230
Reeve, Clara, 30–1, 32
  *Progress of Romance*, 31
Robertson, W. Graham, 159, 160
Rohmer, Sax, 131
  *The Green Eyes of Bast*, 131
Rudbeck, Olof, 18–9
  *Atlantica*, 18

Shaw, George Bernard, 161, 163, 164, 165
Smith, Pamela Colman, 12, 97, 159, 164, 165–6, 168–70, 170–1n
  *Annancy Stories*, 168
  *Susan and the Mermaid*, 168
Simmons, Dan, 212
  *Children of the Night*, 212
Sligo, 5–6
St John, Christopher, 161
Strigoi, 68
Stoker, Bram, *passim*
  Fictionalized, 212–20
  Works:
  'Americans as Actors', 52
  'The Coming of Abel Behenna', 177, 178, 183n, 204–5
  *Dracula*, 3, 4, 6, 7, 8, 9, 10, 11, 12, 28, 30, 36–8, 40–2, 43–6, 49, 50, 52, 53, 55, 58, 63, 64–6, 67, 69–77, 78–84, 85, 86–91, 92–3, 95, 96, 98, 99, 101–2, 103, 105–6, 110–17, 118–9, 120, 121, 127, 131, 132, 134, 149, 150, 152, 160, 162, 163–4, 170, 172, 173, 174, 175–6, 177, 178, 179, 180, 183n, 183–4n, 186, 191, 194, 196–202, 204, 205, 207, 208, 211, 216, 230, 237, 248, 252
  and disease, 3, 4, 6, 7, 8, 9, 10
  and Invasion, 79–82, 86–90, 92–3, 96, 103, 150
  and science, 12, 105–6, 110–17
  and sexuality, 58, 86–90, 118–9, 132
  and New Woman, 36–7, 44–5, 162, 199–200
  *Duties of Clerks of Petty Sessions in Ireland*, 94
  *Famous Impostors*, 159
  *A Glimpse of America*, 48, 94, 100, 150, 210
  'The Invisible Giant', 4, 6
  *The Jewel of Seven Stars*, 12, 92, 94–6, 118, 119, 120, 121, 122–32, 133, 136, 170, 174, 205
  *The Lady of the Shroud*, 12, 92, 102, 149, 150–4, 157–8n, 222, 233, 248, 251–2

*The Lair of the White Worm*, 12, 92, 96, 97–8, 102–3, 159, 169
*The Man* [*The Gates of Life*], 28, 29n, 92, 96–7, 100, 102
*The Mystery of the Sea*, 92, 100, 102, 150
*Personal Reminiscences of Henry Irving*, 4, 5, 49, 53, 61, 173, 179, 180, 181, 183n, 184n, 208, 209, 210, 211
'The Secret of Growing Gold', 59–60
*The Shoulder of Shasta*, 49, 100–101, 150
'The Squaw', 11, 12, 48, 49, 53, 54–62, 92, 99–100, 118, 119, 120, 121, 130, 131, 132–7
*The Snake's Pass*, 92, 102, 173
*Snowbound*, 94
*Under the Sunset*, 6
*The Watter's Mou*', 132, 177, 183n
Stoker, Charlotte, 5–6, 86, 132, 209
Stoker, Dacre, 53, 216–9
Stoker, Dacre, and Holt, Ian, *Dracula, The Un-Dead*, 216–9
Sturluson, Snorii, 15, 16, 23

Temple, William, 20
'Of Heroick Virtue', 20
'Of Poetry', 20
Terry, Ellen, 159, 160–5, 166, 169, 171n
*The Story of My Life*, 169
Tepes, Vlad, [Vlad the Impaler], 68–9
Tolkien, J. R., 223, 244, 248
Transylvania, 11–12, 94, 197
In literature, 63–77, 78, 80, 81–5, 88, 95, 98–9, 114, 150, 201–2, 217
Tree, Beerbohm, 164, 191
Tumblety, Francis, 174–5

*Vagina dentata*, 118, 119, 121, 122, 125, 130, 131, 132, 134, 135, 136
Vasari, Giorgio, 15–6, 25
*Lives of the Artists*, 15–6

Verelius, Olaus, 18, 21, 25
*The Saga of Hervar and Heidrik*, 18
Verstegen, Richard, 20
*A Restitution of Decayed Intelligence in Antiquities*, 20

Walpole, Horace, 11, 14, 24, 25–28, 29n, 55, 222
*The Castle of Otranto*, 14, 25, 27, 28, 222
Wells, H. G., 92, 138, 139–40, 147–8, 152, 153, 157n, 182, 213
*The War in the Air*, 138, 139–40, 147–8, 157n
*War of the Worlds*, 92
*The World Set Free*, 153, 154
Whitby, 10, 12–13, 68, 92, 186–9, 191–4, 195–6, 196–7, 205, 206n, 214, 221n4
in literature, 10, 55, 80–1, 88, 112, 152, 157–8n, 185–9, 191, 193, 196–202, 204, 213–4, 215, 216
Whitman, Walt, 49, 50–1, 150, 163, 173, 177, 210
Wilde, Oscar, 159, 207, 217
*Dorian Gray*, 217
Wilkinson, William, 63, 68, 69
*An Account of the Principalities of Wallachia and Moldavia*, 63, 68, 69
Wollstonecraft, Mary, 11, 30, 31, 32–6, 37, 38, 39–40, 42–3, 45–7
*Letters on the Management of Infants*, 32
*A Vindication of the Rights of Woman*, 32, 47n
*The Wrongs of Woman; or Maria*, 30, 32–6, 37, 39–40, 42–3, 45–7
Worm, Ole, 17, 18, 19, 20, 21, 22, 24, 25
*RUNIR*, 17
Wright Brothers, 138, 140

Yeats, W. B., 146, 157n, 165, 166–7, 168